CCNP: Building Cisco Re
Study Guide

S

Exam number 642-821

OBJECTIVE	CHAPTER
GENERAL KNOWLEDGE	
Describe how different WAN technologies can be used to provide remote access to a network, including asynchronous dial-in, Frame Relay, ISDN, cable modem, and DSL.	1, 2, 5, 6, 7, 8
Describe traffic control methods used to manage traffic flow on WAN links.	8, 9
Explain the operation of remote network access control methods.	3, 4, 11
Identify PPP components, and explain the use of PPP as an access and encapsulation method.	3, 4, 7
Describe the structure and operation of virtual private network technologies.	1, 7
Describe the process of Network Address Translation (NAT).	10
IMPLEMENTATION AND OPERATION	
Configure asynchronous modems and router interfaces to provide network access.	2
Configure an ISDN solution for remote access.	5
Configure frame relay operation and traffic control on WAN links.	8, 9
Configure access control to manage and limit remote access.	11
Configure DSL operation using Cisco IOS.	6
Configure VPN operation using Cisco IOS.	7
Configure Network Address Translation (NAT).	10
PLANNING AND DESIGN	
Design a Cisco remote access solution using asynchronous dial-up technology.	1, 2
Plan a Cisco ISDN solution for remote access or primary link back-up.	1, 5
Design a Cisco frame relay infrastructure to provide access between remote network components.	1, 8
Design a solution of access control to meet required specifications.	7, 11
Plan traffic shaping to meet required quality of service on access links.	8, 9
TROUBLESHOOTING	
Troubleshoot non-functional remote access systems.	2, 3, 5, 6, 7, 8, 10
Troubleshoot a VPN system.	7
Troubleshoot traffic control problems on a WAN link.	1, 2, 3, 4, 5, 6, 7, 8, 11

Exam objectives are subject to change at any time without prior notice and at Cisco's sole discretion. Please visit Cisco's website (http://www.cisco.com) for the most current exam objectives listing.

SYBEX

CCNP:
Building Cisco Remote Access Networks
Study Guide

CCNP®:
Building Cisco Remote
Access Networks
Study Guide

Robert Padjen

San Francisco • London

Associate Publisher: Neil Edde
Acquisitions Editor: Maureen Adams
Developmental Editor: Maureen Adams
Production Editor: Liz Burke
Technical Editor: Toby Skandier
Copyeditor: Sharon Wilkey
Compositor: Scott Benoit
Graphic Illustrator: Scott Benoit
CD Coordinator: Dan Mummert
CD Technician: Kevin Ly
Proofreaders: Laurie O'Connell, Nancy Riddiough, Emily Hsuan
Indexer: Ted Laux
Book Designer: Bill Gibson
Cover Design: Archer Design
Cover Photograph: Andrew Ward/Life File

Library of Congress Card Number: 2003109128

ISBN: 0-7821-4296-6

SYBEX

To Our Valued Readers:

Thank you for looking to Sybex for your CCNP certification exam prep needs. We at Sybex are proud of the reputation we've established for providing certification candidates with the practical knowledge and skills needed to succeed in the highly competitive IT marketplace. Sybex is proud to have helped thousands of Cisco certification candidates prepare for their exams over the years, and we are excited about the opportunity to continue to provide computer and networking professionals with the skills they'll need to succeed in the highly competitive IT industry.

We at Sybex are proud of the reputation we've established for providing certification candidates with the practical knowledge and skills needed to succeed in the highly competitive IT marketplace. It has always been Sybex's mission to teach individuals how to utilize technologies in the real world, not to simply feed them answers to test questions. Just as Cisco is committed to establishing measurable standards for certifying those professionals who work in the cutting-edge field of internetworking, Sybex is committed to providing those professionals with the means of acquiring the skills and knowledge they need to meet those standards.

The author and editors have worked hard to ensure that the Study Guide you hold in your hand is comprehensive, in-depth, and pedagogically sound. We're confident that this book will exceed the demanding standards of the certification marketplace and help you, the Cisco certification candidate, succeed in your endeavors.

As always, your feedback is important to us. Please send comments, questions, or suggestions to support@sybex.com. At Sybex we're continually striving to meet the needs of individuals preparing for IT certification exams.

Good luck in pursuit of your CCNP certification!

Neil Edde
Associate Publisher—Certification
Sybex, Inc.

Software License Agreement: Terms and Conditions

Dedicated to the memory of Marcia Goldberg.

Acknowledgments

Most readers have little knowledge of the work involved in publishing a book like this, and, perhaps, that is good and it means that we are doing our jobs. In a technical text like this there are literally thousands of processes that have to come together in scant months.

Within Sybex I need to thank Liz Burke, Neil Edde, and Maureen Adams. Their tireless work behind the scenes is the sole reason this book is in your hands. Todd Lammle, sometimes called the Barry Bonds of Sybex, is a good friend who I must also thank, and I can think of no one better deserving of snow in September!

I also need to single out my, at times, infuriating, technical editor, Toby Skandier, who challenged virtually every word, but made the book much, much better as a result. I should also thank Wade and Scott for their contributions to the material.

It is impossible to thank my family sufficiently for all of their help and support. Kristie, my wife, who helps maintain a balance against my ISTJ tendencies. Edward, who is turning into a wonderful young man and provides excellent help with his siblings, which, during book deadlines, is imperative and perhaps not praised often enough. Tyler, the five-year-old who reminds me of me, and who perhaps reminds me too much of me. And lastly, Shayna, the image of her mother, who makes me appreciate telecommuting and playing.

My co-workers are a constant source of professional challenge, and I am very grateful for that. Sean Stinson, Art Pfund, Roger Wong, Theran Lee, Cameron Bunt, John Nai, Dat Pham and the rest of the Schwabbies – thank you.

I should also thank my parents. Dad, thank you for reminding me that sometimes life isn't fair and that we all view it through our own eyes. Mom, thank you for everything, including the too rarely shared flights.

Lastly, I need to thank the readers who invest their time in not only reading this material, but, often, provide feedback on how to constantly improve it.

Contents at a Glance

Introduction			*xix*
Assessment Test			*xxxi*
Chapter	**1**	Cisco Solutions for Remote Access	1
Chapter	**2**	Asynchronous Connections	49
Chapter	**3**	Point-to-Point Protocol	77
Chapter	**4**	Using Microsoft Windows 95/98/2000/XP	121
Chapter	**5**	Integrated Services Digital Network (ISDN)	147
Chapter	**6**	Remote Access with Digital Subscriber Line	211
Chapter	**7**	Remote Access with Cable Modems and Virtual Private Networks	231
Chapter	**8**	Frame Relay	251
Chapter	**9**	Queuing and Compression	291
Chapter	**10**	Network Address Translation (NAT) and Port Address Translation (PAT)	325
Chapter	**11**	Centralized Security in Remote Access Networks	359
Glossary			387
Index			*407*

Contents

Introduction   *xix*

Assessment   *xxxi*

Chapter   1   Cisco Solutions for Remote Access   1

What Is Remote Access?   2
    WAN Connection Types   3
    WAN Encapsulation Protocols   14
    Selecting a WAN Protocol   16
Choosing Remote Connection Cisco Products   23
    Fixed Interfaces   24
    Modular Interfaces   25
    Product Selection Tools   25
Cabling and Assembling the WAN   26
    Internetworking Overview and Remote Access Interface
        Options   26
    Identifying Company Site Equipment   28
    Verifying a Network Installation   35
Summary   39
Exam Essentials   39
Key Terms   41
Written Lab   42
Review Questions   43
Answers to Written Lab   46
Answers to Review Questions   47

Chapter   2   Asynchronous Connections   49

Understanding Asynchronous Modems   50
    Signaling and Cabling   53
    Modulation Standards   55
Configuring Asynchronous Modem Connections   58
    Automatic Configuration   58
    Manual Configuration   62
Summary   65
Exam Essentials   66
Key Terms   67
Written Lab   68
Hands-on Labs   68
    Lab 1   68
    Lab 2   69

Review Questions	71
Answers to Written Lab	74
Answers to Review Questions	75

Chapter	**3**	**Point-to-Point Protocol**	**77**

PPP Overview and Architecture	78
The Flag Field	79
The Address Field	80
The Control Field	80
The Protocol Field	80
The Information Field	82
The Frame Check Sequence (FCS) Field	82
Configuring Access Servers	82
Configuring PPP	82
Dedicated or Interactive PPP	83
Interface Addressing Options for Local Devices	83
PAP and CHAP Authentication	91
Password Authentication Protocol (PAP)	91
Challenge Handshake Authentication Protocol (CHAP)	92
PPP Callback	93
PPP Compression and Multilink	97
Compression Configuration	98
Multilink Configuration	99
Verifying and Troubleshooting PPP	101
The *debug ppp authentication* Command	101
The *debug ppp negotiation* Command	102
The *debug ppp packet* Command	106
Summary	109
Exam Essentials	110
Key Terms	111
Written Lab	111
Hands-on Lab	112
Lab 3.1: PPP and DHCP Configuration	112
Review Questions	114
Answers to Written Lab	117
Answers to Review Questions	118

Chapter	**4**	**Using Microsoft Windows 95/98/2000/XP**	**121**

Reasons to Use Dial-Up Networking	122
Configuring Dial-Up Networking with Windows 95/98	123
Configuring a Dial-Up Connection Client	124
Dial-Up Networking Application	124

Make New Connection Wizard 125
Connection Properties 127
Setting Additional Configuration Options 135
Lock DTE Speed 135
Launch Terminal Windows 136
Verifying a Dial-Up Connection 137
Summary 137
Exam Essentials 138
Key Terms 139
Written Lab 139
Review Questions 140
Answers to Review Questions 144
Answers to Written Lab 145

Chapter   **5**   **Integrated Services Digital Network (ISDN)**   **147**

What Is Integrated Services Digital Network (ISDN)? 149
ISDN Line Options 150
Basic Rate Interface (BRI) 151
Primary Rate Interface (PRI) 153
ISDN Function Groups 154
ISDN Reference Points 155
ISDN Protocols 156
LAPD Frames 157
Layer 2 Negotiation 160
ISDN Call Setup and Teardown 163
ISDN Configuration 166
Authentication 171
Password Authentication Protocol (PAP) 171
Challenge Handshake Authentication Protocol (CHAP) 173
Dial-on-Demand Routing (DDR) 175
Configuring DDR 176
Using Optional Commands 179
Using DDR with Access Lists 179
Verifying the ISDN Operation 180
Dial Backup 181
Setting Up Dial Backup 181
Testing the Backup 183
Bandwidth on Demand 190
Channelized T-1/E-1 (PRI) 192
Configuring ISDN PRI 192
Configuring E-1 194
Summary 195
Exam Essentials 195
Key Terms 196

Written Lab   197
Hands-on Labs   197
     Lab 5.1: DDR   197
     Lab 5.2: Configuring PRI and BRI   200
Review Questions   204
Answers to Review Questions   208
Answers to Written Lab   209

Chapter   6   Remote Access with Digital Subscriber Line   211

What is Digital Subscriber Line?   212
The Different Flavors of DSL   213
     Asymmetric Digital Subscriber Line   214
     G.lite   215
     High Bit-Rate DSL   216
     Symmetric DSL   216
     ISDN DSL   216
     Very-High Data Rate DSL   216
Cisco DSL Routers   217
Configuring DSL   218
Troubleshooting DSL   220
Summary   221
Exam Essentials   222
Key Terms   223
Written Lab   223
Hands-on Lab   223
Review Questions   224
Answers to Written Lab   228
Answer to Hands-on Lab   228
Answers to Review Questions   229

Chapter   7   Remote Access with Cable Modems and Virtual Private Networks   231

What is a Cable Modem?   232
     DOCSIS   233
Cisco's Cable Modem Product Line   234
Cisco Cable Manager   235
Virtual Private Networks   235
     IPSec   235
Summary   240
Exam Essentials   241
Key Terms   241
Written Lab   242
Hands-On Lab   242

Review Questions   244

Answers to Written Lab   247

Answer to Hands-on Lab   248

Answers to Review Questions   250

Chapter   8   Frame Relay   251

Understanding Frame Relay.   252

What is Frame Relay?   252

A Brief History of Frame Relay   253

Frame Relay Virtual Circuits   253

Switched Virtual Circuits   254

Permanent Virtual Circuits   255

Data Link Connection Identifier (DLCI)   255

DCLI Mapping   256

Frame Relay Local Management Interface (LMI)   258

Configuring Frame Relay   259

Frame Relay Congestion Control   260

Factors Affecting Performance   260

Congestion Handling by Frame Relay Switches   261

Congestion Handling by Routers   262

Point-to-Point and Multipoint Interfaces   263

Verifying Frame Relay   266

The *show interface* Command   266

The *show frame-relay pvc* Command   267

The *show frame-relay map* Command   268

The *show frame-relay lmi* Command   269

The *debug frame-relay lmi* Command   269

Frame Relay Switching   270

Frame Relay Switching Commands   271

Frame Relay Traffic Shaping   274

Using Traffic Shaping Techniques   274

Configuring Traffic Shaping   275

Summary   277

Exam Essentials   278

Key Terms   279

Written Lab   279

Hands-on Labs   280

Lab 8.1: Configuring Frame Relay with Subinterfaces   280

Lab 8.2: Frame Relay Traffic Shaping   282

Review Questions   283

Answers to Written Lab   287

Answer to Review Questions   289

Chapter   9   Queuing and Compression   291

Queuing   292
   Traffic Prioritization   293
   Queuing Policy   293
IOS Queuing Options   294
   Weighted Fair Queuing   295
   Priority Queuing   298
   Custom Queuing   301
Cisco's Newer Queuing Technologies   308
   Low Latency Queuing   309
   Class-Based Weighted Fair Queuing   309
   Committed Access Rate   310
Compression   310
   TCP Header Compression   311
   Payload Compression   312
   Link Compression   312
   Compression Considerations   313
   Viewing Compression Information   314
Summary   314
Exam Essentials   315
Key Terms   316
Written Lab   316
Hands-on Lab   317
   Lab 9.1: Queuing   317
Review Questions   319
Answers to Written Lab   322
Answers to Review Questions   323

**Chapter   10   Network Address Translation (NAT) and Port
Address Translation (PAT)   325**

Understanding Network Address Translation (NAT)   327
   NAT Terminology   327
   How NAT Works   328
   Advantages of NAT   329
   Disadvantages of NAT   330
   NAT Traffic Types   330
Performing NAT Operations   331
   Translating Inside Local Addresses   332
   Overloading Inside Global Addresses   333
   Using TCP Load Distribution   334
   Overlapping Networks   335
Configuring NAT   336
   Configuring Static NAT   337

Configuring Dynamic NAT, Inside Global Address
    Overloading, and TCP Load Distribution   338
Configuring NAT to Perform Overlapping Address
    Translaton   340
Verifying NAT Configuration   341
Troubleshooting NAT   342
Clearing NAT Translation Entries   343
Using Port Address Translation (PAT)   344
Disadvantages of PAT   344
Configuring PAT   345
Monitoring PAT   347
Summary   348
Exam Essentials   348
Key Terms   349
Written Lab   349
Hands-on Lab   350
Lab 10.1: Static NAT   350
Review Questions   352
Answers to Written Lab   356
Answers to Review Questions   357

Chapter   11   Centralized Security in Remote Access Networks   359

Security Terminology   360
Cisco Access Control Solutions   361
CiscoSecure   362
Authentication, Authorization, and Accounting   363
How AAA Works   364
Router Access Modes   365
Character-Mode Connections   365
Packet-Mode Connections   366
AAA Configuration   367
Authentication Configuration   368
Authorization Configuration   370
Accounting Configuration   374
Virtual Profiles   376
Summary   377
Exam Essentials   377
Key Terms   378
Written Lab   378
Hands-on Lab   379
Configuring TACACS+   379

Review Questions   380
Answers to Written Lab   384
Answers to Review Questions   385

Glossary   **387**

Index   *407*

Introduction

This book is intended to help you continue on your exciting new path toward obtaining your CCNP certification. Before reading this book, it is important to have at least read the Sybex *CCNA: Cisco Certified Network Associate Study Guide*, Fourth Edition. You can take the CCNP tests in any order, but you should have passed the CCNA exam before pursuing your CCNP. Many questions in the Building Cisco Remote Access Networks (BCRAN) exam are built on the CCNA material. However, we have done everything possible to make sure that you can pass the BCRAN exam by reading this book and practicing with Cisco routers.

Cisco Systems' Place in Networking

Cisco Systems has become an unrivaled worldwide leader in networking for the Internet. Its networking solutions can easily connect users who work from diverse devices on disparate networks. Cisco products make it simple for people to access and transfer information without regard to differences in time, place, or platform.

Cisco Systems' big picture is that it provides end-to-end networking solutions that customers can use to build an efficient, unified information infrastructure of their own or to connect to someone else's. This is an important piece in the Internet/networking-industry puzzle because a common architecture that delivers consistent network services to all users is now a functional imperative. Because Cisco Systems offers such a broad range of networking and Internet services and capabilities, users needing regular access to their local network or the Internet can do so unhindered, making Cisco's wares indispensable.

Cisco answers this need with a wide range of hardware products that form information networks using the Cisco Internetwork Operating System (IOS) software. This software provides network services, paving the way for networked technical support and professional services to maintain and optimize all network operations.

Along with the Cisco IOS, one of the services Cisco created to help support the vast amount of hardware it has engineered is the Cisco Certified Internetworking Expert (CCIE) program, which was designed specifically to equip people to effectively manage the vast quantity of installed Cisco networks. The business plan is simple: If you want to sell more Cisco equipment and have more Cisco networks installed, ensure that the networks you installed run properly.

However, having a fabulous product line isn't all it takes to guarantee the huge success that Cisco enjoys—lots of companies with great products are now defunct. If you have complicated products designed to solve complicated problems, you need knowledgeable people who are fully capable of installing, managing, and troubleshooting them. That part isn't easy, so Cisco began the CCIE program to equip people to support these complicated networks. This program, known colloquially as the Doctorate of Networking, has also been very successful, primarily due to its extreme difficulty. Cisco continuously monitors the program, changing it as it sees fit, to make sure that it remains pertinent and accurately reflects the demands of today's internetworking business environments.

Building on the highly successful CCIE program, Cisco Career Certifications permit you to become certified at various levels of technical proficiency, spanning the disciplines of network design and support. So, whether you're beginning a career, changing careers, securing your present position, or seeking to refine and promote your position, this is the book for you!

Cisco's Certifications

Cisco has created several certification tracks that will help you become a CCIE, as well as aid prospective employers in measuring skill levels. Before these new certifications, you took only one test and were then faced with the lab, which made it difficult to succeed. With these new certifications that add a better approach to preparing for that almighty lab, Cisco has opened doors that few were allowed through before. So, what are these new certifications, and how do they help you get your CCIE?

Cisco Certified Network Associate (CCNA)

The CCNA certification is the first certification in the new line of Cisco certifications and it is a precursor to all current Cisco certifications. With the new certification programs, Cisco has created a type of stepping-stone approach to CCIE certification. Now, you can become a Cisco Certified Network Associate for the meager cost of the Sybex *CCNA: Cisco Certified Network Associate Study Guide*, Fourth Edition, plus $125 for the test. And you don't have to stop there—you can choose to continue with your studies and select a specific track to follow. The Installation and Support track will help you prepare for the CCIE Routing and Switching certification, whereas the Communications and Services track will help you prepare for the CCIE Service Provider certification. It is important to note that you do not have to attempt any of these tracks to reach the CCIE, but it is recommended.

Cisco Certified Network Professional (CCNP)

The Cisco Certified Network Professional (CCNP) certification has opened up many opportunities for the individual wishing to become Cisco-certified but who is lacking the training, the expertise, or the bucks to pass the notorious and often failed two-day Cisco torture lab. The new Cisco certifications will truly provide exciting new opportunities for the CNE and MCSE who just don't know how to advance to a higher level.

So, you're thinking, ìGreat, what do I do after I pass the CCNA exam?î Well, if you want to become a CCIE in Routing and Switching (the most popular certification), understand that there's more than one path to the CCIE certification. The first way is to continue studying and become a Cisco Certified Network Professional (CCNP). That means taking four more tests in addition to obtaining the CCNA certification.

We'll discuss requirements for the CCIE exams later in this introduction.

The CCNP program will prepare you to understand and comprehensively tackle the internetworking issues of today and beyond—not limited to the Cisco world. You will undergo an immense metamorphosis, vastly increasing your knowledge and skills through the process of obtaining these certifications.

 Remember that you don't need to be a CCNP or even a CCNA to take the CCIE lab, but to accomplish that, it's extremely helpful if you already have these certifications.

What Are the CCNP Certification Skills?

Cisco demands a certain level of proficiency for its CCNP certification. In addition to those required for the CCNA, these skills include the following:

- Installing, configuring, operating, and troubleshooting complex routed LAN, routed WAN, and switched LAN networks, and Dial Access Services.

- Understanding complex networks, such as IP, IGRP, IPX, Async Routing, extended access lists, IP RIP, route redistribution, route summarization, OSPF, VLSM, BGP, Serial, IGRP, Frame Relay, ISDN, ISL, DDR, PSTN, PPP, VLANs, Ethernet, access lists, and transparent and translational bridging.

To meet the Cisco Certified Network Professional requirements, you must be able to perform the following:

- Install and/or configure a network to increase bandwidth, quicken network response times, and improve reliability and quality of service.

- Maximize performance through campus LANs, routed WANs, and remote access.

- Improve network security.

- Create a global intranet.

- Provide access security to campus switches and routers.

- Provide increased switching and routing bandwidth—end-to-end resiliency services.

- Provide custom queuing and routed priority services.

How Do You Become a CCNP?

After becoming a CCNA, the four exams you must take to get your CCNP are as follows:

Exam 642-801: Building Scalable Cisco Internetworks (BSCI)   A while back, Cisco retired the Routing (640-603) exam and now uses this exam to build on the fundamentals of the CCNA exam. BSCI focuses on large multiprotocol internetworks and how to manage them. Among other topics, you'll be tested on IS-IS, OSFP, and BGP. This book covers all the objectives you need to understand for passing the BSCI exam. The BSCI exam is also a required exam for the CCIP and CCDP certifications, which will be discussed later in this introduction.

Exam 642-811: Building Cisco Multilayer Switched Networks (BCMSN)   The Building Cisco Multilayer Switched Networks exam tests your knowledge of the 1900 and 5000 series of Catalyst switches.

Exam 642-821: Building Cisco Remote Access Networks (BCRAN)   The Building Cisco Remote Access Networks (BCRAN) exam tests your knowledge of installing, configuring, monitoring, and troubleshooting Cisco ISDN and dial-up access products. You must understand PPP, ISDN, Frame Relay, and authentication.

Exam 642-831: Cisco Internetwork Troubleshooting Support (CIT)   The Cisco Internetwork Troubleshooting Support (CIT) exam tests you on troubleshooting information. You must be able to troubleshoot Ethernet and Token Ring LANS, IP, IPX, and AppleTalk networks, as well as ISDN, PPP, and Frame Relay networks.

If you hate tests, you can take fewer of them by signing up for the CCNA exam and the CIT exam, and then take just one more long exam called the Foundation R/S exam (640-841). Doing this also gives you your CCNP—but beware, it's a really long test that fuses all the material listed previously into one exam. Good luck! However, by taking this exam, you get three tests for the price of two, which saves you $125 (if you pass). Some people think it's easier to take the Foundation R/S exam because you can leverage the areas that you would score higher in against the areas in which you wouldn't. There is also an option to take three tests: the BCRAN and CIT exams, and the Composite Exam (642-891), which fuses the BSCI and BCMSN exams.

Remember that test objectives and tests can change at any time without notice. Always check the Cisco website for the most up-to-date information (www.cisco.com).

Sybex has a solution for each one of the CCNP exams. Each study guide listed in the following table covers all the exam objectives for their respective exams.

Exam Name	Exam #	Sybex Products
Building Scalable Cisco Internetworks	642-801	CCNP: *Building Scalable Cisco Internetworks Study Guide* (ISBN 0-7821-4293-1)
Building Cisco Multilayer Switched Networks	642-811	CCNP: *Building Cisco Multilayer Switched Networks Study Guide* (0-7821-4294-X)
Building Cisco Remote Access Networks	642-821	CCNP: *Building Cisco Remote Access Networks Study Guide* (0-7821-4296-6)
Cisco Internetwork Troubleshooting	642-831	CCNP: *Cisco Internetwork Troubleshooting Study Guide* (0-7821-4295-8)

Also available is the *CCNP Study Guide Kit, 3rd Ed.* (0-7821-4297-4), which covers all four exams.

Cisco Certified Internetwork Professional (CCIP)

After passing the CCNA, the next step in the Communications and Services track would be the CCIP. The CCIP is a professional-level certification.

The CCIP will present you with the skills necessary to understand and tackle the complex internetworking world of the service provider. The skills you will obtain will prepare you to move forward toward the ever-elusive CCIE Communications and Services certification.

What Are the CCIP Certification Skills?

Cisco demands a certain level of proficiency for its CCIP certification. In addition to those required for the CCNA, these skills include the following:

- Perform complex planning, operations, installations, implementations, and troubleshooting of internetworks.

- Understand and manage complex communications networks—last mile, edge, or core.

How Do You Become a CCIP?

After becoming a CCNA, you must take two core exams and an elective. The core exams are listed here:

Exam 642-801: Building Scalable Cisco Internetworks (BSCI)   A while back, Cisco retired the Routing (640-603) exam and now uses this exam to build on the fundamentals of the CCNA exam. BSCI focuses on large multiprotocol internetworks and how to manage them. Among other topics, you'll be tested on IS-IS, OSFP, and BGP. This book covers all the objectives you need to understand for passing the BSCI exam.

Exam 642-641: Quality of Services (QoS)   This exam tests your knowledge of quality of service for internetworks.

Exam 640-910: Implementing Cisco MPLS (MPLS)   This exam tests your knowledge of multiprotocol label switching and its implementation. The Sybex *CCIP: MPLS Study Guide* covers all the exam objectives.

Exam 642-661: Border Gateway Protocol (BGP)   This exam tests your knowledge of Border Gateway Protocol (BGP). When you complete this exam, you should be able to manage a large BGP network.

Cisco's Network Design and Installation Certifications

In addition to the Network Installation and Support track and the Communications and Services track, Cisco has created another certification track for network designers. The two certifications within this track are the Cisco Certified Design Associate (CCDA) and Cisco Certified Design Professional (CCDP) certifications. If you're reaching for the CCIE stars, we highly recommend the CCNP and CCDP certifications before attempting the CCIE R/S Qualification exam.

These certifications will give you the knowledge to design routed LAN, routed WAN, and switched LAN.

Cisco Certified Design Associate (CCDA)

To become a CCDA, you must pass the DESGN (Designing for Cisco Internetwork Solutions) test (640-861). To pass this test, you must understand how to do the following:

- Design simple routed LAN, routed WAN, and switched LAN and ATM LANE networks.
- Use network-layer addressing.
- Filter with access lists.
- Use and propagate VLAN.
- Size networks.

Cisco Certified Design Professional (CCDP)

If you're already a CCNP and want to get your CCDP, you can simply take the CCDA and the Designing Cisco Network Architectures (ARCH) 642-871 tests. If you're not yet a CCNP, however, you must take the CCDA, CCNA, BSCI, BCMSN, BCRAN, and ARCH exams.

CCDP certification skills include the following:

- Designing complex internetworks with hierarchical network designs
- Implementation of quality of service
- Understanding of advanced networking concepts, including VLSM, IP multicast, AVVID, VPN, and wireless

Cisco's Security Certifications

There are quite a few Cisco security certifications to obtain. All of the Cisco security certifications also require a valid CCNA.

Cisco Certified Security Professional (CCSP)

You have to pass five exams to get your CCSP. The pivotal one of those is the SECUR exam. After you pass the SECUR exam, you need to take only four more. Here they are—the exams you must pass to call the CCSP yours:

Exam 642-501: Securing Cisco IOS Networks (SECUR)   This exam tests your understanding of such concepts as basic router security, AAA security for Cisco routers and networks, Cisco IOS firewall configuration and authentication, building basic and advanced IPSec VPNs, and managing Cisco enterprise VPN routers. Sybex can help you pass the SECUR exam with the *CCSP: Securing Cisco IOS Networks Study Guide* (ISBN 0-7821-4231-1).

Exam 642-521: Cisco Secure PIX Firewall Advanced (CSPFA)   This exam challenges your knowledge of the fundamentals of Cisco PIX Firewalls, as well as translations and connections, object grouping, advanced protocol handling and authentication, and authorization and accounting, among other topics. You can tackle the CSPFA exam with the help of Sybex's *CCSP: Secure PIX and Secure VPN Study Guide* (ISBN 0-7821-4287-7).

Exam 642-511: Cisco Secure Virtual Private Networks (CSVPN)   The CSVPN exam covers the basics of Cisco VPNs as well as configuring various Cisco VPNs for remote access, hardware client, backup server and load balancing, and IPSec over UDP and IPSec over TCP. Again, using the Sybex *CCSP: Secure PIX and Secure VPN Study Guide* (ISBN 0-7821-4287-7), you'll approach the CSVPN exam with confidence.

Exam 642-531: Cisco Secure Intrusion Detection System (CSIDS)   The CSIDS exam will challenge your knowledge of intrusion detection technologies and solutions, and test your abilities to install and configure ISD components. You'll also be tested on managing large-scale deployments of Cisco IDS sensors using Cisco IDS management software. Prepare for the CSIDS exam by using Sybex's *CCSP: Secure Intrusion Detection and SAFE Implementation Study Guide* (ISBN 0-7821-4288-5).

Exam 9E0-131: Cisco SAFE Implementation (CSI)   This exam tests such topics as security and architecture fundamentals, SAFE network design for small and medium corporate and campus situations, and SAFE remote-user network implementation. See Sybex's *CCSP: Secure PIX and Secure VPN Study Guide* (ISBN 0-7821-4287-7).

Cisco Firewall Specialist

Cisco Security certifications focus on the growing need for knowledgeable network professionals who can implement complete security solutions. Cisco Firewall Specialists focus on securing network access by using Cisco IOS Software and Cisco PIX Firewall technologies.

The two exams you must pass to achieve the Cisco Firewall Specialist certification are Securing Cisco IOS Networks (SECUR) and Cisco Secure PIX Firewall Advanced (CSPFA).

Cisco IDS Specialist

Cisco IDS Specialists can both operate and monitor Cisco IOS Software and IDS technologies to detect and respond to intrusion activities.

The two exams you must pass to achieve the Cisco IDS Specialist certification are Securing Cisco IOS Networks (SECUR) and Cisco Secure Intrusion Detection System (CSIDS).

Cisco VPN Specialist

Cisco VPN Specialists can configure VPNs across shared public networks using Cisco IOS Software and Cisco VPN 3000 Series Concentrator technologies.

The exams you must pass to achieve the Cisco VPN Specialist certification are Securing Cisco IOS Networks (SECUR) and Cisco Secure Virtual Networks (CSVPN).

Cisco Certified Internetwork Expert (CCIE)

Cool! You've become a CCNP, and now your sights are fixed on getting your Cisco Certified Internetwork Expert (CCIE) certification. What do you do next? Cisco recommends a *minimum* of two years of on-the-job experience before taking the CCIE lab. After jumping those hurdles, you then have to pass the written CCIE Exam Qualifications before taking the actual lab.

There are actually four CCIE certifications, and you must pass a written exam for each one of them before attempting the hands-on lab:

CCIE Communications and Services (Exams 350-020, 350-021, 350-022, 350-023)   The CCIE Communications and Services written exams cover IP and IP routing, optical, DSL, dial, cable, wireless, WAN switching, content networking, and voice.

CCIE Routing and Switching (Exam 350-001)   The CCIE Routing and Switching exam covers IP and IP routing, non-IP desktop protocols such as IPX, and bridge- and switch-related technologies.

Sybex can help you pass the CCIE Routing and Switching exam with the *CCIE: Cisco Certified Internetworking Expert Study Guide*, Second Edition (ISBN 0-7821-4207-9).

CCIE Security (Exam 350-018)   The CCIE Security exam covers IP and IP routing as well as specific security components.

CCIE Voice (Exam 351-030)   The CCIE Voice exam covers those technologies and applications that make up a Cisco Enterprise VoIP solution.

What Does This Book Cover?

This book covers everything you need to know for the Remote Access examination; in addition to addressing the real-world materials that you need to understand connectivity options in production networks. Each chapter starts with a list of the topics included as they relate to the exam, so please take a moment to review them before delving into the chapter.

Chapter 1 introduces Remote Access, including a high-level presentation of the different connectivity types and their usage. We also review some of the hardware choices available for remote connectivity.

Chapter 2 presents asynchronous connections, or modem services on telephone lines. While not as glamorous as DSL or Frame Relay, asynchronous connections are the most ubiquitous.

Chapter 3 delves into the details of the Point-to-Point Protocol, which can be used to provide a common transport for users. The protocol also includes authentication options, which are further presented in the chapter.

Chapter 4 presents Microsoft Windows and networking with this popular operating system. There are few, if any, questions remaining on the examination regarding this product, but the coverage is good for real-world implementations and the possibility of a question or two remaining on the exam. The discussion on DHCP is relevant for most readers and should be reviewed.

Chapter 5 discusses Integrated Services Digital Network (ISDN) technologies, which are still common in many countries. Although cable modems and DSL are quickly replacing ISDN, there are benefits in its use and it does provide some historical information applicable to the newer transports.

Chapter 6 addresses Digital Subscriber Line (DSL), one of the fastest growing consumer connectivity options. Businesses are finding economical, high-bandwidth benefits to the technology as well.

Chapter 7 deals with two key technologies. Cable modems are competing well with DSL and provide advantages and disadvantages for remote users. The second part of the chapter presents VPN technologies, including IPSec, and ties together cable modems with tunneling. Although they are independent technologies, they can be complementary and have been presented as such in this chapter.

Chapter 8 returns to what might be the most prevalent remote access technology for enterprise customers—Frame Relay. We examine the technology, its features, and future uses.

Chapter 9 leaves the transport technologies and presents two services that can be important on lower throughput links—queuing and compression. With the deployment of Voice over IP (VoIP) and other time-sensitive traffic on data networks, the ability to prioritize and control bandwidth is critical to success.

Chapter 10 continues with services that augment remote connections by delving into address translation services. These options can greatly help the administrator in remote access deployments.

Chapter 11 concludes with what some would argue is the most important aspect of networking—security. Specifically this chapter examines AAA (authentication, authorization, and accounting) and these functions' role in internetworking.

Each chapter ends with review questions that are specifically designed to help you retain the knowledge presented. To really nail down your skills, read each question carefully and take the time to work through the hands-on labs in some of the chapters.

Where Do You Take the Exam?

You can take the exams at any of the Sylvan Prometric or Virtual University Enterprises (VUE) testing centers around the world. For the location of a testing center near you, call Sylvan at (800) 755-3926 or VUE at (877) 404-3926. Outside of the United States and Canada, contact your local Sylvan Prometric Registration Center.

To register for a Cisco Certified Network Professional exam:

1. Determine the number of the exam you want to take. (The BCRAN exam number is 642-821.)

2. Register with the nearest Sylvan Prometric or VUE testing center. At this point, you will be asked to pay in advance for the exam. At the time of this writing, the exams are $125 each and must be taken within one year of payment. You can schedule exams up to six weeks in advance or as soon as one working day prior to the day you wish to take it. If something comes up and you need to cancel or reschedule your exam appointment, contact the testing center at least 24 hours in advance. Same-day registration isn't available for the Cisco tests.

3. When you schedule the exam, you'll get instructions regarding all appointment and cancellation procedures, the ID requirements, and information about the testing-center location.

Tips for Taking Your CCNP Exam

The CCNP BCRAN test contains about 66 questions to be completed in about 90 minutes. However, understand that your test might vary.

Many questions on the exam have answer choices that at first glance look identical—especially the syntax questions! Remember to read through the choices carefully because "close" doesn't cut it. If you put commands in the wrong order or forget one measly character, you'll get the question wrong. So, to practice, do the hands-on exercises at the end of the chapters over and over again until they feel natural to you.

Unlike Microsoft or Novell tests, the exam has answer choices that are really similar in syntax—although some syntax is dead wrong, it is usually just *subtly* wrong. Some other syntax choices might be right, but they're shown in the wrong order. Cisco does split hairs, and is not at all averse to giving you classic trick questions. Here's an example:

`access-list 101 deny ip any eq 23` denies Telnet access to all systems.

This item looks correct because most people refer to the port number (23) and think, "Yes, that's the port used for Telnet." The catch is that you can't filter IP on port numbers (only TCP and UDP). Another indicator is the use of an extended access list number but no destination address or ìanyî for the destination.

 For further practice with routers and switches, check out the CCNP Virtual Lab from Sybex. For information on the current version of this product, please go to www.sybex.com.

Also, never forget that the right answer is the Cisco answer. In many cases, more than one appropriate answer is presented, but the *correct* answer is the one that Cisco recommends.

Here are some general tips for exam success:

- Arrive early at the exam center, so you can relax and review your study materials.

- Read the questions *carefully*. Don't just jump to conclusions. Make sure that you're clear about *exactly* what each question asks.

- Don't leave any questions unanswered. They count against you.

- When answering multiple-choice questions that you're not sure about, use the process of elimination to get rid of the obviously incorrect answers first. Doing this greatly improves your odds if you need to make an educated guess.

- As of this writing, the written exams still allow you to move forward and backward. However, it is best to always check the Cisco website before taking any exam to get the most up-to-date information.

After you complete an exam, you'll get immediate, online notification of your pass or fail status, a printed Examination Score Report that indicates your pass or fail status, and your exam results by section. (The test administrator will give you the printed score report.) Test scores are automatically forwarded to Cisco within five working days after you take the test, so you don't need to send your score to them.

How to Use This Book

This book can provide a solid foundation for the serious effort of preparing for the CCNP BCRAN exam. To best benefit from this book, use the following study method:

1. Take the Assessment Test immediately following this Introduction. (The answers are at the end of the test.) Carefully read over the explanations for any question you get wrong, and note which chapters the material comes from. This information should help you plan your study strategy.

2. Study each chapter carefully, making sure that you fully understand the information and the test topics listed at the beginning of each chapter. Pay extra-close attention to any chapter where you missed questions in the Assessment Test.

3. Complete all hands-on exercises in the chapter, referring to the chapter so that you understand the reason for each step you take. If you do not have Cisco equipment available, make sure to study the examples carefully. Also, check www.routersim.com for a router simulator. Answer the Review Questions related to that chapter. (The answers appear at the end of the chapter, after the Review Questions.)

4. Note the questions that confuse you, and study those sections of the book again.

5. Before taking the exam, try your hand at the two Bonus Exams that are included on the CD that comes with this book. The questions in these exams appear only on the CD. This will give you a complete overview of what you can expect to see on the real thing.

6. Remember to use the products on the CD that is included with this book. The electronic flashcards and the EdgeTest exam-preparation software have all been specifically picked to help you study for and pass your exam. Study on the road with the *CCNP: Building Cisco Remote Access Networks Study Guide* e-book in PDF, and be sure to test yourself with the electronic flashcards.

The electronic flashcards can be used on your Windows computer, Pocket PC, or on your Palm device.

7. Make sure you read the Key Terms list at the end of each chapter. Appendix A includes all the commands used in the book, along with an explanation for each command.

To learn all the material covered in this book, you'll have to apply yourself regularly and with discipline. Try to set aside the same time every day to study, and select a comfortable and quiet place to do so. If you work hard, you will be surprised at how quickly you learn this material. All the best!

What's on the CD?

We worked hard to provide some really great tools to help you with your certification process. All of the following tools should be loaded on your workstation when studying for the test.

The Sybex Test Engine for Cisco BCRAN Test-Preparation

New from Sybex, this test-preparation software prepares you to successfully pass the BCRAN exam. In this test engine, you will find all of the questions from the book, plus two additional Bonus Exams that appear exclusively on the CD. You can take the Assessment Test, test yourself by chapter, or take the two Bonus Exams that appear on the CD.

Electronic Flashcards for PC, Pocket PC, and Palm Devices

After you read the CCNP: *Building Cisco Remote Access Networks Study Guide,* read the Review Questions at the end of each chapter and study the Bonus Exams included in the book and on the CD. But wait, there's more! Test yourself with the flashcards included on the CD. If you can get through these difficult questions, and understand the answers, you'll know you'll be ready for the CCNP BCRAN exam.

The flashcards include 150 questions specifically written to hit you hard and make sure you are ready for the exam. Between the Review Questions, practice exams, and flashcards, you'll be more than prepared for the exam.

CCNP: Building Cisco Remote Access Networks Study Guide in PDF

Sybex offers this Cisco Certification book on the accompanying CD so that you can read the book on your PC or laptop. It is in Adobe Acrobat format. Acrobat Reader is included on the CD as well. This could be extremely helpful to readers who travel and don't want to carry a book, as well as to readers who find it more comfortable reading from their computer.

About this book

It would be unfair to publish this text with only one name on the cover without noting that a lot of people were involved in its construction, including co-authors. Materials that were used in the second edition have been revised and updated, but many pages are unchanged as the technology and exam focuses are unchanged. This has allowed all those working on this project to focus on new materials and the new examination focuses to provide greater value to the reader.

How to Contact the Authors

You can reach Robert Padjen at `remoteaccess3@yahoo.com`.

Assessment Test

1. What type of queuing is the default for serial links under 1.544Mbps on Cisco routers?

    A. Link

    B. Payload

    C. Weighted Fair Queuing

    D. Header

2. Which of these is not a Primary Rate Interface (PRI) switch option?

    A. `primary-ni`

    B. `primary-dms100`

    C. `primary-4ess`

    D. `primary-net5`

3. Which of the following commands will show the custom queues configured on your router?

    A. `show custom`

    B. `show all queues`

    C. `show queuing custom`

    D. `show queueing custom`

4. The most commonly available WAN technology is _____.

    A. Analog dial-up

    B. Frame Relay

    C. Cable modem

    D. ISDN

5. What is the component in a cable modem that is responsible for converting the radio frequency into digital data?

    A. Modulator

    B. Demodulator

    C. DHCP

    D. CMTS

6. The command `aaa authorization if-authenticated` performs which of the following functions?

   A. Allows only authorized resources to attempt authentication

   B. Allows only connections via console connections

   C. Allows all functions, if the user is correctly authenticated

   D. None of the above

7. Which of the following does a UART perform?

   A. Compression

   B. Error correction

   C. Buffering

   D. Compression and error correction

8. An address pool or DHCP might be preferred to manual address allocation for which of the following reasons? (Select all that apply.)

   A. Conservation of addresses

   B. Exhaustion of addresses

   C. Simplification of client configuration

   D. Complexity of client configuration

9. True or False: NAT enables you to increase or decrease the number of globally routable addresses without changing any hosts on the network, with the exception of the NAT border router.

   A. True

   B. False

10. True or False: Windows 95 supports the IP protocol with Cisco remote access servers.

    A. True

    B. False

11. True or False: The Windows Control Panel is used to configure dial-up networking.

    A. True

    B. False

12. The LZW algorithm performs what function?

    A. Error correction

    B. Compression

    C. Hardware flow control

    D. None of the above

13. To provide authentication without requiring the password to be sent in clear-text, what should the administrator configure?

   A. CHAP

   B. PAP

   C. MP

   D. TCP

14. When you are setting up a long-distance connection, which of the following is typically the lowest-cost solution?

   A. Frame Relay

   B. ISDN

   C. Leased line

   D. Analog dial-up

15. Which is *not* true regarding PPP callback?

   A. The access server will not make repeated attempts for a callback.

   B. The user must authenticate before callback is initiated.

   C. PPP callback is defined in RFC 1570.

   D. The user must enter the callback phone number.

16. What is the default encapsulation for serial circuits on Cisco routers?

   A. PPP

   B. ATM

   C. HDLC

   D. SDLC

17. Which of the following is true regarding ISDN PRI in Europe and the United States?

   A. The standards are identical.

   B. Primary rate in Europe is equal to BRI in the U.S.

   C. The two are different because of Europe's E-1-based carrier. The U.S. uses T-1.

   D. ISDN is not available in Europe.

18. What is the modemcap database?

   A. A table of modem configuration information

   B. A listing of hostnames

   C. A set of compression formulas

   D. None of the above

19. True or False: Port Address Translation (PAT) will deny traffic from all well-known port numbers, such as ports used by FTP by default.

    A. True

    B. False

20. What protocol is used for signaling on ISDN?

    A. LAPB

    B. LAPD

    C. LAXD

    D. ITU I.430

21. What does the *MD* in MD4 and MD5 stand for?

    A. Manual distribution

    B. Multilink datagram

    C. Message digest

    D. Message distribution

22. What is the interface name for the D channel on a T1-based PRI?

    A. Port 0:d

    B. Interface ISDN PRI0/0

    C. Interface BRI0

    D. Interface Serial0:23

23. Token-based security solutions are sometimes called which of the following?

    A. Something you have and something you know

    B. Random key

    C. Lock and key

    D. IPSec

24. The command `debug isdn q.931` provides information about which of the following?

    A. TEI negotiation

    B. Bearer capability

    C. B channel ID

    D. B and C

25. Which of the following is *not* a primary difference between ADSL and SDSL?

  A. ADSL provides faster download speeds than upload.

  B. SDSL provides the ability to run voice over the same line.

  C. ADSL provides the ability to run voice over the same line.

  D. Common ADSL currently faster than most varieties of SDSL.

26. What is the correct syntax for an ISDN dialer map?

  A. `dialer map ip 192.168.254.2 8358661`

  B. `dialer string 8358661`

  C. `isdn dialer map 192.168.254.2 name R2 8358661`

  D. `isdn dialer string 8358661`

27. Which of the following commands is a valid map class?

  A. `RouterA#frame-relay map-class name`

  B. `RouterA(config-if)# frame-relay map-class name`

  C. `RouterA(config-if)#map-class frame-relay name`

  D. `RouterA(config)#map-class frame-relay name`

28. What specification is used to standardize cable modem functions and services?

  A. IPSec

  B. DOCSIS

  C. DOCSYS

  D. VPN

29. Which of the following best describes a protocol framework that defines payload formats, the mechanics of implementing a key exchange protocol, and the negotiation of a security association?

  A. ISAKMP

  B. L2TP

  C. Shared keys

  D. Diffie-Hellman

30. Which of the following is *not* an advantage of VPN technology?

  A. Provides secure communications

  B. Allows use of the public Internet for private communications

  C. Can greatly reduce connectivity costs

  D. Works only with Frame Relay PVCs

  E. Is topology independent

31. Which of the following enables traffic shaping on an interface?

   A. RouterA(config-if)#frame-relay class *name*

   B. RouterA(config)#frame-relay class *name*

   C. RouterA(config)#frame-relay traffic-shaping

   D. RouterA(config-if)#frame-relay traffic-shaping

32. An administrator needs to configure compression on an AS5300 for a remote user pool that includes 1600 and 700 series routers. The administrator should use which of the following?

   A. MPPC

   B. Stac

   C. Predictor

   D. All of the above

33. Which of the following would the administrator use to prioritize a class of traffic at the router?

   A. Weighted Fair Queuing

   B. Custom Queuing

   C. Class-Based Weighted Fair Queuing

   D. Classful Queuing

34. A Frame Relay switch is getting congested. What type of message would it transmit to the sender of the frame, indicating that congestion is occurring?

   A. BECN

   B. FECN

   C. DE

   D. CIR

   E. CR

35. What type of compression compresses only the data, not the header?

   A. Cisco

   B. IETF

   C. TCP header

   D. Payload

   E. Link

36. What compression method compresses both the header and data fields?

    A. Cisco

    B. IETF

    C. TCP header

    D. Payload

    E. Link

37. True or False: NAT hides end-to-end IP addresses, rendering some applications unusable.

    A. True

    B. False

38. Packet-mode connections usually

    A. Pass through the router.

    B. Terminate at the router.

    C. Require the use of PPP.

    D. Either A or B.

39. You have one corporate office and many small remote offices that transmit only bursty data transfers. Which WAN technology should you consider?

    A. Frame Relay

    B. Cable modem

    C. Dedicated circuit

    D. TDM circuit

    E. Not possible

40. Which of the following commands is correct for configuring a custom queue list that takes all packets received on Ethernet 0 and places them in the first queue?

    A. `queue-list 1 interface Ethernet0 1`

    B. `interface ethernet 0 queue-list 1`

    C. `queueing-list 1 ethernet 0 1`

    D. `queue-list e0 list 1`

41. Which of the following types of entries in the NAT table indicates an IP address and port pair?

    A. Simple translation entry

    B. Extended translation entry

    C. Global translation entry

    D. Inside translation entry

42. Which of the following is a valid DLCI for use on a serial interface?

   A. 0

   B. 15

   C. 1008

   D. 1023

   E. None of the above

43. True or False: You should implement an access list to deny all inside IP addresses so they do not filter through the router into the outside network.

   A. True

   B. False

44. True or False: European PRI connections operate over T-1 access circuits.

   A. True

   B. False

Answers to Assessment Test

1. C. Weighted fair Queuing (WFQ) is the default for serial links on Cisco routers. See Chapter 9 for more information on queuing.

2. A. The National 1 is a BRI switch option. For more information, see Chapter 5.

3. D. The command is `show queueing custom`. (Yes, the alternate spelling, *queueing*, is used.) See Chapter 9 for more information on queuing.

4. A. Analog dial-up ports for modem connections are available worldwide in virtually all locations. These connections are relatively slow and costly but can provide access with a minimum of lead time. See Chapter 1 for more information.

5. B. A demodulator takes a radio-frequency signal that has had information encoded in it by varying both the amplitude and phase of the wave, and turns it into a simple signal that can be processed by the analog-to-digital (A/D) converter. See Chapter 7 for more information.

6. C. The `authorization if-authenticated` command is quite powerful—it authorizes all authenticated connections. See Chapter 11 for more information.

7. C. A UART buffers incoming serial data. More advanced UARTs buffer outbound data as well. For more information, see Chapter 2.

8. A, C. DHCP can greatly simplify client configuration—in fact, DHCP can negate the need for any client configuration. In addition, DHCP can conserve addresses as only concurrent stations within the lease period require an address, as opposed to the total number of stations. To learn more about DHCP, see Chapter 3.

9. A. NAT is configured only on the router between the inside network and the outside network. NAT translates addresses for the inside network, and a simple change in the NAT configuration on the NAT border router can change the global address pool without any manual change required on any network host. For more information on globally routable IP addresses, see Chapter 10.

10. A. Windows and Cisco remote access services support the IP protocol. This is the most common protocol in use today. See Chapter 4 for more information.

11. B. The Dial-Up Networking options, unlike other Windows network settings, are controlled under Start ➢ Programs ➢ Accessories ➢ Communications ➢ Dial-Up Networking. See Chapter 4 for more information.

12. B. Lempel, Ziv, and Welch developed a compression algorithm. For more information, see Chapter 2.

13. A. The Challenge Handshake Authentication Protocol (CHAP) is used to authenticate sessions. The protocol sends a hash of the password, as opposed to the actual text. This differs from PAP, which provides authentication but transmits the password in clear-text. See Chapter 4 for more information.

14. A. Frame Relay provides the advantage of being distance insensitive, thus reducing its cost. For more information, see Chapter 8.

15. D. Using a Cisco access server, the user will not be able to enter the callback phone number. All other options are true. To learn more about PPP callback, see Chapter 3.

16. C. The HDLC encapsulation is used by default on Cisco's serial interfaces. For more information on serial encapsulations, see Chapter 8.

17. C. Europe's phone system was designed around a 2.048Mbps E-1 carrier, which differs from the U.S. T-1 standard. This difference is carried into the ISDN environment, which uses T-1 and E-1 for PRI interfaces and aggregation. For more information, see Chapter 5.

18. A. The modemcap database contains modem configuration information that the router can send to the modem in order to interoperate. For more information, see Chapter 2.

19. B. PAT does not deny any traffic from well-known addresses by default. For more information on PAT and how PAT translates well-known IP addresses, see Chapter 10.

20. B. Link Access Procedure, Data (LAPD) is used to carry ISDN signaling information over the D channel. For more information about LAPD, see Chapter 5.

21. C. Message digest, types 4 and 5, is used to hash passwords in Windows dial-up networking. For more information, see Chapter 3.

22. D. The PRI D channel on a T-1-based PRI is channel 23. B channel numbers start at zero (0), with 23 being the 24th channel. For more information about PRIs, see Chapter 5.

23. A. Tokens work like ATM cards—you have the card, but you still need the PIN (personal identification number) when you go to the bank. The other answers are intended to sound similar. For more information, see Chapter 11.

24. D. Debug ISDN Q.931 provides information about Layer 3, including information about bearer capability and channel ID. For more information about Q.931, see Chapter 5.

25. B. SDSL requires a dedicated line and cannot have integrated voice over the same wire. For more information see Chapter 6.

26. A. A dialer map statement is used to map a destination IP address to a dial number or username. For more information about dialer maps, see Chapter 5.

27. D. To create a map class, use the global `map-class frame-relay` *name* command. See Chapter 8 for more information on Frame Relay traffic shaping.

28. B. DOCSIS is a specification for cable modem services. See Chapter 7 for more information.

29. A. Internet Security Association and Key Management Protocol (ISAKMP) is a framework for establishing trusted interactions among entities using TCP/IP. For more information, see Chapter 6.

30. D. VPN services do not require Frame Relay. To learn more about VPN services, see Chapters 6 and 7.

31. D. The interface command `frame-relay traffic-shaping` is used to enable an interface to accept map class parameters. See Chapter 8 for more information on traffic shaping with Frame Relay.

32. B. Recall that the Cisco 700 supports only Stac, making this the only viable option. For more information, see Chapter 9.

33. C. Class-Based Weighted Fair Queuing allows for traffic prioritization. See Chapter 9 for more information.

34. A. Backward Explicit Congestion Notification is used to tell a transmitting router that the frame switch is congested and to slow the transmit rate. See Chapter 8 for more information on congestion control with Frame Relay.

35. D. Payload compression does not compress the header of a packet, only the data field. See Chapter 9 for more information on compression.

36. E. Link compression compresses the header and data fields of a packet. See Chapter 9 for more information on compression.

37. A. Some applications that use IP addressing stop functioning when NAT is used because NAT hides the end-to-end IP address. This can be overcome by using fully qualified domain names or implementing static mappings. For more information on end-to-end IP addresses, see Chapter 10.

38. A. Although packet mode includes PPP, among others, these connections generally pass through the router. PPP is not required. See Chapter 11 for more information on packet-mode connections.

39. A. Frame Relay is perfect for companies with many remote sites that have bursty data transfers. See Chapter 8 for more information on Frame Relay.

40. A. The command is `queue-list [#] interface` *`interface queue number`*. See Chapter 9 for more information on queuing.

41. B. An extended translation entry into the NAT table indicates an entry with an IP address and port pair. The single translation entry indicates an inside IP address to globally routable IP address translation. For more information on NAT table entries, see Chapter 10.

42. E. Valid DLCI assignments are 16–1007. For more information about Frame Relay, see Chapter 8.

43. B. Just the opposite is true. An access list should be created with a permit statement to enable the inside addresses to be handled by NAT for translation from the inside network to the outside network. This process occurs after policy routing is applied. For more information on how access lists work in conjunction with NAT and PAT, see Chapter 10.

44. B. European circuits are configured under the E-1 standard. T-1 is used in North America. See Chapter 1 for more information.

Chapter

1

Cisco Solutions for Remote Access

EXAM TOPICS COVERED IN THIS CHAPTER INCLUDE:

✓ Specify Cisco products that best meet the connection requirements for permanent or dial-up access WAN connections.

✓ Know the benefits and detriments of WAN connection types.

✓ Select appropriate WAN connection for specific site connection considerations.

✓ Choose Cisco equipment that addresses the specific needs of the WAN topology.

✓ Identify the components necessary for WAN connections such as Frame Relay and ISDN PRI from the central site to a branch office.

✓ Identify the requirements for ISDN connections.

✓ Understand the placement of Cable Modem and DSL technologies in Remote Access solutions.

As the computer industry has evolved, the number of access solutions available to the network designer has also increased. Modern networks require a substantial number of solutions to address the wide array of industry needs. Corporations, home office users, and mobile workers all require connectivity options that stress the divergent goals of cost control, bandwidth, and availability.

Cisco has greatly augmented its product line to address some of these needs. The material covered in this book focuses on your ability to apply Cisco-centric solutions to the production networks of today. Architects and designers should always evaluate all vendors' solutions for each problem that they face; however, there is some merit to coming up with a strategic solution that maintains consistency along vendor and product lines. Many problems can arise from the interoperability issues that can result from the use of multiple vendors.

This text focuses on two goals. As with other Study Guides, the ultimate goal is to provide a substantial foundation of knowledge so you can successfully pass the Remote Access exam. The second goal is to provide information that relates to the live production networks that you will be challenged by every day. The benefit of this approach is that the live network experience you will encounter while reading will help you attain certification, and the certification will in turn provide you with a foundation to get experience with a live network.

This chapter begins with an overview of the fundamentals of remote access. In the first section, you will learn about the various wide area network (WAN) connection types, WAN encapsulation protocols, and how to select a WAN protocol. In the next section, you will learn how to choose from among Cisco's remote connection products. And, in the final section, you will learn about WAN cabling and assembly issues. Developing a solid foundation in these topics is an extremely important part of your preparation for Cisco's Remote Access exam because it provides a framework for the subsequent chapters and the exam, not to mention real-world applications.

What Is Remote Access?

The term *remote access* is broadly defined as those services used to connect offices over a wide geographical area. These services are typically encompassed under the guise of a *wide area network (WAN)*. Traditionally, a wide area network uses a telecommunications provider to link distant locations; however, this definition is undergoing substantial change. Many providers are starting to offer Ethernet technologies over significant distances, although Ethernet is typically a local area network (LAN) technology. Unlike LANs, WANs usually use the telecommunications infrastructure—a group of services that are leased from service providers and phone companies.

Historically, the most common remote access installations have provided connectivity between fixed locations and a corporation's headquarters. Such installations are relatively simple once a design has been selected because the solution used for the first office is applicable to the hundredth. Designers need concern themselves only with scalability and availability—as long as the bandwidth needs of each office are comparable.

In the modern remote access design, the architect needs to focus on multiple solutions to address not only the branch office, but also the sales force (a typically mobile group) and tele-commuters working from their homes. Residential installations usually have a different set of needs than office configurations, and T-1 and other high-speed access technologies are usually not available for home use.

 With the deployment of Digital Subscriber Line (DSL) technologies, designers can provide the equivalence of T-1 bandwidth, and more, to the residential user. Actual T-1s are generally not available in residential settings but have been installed when the expense was warranted. This chapter presents various remote access technologies, including ISDN, Frame Relay, and asynchronous dial-up.

WAN Connection Types

The Remote Access exam is concerned primarily with six types of WAN connections. These are predominantly older, more established technologies. The following are WAN connection types you can expect to see on the Remote Access exam:

- Asynchronous dial-up
- Integrated Services Digital Network (ISDN)
- Frame Relay
- Leased lines
- Digital Subscriber Line (DSL)
- Cable modems

Notably absent from this list are Asynchronous Transfer Mode (ATM), wireless, and cellular technologies. Although the Remote Access exam was revised in 2003, and cable modems and DSL were added to the topics addressed, these other remote access technologies remain absent.

Even though these newer technologies are not covered yet, it is important to know a bit about them. For instance, wireless technologies have greatly enhanced the options available to home users. The primary benefit of wireless services is little to no provisioning time, but roaming and cheaper deployment also can be found with these solutions, as discussed later in this chapter. *Asynchronous Transfer Mode (ATM)* is a cell-based system similar in many respects to Frame Relay, although the use of fixed-length cells can make ATM better suited to installations that integrate voice, video, and data. Wireless technologies include microwave, 802.11 LANs, and laser and satellite systems, which typically require a fixed transmitter and receiver, although major strides are being made to add mobility. Cellular systems are very mobile but do not provide substantial bandwidth; however, the technology is being improved and cellular can now provide ISDN-comparable data rates.

If you are a designer who is building a remote access solution, you will need to augment the technical material in this text in order to compose the best remote access solutions for your customers' needs.

 For network architects and designers, we recommend that you read *CCDP: Cisco Internetwork Design Study Guide* by Robert Padjen with Todd Lammle (Sybex, 2000) for more information on designing and integrating remote access solutions into the corporate network.

Asynchronous Dial-Up

Asynchronous dial-up is traditional modem-based access over the public analog phone network. The primary advantage of asynchronous dial-up is that it is available virtually everywhere. Unfortunately, its greatest limitation is bandwidth, which is currently limited to less than 56 kilobits per second (Kbps). In addition, asynchronous dial-up connections require a negotiation period, during which time traffic must be buffered and the user experiences delay.

Because hotels, homes, and customer sites are already supplied with the traditional level of connectivity, dial-up connections are primarily suited to those members in the workforce who are mobile. Such connections are a substantial benefit when compared to the other remote access technologies, each of which must be predefined or preprovisioned.

Given the universal availability of analog circuits, most designers find that they still require dial-up installations to be a part of their remote access solution. Typically, ISDN installations lend themselves to a dual role—as an ISDN Primary Rate Interface (PRI) that can terminate 23 analog connections, or an assortment of ISDN B channels (user data bearer channels) and analog connections. This ability to service both ISDN digital connections and asynchronous dial-up connections can greatly ease facilities, configuration, and administration burdens.

Analog circuits are best suited for short-duration, low-bandwidth applications. Examples of this type of traffic include terminal emulation and e-mail services. Limited file-transfer and client/server-based application activity could also use this connection.

 In this Study Guide, you will see the terms *asynchronous dial-up* and *analog* used synonymously.

X.25

X.25 is a reliable Layer 2 and Layer 3 protocol that can scale up to 2 megabits per second (Mbps), although most installations stop at 56Kbps. The X.25 protocol was intended to provide reliable data transfer over unreliable circuits. Currently, X.25 is typically used for terminal emulation and small file transfers. Due to its low bandwidth and high overhead, X.25 is losing favor as a remote access technology. Originally, it was designed to address the higher error rates that were experienced on analog circuits. This high degree of overhead makes the protocol very inefficient but well suited to less-advanced telecommunications infrastructure, such as old carrier management systems.

Designers typically find that X.25 is one of the most widely available technologies on an international basis. This availability greatly adds to the desirability of the protocol. However, it is likely that demands for greater bandwidth and the proliferation of fiber-based networks will continue to erode X.25's market share. Although a migration to Ethernet has already begun, it is important to note that many telecommunications carriers continue to use X.25 for management of their switches and other systems.

Integrated Services Digital Network (ISDN)

Integrated Services Digital Network (ISDN) is the result of efforts to remove analog services from the telecommunications network. In the 1960s, the American phone company, AT&T, realized that their network would be more efficient with digital services throughout. This included the residence, where most ISDN BRI (explained next) is found. However, the model scaled beyond this, and included aggregation and other interfaces that allowed efficient *MUXing*, or the consolidation of multiple small links into one large one.

Two types of ISDN services are available. The first, ISDN *Basic Rate Interface (BRI)*, provides for two 64Kbps channels (the bearer, or B, channels) and one 16Kbps channel (the D channel), which can carry user data. The second type of ISDN service, called *Primary Rate Interface (PRI)*, can provide twenty-three 64Kbps B channels for user data and one 64Kbps channel (D channel) for signaling, based on the North American T-1 standard. The E-1 European standard provides 2.048Mbps worth of bandwidth and a corresponding increase in the number of B channels.

Please note that the 16Kbps channel in ISDN BRI is used for signaling; however, many providers permit the transit of user data using this bandwidth. This is frequently marketed as "always-on" ISDN. ISDN PRI uses a single 64Kbps channel for signaling.

    Some ISDN BRI installations limit each B channel to 56Kbps.

The primary advantage of ISDN is its capability to provide faster access than would be available from traditional asynchronous dial-up connections. Unfortunately, the service is not as widely available as traditional analog services and it tends to be more costly. ISDN is typically used in scenarios including low-bandwidth video, low-bandwidth data, and voice services. It is important to note that each of the two ISDN channels can provide the user with a traditional analog dial-up connection.

ISDN services are quickly being replaced in the United States by DSL services. Digital Subscriber Line connections are currently available at over 1Mbps, and some provide over three times this rate. However, substantial restrictions exist regarding the distance over which these connections can be set up (the maximum distance is 18,000 feet, or under 3 miles from the central office to the residence), and some sources predict that up to 40 percent of homes will be too far from the central office to receive the service. As of this writing, DSL still failed to compete with cable modem and ISDN installations in terms of number of deployments in the United States.

ISDN is well suited for most applications, including file transfers. However, its high per-minute pricing (depending on service package) makes it impractical when it is needed for more than a couple hours per day. Frame Relay, which you will learn about next, is typically a better solution for higher-bandwidth, long-duration connections.

Frame Relay

Frame Relay is a logical, low-overhead transport protocol that removes much of the overhead found in X.25. Frames are marked with a data link connection identifier (DLCI) that provides direction to the switch regarding frame forwarding. As such, frames in Frame Relay are Layer 2 elements. In many companies, setting up Frame Relay services between central locations and remote offices is very popular. The primary benefit of Frame Relay is that it is traditionally tariffed to be distance insensitive—this means that a connection that crosses the United States will be comparable in cost to that of a connection across town. In addition, Frame Relay services are available internationally from many providers.

Frame Relay, in addition to DSL, is becoming more accepted in the telecommuter workspace. Telecommuters are finding that connections are required for more than a few hours per day— a threshold that makes ISDN more costly than the other options. In addition, ISDN is incapable of expanding beyond 128Kbps without using PRI services or bonding. Frame Relay is available in a myriad of bandwidths, up to and including DS3. New variations on Frame Relay are increasing this performance characteristic.

Note that ISDN cannot scale beyond 128Kbps in user data on a single pair of B channels. Just as two B channels can be bonded together into a single logical data conduit, it is possible to bond multiple ISDN BRI circuits into a single logical data stream. Chapter 3 discusses PPP bonding in greater detail, and Chapter 5 discusses ISDN bonding.

For the network designer, there are two factors to consider when deploying Frame Relay: Frame Relay is available with a *Committed Information Rate (CIR)*, and Frame Relay enables multiple *Permanent Virtual Circuits (PVCs)* to terminate at a single physical connection point on the router. A PVC is a previously defined logical path through the network. The DLCI is used to determine which PVC is to be used. *Switched Virtual Circuits (SVCs)* are alternatives to PVCs. SVCs are similar to PVCs, but they are not predefined and static. Before data can be transmitted by using SVCs, a path must be established dynamically through the network.

The CIR is best thought of as a guaranteed amount of bandwidth available on a PVC. This figure might be substantially lower than the capacity of the circuit itself. The corporation will pay for the bandwidth guaranteed by the CIR, and any traffic that exceeds the CIR will be handled on a best-effort basis. Thus, a company can obtain better throughput than that for which it is being charged.

The capability of Frame Relay to enable multiple PVCs to terminate at a single physical connection point on the router is a powerful tool. This means that a designer need not purchase additional interfaces to accommodate multiple connections. In addition, there's a substantially lowered lead-time for new connections, and such connections can be provisioned without a visit to the head-end location.

The Frame Relay protocol is primarily designed to encapsulate data on reliable, digital connections. Its benefits include low overhead when compared to X.25 (X.25 using protocol overhead for data reliability), lower costs when compared to point-to-point connections, and a single access point on the router that can terminate multiple virtual circuits (each of which can go to different destinations). This last benefit greatly reduces the costs associated with the router hardware. The Frame Relay protocol and its benefits are explored in more detail in Chapter 8.

Due to its relatively low cost and high bandwidth, Frame Relay is better suited for higher-bandwidth demands than other access technologies, including ISDN.

Leased Lines

Leased lines are commonly referred to as dedicated connectivity options. This means that the connection between the two endpoints is permanent in nature and that 100 percent of the capacity is available to the end user. Leased lines are owned by the telecommunications carrier and are often provided in the form of a T-1. These connections are also called point-to-point links because the capacity of a leased line is dedicated to the corporation. Unfortunately, because bandwidths cannot be shared, this type of connection is more expensive than Frame Relay or ATM.

In addition, leased lines are also distance sensitive. Unlike Frame Relay, with leased lines, the telephone company will charge the end user for both the local loop and the transit network. For short distances, the differences in costs might be negligible, but for long distances, the costs increase dramatically. For example, a 200-mile Frame Relay connection might cost $200 a month, which would be the same as a 2,000-mile Frame Relay connection. The leased line installation might also cost $200 a month for 200 miles, but most likely, it would cost $3,000 a month for the 2,000-mile link. The most common leased-line service available in the United States is called a T-1. This provides the corporation with 1.544Mbps of dedicated bandwidth. Older leased lines were digital data service (DDS) circuits and yielded up to 56Kbps of bandwidth. These connections were popular for mainframe connectivity at both the 9.6Kbps and 56Kbps levels.

Digital Subscriber Line

Digital Subscriber Line (DSL) technologies were developed to be the magic bullet of the telecommunications industry. Primarily designed to add bandwidth to the home without installing fiber optics, the various DSL protocols, referred to in the generic as xDSL, have the potential to provide 52Mbps over already installed copper wire—a marked increase in performance. This feat is accomplished with special encoding of the digital signal.

At present, DSL technologies are being used as a replacement for ISDN and analog Internet Service Provider (ISP) connections. However, as DSL technologies are accepted into the home and office, they will likely be used for primary and backup data transfer and for high-demand services such as live video. DSL currently lags behind cable modem installations, but some vendors, including Next Level Communications (www.nlc.com), have equipment in production that demonstrates the long-term potential of this technology. The NLC-based systems can provide voice (plain old telephone system, or POTS, based), video, and high-speed Internet service over DSL technologies, and are priced competitively when compared to obtaining these services independently.

The different DSL standards provide for varying amounts of upstream and downstream bandwidth based on the equipment in use and the distances between this equipment. As a result of the distance sensitivity of xDSL, connections typically must terminate within 3 miles of the central office, but access technologies can be employed to extend the range. Access products connect a remote termination device to the central office via fiber optics, which greatly extends the reach of xDSL. Figure 1.1 illustrates a typical installation of xDSL with and without an access product. As shown, a home 4 miles away cannot obtain xDSL access without an access product. Please note that most xDSL technologies support distances between 1,800 feet and 18,000 feet.

FIGURE 1.1   xDSL installations

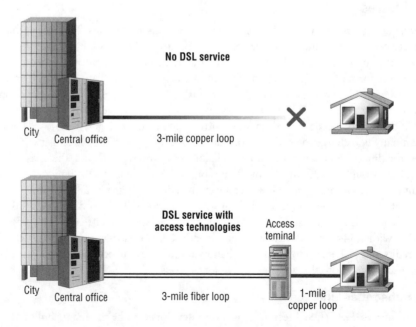

As of this writing, vendors are deploying DSL at fairly low speeds and as an Internet connectivity solution. Most vendors provide 1.544Mbps downstream bandwidth as viewed from the central office site, and 128Kbps to 384Kbps upstream. These bandwidths greatly surpass ISDN and analog offerings, but they cannot provide the multiservice goals of xDSL—primarily MPEG-2 video streaming. Table 1.1 shows the various xDSL technologies available.

TABLE 1.1   The Various xDSL Technologies

Standard	Characteristics
Asymmetric DSL (ADSL)	There are a number of flavors to Asymmetric DSL; the two most popular are G.lite and G.dmt (discrete multitone). The G.lite specification provides 1.5Mbps/384Kbps bandwidth and typically invokes lower capital costs. The G.dmt specification can provide 8Mbps downstream and 1.5Mbps upstream.
High bit-rate DSL (HDSL)	HDSL is similar to SDSL but uses double and triple pairs of copper wire. Most other DSL technologies operate over a single pair, which can simplify installation compared to HDSL. HDSL typically provides distances reaching 15,000 feet.
ISDN-based DSL (IDSL)	ISDN-based DSL typically allows the greatest distances but is limited to 144Kbps.
Symmetric DSL (SDSL)	Symmetric DSL provides 2Mbps bidirectional bandwidth over a single pair of copper wires. Distances are typically limited to 10,000 feet.
Very high bit-rate DSL (VDSL)	VDSL can provide up to 52Mbps downstream bandwidth, but its distance is limited to less than 4,500 feet. This is usually the shortest-range DSL service.

Most vendors deploy one of the following two xDSL implementation models: ISP-based installation (Layer 3) and Remote LAN (RLAN, or Layer 2). The traditional ISP-based installation simply substitutes ISDN or analog dial-up for xDSL. Because DSL is an always-on technology, there is no call setup or teardown process, and the connection to the Digital Subscriber Line Access Multiplexer (DSLAM) is always active. There is a single link to the service provider, and all packets are routed to their destination. RLAN, on the other hand, places the DSL connection on par with Frame Relay or point-to-point links in the WAN. This provides more secure connectivity that can support nonroutable protocols. This solution is being deployed for telecommuters as opposed to interoffice connections. Ultimately, designers might find that the consumer level of support currently offered in DSL will be augmented, and the lower price for setup will encourage companies to replace Frame Relay and leased-line installations for interoffice traffic with DSL as well.

Both of these implementation methods can make a modern network design perform better. However, some caveats should be considered. At present, most DSL vendors offer a single PVC with DSL installations. This limits connectivity options and makes redundancy difficult. A second PVC could provide a link to another head-end, perhaps a distribution layer aggregation point, and most vendors have multiple DSLAMs in the central office. An SVC-based solution would also make a fault-tolerant design more successful.

Another concern with current DSL installations is that most products do not offer security solutions. The RLAN model greatly reduces this risk because the links are isolated at Layer 2, but all connectivity must be provided by the head-end, including Internet connectivity. For Internet connections, the risk is significantly greater, especially when the bandwidth available for an attack and the use of static IP addresses or address pools are considered. A number of significant attacks have already occurred as a result of these issues, and although they should not deter the use of the technology, the risks should be addressed with firewall technology.

A third consideration in DSL is the installation delay compared to other technologies. Vendors are moving toward splitterless hardware so that the phone company does not have to install a splitter in the home. The splitter divides the traditional phone signals from the data stream and provides a jack for standard telephones—DSL transport data and voice over the same twisted-pair wiring used for standard analog phone service. At present, because the circuit to the home and the installation of the splitter need to be validated, installations require weeks to complete.

 DSL technologies are presented in greater detail in Chapter 6.

Cable Modems

It would be unfair to present the DSL technologies without providing some space to discuss the alternative: cable modems. *Cable modems* operate over the same cabling system that provides cable television service; in other words, they use the same coax cable that is already used in the homes with cable television. Most cable installations provide two cables—one for the television and one for the data converter—but the signaling and the system are the same. This is accomplished by allocating a television channel to data services. Bandwidth varies with each installation; however, many installations provide up to 2Mbps in the downstream direction and 128Kbps to 256Kbps in the upstream one. *Downstream* is a common term for traffic from the provider to the customer; *upstream* is return traffic. This type of asymmetric connection is sufficient for most Internet users, because these users typically pull more information (bits) to their machines than they send.

Detractors of cable modem technology are quick to point out that these installations are shared bandwidth, similar to Ethernet, which results in contention for the wire among neighbors. This shared bandwidth also introduces a security risk, in that network analysis is possible, although vendors have addressed this concern with switching and encryption technology. This issue does not exist in DSL because the local loop connection to the home is switched. In DSL, traffic is not integrated until it reaches the central office, and at that point, the switch will forward only traffic destined for the end station based on the media access control (MAC) address.

Basically, cable modems are a shared technology—hub-based Ethernet versus switched. Along the same lines, a cable modem is really a broadband Ethernet bridge to the cable.

> There is a lot of confusion in the marketplace regarding oversubscription and performance in the residential DSL and cable modem markets. DSL is usually oversubscribed 10 to 1 at the central office; if a DS3 is used to link the DSLAM to the Internet, as many as 300 homes could be connected to the DSLAM. None of those users would be oversubscribed on their connection to the DSLAM. Cable modems typically share bandwidth before the head-end. As a result, users contend for bandwidth both before and after the head-end.

Network designers might wish to consider cable modems as part of a Virtual Private Network (VPN) deployment because the technology will not lend itself to the RLAN-type designs available in DSL. Recall that an RLAN requires Layer 2 isolation—a service not offered by cable modem providers at present. This might change in the future if channels can be isolated to specific users. This might be especially true in very remote rural areas, where cable is available and DSL is not.

> Cable modem technology, including the features of Data over Cable Service Interface Specification (DOCSIS), is presented in Chapter 7.

New WAN Connection Technologies

As noted previously, there are many new technologies with which designers and administrators should be familiar, but they aren't covered on the current Remote Access exam. These include Asynchronous Transfer Mode (ATM), and wireless (802.11) and cellular services.

Asynchronous Transfer Mode (ATM)

ATM does not relate in any way to asynchronous dial-up connections. Rather, it refers to the transmission of fixed-length cells and the transport of data, voice, and video services. The majority of the public telephone network has already converted to this technology for the aggregation of phone lines. Cells are fixed in length, and therefore latency and delay can be determined and controlled accurately.

ATM is rarely used as a remote access technology in the context applied to the exam, and it would be best to think of it as a potential replacement for Frame Relay installations. Typically, residential ATM installations appear in the form of DSL—ATM being the underlying Data Link (Layer 2) technology.

Wireless and Cellular

Wireless technologies, including cellular systems, provide a mobile access method. Typically, these technologies offer substantially lower bandwidth than wire line services.

For wireless solutions (wireless LAN), the current standard is based on IEEE 802.11, with interoperability between systems certified by the Wi-Fi committee. This technology is well suited for short-range deployments within a building or campus environment, and provides for bandwidths up to 54Mbps. Security, a long-time stumbling block for deployment (the original security provided by wireless LANs, Wired Equivalent Protocol (WEP), was relatively poor and subject to hacking), has been addressed by vendors and will be part of the 802.11i specification when ratified. Current solutions include Temporal Key Integrity Protocol (TKIP), and it is likely that 802.1x (an authentication model) and Advanced Encryption Standard (AES) will be found in both wireless LAN and wired solutions.

Three standards are available for wireless LAN installations, as described in Table 1.2.

TABLE 1.2   802.11 Standards

Standard	Frequency Used	Bandwidth Available (Maximum Rated)	Range	Features
802.11b	2.4GHz	11Mbps	Longest	Original specification and most widely used today. Provides three non-overlapping channels of 11Mbps, but prone to interference from cordless phones and microwave ovens.
802.11a	5.0GHz	54Mbps	Shortest	Uses frequency space that is less prone to interference.
802.11g	2.4GHz	54Mbps (standard ratified at 22 Mbps)	Medium to long	Backward compatible with 802.11b.

Because wireless LAN is outside of the scope of the Remote Access exam, it is presented here only as an introduction. This technology could be deployed as part of remote access solutions in the future. For further information, we suggest consulting the 802.11 Planet website at www.80211-planet.com.

 This text was written following the acquisition of Linksys by Cisco Systems. This acquisition is a strong signal of the future of wireless technology for small office and home office (SOHO) users, of which remote access is a critical component.

Another area not addressed on the current Remote Access exam is cellular communications. Although historically used in voice communications, the latest Global System for Mobile Communications (GSM) and code division multiple access (CDMA) technologies provide sufficient bandwidth for lower-demand applications. Although the technical characteristics and benefits of each technology are beyond the scope of this text, this technology is important for real-world application of remote access design. Not only will cellular-based systems provide for roaming and small form factor connectivity, but they will ultimately link small offices and other services while removing the last mile that is typically the most costly and time consuming portion of a remote access link. The term *last mile* refers to the connection between the telecommunications providers and the end-customer.

Summarizing WAN Connection Technologies

Table 1.3 summarizes the WAN connection technologies discussed in this chapter in order to provide comparisons among them.

TABLE 1.3   Summary of WAN Connection Technologies

Connection	Max Throughput	U.S. Availability	Relative Cost
Asynchronous dial-up 56Kbps/DDS	56Kbps	Widely available	Low
Leased line T-1/E-1	1.544Mbps/2.048Mbps	Widely available in the U.S.	Medium
Leased line DS3	44.736Mbps/ 34.368Mbps(E-3)	Widely available	High
ATM	10Gbps. However, it is virtually unlimited from a protocol perspective	Moderately available	Very high
ISDN BRI	128Kbps for user, 16Kbps for control data, and 48Kbps for overhead	Moderately available	Low. However, per-minute tariffs can quickly alter this
ISDN PRI	1.5Mbps T-1, and about 2Mbps E-1	Moderately available	Medium
DSL	128Kbps to 2Mbps (some installations up to 52Mbps)	Available in larger cities, becoming more available in rural areas	Low
Frame Relay	Wide range of speeds, from 56K over T1 to DS3 (45Mbps)	Widely available	Low
Cable modem	From 128 Kbps to 3Mbps	Widely available	Low

WAN Encapsulation Protocols

There are many WAN encapsulation protocols, which operate at Layer 2 to provide consistent transport at the Data Link Layer. It is important to note that some of these protocols extend into Layer 3, especially X.25. These protocols include the Point-to-Point Protocol (PPP); the X.25 Link-Access Procedure, Balanced (LAPB) protocol; and the Frame Relay protocol. Additional WAN encapsulation protocols include the Serial Line Internet Protocol (SLIP), the High-Level Data Link Control (HDLC) protocol, and Asynchronous Transfer Mode (ATM).

Again, the Remote Access exam omits many these protocols, both older and newer encapsulations. SLIP has been largely replaced by PPP, and ATM is quite common, but both are outside the scope of the exam. The omission of HDLC is significant if only because this protocol is the foundation for many other transports. In addition, it remains the default encapsulation for Cisco serial interfaces.

The encapsulations covered within the Remote Access exam include the following:

- Point-to-Point Protocol
- X.25
- Frame Relay

In later sections of this chapter and in other chapters, you will learn about each of these in greater detail.

 The current Remote Access exam does not include ATM, HDLC, or SLIP. Here you will find brief descriptions of these three protocols for reference only.

Asynchronous Transfer Mode (ATM)

You might be asking what the difference is between the technology and the encapsulation type. ATM as a technology is different from the protocol itself. Unfortunately, it would be inappropriate to go into significant detail regarding ATM in this chapter—both because this chapter functions as an introduction and because this material is not on the exam. However, to understand ATM as an encapsulation type, you need to look at ATM adaptation layers (AAL) and cell header formats.

ATM is a cell-based service that breaks data into 53-byte packets. This fixed length enables processing to be handled in hardware, which reduces delay and provides for deterministic latency. ATM is primarily designed to integrate voice, data, and video services.

High-Level Data Link Control (HDLC)

High-Level Data Link Control (HDLC) is the encapsulation method used by serial links and is the default on Cisco serial interfaces. The protocol provides for a 32-bit checksum and three transfer modes: normal, asynchronous response, and asynchronous balanced. Many point-to-point connections using Cisco routers continue to make use of the HDLC protocol.

Serial Line Internet Protocol (SLIP)

The *Serial Line Internet Protocol (SLIP)* is designed for point-to-point serial connections using TCP/IP. The Point-to-Point Protocol (PPP), which you will learn about next, has effectively replaced SLIP. Some installations, however, still rely on SLIP because of its simplicity.

Point-to-Point Protocol (PPP)

The *Point-to-Point Protocol (PPP)* is a standard, efficient Layer 2 technology designed for connections between two endpoints. As such, it doesn't include addressing functionality as Ethernet's MAC address does, but it can be augmented to operate in point-to-multipoint installations. The PPP has effectively replaced SLIP and is commonly found in lower-bandwidth applications, although it is also used as a ubiquitous protocol for a wide range of higher-bandwidth installations. One of the most innovative benefits of PPP is its support for multiple upper-layer protocols. This is accomplished by the use of the Network Control Protocol (NCP), which encapsulates the upper layers. The Link Control Protocol (LCP) is used to negotiate connections on the WAN data link, and in PPP, it provides for authentication and compression. Use of PPP permits the binding of connections, also called multilink PPP.

 PPP is covered in more detail in Chapter 3.

The X.25 Protocol

The X.25 protocol really comprises many protocols, including LAPB and X.25 itself, which is a Layer 3 protocol. X.25 also uses various standards, including X.121, X.75, and X.3, among others.

 We have included information regarding X.25 in this text; however, it is very likely that this information will not be included in the exam as it is modified in the future. Readers can expect to see questions relating to the technology, and given its historical significance, learning about X.25 is not unwarranted.

LAPB operates at Layer 2 of the Open System Interconnect (OSI) model and is responsible for providing reliability. Specifically, LAPB provides windowing functions and detects missed frames.

 Readers who wish to review the OSI model should refer to *CCNA: Cisco Certified Network Associate Study Guide,* Third Edition by Todd Lammle (Sybex, 2002).

X.25 (which can be described as also belonging to Layers 1 through 3) was designed to catch errors, because it was developed to operate on poor-quality telecommunications systems. At

Layer 3, X.25 describes the formation of data packets and the methods to be used for connectivity, in addition to addressing.

Some consider the X.25 standards to be recommendations from the International Telecommunications Union–Telecommunication (ITU-T) Standardization Sector. In practice, this can be accurate because private X.25 networks are free to operate over any methodology that works. However, the standards can simplify matters and become very important in public X.25 networking.

The X.25 addressing standard is X.121. X.121 addresses are composed of a Data Network Identification Code (DNIC) and a Network Terminal Number (NTN). These numbers work similarly to the way area codes and phone numbers work—the DNIC is akin to an area code that is defined on a country basis. The NTN is a specific node identifier.

Frame Relay

The Frame Relay protocol is quite simple compared to X.25 because the error correction functions have been removed. This enables the protocol to scale up to 45Mbps in currently available offerings, although this is more a practical limit than a technology-based one. The greatest benefit of Frame Relay is its availability and its low cost over long distances at high bandwidths.

The protocol itself is used to define virtual circuits, which adds an additional benefit to Frame Relay: a single physical port can terminate numerous logical virtual circuits. This can greatly reduce the hardware costs associated with an installation. Each virtual circuit is defined with a DLCI.

Frame Relay is formally presented in Chapter 8, but in the context of this chapter, the protocols of this international standard should be noted. The specifics of the protocol are defined in the following standards:

- ANSI T1.617
- ITU-T Q.933
- ITU-T Q.922

To remember the function of each standard, look at the second digit of the ITU number. As could be inferred, Q.933 is a Layer 3 (OSI model) protocol, whereas Q.922 operates at Layer 2.

Selecting a WAN Protocol

You should consider the following factors when selecting a WAN type:

- Availability
- Bandwidth
- Cost
- Manageability

- Applications in use
- Quality of service
- Reliability
- Security

Many of these elements are common to any network design regardless of its WAN or LAN delineation. This section defines each of these factors and provides some guidance as to how they might apply to remote access deployments.

Availability

Unfortunately, not all of the WAN technologies introduced in this chapter are available in all locations. Although this is frequently true in more rural locations, it might also be true on a country-by-country basis. Distance, technology, and infrastructure all play a role in determining what services will be available in a particular location. Table 1.4 summarizes the technologies and general availability throughout the world.

TABLE 1.4   Worldwide Availability of WAN Technologies

Technology	Availability
Asynchronous dial-up	Widely available
X.25	Widely available
ISDN	Moderately available
Frame Relay	Widely available
Leased lines	Widely available
DSL	Moderately available
Cable modem	Widely available (U.S.)

Bandwidth

Applications might demand more bandwidth than is readily available with some WAN technologies. For example, an asynchronous dial-up connection is limited to 56Kbps. Should the application require the movement of more data than will fit in this constraint, the network architect will be required to select a different technology.

Frequently, selecting another technology will increase overall costs; for example, a T-1 circuit will cost substantially more than a standard analog connection at a remote location. Some technologies provide high levels of bandwidth for relatively low cost. Frame Relay is an example of one such technology.

Table 1.5 compares available bandwidth of common WAN technologies.

TABLE 1.5   Bandwidth Comparison of WAN Technologies

Technology	Bandwidth
Asynchronous dial-up	Low
X. 25	Low
ISDN	Moderate
Frame Relay	High
Leased lines	High
DSL	Moderate
Cable modem	Moderate

Cost

Cost is almost always the single most important criteria in the network design. As such, network designers and architects are required to weigh the relative cost of a WAN technology against the services that it provides. Again, Frame Relay frequently reduces the costs of a WAN circuit compared to a point-to-point leased line. The network architect needs to weigh this cost differentiation against the other factors used in determining the appropriate WAN protocol to use.

Table 1.6 compares the costs of various WAN technologies.

TABLE 1.6   Cost Comparison of WAN Technologies

Technology	Cost
Asynchronous dial-up	Low. However, per-minute and distance charges can significantly increase total cost.
X.25	Low. However, per-minute and distance charges can significantly increase total cost.
ISDN	Low. However, per-minute and distance charges can significantly increase total cost.
Frame Relay	Low.

TABLE 1.6   Cost Comparison of WAN Technologies *(continued)*

Technology	Cost
Leased lines	High.
DSL	Low.
Cable modem	Low.

Manageability

The best networks cannot hope to operate without being manageable. In local area networks, this is fairly simple because the administrator controls everything from the wall jack to the server or WAN router. In remote access, these advantages no longer exist because the ability to physically access the remote end has been removed. When the connection is down or disconnected (reflecting the potential differences between dedicated circuits and on-demand connections), it is not possible to logically connect to the remote equipment. Either of these limitations can greatly work against quick problem resolution.

For remote access manageability, the designer and administrator will frequently try to automate as many functions as possible. This can be accomplished with tools including Dynamic Host Configuration Protocol (DHCP), which automatically assigns IP addresses; and authentication servers, including Enhanced Terminal Access Controller Access Control System (TACACS+), which can centralize the user-authentication database. Administrators prefer centralization, instead of the alternative, which would require placing each user and password on every access resource manually. This centralizing of the security function will also make the network more secure; removing a single terminated employee will remove their access account from all entrances into the network.

Table 1.7 shows the difference in manageability of various WAN technologies.

TABLE 1.7   Manageability Comparison of WAN Technologies

Technology	Manageability
Asynchronous dial-up	Little.
X. 25	Some, including congestion statistics.
ISDN	Some.
Frame Relay	High.
Leased lines	High.

TABLE 1.7   Manageability Comparison of WAN Technologies *(continued)*

Technology	Manageability
DSL	Some.
Cable modem	Some. Very little controllable by the end-user, but the carrier can perform some management functions on their behalf.

Remote Access in the Field: Manageability

The benefits of centralized access control cannot be overemphasized, but a certain amount of care must accompany this process. Many older security products would store the password file in clear-text, which could be read by anyone with access to the server. This, coupled with no requirement to change the passwords on a regular basis, made centralized security less secure than one that stores passwords in an encrypted form or one that uses tokens or other mechanisms than passwords.

Obviously, the trick is to make sure that the central access control database and server are secure. This again yields a benefit to the administrator because this can be accomplished easily when there are one or two security servers (remember, redundancy is an important consideration). Although the remote access devices will also demand a degree of security, it is far easier to protect a single resource than tens or hundreds—the basis for perimeter firewalls.

A note regarding forcing regular password changes: it can be taken too far. Consider an organization that requires monthly password changes. Our first guess at everyone's password would be some combination of month and year—jun00, for example. Incremented passwords, such as Tyler7, Tyler8, and so on, would also be common; of course, substitute the name of your child, pet, or significant other in the string.

Applications in Use

Network designers are concerned with two specific characteristics of the traffic when selecting a WAN protocol. The first consideration relates to the upper-layer protocol that will be used. For example, it is not possible to use SLIP with any other upper-layer protocol except IP. To use a different protocol, the administrator would have to select another lower-level protocol (PPP, for example) to transport native Internetwork Packet Exchange (IPX) packets. The second consideration has to do with the acceptability of delay on the part of the upper-layer protocol. Systems Network Architecture (SNA), a mainframe protocol, traditionally cannot accept a high level of delay.

Fortunately, most applications can use many transport protocols and most operate using IP. This enables the remote access solution to focus on supporting a single protocol in most cases, and it enables the use of a protocol that does not suffer significantly from the delay present in low-bandwidth and on-demand connections. Because of this, many vendors and designers will opt to use PPP as a transport protocol.

Quality of Service (QoS)

Unlike the marketing term "quality of service" that is based on traffic shaping and control, this *quality of service (QoS)* refers to the reliability of the connection and its capability to process nondata traffic. This simpler view is controlled less by configuration and software and is more reliant on the physical and logical characteristics of the standard.

There are two factors to consider when evaluating quality of service requirements on a WAN link. The first factor involves the type of application traffic that will traverse the link—whether data and voice traffic will both share the available bandwidth, for example. The second factor focuses more upon the reliability of the connection; for example, dial-up analog connections are frequently considered less reliable than a point-to-point link. As a result, designers might wish to incorporate backup technologies based on both the criticality of the data and the reliability of the selected WAN protocol. For instance, Frame Relay, though it is considered a reliable protocol, is frequently backed up with analog connections or ISDN.

Reliability

Reliability is a quality of service characteristic; however, it is relatively important and warrants separate consideration. As noted in the quality of service description, reliability is frequently a factor in determining whether a backup link is required. Some designers will use multiple PVCs to provide a greater level of reliability when problems are anticipated in the WAN cloud; this differs from those situations when the designer is concerned with reliability in the local loop or in the last portion of the circuit. In these situations, a separate connection is warranted.

The designer might also wish to use separate components in remote locations to further augment reliability. This migrates the objective into the category of redundancy. It would require disparate routers, circuits, Data Service Unit/Channel Service Unit (DSU/CSU) terminations, and electrical systems to become fully fault tolerant, although it might also require placing the equipment in two separate telephone closets with different building entrances to different service providers' offices. Different providers would further add to the redundancy of the design and its ultimate survivability, which is synonymous to reliability. See Table 1.8 for a comparison of various WAN technologies. Please note that this table refers to the technology's inherent capability to recover from data corruption, error, or topology change.

TABLE 1.8   Reliability Comparison of WAN Technologies

Technology	Reliability
Asynchronous dial-up	Low
X. 25	High

TABLE 1.8   Reliability Comparison of WAN Technologies *(continued)*

Technology	Reliability
ISDN	Moderate
Frame Relay	Moderate
Leased lines	Moderate
DSL	Moderate
Cable modem	Moderate

Examining this table further, it is important to consider each factor of reliability. Dial-up connections cannot recover errors within packets and cannot automatically find a new path through the network except when the circuit is emulated over ATM or another technology within the carrier's cloud. X.25 is considered highly reliable by most, including Cisco, because the protocol provides for error correction and other mechanisms to protect data without relying on upper-layer protocols.

The technologies rated with moderate reliability are typically quite robust and will work for most users without any problems. Historically, however, Cisco presented the position that these technologies were more prone to problems, including lower service guarantees. Although none of the technologies rated moderate provide for error correction as X.25 does, the quality of cables, equipment, and software makes errors very rare and easily addressed by the upper-level protocols.

Carriers are turning to Multi Protocol Label Switching (MPLS) for their voice and data clouds and IP datagrams for all services. This will eventually position each of these technologies as a last mile service; the technology within the cloud will be transparent to the user and data. Table 1.8 focuses on the end-to-end use of the noted technologies.

Security

Security is an important consideration when selecting a WAN protocol—security relating to protection from corruption, theft, or misuse of digital transmissions. Some applications, such as financial ones, require a high level of security. For example, many designers in financial institutions will select private point-to-point connections over fiber-optic cable. In installations that require less security, the designer might opt for a public connection, which frequently has a substantially reduced cost.

Remote access solutions can alter the security model of a corporation substantially, as it is reasonable to assume that some business data will be stored remotely. This immediately causes a security concern because a lost or stolen notebook can quickly lead to the release of corporate data. The network designer will typically be more concerned with the security requirements that will prevent unauthorized access to the network. This, again, is a fairly simple model because the majority of the security configuration will be placed on the remote access servers.

Virtual Private Networks (VPNs)

In recent years, the use of *virtual private network (VPN)* technology has entered into the remote access landscape. VPNs allow secure connections over public networks—typically making use of the Internet. Data is encrypted for transport in a virtual tunnel between source and destination, and its costs are greatly reduced without a substantial decrease in security. As such, a VPN is a system of these tunnels used to create a logical system of conduits that transport user data.

Although most VPN software is very solid, it is important to note that most companies bristle at the thought of using only basic software to secure data. In addition, the processing demands required by some encryption technologies are high, and many implementations will likely require newer processors or coprocessed implementations. Coprocessors offload specific functions from the main processor; video adapters have used them for years to provide better graphics output. Encryption can benefit from this coprocessor design as well.

Two common VPN technologies are in use today: IPSec and SSL. The IP Security Protocol (IPSec) is an encapsulation mechanism that operates at Layer 3 of the OSI model. It is useful in providing a virtual end-to-end connection between points regardless of the technology. In IPSec the client is on the network and can use most software and applications. IPSec uses triple-DES (Data Encryption Standard) in most instances, but this will be replaced in the near future by the less demanding, and possibly more secure, AES, or Advanced Encryption Standard. Both technologies encrypt data so it cannot be modified or intercepted en route.

Secure Sockets Layer (SSL) is commonly used to secure web sessions and transactions; however, it is being used more and more by application emulators and remote access technologies. These installations provide a screen presence to the remote user—all the processing occurs at the central, hosting, location. As networking evolves, it is quite likely that VPNs and technology independence will become common, and customers will use any physical connectivity technology, including Ethernet, to access remote locations.

Choosing Remote Connection Cisco Products

Cisco offers a wide range of router products available for use in remote access solutions. Most of these fall into one of two general categories: fixed interface or modular interface. Fixed-interface solutions are fairly common in remote deployments, whereas modular interfaces are found in central locations. This placement also relates well to their characteristics: Fixed interface solutions are very limited and lack upgradeability. Modular routers are expandable and usually provide better performance.

In addition to the interface types, different software options are available in the Cisco product line. Many products take advantage of the Cisco Internetwork Operating System (IOS), which simplifies administration and training expenses because administrators need to learn only one operating system. Routers based on this software also support more features under most circumstances. Other Cisco routers make use of the Cisco Broadband Operating System (CBOS), which can be found on the 600 series products. The CBOS software is limited in functionality, and many of its commands differ from their IOS counterparts. However, the 600 series routers can reduce acquisition costs by more than half compared to an IOS-based platform—a substantial cost difference when magnified against the hundreds of routers that might be acquired in a large-scale remote access deployment.

Remote Access in the Field: Outsourcing Remote Access Solutions

Given the complexity of managing equipment in hundreds of locations internationally, many companies have selected to outsource their remote access solutions. This option provides a great deal of support flexibility because the outsourcing company can frequently provide technicians over a larger geographical area. As a result, outsourcing provides a great deal of benefit because it can provide faster response times and can free corporate support personnel from the responsibility of responding themselves.

Outsourcing solutions can also provide cost savings in the form of leasing options for remote access equipment. Although the final cost of leasing might be greater, many companies use this financing option as a means to reduce corporate taxes.

By no means should companies use outsourcing as a panacea. Significant downsides exist, including the real risk of outsourcing too many components of the network. Should the outsourcing company be unable to comply with service-level agreements, or unable to provide a reasonable level of service, the remote users will suffer and the ultimate recourse will be to change outsourcing companies—a process that is time-consuming and costly.

Companies should seriously evaluate the benefits of outsourcing against their overall corporate strategy. Selective use of outsourcing, in addition to leasing, can greatly facilitate remote access solutions.

Fixed Interfaces

Early routers were little more than Unix workstations and PCs equipped with two Ethernet interfaces. The first fixed-purpose routers were typically fixed interface as well—there was no provision for adding an additional interface or a new type of interface. As router products evolved, the capability to add modularity to the products increased. A fixed-interface router cannot be expanded, so one with two Ethernet interfaces will always have only two Ethernet interfaces. When you need a third, you must replace the router or augment it with another.

Fixed-interface routers typically reduce the costs associated with acquisition, which directly relates to the initial capital expense. Many organizations try to reduce capital costs, even when this leads to ultimate replacement requirements. In addition, they are simpler to install than modular routers, especially by less experienced staff and vendors. Fixed-interface equipment lacks an upgrade path, however. It is impossible to add features without requiring a complete replacement of the equipment. Replacing equipment can quickly offset the savings you made with the initial purchase. Therefore, designers should seriously evaluate the life span of the equipment and the growth potential for the environment before they make any irreversible decisions. Typically, sites with more than 30 users will quickly outgrow fixed-configuration routers, although different environments yield different thresholds.

Cisco offers two alternatives to the fixed router. The modular router enables network modules or port adapters to be installed by supplying the type and volume of interfaces needed; this is discussed in the next section. In addition, routers are also available for expansion with fixed interfaces and one or more modular ports. The Cisco 1600 is a good example of this hybrid router type and is discussed later in this chapter.

Modular Interfaces

The modular-interface remote access products provide the designer with a few benefits, including an upgrade path, and, typically, higher densities that are unavailable in the fixed-interface models. This flexibility comes at a price; however, and the costs associated with the removal and replacement of network equipment easily offsets this initial cost difference.

The benefits of the modular router also lead to potential savings in the initial acquisition of the device. Sometimes the fixed-interface router provides interfaces that are not needed—Cisco still charges for the unused ports. Although port disparity is uncommon given the wide array of fixed-configuration routers in the Cisco product line, it is possible to find situations in which a high number of Ethernet ports also require a high number of serial ports on a fixed router, which greatly adds to the cost. Modular routers provide the following positives and negatives:

Pros	Cons
Defined upgrade path	Higher cost
Potentially lower total cost of ownership	More complex installation
	More difficult and costly to stock spare equipment

Again, it is usually best to select modular routers to avoid forklift upgrades in the future—ones that require the complete replacement of the chassis. However, the use of modular routers comes at higher initial and support costs.

Product Selection Tools

Most designers find that the best information regarding Cisco's product line comes from their sales representatives. The sales force, though, relies upon information on Cisco's website. Cisco has provided a product selection tool that enables the designer to define the features needed for their particular WAN project. As of this writing, this service is

available at www.cisco.com/pcgi-bin/front.x/corona/prodtool/select.pl; however, Cisco does change its site from time to time.

The end of this chapter provides a high-level presentation of the major remote access platforms provided by Cisco.

Cabling and Assembling the WAN

The cabling of the WAN will vary depending on the technologies used and the equipment locations. For example, central sites typically use modular, high-capacity routers, whereas branch
offices typically use modular or fixed-configuration routers. Usually telecommuter equipment
entails fixed-configuration devices and attempts to place all components of the Customer
Premise Equipment (CPE) in a single chassis.

The cabling will also depend on the media to be used. For example, RJ-45 interfaces are typically used to terminate Ethernet connections, whereas serial connections are typically terminated with RS-232 or V.35 cables. Cisco also provides integrated Data Service Units (DSUs)
that can accept the T-1 connection or DS3's COAX connection directly—a serial port uses an
external DSU and is the focus of the Remote Access certification.

This section supplies an overview of the cable connections used with different WAN types.
You will learn about interfacing and terminating options for remote access equipment, identifying appropriate equipment, and verifying a network installation. Subsequent chapters will
expand upon many of the concepts introduced here, including ISDN, X.25, Frame Relay, PPP,
security, and the types of telecommuters and specific equipment in the Cisco product line.

Internetworking Overview and Remote Access Interface Options

Selecting interface types and determining their interoperability for the various cable connections
are a couple of the most critical components used to construct an internetwork. Although it is
possible to perform media conversion for some interfaces, it is far easier to maintain consistency
throughout the design. For example, if a fiber connection is needed to link the router to the
switch, it is generally preferred to use a fiber interface on the router, as opposed to using a copper interface and then using a copper-to-fiber converter upstream. This is also applicable for
serial connectors—it is far easier to manage the network when all cables and interfaces are the
same and relevant to that provided by the vendors. To successfully design this standardization,
it is important to know the functionality of each connection and how it might be used to terminate network interfaces; each of these connections is presented next.

Asynchronous or Analog Connections

Standard telephone service typically terminates with an RJ-11 interface, which connects the
modem to the telephone company's jack. External modems are attached to a Cisco router with

an RS-232 cable. This is also referred to as an EIA/TIA-232 cable. The router end of this connection uses the Cisco DB-60 connector, a 60-pin termination specific to Cisco routers, and a DB-25 connector, which interfaces to the modem. The DB-25 connector is quite common in telecommunications equipment.

ISDN BRI

ISDN BRIs are common in branch and telecommuter installations in which higher than asynchronous bandwidth is needed. The BRI specification avails two 64Kbps bearer channels (B channels) for user traffic, and it uses a single 16Kbps D channel for management and signaling. It is important to remember that these connections are circuit switched and that the data link protocol on the D channel is Link Access Procedure, Data (LAPD). This differs from the X.25 protocol, which uses LAPB. The ISDN B channel is similar to a standard voice channel in terms of bandwidth, and therefore most systems allow the use of a B channel for a traditional analog call. Although the single channel is encoded digitally from the ISDN device to the switch—unlike an analog connection from a phone to a phone switch—the overall mechanics between them are similar.

Some installations of ISDN allow only 56Kbps for each B channel. The reference to X.25 is incorporated in this section due to the comparison provided by the protocol. X.25 is a highly robust protocol, but is not commonly deployed and is no longer part of the exam.

The ISDN BRI is terminated with different connections, but the network (phone company) is usually terminated with an RJ-11 or RJ-45 interface. According to the specifications, the termination should always be accomplished with an RJ-45, which provides for additional signaling and visually distinguishes the ISDN interface from analog connections. However, the exterior pins (1, 2, 7, and 8) of the RJ-45 are frequently unused, so some providers use RJ-11 instead. If you can control this part of the installation, specify RJ-45 and use a specific color to differentiate it from Ethernet, T-1, and other connections.

ISDN PRI (North America)

In North America, ISDN PRIs are provisioned over T-1 standards. The T-1 standard, also called DS1, is capable of servicing 24 64Kbps channels—each channel being historically provisioned for a single voice connection. From this, 23 B channels are allocated, with the last 64Kbps channel used for D channel signaling.

The most important thing to note, in addition to the channels of ISDN PRI, is that ISDN PRI operates over *channelized T-1* connections. This means that at its core, each B channel is one time slot in the T-1 specification, although clearly, there is additional functionality. PRI requires only two pairs of copper wire (the same as T-1); however, all installations should use RJ-45, which has four pairs. This provides a visual variance to RJ-11 ports, and typically RJ-45 provides a better, cleaner connection.

ISDN PRI (Europe)

The European telecommunications standard comparable to T-1 services is called *E-1*, and it provides for 31 channels (time slot 0 is used for signaling and is not a channel in the ISDN framework). The last channel (actually channel 16) is used as a D channel for signaling, yielding a total of 30 user bearer channels. As a significant aside, in Europe, the vendor typically provides the network termination, whereas in the U.S., the customer usually provides it.

> It is important to understand the differences between the North American and European specifications.

Consult with the vendor to determine the proper termination for E-1 PRI installations. These should differ little from American installations; however, there might be small alterations, which could include, for example, providing the demarcation point on a wiring block. ISDN remains popular in Europe and is likely to continue as an access technology there for some time. On a recent trip to Germany and Italy, we noted many advertisements for the service, but we didn't see any evidence of DSL proliferation.

> Chapter 5 addresses some of the differences in European ISDN specifications, as compared to North American installations, in greater detail; however, it is important to note that the middle channel of the E-1 circuit (16) is the D channel, contrasted with 24 in the T-1 specification. In addition, T-1 starts numbering at 0, and E-1 starts with 1 (as noted before, channel 0 is used for framing).

Frame Relay

Using Frame Relay is a powerful way of getting remote access and WAN connectivity. As a packet-switched technology, Frame Relay operates at bandwidths up to 45Mbps, although older networks might limit this to 1.544 (DS3 versus T-1).

> Please check with your vendor for the latest information regarding access loop capacity. Also remember that DS3 is sometimes—incorrectly—called T-3, but in normal conversation the two terms indicate the same amount of bandwidth.

Frame Relay is supported on Cisco routers with EIA/TIA-232, EIA/TIA-449, V.35, X.21, and EIA-530 signaling, but the DB-60 serial cable is almost always used. The network side of the DSU/CSU connection is RJ-45.

Identifying Company Site Equipment

One of the key challenges for the network designer is selecting the equipment that is appropriate to both the current and future demands of the network. This becomes even more difficult when cost constraints are taken into account.

Designers need to select equipment based primarily on the port type and density required for their application. *Port type* refers to the topology, interface, and protocol (T-1, PRI ISDN with an RJ-45 connector, for example). *Port density* is a simplified way of noting the number of ports that can be squeezed into a particular slot or chassis. Frequently changing connectors will allow greater density; however, a larger chassis can also increase the density. As a result, equipment purchased for the central site will frequently require larger and more modular platforms. Equipment for remote locations tends to be simpler and less expensive—primarily to simplify administrative costs.

Although the current version of the Remote Access exam is relatively new, some of Cisco's recommendations and questions might refer to end-of-life or end-of-sales equipment. Please consider this when deploying a production remote access solution, and consult the Cisco website, www.cisco.com, for the most current information.

Central Site

The central site has different requirements compared to the remote branch and telecommuter locations. Unlike those locations, the central site is an aggregation point for all of the other links, and, as such, it requires greater bandwidth, larger equipment, and additional administration.

As of this writing, Cisco suggests four high-end routers to meet the demands of the central site. Designers should consider protocols, interfaces, and scalability when selecting a piece of network equipment. The recommended platforms are as follows:

- Cisco 3600XM and 3700
- Cisco AS5x00
- Cisco 7000/7500

It should be noted that each of these platforms is modular in nature. In addition, Cisco continually introduces new platforms into the product line and will most likely continue to do so as part of its AVVID initiative. *AVVID* stands for *Architecture for Voice, Video, and Integrated Data*, and although it is a marketing term, it will likely define an entire class of equipment for some time. Historically, remote access technologies have been centered on data transport, with support for voice—ISDN and the use of a B channel, for example. Demands will increase for video, voice integration, and data transport in the future; in fact, these demands are already surfacing today.

The following sections provide a more detailed overview of these platforms.

The Cisco 3600 Platform

The Cisco 3600 and 3600XM router platform is well suited to smaller aggregation point deployments and is currently available in the 3620, 3640, and 3660 models. The third digit in these numbers reflects the number of slots available for modules: two, four, and six, respectively. The 3600 was originally designed to address high-bandwidth services and integration of voice and video, along with traditional data services. Due to these characteristics, the platform is also well suited to the remote branch application.

Many production networks have deployed this system in the remote branch locations as well, when high-speed or multiple interfaces are required. The OC-3 ATM port adapter and the newer inverse multiplexing for ATM (IMA) adapter are benefits to the 3600 platform in remote branch installations. Prior to the release of the 3660, the 3600 series was limited to a single internal AC power supply, which reduced its acceptance in the data center or central site—the 3620 and 3640 routers were provisioned with only a single power supply. These boxes could, however, be outfitted with external DC-based redundant systems, but this solution was never clean from a wiring and simplifying perspective.

Many different types of equipment can be used in the central site, but Cisco recommends the 3600 platform overall. As one of the newest routers, the 3600 does provide a solid service offering for designers. The AS5x00 platform is also well suited to ISDN and dial-up terminations in the central site.

The Cisco 3700 Platform

The Cisco 3700 series is a newer version of the 3600, with significantly greater expandability options. As of this writing there are two versions of the platform: the 3725 and the 3745. The third digit in the model number relates to the number of Network Module (NM) slots in the chassis.

Both versions of the 3700 router provide two 10/100 Ethernet ports, two advanced integration module slots (AIM) and three WAN Interface Card (WIC) slots. The platforms are well suited to branch installations, particularly when Voice over IP (VoIP) services might be installed. The platform supports switched Ethernet services with inline power as well.

The Cisco AS5x00 Platform

The Cisco AS5x00 access servers are designed to terminate ISDN and analog dial-up connections. These systems differ substantially from other router platforms in the central site. The primary benefit of these systems is that the routing, switching, channel services, and modems are all integrated into a single chassis, which reduces the number of external connections and space requirements in the rack. These devices can terminate hundreds of connections.

The Cisco 7000/7200/7500 Platforms

Prior to the release of the Gigabit Switch Router (GSR), or Cisco 12000 series, the 7000 series was the flagship of the Cisco router line. The 7000 series is still well suited to the task of remote access aggregation, which is typically less demanding than the high-speed ISP niche of the GSR.

The 7200 platform is most frequently used in new remote access installations. Cisco positions this box as a high-performance, high-density central site router for terminating LAN and WAN connections. Many companies use the 7500 (specifically the 7513) in their network cores, and the platform is still one of the most capable multiprotocol routers in production.

The GSR is beyond the scope of this text and is currently used in high-end data centers and ISP environments. It is designed to forward IP packets only.

Remote Branch

The concept of a remote branch is highly variable, depending upon the individual location and services needed. A branch office might contain two or a hundred users, and their demands might be substantial in terms of redundancy, bandwidth, and supportability.

Typically, a remote branch services a population of users rather than a single user. In addition, the level of technical expertise in the remote location is usually limited. Platforms typically recommended for the remote branch include the following:

- Cisco 1600 platform
- Cisco 1700 platform
- Cisco 2600XM platform

The Cisco 1600 Platform

The Cisco 1600 provides an ISDN BRI termination in addition to a WAN expansion slot. This enables the router to accept a WIC, which can be used for a serial connection or integrated T-1/fractional T-1 services. The WIC can also be used for Frame Relay terminations. The router is commonly deployed in remote branch facilities because it can link the Ethernet interface to a Frame Relay network with ISDN BRI backup. This configuration does not provide router redundancy but can greatly augment circuit fault tolerance.

As an IOS-based router, the 1600 can support most features, including Network Address Translation (NAT), access-list control, and multiprotocol support, including IP, IPX, and AppleTalk.

The Cisco 1700 Platform

The Cisco 1700 series routers provide two modular card slots for WAN interfaces, in addition to VPN features. This platform can support Ethernet and Fast Ethernet LANs. Expansion cards are interchangeable with other platforms in the Cisco line, including the 3600.

The Cisco 2500 Platform

The Cisco 2500 series router is available in a wide array of fixed configurations, and depending on the model, it can support Ethernet, Token Ring, serial, and ISDN BRI connections. Some models include an integrated Ethernet hub.

Most of the 2500 series routers are end-of-sale and cannot be ordered. The 2600XM series provides the best replacement; however, some users might wish to review the 3700 series for more advanced branch and small office installations. Cisco continues to sell the 2509, 2511, AS2509, and AS2511 platforms, but prudence dictates review of newer platforms before ordering.

The Cisco 2600XM Platform

The Cisco 2600XM platform builds upon the 2500 series with the addition of two modular card slots for WAN interfaces, including T-1, ISDN PRI, and Frame Relay.

Telecommuter

In the real world, telecommuters fall into two distinct categories: remote users and telecommuters. The remote user requires access from multiple locations because they might be at home, at a customer's site, or in a hotel. Typically, these users use analog dial-up connections; however, wireless technologies are becoming increasingly popular with these users. Most remote users use a modem connected to (or built into) their PC.

Telecommuters operate from a home office or an otherwise fixed location. For telecommuters, the smaller, fixed-configuration routers are best suited to the task, and therefore, the technologies recommended by Cisco for remote access mesh well with their needs. These platforms include the following:

- Cisco 700 series
- Cisco 800 series
- Cisco 1000 series

The primary characteristics of these platforms include simple options and fixed configurations, both of which can lower the cost of these systems.

The 700 Series

The 700 series was designed for telecommuters and supports ISDN. Routing services are provided for IP and IPX, and this router uses the Cisco IOS-700 software as opposed to the standard IOS. This can add to the training requirements for a corporation since the differences in syntax can be substantial.

 You might be confused that this section is devoted to the Cisco 700 series routers, as this platform has been removed from the product line. The 700 series also will likely be removed from the exam; however, you see a question or two regarding the platform, particularly as it relates to various connectivity options. Unfortunately, the Cisco certification exams do not always parallel the current level of technology being deployed and marketed.

The 700 series has three models. These are outlined in Table 1.9.

TABLE 1.9   Cisco 700 Series Platform Features

Platform	Cisco 761	Cisco 775	Cisco 776
ISDN interface	S/T	S/T	S/T and U
Analog ports	No	Yes, RJ-11	No
Ethernet	10-BaseT	Four-port 10-BaseT	10-BaseT

Cisco claims that each of the 700 series routers can support up to 30 users; however, in practice, the limitations of ISDN and the platform realistically place fewer than 10 users as a more reasonable population.

The 700 series also supports the following configuration features:

DHCP Relay   This can forward DHCP client requests to an off-subnet DHCP server. DHCP provides automatic IP addressing, which can greatly reduce the administration overhead of manual addressing.

DHCP Server   This feature enables the 700 series router to provide the DHCP server function as opposed to forwarding DHCP requests to an external server. Although this feature might have some benefits, most large corporations prefer to use a centrally located and administered server and leave the routing function to the routers.

Port Address Translation (PAT)   This is an interesting feature for the designer and administrator to consider. It can significantly conserve address space because all devices share a single IP address to the outside network. The router alters the port number and maintains a dynamic one-for-one relationship between the source IP address and port and the altered port assignment. Unfortunately, PAT and its associated feature Network Address Translation (NAT) do not function correctly with protocols that embed the IP address, including NetBIOS packets. This makes these features difficult to implement in Windows installations that rely on NetBIOS functions.

Compression   The 700 series routers can compress data by using the Stacker compression algorithm when communicating with Cisco IOS-based routers. Compression is a method by which computing devices substitute longer strings of repeated sequences with token or symbolic notation; the net result is a reduction in the number of bits required to send data. There is a performance penalty because the routers must compress and decompress the data stream; however, this is negligible in lower-bandwidth instances.

IPX and IP routing   All 700 series routers support IPX and IP packet routing. Bridging is offered for support of other protocols. This is not a major issue for many corporations because IP is easily the dominant protocol; however, it does mean that Macintosh environments that have not migrated to IP will likely wish to select another platform. Stated another way, AppleTalk is not included in the 700 series and is not on the exam.

Bonding   The Cisco 700 series routers support *Multilink Protocol (MP) bonding*, which allows for the aggregation of two or more channels into a single logical connection. Bonding can be used to improve the throughput when only low-bandwidth links are available.

Management   Simple Network Management Protocol (SNMP) management is available with routers in the 700 series. This allows for pooling and trap alarm messages. Some organizations do not opt to manage their remote equipment (home based) due to the volume of false error messages and the sheer number of devices.

Multinational support   The 700 series routers support both North American and international applications, including most major ISDN switches. The platform is certified for use in more than 25 countries. Administrators should check with the Cisco website or their sales representative for a current listing of countries and remember to verify power requirements for their installation.

Support for telephone services   Specific models of the Cisco 700, including the 765, 766, 775, and 776, provide telephone services over ISDN, including call-waiting, call-hold, and call-retrieve. The telecommunications service provider must make these services available.

Snapshot routing   The *Routing Information Protocol (RIP)* is a fairly chatty protocol, sending a full update every 30 seconds. *Snapshot routing* resolves the problems that result from using RIP on an ISDN circuit; because ISDN is tariffed on a per-minute basis in most installations, it would not be cost-effective to have the circuit open all the time just for routing updates. Snapshot routing caches the dynamic routing information and maintains it in the router's route table even when the link is down.

Product Selection and Outsourcing

When recommending a router product, we generally steer away from platforms such as the 700 series. The limitations of the platform and the differences in command syntax generally add to the total cost of ownership, and the price difference, with discounts, is generally not that significant compared to IOS-based routers. Of course, when magnified over thousands of routers, a $200 difference per unit is suddenly $200,000 or more. Corporate budgets might bristle at that increase unless the consultant or designer can justify the extra expense with extra benefits.

One alternative that some companies choose is outsourcing their remote access platforms. This generally appears as a lease, which can be advantageous to the accountants and can off-load the support and repair functions from the staff.

The 800 Series

Cisco's lowest-price IOS-based routers are found in the 800 series. For remote access, these routers offer ISDN BRI terminations and basic telephone service ports. Recall that ISDN BRI can be used for two traditional analog services. As of this writing, the 800 series includes ADSL, Ethernet, HDSL, ISDN, and serial terminations, as noted in the following list:

- Cisco 837 ADSL Broadband Router
- Cisco 836 ADSL over ISDN Broadband Router
- Cisco 831 Ethernet Broadband Router
- Cisco 828 G.SHDSL Router
- Cisco 827 ADSL Router
- Cisco 827H ADSL Router
- Cisco 827-4V ADSL Router
- Cisco 826 ADSL Router
- Cisco 813 ISDN Router
- Cisco 811 ISDN Router
- Cisco 806 Broadband Router

- Cisco 805 Serial Router
- Cisco 804 ISDN Router
- Cisco 803 ISDN Router
- Cisco 802 ISDN Router
- Cisco 801 ISDN Router

In addition, Cisco has released the SOHO (small office, home office) 7X and 9X platforms. Their Linksys product line, recently acquired, is being offered as an independent series and is not included in the 800 series, but these systems do compete in many instances.

The latest information regarding the 800 series is available at `http://www.cisco.com/en/US/customer/products/hw/routers/ps380/index.html`.

> Please be careful with this statement: the 800 series is currently the *lowest* cost *IOS*-based router. This does not make it the cheapest router mentioned. The 700 series is generally the *lowest* cost router.

The 1000 Series

The Cisco 1000 series routers are based on a fixed configuration; however, they provide for WAN options beyond ISDN. The Cisco 1005 router provides a traditional serial interface for expansion. Most corporations appear to be selecting other platforms than the 1000 series.

Verifying a Network Installation

Verification of the network installation is encompassed in three phases:

- Bit error rate tests and validation diagnostics
- Connection of customer premise equipment
- Configuration

The telephone company installer usually performs bit error rate tests and other validation diagnostics, the first component of verification. The second phase of verification typically requires connecting the customer premise equipment—the router or DSU. After the equipment is connected, the installer can use the LED information to provide a high-level overview of the usability of the link. The third phase of verification uses an actual configuration. For example, the installer or network architect might configure one of the PVCs to carry an upper-layer protocol for simple connectivity tests. For the purposes of the exam, Cisco is primarily interested in the use of the LED indicators.

Verifying the Central Site

As explained previously, Cisco recommends using its 3600 series routers (XM) for the central site, although other platforms are also available. Therefore, the following text focuses on the verification steps for installation of the 3600 platform.

Figure 1.2 shows the front of the 3600 router (in this case, it is a 3640 router). As you will notice, the router is fairly limited in the amount of diagnostic information it can provide. LEDs are limited in the same way idiot lights are more limited than gauges in an automobile: they can alert you when there is a problem, but full instrumentation (in a car this would include gauges and a tachometer) can provide details and advanced warning. However, it is a good place to start the process of troubleshooting, just as an oil warning light in the car helps you eliminate the brakes as a problem area.

FIGURE 1.2   The 3640 router front view

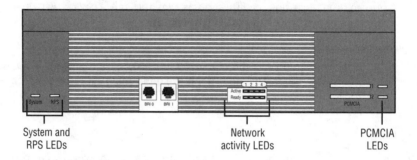

The front panel LEDs are presented as follows:

System   The System LED is used to show both the system power and operation characteristics. When the LED is off, the router is not receiving power; a solid green LED denotes proper, powered operation. An amber indicator shows that the router is not functioning correctly, but that power is connected. A blinking green light indicates that the router is powered and working properly, but that it is in ROM monitor mode. Alternating amber and green show that the self-test is running. As indicated, a single LED can provide a great deal of information.

RPS   The RPS LED denotes the status of the redundant power supply. On the 3640, only one power supply can be operational at a time. An off LED reflects that the RPS is not installed. A blinking green LED denotes that both the internal and redundant power supplies are operational; administrators should reconfigure the installation to run on one or the other system. A solid green LED denotes that the RPS is operational, and amber shows that the RPS is installed but not in operation.

Network Activity   There are two sets of LEDs in the Network Activity section of the router. There are four LEDs per set, with one per slot. The Ready LEDs illuminate to show that a module is installed in the slot and operational. An off LED indicates that nothing is installed in the slot or that it is not functioning. The Active LEDs blink to indicate activity.

PCMCIA   The PCMCIA (or PC Card) LEDs light up to show activity on that slot. This should serve as a warning to not remove the flash card when reading or writing data. Flash cards are also called PCMCIA memory cards and they store the router's flash image.

The module LEDs vary widely depending on the type of interface; however, most include at least a link or enable the LED to denote connectivity. Many also include activity indicators—the serial module, for example, also includes clocking indicators to show the presence or absence of synchronization.

Verifying the Remote Branch

As noted previously, Cisco recommends the 1600 series router for remote branch installations. This platform provides an IOS-based system with expandability. Figure 1.3 illustrates the front of the Cisco 1600 router.

FIGURE 1.3   The Cisco 1600 LEDs

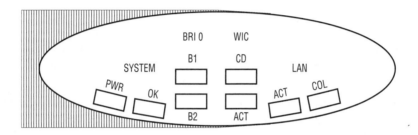

You should understand what each indicator means, as explained in the following list:

System PWR   The green System power LED illuminates to show that the system is on and receiving power.

System OK   The green System OK LED blinks during the boot cycle. After the boot cycle is complete, this LED is steady.

BRI0 B1 and BRI0 B2   These LEDs display active connections on the BRI0 B1 and B2 channels, respectively. BRI 0 is the first ISDN BRI interface on the router.

WIC CD   This LED denotes a connection on the WAN Interface Card. This indication can be helpful when troubleshooting DSU/CSU issues.

WIC ACT   The WAN Interface Card activity LED can be used to indicate circuit use, although it is helpful to use the command-line interface to see the direction and characteristics of the traffic itself.

LAN ACT   The LAN activity LED is similar to the WIC activity LED but it represents traffic on the Ethernet interface.

LAN COL   The LAN collision LED indicates a collision on the Ethernet segment. It is yellow, unlike the other LEDs, which are all green.

Verifying the Telecommuter Installation

Cisco generally recommends the use of the Cisco 700 router in telecommuter installations. One example of this device is the 766 router. This device includes a substantial number of diagnostic LEDs, shown in Figure 1.4.

FIGURE 1.4   The Cisco 766 LEDs

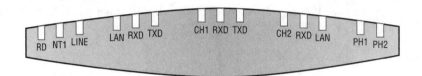

These LEDs are read as follows:

RD   The ready LED is illuminated when the router is operating normally. You can use it to verify that a successful power-on self-test (POST) has been completed and that power is available to the device.

NT1   For routers with an internal ISDN NT1, this LED displays the status of the ISDN connection. When steady, the ISDN switch and the NT1 are synchronized; when it is blinking, the connection is attempting synchronization.

LINE   The LINE LED indicates that framing between the router and the ISDN switch has been established.

LAN   This light indicates that the Ethernet interface on the router is active and that a frame has been sent or received within the past 60 seconds. A link light on the back of the router denotes a valid connection.

LAN RXD   The LAN received LED blinks upon receipt of a frame on the Ethernet interface.

LAN TXD   The LAN transmitted LED blinks when frames are sent from the router onto the Ethernet link.

CH1 and CH2   These LEDs indicate the status of the two B channels on the ISDN BRI. They illuminate steadily when the connection is established and blink during the negotiation process.

CH1 RXD and CH2 RXD   These LEDs reflect the receipt of packets on their respective ISDN BRI channels. Each packet generates a blink of the LED.

CH1 TXD and CH2 TXD   These LEDs reflect the transmission of packets on the respective ISDN BRI channel. Each packet generates a blink of the LED.

PH1 and PH2   For routers so equipped, these LEDs provide information regarding the use of the POTS ports on the router. These ports can be used for telephone, fax, or analog modem services.

Remember the significance of each LED, including its color, for the exam. This information can be helpful in live troubleshooting as well.

Summary

As with most aspects of networking, the physical layer provides the foundation for both LAN-based solutions and remote access ones. *Remote access* refers to the use of longer range solutions than the 100-meter Ethernet solutions commonly found in local area networks (LANs).

Remote access technologies include dial-up lines, ISDN BRI and PRI technologies, leased lines, Frame Relay, cable modem, and xDSL. Each of these solutions provides the designer with various benefits and detriments, including availability, cost, and complexity. For example, dial-up lines are widely available but are relatively expensive and of lower capacity than Frame Relay.

In addition to the physical circuits between remote locations, remote access solutions also require the physical termination equipment. This Customer PremisesEquipment (CPE) includes the router, a DSU/CSU where necessary, or a modem. ISDN also incorporates different types of terminations that the administrator needs to keep in mind.

Routers for remote access solutions vary widely within the Cisco product line. The Cisco 800 series routers are well suited to small offices and home users, whereas the Cisco 3600XM/3700 platform affords more expansion capabilities and performance.

The Remote Access materials might continue to focus on the older Cisco 700 series ISDN routers. Although these routers are no longer available, success on the Remote Access exam requires a high level of understanding of the platform and its characteristics. Specific attention should be paid to the interface types of the model, in addition to the fact that the 700 series does not run an IOS image.

It is also important to note that the materials in this chapter focus on the exam and the information needed for the exam, rather than the solutions necessary in modern remote access solutions. For example, the Remote Access exam fails to note ATM technologies, which are quite common in many networks today. This failure should be of concern to the reader and warrants further augmentation beyond the focus of this text.

Exam Essentials

Understand the ISDN terminations of the Cisco 700 series platforms. The Cisco 776 router includes both the S/T and the U type ISDN interfaces, for example, whereas the other 700 series platforms presented provide only the S/T interface. More information regarding these interfaces is included in Chapter 5.

Know which remote access platforms are best suited to small offices and home offices.   Cisco recommends that users consider the Cisco 700, 800, 1000, and 1600 platforms for inexpensive remote connectivity to small user populations.

Be familiar with the WAN connection types.   Readers should be comfortable with Frame Relay, ISDN, analog, leased line, and X.25 connection options. As presented in the chapter, analog connections are the most common. They are highly available; however, the bandwidth provided is quite limited and the costs associated with usage are quite high. X.25 is a reasonable option, particularly outside of the United States, and it is well suited to poor line conditions. Leased line and Frame Relay typically provide the highest bandwidth capabilities, with Frame Relay adding the benefit of distance-insensitive pricing.

Know the differences between ISDN BRI and PRI technologies.   ISDN BRI services operate over a 144Kbps connection, divided into two 64Kbps channels (B, or bearer) and a single 16Kbps channel (D, or data). This is best used for the remote side of a remote access solution. The ISDN PRI technology uses a T-1 or E-1 connection for transport and can provide 23 or 30 B channels, respectively.

Understand the differences between North American and European standards.   The ISDN Primary Rate Interface (PRI) in North America and Japan offers twenty-three B channels and one D channel for a total interface rate of 1.544Mbps. ISDN PRI in Europe, Australia, and other parts of the world provide thirty B channels plus one 64Kbps D channel.

Be familiar with the high-end router platforms for central office termination.   Cisco recommends a wide variety of platforms for aggregation points, including the AS5300 series, the Cisco 7000 series routers, and the smaller 3600 systems. Admittedly there is some inconsistency in selecting these platforms; test takers would be advised to understand the platforms and select the best answer for each question.

Understand the router platforms' flexibility regarding configuration.   Fixed configuration routers are limited with regard to future enhancements. These platforms include the 700 and 800 series. Modular routers, including the 1600, 2600XM, and 3600/3700 series, allow for the addition or replacement of specific components, which can be used to add features without the need for a forklift upgrade.

Key Terms

Before you take the exam, be certain you are familiar with the following terms:

asynchronous dial-up

Asynchronous Transfer Mode (ATM)

Architecture for Voice, Video, and Integrated Data (AVVID)

Basic Rate Interface (BRI)

cable modems

channelized T-1

Committed Information Rate (CIR)

Digital Subscriber Line (DSL)

E-1

Frame Relay

High-Level Data Link Control (HDLC)

Integrated Services Digital Network (ISDN)

leased lines

Multilink Protocol (MP) bonding

MUXing

Permanent Virtual Circuits (PVCs)

Point-to-Point Protocol (PPP)

port density

port type

Primary Rate Interface (PRI)

quality of service (QoS)

reliability

remote access

Routing Information Protocol (RIP)

Serial Line Internet Protocol (SLIP)

Snapshot routing

Switched Virtual Circuits (SVCs)

virtual private network (VPN)

wide area network (WAN)

X.25

Written Lab

1. The system LED on the 3640 indicates _____.

2. A reliable protocol for poor-quality circuits is ____.

3. A low-overhead, low-cost protocol is _____.

4. You believe that data is being received on the first B channel of a 700 series router. What would indicate this?

5. A modern alternative to ISDN is ____.

6. A common protocol for remote access is _____.

7. The most widely available remote access technology is _____.

8. The _____ series is the lowest model number IOS-based router platform.

9. The 7000/7200/7500 series routers would likely be found in the ____.

10. The 700 series router would likely be found in _____.

Review Questions

1. Which of the following remote access connection types provides the advantage that it is widely available?

    A. ATM

    B. ISDN

    C. Asynchronous dial-up

    D. Frame Relay

2. Which of the following remote access technologies provides the user with two 64Kbps channels for data traffic?

    A. Frame Relay

    B. Leased line

    C. ATM

    D. ISDN BRI

3. Which of the following is not a consideration in remote access design?

    A. Cost

    B. Availability

    C. Bandwidth

    D. Compression

4. Which of the following might be the best solution for use in an international remote access installation with poor cable quality?

    A. X.25

    B. ISDN

    C. Frame Relay

    D. Leased line

5. The administrator sees intermittent flashing on the CH1 RXD LED on a 700 series router. This most likely means

    A. That the asynchronous interface is bad.

    B. That the first Frame Relay channel is receiving data.

    C. That the first ISDN D channel is receiving data.

    D. That the first ISDN B channel is receiving data.

    E. That the first ISDN B channel is negotiating connectivity with the remote location.

6. Of the following, which series offers the lowest priced IOS-based router?

   A. The 700 series

   B. The 800 series

   C. The 1600 series

   D. The 7000 series

7. Of the following, which router provides an Ethernet and ISDN BRI termination, in addition to a single WAN expansion slot?

   A. The 700 series

   B. The 800 series

   C. The 1600 series

   D. The 7000 series

8. The 700 series routers can support which of the following? (Select all that apply.)

   A. AppleTalk

   B. IPX

   C. IP

   D. All of the above

9. The administrator observes that the power and OK LEDs are illuminated on a Cisco 1600 series router. From this, the administrator can deduce that

   A. The router is on.

   B. The router is on and successfully booted.

   C. The router is on and the Ethernet interface is receiving packets.

   D. The router is on and the ISDN interface is receiving packets.

10. An ISDN PRI in London, England, provides which of the following?

   A. 23 B channels

   B. 30 B channels

   C. 23 D channels

   D. 30 D channels

11. Of the following, which series of routers does Cisco recommend for use in central sites?

   A. The 700 series

   B. The 1000 series

   C. The 1600 series

   D. The 3600 series

12. Typically, which of the following connectors would be used to terminate an analog modem to a router?

   A. V.35

   B. 10-BaseT

   C. RS-232

   D. RS-449

13. According to Cisco, quick verification of a remote access installation can use which of the following?

   A. Router LEDs

   B. CiscoWorks

   C. Telnet

   D. Cable testers

14. The Data Link Layer of ISDN's D channel is which of the following?

   A. LAPB

   B. LAPD

   C. X.25

   D. PPP

15. ISDN is typically defined as a

   A. Packet-switched connection.

   B. Cell-switched connection.

   C. Circuit-switched connection.

   D. Frame-switched connection.

16. Modems are limited to a maximum bandwidth of

   A. 28.8Kbps

   B. 33.6Kbps

   C. 56Kbps

   D. 56Mbps

17. Which router is a high-performance, high-density LAN and WAN router positioned by Cisco for the central office?

   A. The 700 series

   B. The 1000 series

   C. The 1600 series

   D. The 7200 series

18. Which product would you use to terminate a DSL connection at an employee's home?

    A. The Cisco 827 router

    B. The Cisco 813 router

    C. The Cisco 2600XM router

    D. The Cisco 7500 router

19. What is one of the benefits of routers with fixed interfaces?

    A. High cost

    B. Lower cost

    C. More flexibility

    D. Harder configuration

20. Frame Relay is best suited for connections from the central site to which of the following?

    A. Telecommuter homes

    B. Hotel room access

    C. Branch offices

    D. All of the above

Answers to Written Lab

1. System power and operation characteristics

2. X.25

3. Frame Relay

4. The B1 RX LED

5. DSL

6. PPP

7. Asynchronous dial-up

8. 800

9. Network core, central site, or central office

10. A small office or home office

Answers to Review Questions

1. C. Asynchronous dial-up is found in virtually every residential and business setting. It is the most basic of telecommunications services. It might be possible to install the other services in many places, but asynchronous dial-up is the most ubiquitous connection type.

2. D. ISDN BRI provides two user channels of 64Kbps each.

3. D. Although compression might be a desired feature, it is not a consideration in the design.

4. A. X.25 is widely available in international markets and was designed to operate on poor-quality circuits.

5. D. Remember that the LED reflects the receipt of a packet, so the intermittent flashing will be faster under heavy loads and slower under idle periods.

6. B. The 800 series is the lowest priced IOS-based router. The 700 series uses a different operating system.

7. C. Make sure that you are familiar with the ports, slots, and modules of the Cisco router products. Of the choices, only the 1600 offers the configuration presented.

8. B, C. The Cisco 700 routers do not run the full Cisco IOS and, because of this, provide limited features.

9. B. Remember the significance of the colors and indicators on the LEDs.

10. B. European E-1 standards provide for thirty B channels and one D channel.

11. D. Although Cisco recommends the 3600 for central sites, in reality, this decision should be based on requirements. Of the choices given here, however, the 3600 is the most scalable and best performing and typically matches well with central site requirements.

12. C. The other choices are for Ethernet (10-BaseT) or high-speed serial connections (V.35 and RS-449).

13. A. The fastest and simplest way to check the status of a network device is to look at the LEDs. The other solutions require additional equipment and time. However, only high-level problems can be resolved by using this method.

14. B. The easiest way to remember that LAPD is the correct answer is because it has a *D* at the end.

15. C. ISDN operates by establishing a circuit pathway for packets. There is no addressing information as part of the frame.

16. C. In the United States, the figure is actually 53Kbps due to Federal Communications Commission (FCC) regulations; however, the theoretical bandwidth is 56Kbps.

17. D.   Of the choices provided, the 7200 router provides the highest density and performance. It is for these reasons that it is Cisco's recommended platform.

18. A.   The Cisco 827 router provides an ADSL termination. The Cisco 813 is used for ISDN terminations. The 2600XM and 7500 series routers would not be used in a residential setting.

19. B.   Fixed-interface routers are cheaper to build and thus have a lower cost. They are also generally easier to support.

20. C.   Homes and hotels rarely provide the appropriate facilities for Frame Relay. Typically, only asynchronous dial-up is available; however, some hotels are providing T-1-based Internet connectivity from an office area or individual rooms.

Chapter

2

Asynchronous Connections

EXAM TOPICS COVERED IN THIS CHAPTER INCLUDE:

✓ Know the commands and procedures necessary to configure an access server for modem connectivity so telecommuters can access the central site.

✓ Know the commands and procedures to configure dial-out connections.

✓ Know the commands used for reverse Telnet.

✓ Understand how to configure the modem for basic asynchronous operations.

✓ Know the commands and procedures used for the modem autoconfiguration feature.

As noted in Chapter 1, asynchronous (analog) remote access solutions are extremely popular, primarily because little preparation is needed on the remote side of the connection. Unlike Frame Relay, ISDN, and X.25, *asynchronous connections* use standard phone lines and are available virtually everywhere. With cellular modems, these services are even available on a wireless basis (this is different from the CDMA and GSM data connections briefly noted in Chapter 1). This wide availability provides a huge advantage over other remote access solutions and effectively mandates the inclusion of asynchronous connections in modern implementations. Unfortunately, analog-based modems suffer from low performance and relatively high cost per kilobyte.

With a digital connection at the service provider's side of the connection, it is possible to provide up to 56Kbps of theoretical bandwidth to remote users; however, the Federal Communications Commission (FCC) limits this to 53Kbps in the United States. Also, asynchronous connections require a lengthy call-setup time—sometimes more than one minute—which can substantially affect user and application performance.

Administrators frequently look for other technologies to replace asynchronous modems, or dial-up connections, in order to improve performance. Even with the proliferation of ISDN, DSL, cable modems, and other technologies, no system has yet successfully dethroned simple dial-up services.

Understanding Asynchronous Modems

Technically, *modems* are modulator/demodulators, but most people define them by their high-level function: modems connect devices to the telephone network. The modem connects the computer or router to the phone network and might incorporate a pass-through for an analog phone set. Although the phone cannot be used while the computer is connected to a remote location, this does afford a nonconcurrent role for the installation—only the phone or the data connection can be used at any given time.

Modems are considered *Data Communications Equipment (DCE)*, whereas computers and routers are *Data Terminal Equipment (DTE)*. The connection between the modems, or DCEs, is *analog* in nature, meaning that bits are defined by an analog waveform that is continuous and variable. DTE connections are *digital* in nature; this means that each bit has a clear 0 or 1 value defined by voltage to denote the bit. It is important to remember that asynchronous refers to clocking and not a digital or analog transmission. *Clocking* is provided in asynchronous connections with start and stop bits, which typically results in 10 bits per byte of data—8 for the byte of data and 1 each for the start and stop markers. Unlike asynchronous connections, synchronous connections have precise clocking to denote the data bits; in these connections, bytes can begin only on the downbeat of the synchronous drum, for example. There really isn't a drum in synchronous signaling. Rather, bits are sent in sync with the clocking pulse; it's similar to taking a dance step for every drumbeat, with the dance step being the data. For an asynchronous connection there are actually three distinct connections (DTE to DCE, DCE to DCE, and DCE to DTE), which are shown in Figure 2.1.

FIGURE 2.1 An asynchronous end-to-end connection

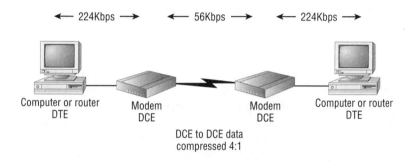

As shown in Figure 2.1, the DTE-to-DCE bandwidth is uncompressed and is four times that of the modem connection, assuming optimum compression. Remember that this figure represents an optimal situation rather than a realistic one. Therefore, it is unlikely that either the DTE-to-DCE or DCE-to-DCE connections will normally see this level of performance. Some of this is attributable to the DCE-to-DCE limitations; however, limitations also exist in the serial interface from the PC to the modem.

 Real World Scenario

Remote Access with Modems

When discussing the limitations of serial signaling, it would be remiss not to discuss the limitations of the public phone system and the analog technology available today. As noted earlier in this chapter, asynchronous connections are limited to 56Kbps, or 53Kbps by FCC order. Distance and line quality further limit this amount of bandwidth, possibly reducing throughput to 28.8Kbps or less. (This was written in a Boston hotel room, where there was no reliable connection beyond 26Kbps.) In addition, connections might take up to a minute to establish and might be further impeded by load coils and analog-to-digital conversions between you and the central office (CO). Load coils are amplifiers used to accommodate longer distances than normal, and analog-to-digital conversions are often used in new housing developments to convert the copper pairs to fiber, again extending the length of the link. It is far cheaper to run a few pairs of fiber to an access terminal (a small cabinet that sits in the neighborhood and converts the fiber to copper) where the copper runs, than it is to extend into the home.

You need to remember that the plain old telephone service (POTS) is exactly that—old. It was developed from the same technology that Alexander Graham Bell developed in his lab over a hundred years ago and was never intended to address the needs of video and data. That's the first problem with analog connections: they were never designed to allow millions of bits of data to flow from one point to another.

The second problem with analog connections is their inefficiency. Voice is a specific type of data and fits in a single 64Kbps channel. You might already be aware of the channels of voice aggregation, or T-1 circuits—where 24 voice signals (DS0, digital signal) fit into a T-1 or DS1. Data is unlike voice, however, which leads to inefficiency. Voice demands that the idle (or no data) points in the conversation be communicated as well, so there is always a constant flow of information. Data doesn't work that way; if no data is transmitted, there is little need for the bandwidth to be consumed. By using only the available bandwidth that is necessary, it is possible to service more connections with data than voice. You might have heard of convergence or time division multiplexing (TDM), two very different concepts that relate to this topic. *Convergence* is the concept of voice, video, and data all using the same network, whereas *TDM* is the old voice channel model—each channel always given the same amount of access to the network regardless of the need. Convergence will remove TDM from the network and place everything into packets that can then use only the required amount of bandwidth, as opposed to reserving more than is necessary.

However, convergence will also effectively eliminate the analog network (an event that has already occurred in the core of the telephone world). But before that comes to fruition, network administrators will need to contend with the problems of the current network, including long call-setup times, poor- quality connections, and low bandwidths.

These problems, just for the record, already have solutions in many cases. Although it is true that analog connections are the most prevalent in the world, the availability of DSL, cable, ISDN, Frame Relay, wireless, and Long Reach Ethernet (LRE) enables designers to incorporate alternatives into their installations and provides an indication of what will happen in the near future.

At the beginning of this sidebar, we noted problems with analog service and the phone network. While discussing these problems, we failed to address what is possibly the most important problem—cost. Readers of the *CCDP: Cisco Internetwork Design Study Guide* (Sybex, 2000) will recall the emphasis on business concerns when designing the network. Cost is frequently the single biggest business factor, period. Business managers who do not understand bits and protocols certainly understand the benefits of a $40-a-month fixed cost per employee compared to a variable bill that could surpass $100 a month.

One last item: virtual private networks. *Virtual private networks (VPNs)* are encrypted sessions between two devices over the public network, typically the Internet. These sessions are virtually private because the encrypted data is, conceptually, protected from snooping. Users, however, will still be affected by delay and bandwidth limitations that could be better controlled in private network installations.

VPNs provide remote access designers with two benefits. The first is low cost, which, as noted in the previous paragraph, is a powerful business case argument. The second benefit is universality—or the capability to allow access from different technologies. With VPNs, the administrator no longer cares what technology is used on the remote side of the connection. The remote side simply needs to connect to the Internet via any available transport, or in some cases, an internationally accessible single-vendor network (which can provide service-level agreements and other service guarantees). Once connected, the connection traverses the network and is decrypted at the corporate access point, typically a T-1 or DS3, depending on the bandwidth demands. For smaller support departments, this entire service might be outsourced so the maintenance of the VPN equipment and connections is not an additional burden on the team.

The *Universal Asynchronous Receiver/Transmitter (UART)* is a chip that controls asynchronous communications to and from a device. It can buffer inbound and outbound data. Most UARTs are limited to the speed of 115.2Kbps, which is insufficient for 56Kbps connections, and the most capable UART provides for only a 56-byte receive buffer and a 64-byte transmit buffer. Even with these relatively large buffers this may be insufficient for maximum throughput.

In current computer designs, the UART is virtually disregarded as a component in the communications system. This is because most systems today provide sufficient buffering systems to address the volume of packets that come with 56Kbps asynchronous transmissions—specifically, the 16550 UART (16550 is a part number). In the early days of PCs, the most common chipset was the 8250 UART from National Semiconductor. It contained a single buffer of sorts—it could hold a single byte of data. Any transmission speed greater than 19,200Kbps was too fast for the UART to forward properly. This was a substantial cause of performance problems with the original deployments of 28.8Kbps modems.

Again, this issue is not of much consequence in modern communications systems. Unless you are installing a 386 or older computer (which by mid-2003 is very unlikely), you should find that 16550 UARTs (or better) were used for the serial ports. Please note that most internal modem cards include either the 16550 UART or a proprietary buffering system to alleviate these problems.

Signaling and Cabling

The cables used in various asynchronous connections differ depending on the end equipment plus the type and distance of the connection.

Modems typically use two types of connectors—one for the connection to the host and one for the connection to the phone network. An RS-232-C 25-pin connector typically provides the connection to the host; the RS-232-C connector is also called an EIA/TIA-232 connector. Both terms are still used today, although the EIA/TIA terminology is more current. A standard RJ-11 connector provides the connection to the phone network.

For the connection between the DTE and the DCE, individual wires are used in the serial cable. These wires and their functions are shown in Table 2.1.

TABLE 2.1   DTE to DCE Signaling

Wire	Function
TXD	Transmits data from the DTE to the DCE. All serial connections send their data one bit at a time over a single transmission path. This differs from parallel transmissions that have multiple paths. Printers, for example, send a full octet per signaling window. TX is on pin 2.
RXD	Receives data from the DCE to the DTE and is carried on pin 3. If there is a need to cross two serial ports together, as is the case in DTE-to-DTE connections, pin 2 is linked to 3 and vice versa.
GND	The electrical ground provides a baseline for voltage changes on the TX and RX wires. It is on pin 7.
RTS	Request to send. This signal is used when the DTE would like to send data.
CTS	The Clear To Send signal is used to inform the DTE that the DCE is ready to send data received from the DTE.
DTR	The data terminal ready wire is a modem control signaling wire, which signifies that the DTE can accept a call from the DCE.
CD	Carrier detection indicates that the local DCE has a connection to the remote DCE. It is also a modem control wire.
RI	The Ring Indication/Indicator is used to signal the DTE device that an incoming call is ringing the phone. On nine pin interfaces, RI is on pin 9.

The information in Table 2.1 is important to understand from a troubleshooting perspective; however, it is also nice to know for an overview of wiring. In some instances, such as the extension of a serial connection, it might be necessary to serially link two devices by using Category 5 cable, for example. Hoods are available to make this link, and in fact, many Cisco connections use so few wires in serial connections that console ports are terminated with RJ-45 connections. (*Hood* is a slang term describing the plastic converter that covers the wiring as it changes from RJ to DB connections. Another term for this is *media converter*.)

Refer to the documentation that came with your router or switch regarding console connections. Cisco has been inconsistent with this implementation, sometimes requiring the use of rolled connection cables and at other times needing straight-through patch cords. A rolled connection places pin 1 on one end into the pin 8 position on the other end; thus, pin 2 falls into the pin 7 position, and so forth. Straight-through connections map 1 to 1 and 2 to 2, through to pin 8 connecting to pin 8.

Modulation Standards

Modulation defines the method used to encode the data stream between DCE devices. There are many modulation standards, including several proprietary methods. Modems will negotiate the modulation standard to be used during the connection. Modern modems will alter this negotiation during the connection, should line conditions permit. This can provide improved performance or prevent a connection from terminating, should the line condition degrade. Table 2.2 notes the common modem modulation standards.

TABLE 2.2   Modem Modulation Standards

Modulation	DCE to DCE Bandwidth	Status
V.22	1,200bps	ITU standard
V.22bis	2,400bps	ITU standard
V.32	9,600bps	ITU standard
V.32bis	14.4Kbps	ITU standard
V.32 terbo	19.2Kbps	Proprietary
V.34	28.8Kbps	ITU standard
V.fast	28.8Kbps	Proprietary
V.FC	28.8Kbps	Proprietary
V.34 annex 12	33.6Kbps	ITU standard
K56Flex	56Kbps	Proprietary
X2	56Kbps	Proprietary

TABLE 2.2   Modem Modulation Standards *(continued)*

Modulation	DCE to DCE Bandwidth	Status
V.90	56Kbps	ITU standard
V.92	56Kbps	ITU standard—adds faster call connection capabilities
V.61 or V.34Q	56Kbps	ITU standard—adds simultaneous voice and data capabilities

Most modems support all lower-bandwidth ITU standards for backward compatibility, and many V.90 and V.92 modems also support either X2 or K56Flex. Modems that shipped with X2-only or K56Flex-only support—before the V.90 standard was ratified—can usually be upgraded in the field, frequently with software only. This might not be the case when upgrading from V.90 to V.92. You will have to consult your modem vendor for upgrade capabilities and cost.

The V.92 standard represents three significant modem enhancements. The first is Quick Connect, which reduces the amount of time required for the modems to negotiate a connection. In some instances, a user might see a 50 percent reduction in connection time. Second, the V.92 standard includes Modem on Hold, which enables a user to accept an incoming phone call without terminating their existing connection. For users with only one phone line in their home or office, Modem on Hold enables them to handle both data and voice calls over the same telephone line. Third, V.92 supports PCM Upstream, which allows for faster uploading and sending of large e-mail messages, photos, and documents. With PCM Upstream, users gain faster upstream communication with speeds reaching up to 48,000 bits per second, as compared to 33,600 bits per second with V.90 technology.

The modulation standards also incorporate data compression and error correction specifications, which are detailed next.

Data Compression

Data compression substitutes repetitive data in a a bit stream with fewer bits that will be interpreted, or uncompressed, on the other device. Later in this book, we present a more detailed example of data compression; for this introduction, it is sufficient to know that compression will allow fewer bits of data to represent the total number of bits needed to reconstruct the message accurately. One of the more common compression systems today is V.42bis, which is based on the theoretical works of Professors Jacob Ziv and Abraham Lempel at Technion University in Israel. We visited Technion in 1984 and were extremely impressed with their facilities and the technical capabilities of their students. At that time, they had perfected systems that could convert English text to Hebrew text and they could integrate both texts into a single document. To better understand how impressive this was, consider that this was happening the same year as the first Apple Macintosh release.

The work of Ziv and Lempel was used by Englishman Terry Welch to develop the *LZW algorithm*, named to honor the three men. The LZW process uses two steps to parse character sequences into a table of strings; these strings are then represented with one of 256 codes. The parsing process works by constantly trying to find longer sequences that aren't part of the current 256 values. This enables the compression process to substitute longer and longer strings, which subsequently increases the benefits of the compression.

V.44 is the latest compression standard approved by the ITU and is included with the V.92 standard. V.42bis was created about 10 years ago, so it wasn't designed with the Internet in mind. V.44 was, and it is therefore much more efficient at compressing web pages—up to 100 percent more efficient in some cases.

Error Correction

Error correction validates the integrity of the data and is frequently used with compression to verify that the compression process did not corrupt the data. The impact of a single-bit error can distort substantial amounts of compressed data—instead of just impacting a single bit, it might distort 2 or more bytes, which, in turn, might require retransmission of even more data. When you consider the overhead of asynchronous communications—the start and stop bits require 2 extra bits per 8-bit byte, or 20 percent of the final bit stream data rate—the added overhead that would result from errors involving compressed data only serves to further reduce the actual throughput. Detection, and correction when applicable, of errors as quickly as possible can reduce the amount of data that needs to be retransmitted and, thus, improve total throughput.

The error correction process relies on a checksum value that validates the data. A simple example of this checksum looks like the following:

$$21 + 9 + 6 + 17 + 8 + 29 + 4 + 27 = 121$$

It is reasonably certain that the calculation on the left side of the equal sign is accurate because it does equal the value on the right side. However, it would also be possible for the 21 to be a 22 and for the 9 to be an 8, which also yields an answer of 121. Error correction works on the same premise as this equation; however, most error correction algorithms work to allow for multiple errors and other distortions. Many error correction processes block the binary data and divide that value by a fixed value. This value is then added to the block of data and is transmitted with the user data. On the opposite end of the transmission, the checksum is calculated against the binary value of the data and the division of the same fixed value. If they match the data block, the result is considered true and forwarded. If the values do not match, the data is discarded.

Configuring Asynchronous Modem Connections

Asynchronous connections, like other connections, require configuration before they can be used. In applications using Cisco routers, this configuration can be supplemented with automatic functions or it can be manual. As such, there are three possible configuration options:

- Manual configuration
- Autoconfigure
- Autodiscovery

Manual configuration requires knowledge of the commands required by the modem to establish the parameters that govern flow control, error control, compression, and the number of rings that will occur before the line is answered. Flow control is a function that uses the clear-to-send and ready-to-send pins on the serial cable to govern the bit stream, and it can be serviced by hardware or software.

The *autoconfigure* function is used to automatically configure a modem from a router that has been given the modem type. The configuration information is stored in a database on the router.

The *autodiscovery* function detects the modem type and then supplies the proper initialization string information. This process works by first negotiating the baud, or data rate, and then sending queries to the modem to learn its identity. This is accomplished with standard attention (AT) command sequences based on the router's database. If there is no match, the autodiscovery function will fail.

Stated another way, Cisco routers provide two methods for preparing the modem for operation. These are manual and automatic, and within automatic configuration there are two options, a completely automatic process that learns the type of modem in use and a hybrid that relies on the administrator to define the type of modem connected to the router. This alternative removes the need for a negotiation process; however, it is still considered an automatic process. The modem's configuration must match the router so that communications between the two devices are properly coordinated.

Automatic Configuration

Most modern modems provide the capability to identify their type and specifications, which a computer or router can use to assist in the configuration process. Obviously, the benefit of automatic configuration is that it reduces the number of administrative tasks required during installation; however, the learning process can delay modem availability and can fail. The delay is the result of the interrogation process, and failure can occur if the router fails to understand the responses from the modem. This can happen if the modem is not in the modemcap database, discussed later in this chapter.

Commands for Automatic Configuration

This section introduces the commands used for automatic configuration.

The *modem autoconfigure type* Command

The modem autoconfigure type *modem-type* command is used to instruct the router to automatically configure the modem attached to a port by using the commands in the modemcap database for the modem type specified. The *modemcap database* is a listing of modem configuration commands that provide basic information enabling the modem to operate with the router.

To show this database, use the show modemcap command. The output of this command is shown next. This output provides a list of the modem types that are defined in the database. This list is from a Cisco 2600 series router, and thus it reflects those modem types that are included with that router image.

```
Router_A#show modemcap
default
codex_3260
usr_courier
usr_sportster
hayes_optima
global_village
viva
telebit_t3000
microcom_hdms
microcom_server
nec_v34
nec_v110
nec_piafs
cisco_v110
mica
```

Each modem type has a related AT command-string sequence stored, which is shown with the show modemcap *modem-type* command. AT stands for *attention* and is the prefix for many modem commands. The output of this command, when used for the U.S. Robotics Courier, is shown here:

```
Router_A#show modemcap usr_courier
Modemcap values for usr_courier
Factory Defaults (FD):  &F
Autoanswer (AA):  S0=1
Carrier detect (CD):  &C1
Drop with DTR (DTR):  &D2
```

```
Hardware Flowcontrol (HFL):  &H1&R2
Lock DTE speed (SPD):  &B1
DTE locking speed (DTE):  [not set]
Best Error Control (BER):  &M4
Best Compression (BCP):  &K1
No Error Control (NER):  &M0
No Compression (NCP):  &K0
No Echo (NEC):  E0
No Result Codes (NRS):  Q1
Software Flowcontrol (SFL):  [not set]
Caller ID (CID):  [not set]
On-hook (ONH):  H0
Off-hook (OFH):  H1
Miscellaneous (MSC):  [not set]
Template entry (TPL):  default
Modem entry is built-in.
```

This output is similar to what would happen if you manually sent the modem the sequence AT&FS0=1&C1&D2&H1&R2&B1. This sequence would instruct a Courier to reset its configuration and then answer in one ring, using hardware flow control with DTR dropping and carrier detect.

As denoted, this modem entry is included in the router's operating system—it is built-in. Please note that the database entry must be complete and exact. As shown in the following output, the router will respond with an error message if the entry is abbreviated.

```
Router_A#show modemcap usr_cou
There is no record of modem usr_cou
```

In addition, the command modemcap entry *modem-profile-name* can be used to obtain an abbreviated version of the output, assuming that attributes are not set.

The *modemcap edit* Command

To add entries to the modemcap database, the administrator can use the modemcap edit command followed by the database name: modemcap edit *modem-profile-name*. Configurations provided with the router cannot be modified. Administrators should create a similar user-created entry with their modifications.

To create a user-defined profile by using an existing profile as a template, use the modemcap edit *new-profile-name* template *existing-profile-name* command with the template being the key parameter. This will create a profile with the name *new-profile-name* and copy all settings from the *existing-profile-name*.

Use care when removing modemcap entries. The `no modemcap edit modem-profile-name` command will delete the entire entry, not just a single line. To delete only one line from the profile, use `modemcap edit modem-profile-name attribute`.

It is generally recommended that administrators specify the type of modem that is connected to the router. This reduces the probability of error and hastens the configuration process.

The *modem autoconfigure discovery* Command

The command for discovering and automatically configuring the modem attached to a port is `modem autoconfigure discovery`. The discovery process will try to learn the make and model of the modem automatically. Automatic modem recognition is made possible by the modemcap database. The command is entered in line mode, as shown in the following output:

```
Router_A(config)#line 1
Router_A(config-line)#modem autoconfigure discovery
```

This sequence will instruct the router, or access server, to send an AT command sequence to line 1 at varying baud rates until it receives an acknowledgment from the modem. After it has determined the appropriate speed with which it should communicate to the modem, the router will attempt to determine the modem type with additional AT commands.

We need to define a term here: *baud*. *Baud* is a representation of the signaling speed, and it frequently corresponds to the bits-per-second capacity of the link. However, this assumes a modulation of 1 bit per signaling change—an inconsistent assumption given the wide variety of modulation protocols available in modern modems.

The modem entries in the modemcap database vary based on the version of IOS software and platform.

Automatic modem recognition can take up to five seconds. A default setting will be sent to the modem after a six-second timeout. This will occur if no match is found during the autodiscovery process, which means that a relevant entry was not found in the modemcap database. Specifying the type of modem and using the autoconfigure command should take less than two seconds for modem configuration.

Verifying and Troubleshooting the Automatic Configuration

Cisco provides many troubleshooting services to assist in the diagnostic process, and support for troubleshooting the automatic configuration service is no exception. However, before using the debug commands and other troubleshooting tools, it is best to review the status of the installation and the connections between the modem and the router. Make sure to check for the following:

- The modem is turned on and is receiving power.

- The cable is of the right type and is secured.

- The DIP switches or other physical options on the modem are set to known values or factory defaults. In this case, *known values* means settings that are known to work for this router and modem configuration in other installations; sometimes the factory defaults will not work. In addition, administrators might find that random guessing is required to find the proper settings.

- The modem is plugged into a phone jack and the dial tone is present.

After these steps have been completed, you need to *reverse Telnet* to communicate with the modem. For reverse Telnet to work, the line interface needs the `transport input all` and `modem inout` commands. These commands enable the port to accept input and transfer data to and from the modem. Note that reverse Telnet is not a command but a tool used to provide a connection to a reserved TCP port on the router, which maps to a physical asynchronous port. For example, the physical port on line 4 would map to TCP port 2004. The administrator can Telnet to the router and, by altering the port number (the default TCP port for Telnet is 23), can be connected directly to the attached device, such as a modem. TCP ports starting with 2000 are used for Telnet, whereas 4000 is the start of the range for non-Telnet-specific TCP connections. Ports starting with 6000 are used for binary-mode Telnet. Of these, most administrators find it necessary to use ports only in the 2000 range.

Reverse Telnet is a powerful tool that has been required for practical demonstrations of Cisco expertise and certifications. Readers should be familiar with its functionality.

Manual Configuration

Manual configuration can eliminate the negotiation process required for automatic configuration, but it adds substantially to the configuration process. It requires router configuration changes if the modem is changed, possibly through an upgrade or replacement to a different vendor or model. Manual router configuration requires knowledge of the AT, or Hayes, command instructions.

The attention (AT) commands are used to configure the modem and, for most purposes, are used to create a standard configuration methodology for modems. There are differences from vendor to vendor in the function of each command, but for the most part they have been standardized. AT commands enable configuration and diagnostic services to become fairly advanced, including settings that report the modem's status, the quality of the network (phone company) connection, and the configuration of flow control and other modem functions. Software, including terminal software, will frequently provide these commands upon selection of a menu-driven function, which insulates the user from needing to learn and use the commands.

Please consult with the modem manufacturer regarding the appropriate codes for your modem.

Most modems have a number of commands in common, and many of these are quite useful for the administrator. These are outlined in Table 2.3.

TABLE 2.3   Common AT Commands

Command	Function
&F	The AT&F command resets most modems to their factory defaults.
&C	This command configures the modem-for-modem control (C is for *Carrier Detect*). C1 instructs the modem to use CD to reflect the actual connection status.
S0=1	There are a number of S series commands, of which S0 is the first. S0 controls the number of rings before the modem answers; in this case the modem will answer on the first ring. A setting of at least 2 is suggested for Caller ID installations; some secure installations use fairly high values—perhaps 10 rings or more. This is because most "war dialers" (or automatic dialers) assume the line is not terminated after eight or more rings.
&D	The &D command relates to DTR. With a setting of D3, the modem will hang up the line when the DTR drops. This is the normal configuration.
M0	This command turns off the audio output from the modem. This can provide a great benefit when you are not troubleshooting; the screeching of the modem connection sequence can be quite irritating.
L1	The L commands control the volume on the modem speaker. L3 would turn the volume to maximum. Note that modems with external volume controls, such as the U.S. Robotics Courier, will also require the physical knob to be turned.
&Q6	The &Q6 command is significant because it results in the DTE speed being locked. This is discussed in greater detail in Chapter 4, but basically, this means that locking the DTE speed can improve performance on lower-quality circuits.

From the router's perspective, a number of commands are necessary to configure an asynchronous connection. These are outlined in Table 2.4.

TABLE 2.4   The Asynchronous Router Commands

Command	Function
line *N*	Cisco routers refer to asynchronous ports as lines. *N* is equal to the number of the port and is used before the rest of the commands in this table to get into line configuration mode.
login	The login command is required to force authentication of a connection.
password	This command establishes the password to be used on the line.
flowcontrol	The flowcontrol command can be followed with hardware or software settings. Typically, hardware flow control provides greater control over the data flow and allows for higher communication speeds. Software flow control is not recommended.
speed	The speed command establishes the maximum speed to be used between the modem and access server or router. It defines the speed of both transmit and receive, and it is noted in bits per second (bps). Note that the modem and access server can negotiate a slower speed or data rate.
transport input	The transport input command defines the protocol to use in reverse Telnet connections. This may be LAT, MOP, NASI, PAD, RLOGIN, Telnet, or V120; however, administrators typically use the all keyword to allow all connection types. This is potentially less secure because a hacker could use one of these protocols to gain access or deny service to the router. For example, if there is no business need to use RLOGIN, why leave the access available to allow repeated access attempts from an outsider?
stopbits	Stop bits are used in asynchronous communications to define the end of each byte. Typically, the stopbits value is set to 1 because there is little reason to send additional bits; however, values of 1.5 and 2 are also valid.
modem	The modem command is used to define the type of calls allowed. By default, the router allows dial-in, or incoming, calls only. However, to allow reverse Telnet or dial-out connections, in addition to dial-in, the administrator would use the inout keyword.

It is important to note that each line, or logical interface, (specified with the line command in Table 2.4) has an associated physical interface. This is defined by the router. There is also a line associated with the aux interface. The asynchronous, or async, interface is the physical representation of the interface, and configurations on async interfaces define the protocol characteristics of the connection. This would be used to define a protocol such as Point-to-Point Protocol (PPP) or the addressing mechanism to be used. An async interface can be a capable serial interface configured for asynchronous services with the physical-layer async command, or the aux (auxiliary) port on the router.

Configuration begins with the line command and the number of the interface. This is followed with the specific information that is needed—for example, the login capabilities and DTE-to-DCE speed. A typical configuration might appear as follows:

```
line 3
    modem inout
    stopbits 1
    databits 8
    parity none
    transport output all
    transport input all
    speed 56000
    flowcontrol hardware
    login
    password tplekprp
```

This configuration would allow calls in or out, with all protocols supported and login required. We've also configured the data rate to 56Kbps and added a common set of modem parameters (N, 8, 1) to the configuration. These last parameters define those communications characteristics and must match on both sides of the connection. Hardware flow control would be used. Flow control is used to prevent buffer overruns and maintain an efficient flow of data by signaling the sender that it should slow down or speed up.

If there is a problem with manual configuration, it will be first noted when the administrator attempts to use the modem. Reverse Telnet and use of the diagnostic commands associated with that modem are most likely the best tools available for troubleshooting.

Summary

Asynchronous, or analog, connections are widely available and extremely popular methods for providing remote access in today's networks. They are not without their disadvantages; however, no other technology has come along to replace them entirely.

Modern modems provide a wide range of modulation types, which provides the user with many connection speed options. Connecting modems to an access server is straightforward due to the use of the universal EIA/TIA-232 (RS-232-C) serial connector.

Asynchronous modems provide a challenge for remote access connections, and configuration options include manual, automatic (autoconfigure), or autodiscovery. Each method has its own characteristics. For instance, manual configuration requires the knowledge of which AT commands to use to configure the modem for dial-in access. If using automatic configuration, the only knowledge needed is the type of modem used on the access-server, and the router will try to apply the best match. When using autodiscovery, the administrator does not need to know what type of modem is connected to the access-server; the router will query the modem to determine its type and then apply the best matching parameters.

Exam Essentials

Know how to identify the different connection types in analog communications.   The DTE-to-DCE connection occurs between the router (DTE) and the modem (DCE). The DCE-to-DCE connection occurs between the two modems over the phone network.

Understand the different modulation types and their speeds.   You should know the 14 modulation types and the data rates they provide as listed in Table 2.2. You should also understand that asynchronous connections are limited to 56Kbps, or 53Kbps by FCC order.

Understand the different signals carried in the communications cable.   Make sure you know which signal does what when two devices are communicating over an EIA/TIA-232 (RS-232-C) connection. TXD is used for transmission of data, RXD is for reception of data, CD is used to signal that a connection exists between local and remote DCE, and GND is used as a reference signal. RTS and CTS are used in hardware flow control.

Know the compression and correction standards.   V.42bis is the most widely used data compression standard. V.44 is the more recent kid on the block and is significantly more efficient than V.42bis.

Understand the different IOS modem configuration modes.   Cisco IOS has the capability to automatically configure a modem by using the information in the modemcap database. The router can also automatically discover the modem type and configure that modem for asynchronous communications. You can also manually supply the router with modem configuration commands.

Know the major attention (AT) commands used for manual modem configuration. You should understand what the AT&F command will do to most modems and you should know the other AT commands in Table 2.3.

Know how to create a new modemcap database entry by using an existing database entry as a template. To create a new modemcap database entry, use the modemcap edit *new-profile-name* template *existing-profilename* command with template being the key parameter.

Know which commands to use in line configuration mode and which to use in the logical interface configuration mode. Commands in Table 2.4 are used in line configuration mode to specify the physical characteristics of the asynchronous connection. Commands used in interface configuration mode configure parameters such as encapsulation and addresses used on the asynchronous connection.

Key Terms

Before you take the exam, be certain you are familiar with the following terms:

analog

asynchronous connections

autoconfigure

autodiscovery

baud

clocking

convergence

data compression

Data Communications
Equipment (DCE)

digital

Data Terminal Equipment (DTE)

error correction

known values

LZW algorithm

manual configuration

modem

modemcap database

modulation

reverse Telnet

time division multiplexing (TDM)

Universal Asynchronous Receiver/
Transmitter (UART)

virtual private network (VPN)

Written Lab

1.   The command AT&F performs what function on many modems?
2.   What command is used to select hardware or software data control?
3.   To set the maximum speed between the DTE and DCE, the administrator would use what command?
4.   What command is used to select configuration mode for port 5?
5.   To define the number of bits that define the end of a byte in asynchronous communications, the command _____ is used.
6.   The best theoretical analog modem DCE-to-DCE speed is ____.
7.   In the U.S., the FCC limits DCE-to-DCE speed to no more than _____.
8.   V.34 operates at _____.
9.   Pin 7 in DTE-to-DCE signaling normally provides _____.
10.   The connector for connecting to the public phone network from the DCE is typically _____.

Hands-on Labs

Lab 1

In this lab, you will configure the router for reverse Telnet to a modem attached to Serial 0/0 with a number of parameters. Perform the following functions on a router with an asynchronous serial port:

- Name your router **Toontown**.
- Assign a host only (/32) loopback address of 10.1.0.1.
- Connect a modem to S0/0.
- Configure the interface for asynchronous communications.
- Set hardware based flow control
- Set a data rate of 28.8Kbps.
- Set login restrictions.
- Set a single user password of **bugsbunny**.
- Set parity, data, and stopbit values of **N**, **8**, **1**, respectively.

- Configure the modem for bidirectional traffic allowing all protocols.
- When you are finished, you should be able to issue AT commands to the modem after reverse Telnetting to the line:

```
conf t
en

hostname Toontown

interface loopback 0
  ip address 10.1.0.1 255.255.255.255

interface serial 0/0
  physical-layer async
  no shutdown

line 1
  speed 28800
  flowcontrol hardware
  stopbits 1
  databits 8
  parity none
  modem inout
  transport input all
  transport output all
  password bugsbunny
  login
```

Lab 2

In this lab, you will configure the modem configuration with the AT commands.

1. Reverse Telnet into a modem connected to the router:

```
{Router Ethernet IP address} {port number}
```

Assuming 10.10.10.10, line 1, the command would be 10.10.10.10 2001. Remember that you also need to have the modem inout configuration command and the transport input telnet command.

2. Using the modem's documentation, reset the modem's configuration. Then instruct it to answer on the second ring, use CD, hang up on DTR low, and turn the speaker off.

```
AT&F
ATS0=1
AT&C1
AT&D3
ATM0
```

Note that the command could be entered on a single line as follows:

```
AT&FS0=1&C1&D3M0
```

The &F must appear at the beginning because it is the reset command. Placing it later in the string would erase any modifications made up to that point.

Review Questions

1. What is reverse Telnet?

   A. An encryption technique used by the Telnet protocol

   B. A method for connecting to directly attached asynchronous devices

   C. A function that is available only on the AS5x00 platform

   D. A function that is available only with internal modems

2. Modem-to-modem connections are which of the following?

   A. DTE to DTE

   B. DTE to DCE

   C. DCE to DCE

   D. Dependent upon the modulation used

3. Which of the following options represents the connection between the router and modem?

   A. DTE to DTE

   B. DTE to DCE

   C. DCE to DCE

   D. Analog

4. The UART provides which of the following services?

   A. Compression

   B. Encryption

   C. Error detection

   D. Buffering

5. What is the command to instruct a Cisco router to automatically configure a modem?

   A. modem auto-configure

   B. modem autoconfigure

   C. async modem autoconfigure

   D. modem configuration auto

6. To display the router's initialization string for a U.S. Robotics Courier modem, what would the administrator type?

   A. show modemcap

   B. show modemcap modem usr_courier

   C. show modem usr_courier

   D. show modemcap usr_courier

7.   *Baud* is roughly equivalent to which of the following descriptions?

   A. Bits per minute

   B. Bits per second

   C. Four-to-one encryption

   D. Analog-to-digital encoding

8.   The protocol characteristics of the asynchronous connection are defined by which of the following?

   A. The line interface

   B. The Ethernet interface

   C. The asynchronous interface

   D. The modem interface

9.   The administrator would use which command to configure a modem for both incoming and outgoing calls?

   A. `modem answer`

   B. `modem inout`

   C. `allow modem dial in-out`

   D. `modem both`

10.   Which flow control method is recommended for use by administrators?

   A. Hardware

   B. Software

   C. Varies with the speed of the modem

   D. Varies with the type of router

11.   The `speed` command is applied to which of the following interfaces?

   A. Asynchronous

   B. Modem

   C. Line

   D. Port

12.   The transport protocols do not include which of the following?

   A. Telnet

   B. rlogin

   C. V120

   D. FTP

13. What is the interface used to configure the router locally called?

   A. Serial

   B. Virtual terminal

   C. Console

   D. Management

14. What is the command used to reset most modems to their factory defaults?

   A. ATF&

   B. Reset

   C. AT&E

   D. AT&F

15. What is the function of the ground wire?

   A. To secure the modem to the router

   B. To provide a reference signal for clocking

   C. To provide a reference signal for voltage changes

   D. To allow data bursts

16. The CTS and RTS wires are part of what modem function?

   A. Modem control signaling

   B. Hardware flow control

   C. Data transfer

   D. Compression

17. What is the result of the `modem autoconfigure discovery` command?

   A. The router will interrogate the modem at varying baud rates to automatically configure the modem.

   B. The modem will send an AT string to the router every five seconds following power on, which is used to configure the IOS.

   C. The router will send each of the AT command strings in the modemcap database until one receives an OK response.

   D. None of the above.

18. To permit a connection to a port, the administrator would enter which command in line configuration mode?

   A. `login`

   B. `access`

   C. `permit`

   D. None of the above

19. What is the command to have the modem answer on the second ring?

   A. S0=2

   B. AT=2

   C. AT&D2

   D. ATS0=2

20. What is a DIP switch?

   A. The act of hiring a new network administrator.

   B. A physical configuration pin on a modem.

   C. A logical configuration parameter accessed from AT commands.

   D. DIP is another term for DTR—it controls carrier detection.

Answers to Written Lab

1. It resets the configuration to the default.

2. flowcontrol

3. speed

4. line 5

5. stopbits

6. 56Kbps

7. 53Kbps

8. 28.8Kbps

9. Ground

10. RJ-11

Answers to Review Questions

1. B. Although the term can be confusing, reverse Telnet links an IP port to a physical port on the access device. Thus, it is a method for connecting to directly attached devices.

2. C. Modems are regarded as DCE devices.

3. B. Although the modem is a DCE device, the router is a DTE device.

4. D. UARTs provide a buffer for asynchronous ports.

5. B. Unfortunately, all of these answers seem plausible, and the difference between the first three options is minute. However, the command is `modem autoconfigure`.

6. D. In practice, the administrator would likely use the built-in Help function; however, the command to display the initialization string is `show modemcap usr_courier` and is stored in the modemcap database.

7. B. The baud rate is usually parallel to the data rate in bits per second (bps). Although related, baud is rarely "equivalent" to bit rate these days, due to compression and encoding schemes.

8. C. The asynchronous (logical) interface is responsible for the protocol characteristics.

9. B. Command questions can be the most difficult, and due to the inconsistencies of the IOS, most must be memorized. The `modem inout` command configures the interface to accept and place calls.

10. A. Hardware flow control is recommended because it reduces the processing requirements incurred with software flow control and allows for higher-speed communication.

11. C. The `speed` command is used to set the modem-to-DTE rate and it is applied to a line interface.

12. D. FTP is not included in the transport protocols, which are best thought of as protocols that allow screen-based sessions, such as Telnet.

13. C. The console port is used to initially configure the router. The default data rate is 9,600 baud.

14. D. The Hayes AT command &F resets the modem for compatible modems.

15. C. The ground wire provides a reference for voltage levels. Asynchronous connections do not rely on external clocking, and no data is transferred on the ground wire.

16. B. Clear-to-send and ready-to-send wires provide hardware flow control functions.

17. A. Autoconfigure discovery starts by establishing a baud rate for further connectivity.

18. A. The `login` command is used to require authentication before establishing a connection. The other two commands are used for access lists and security, respectively.

19. D. If you answered S0=2, you jumped the gun. All AT commands must be prefixed with AT. Although S0=2 is the right variable, the command cannot stand on its own. &D2 is a DTR command.

20. B. A DIP switch is a physical switch used to alter a modem's configuration. Hope you chuckled at "the act of hiring a new network administrator." "A logical configuration parameter" implies a logical configuration change.

Chapter
3

Point-to-Point Protocol

EXAM TOPICS COVERED IN THIS CHAPTER INCLUDE:

- ✓ Know the commands and syntax used to configure PPP connections between the central site and branch offices.
- ✓ Understand the commands and syntax to configure PAP or CHAP authentication.
- ✓ Know how to configure Multilink services.
- ✓ Be able to verify and troubleshoot PPP configurations.
- ✓ Know the commands and procedures to configure a PC for dial-up connections.

The Point-to-Point Protocol (PPP) is one of the serial encapsulations that administrators find useful for remote access solutions. PPP operates over a wide range of media and was designed to simplify the transport of multiple protocols (IP, IPX, AppleTalk, and so on) over serial links. Though the protocol does operate over other media, this chapter focuses solely on remote access solutions.

With the intense demand for connectivity by salespeople, remote staff, and telecommuters, it becomes clear that consistent remote access solutions are required. The benefits of using PPP are that it is universal and efficient. PPP on Windows should be able to communicate with PPP on any access server, and the configuration demands on the client side are extremely small, thus resulting in fewer support issues. Although HDLC, SLIP, and Frame Relay encapsulations are also somewhat standardized, the benefits of PPP and its low overhead, along with virtually universal media support, make it an excellent choice for remote access.

This chapter provides an overview of PPP and the commands and processes required to configure this protocol on Cisco access servers.

PPP Overview and Architecture

PPP is documented in RFC 1661 as a standard method for transporting multiple protocols over point-to-point links. This substantially improved upon the Serial Line Internet Protocol (SLIP). SLIP transports IP packets only across serial circuits.

Although beyond the scope of this Study Guide, PPP has evolved to operate over Ethernet (PPPoE), as specified in RFC 2516, and PPP over ATM (PPPoA), as specified in RFC 2364. Packet over SONET (Synchronous Optical NETwork) also uses PPP-based encapsulations.

RFCs for Remote Access Networks

There appear to be two schools of thought on *Request for Comments (RFCs)*—the documents that are used to establish and document standards in computer networking. Some believe that only geeks bother to memorize and recite the various RFC numbers, whereas others believe that such knowledge is critical to the proper design and administration of the network.

Regardless of your individual position, the RFCs that document PPP are worthy of your time and attention. The various protocols are well documented and invaluable in troubleshooting. Some of the RFCs that warrant specific attention include the following:

RFC 1334 includes the PPP authentication protocols.

RFC 1661 includes the current revision of the PPP protocol.

RFC 1990 includes the PPP Multilink protocol, which is discussed later in this chapter.

There are many RFCs that would augment this brief list, but their relevance is highly variable depending on the installation requirements. Appendix B lists several RFCs and websites to assist you in your studying. The Internet Engineering Task Force (IETF) website at www.ietf.org provides links to all RFCs; other sources are available as well.

PPP contains three main components. The first is the encapsulation method used, and for PPP the default is an HDLC-like framing. The second, *Link Control Protocol (LCP)*, is used when establishing, configuring, and testing the data-link connection. The third is actually a family of *Network Control Protocols (NCPs)*, which establishes and configures different Network Layer protocols. PPP, LCP, and NCP are all considered Layer 2 protocols.

The PPP protocol adds a minimal amount of overhead to the packet, as shown in Figure 3.1.

FIGURE 3.1   The PPP frame structure

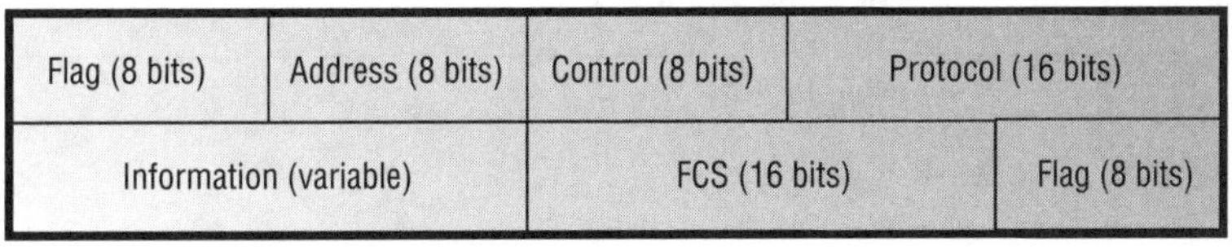

Flag (8 bits)	Address (8 bits)	Control (8 bits)	Protocol (16 bits)	
Information (variable)		FCS (16 bits)		Flag (8 bits)

The remainder of this section describes each of the components found in the PPP frame.

The Flag Field

The *Flag field* is a single octet (8 bits) that indicates the beginning and end of each frame; it has a unique pattern of 01111110. Generally, a single flag ends one frame and begins the next. But, as can be seen in Figure 3.1, distinct start and end frames are also found. Both of these examples use the same pattern. *Bit stuffing* is used to make this pattern unique. Bit stuffing is a technique that alters patterns in the user data that appear the same as the frame delimiter or other framing information. For example, if the sequence 010101111110100 appeared representing two characters, the protocol would interpret this as the start of a frame—01111110. Bit-stuffing will re-represent the characters by altering this flow so that the 01111110 pattern remains unique.

The Address Field

The *Address field* is a single octet (8 bits) with the binary sequence of 11111111 (0xff hexadecimal). This is known as the All-Station Address because PPP does not assign individual station addresses. The field is included to allow addressing; however, as inferred by the term *point-to-point*, the destination is always the opposite end of the link.

The Control Field

The *Control field* is a single octet (8 bits) and contains the binary sequence 00000011 (0x03 hexadecimal), which is the Unnumbered Information (UI) command. This signifies that the following bits will provide information regarding the remaining data—as opposed to the data being part of the PPP protocol.

The Protocol Field

The *Protocol field* is two octets (16 bits) and identifies the upper-layer protocol. An upper-layer protocol would include IPCP, or the IP Control Protocol. The more commonly assigned Protocol fields and their hexadecimal values are listed in Table 3.1. This list is beneficial for two reasons: first, it shows the wide diversity of PPP; second, the list will supplement troubleshooting.

TABLE 3.1   PPP Assigned Protocol Fields

Value (in hex)	Protocol Name
0001	Padding Protocol
0021	Internet Protocol
0023	OSI Network Layer
0025	Xerox NS IDP
0027	DECnet Phase IV
0029	AppleTalk
002b	Novell IPX
002d	Van Jacobson Compressed TCP/IP
002f	Van Jacobson Uncompressed TCP/IP

TABLE 3.1 PPP Assigned Protocol Fields *(continued)*

Value (in hex)	Protocol Name
0031	Bridging PDU
0035	Banyan Vines
0041	Cisco Systems
0201	802.1d Hello Packets
0203	IBM Source Routing BPDU
8021	Internet Protocol Control Protocol
8023	OSI Network Layer Control Protocol
8025	Xerox NS IDP Control Protocol
8027	DECnet Phase IV Control Protocol
8029	AppleTalk Control Protocol
802b	Novell IPX Control Protocol
803d	Multilink Control Protocol
80fd	Compression Control Protocol
c021	Link Control Protocol
c023	Password Authentication Protocol
c025	Link Quality Report
c223	Challenge Handshake Authentication Protocol

Notice that both Password Authentication Protocol (PAP) and Challenge Handshake Authentication Protocol (CHAP) are listed toward the bottom of this table. These two protocols are discussed later in the chapter; however, it is significant to note them here in the context of PPP's broad support for features. Authentication, multilink (the ability to bond different physical channels into a single logical connection), and compression are all supported in PPP and its associated upper-layer protocols.

The Information Field

The *Information field* is also called the *Data field*. This field contains the data of the packet that has been encapsulated in PPP. The Information field's length is determined by the amount of user data offered, which can range from zero to 1,500 octets. The Maximum Receive Unit (MRU) establishes this upper limitation.

The Frame Check Sequence (FCS) Field

The *Frame Check Sequence field* is two octets (16 bits) and provides a cyclical redundancy check (CRC) value, and it is used to validate the packet's integrity. This is also called a *checksum*.

Configuring Access Servers

Although differences can exist in the configuration methodology needed for different platforms, most steps are consistent and similar. Stated another way, commands for a Cisco access server are different from those for a Shiva LanRover, but the functions are similar.

Router ports on remote access devices can terminate standard terminal emulation (exec session)—sometimes thought of as a terminal or VT100 terminal—or a wide array of protocols including PPP, SLIP, and ARAP (AppleTalk Remote Access Protocol). The type of protocol used can be predefined by the administrator or automatically selected by the router. This feature uses the `autoselect` command. When `autoselect` is not enabled, the router will start an exec session on the line.

If `autoselect` is not used, the user can still start a session by using one of the other protocols, but they will need to provide the command to start. With `autoselect`, the router can detect the protocol flag value—0x7E for PPP, 0x10 for ARAP, and 0xC0 for SLIP. A carriage return is interpreted as a request for an exec session.

For the remainder of this section, the PPP protocol will remain our focus.

Configuring PPP

There are a few choices for the administrator or designer to consider when deploying PPP. These choices are above and beyond those that would be used with any other technology, such as IP addressing assignments (the actual addresses, not the method used) and the provisioning of routing protocols. This section focuses on some of the more common issues regarding PPP, including the selection of dedicated or interactive PPP and the implementation of Layer 3 addressing. Later in this chapter we will introduce authentication protocols and multilink technologies.

Dedicated or Interactive PPP

To dedicate a line for use by SLIP or PPP, the administrator can use the `async mode dedicated` command. This command prevents the user from changing the encapsulation protocol and can augment security by restricting the method of access.

The interactive option, configured with the `async mode interactive` command, enables the user to select any encapsulation for the session by entering a command in exec mode.

> The default for each interface is no async mode. As such, neither PPP nor SLIP is available.

Interface Addressing Options for Local Devices

PPP configuration also requires attention to Layer 3 addressing. In this section, IP addressing considerations are presented due to both their complexity and frequency. These include static, IP unnumbered, and dynamic addressing options:

Static addressing   Clearly, the use of static addresses is the most basic IP addressing technique. Static addresses are entered on each interface manually and require administration and documentation. The benefit of static addresses is supportability—troubleshooting is simplified with statics. However, there is a substantial amount of administration overhead. Static addresses are well suited to the central office remote access server.

IP unnumbered   An alternative to static addressing is the use of IP unnumbered. This is not a dynamic solution, which will also be presented, but rather a feature that Cisco provides to allow a point-to-point link to share an IP address from another interface. For example, the remote router might be configured with a static IP address on its Ethernet interface, whereas the serial interface could be configured with an unnumbered interface, effectively using the same IP address assigned to the Ethernet port. The downside of this solution is that the troubleshooting options are more limited. An alternative to using a physical interface is to use the loopback interface. Some argue that this interface is best used with IP unnumbered because, theoretically, it can never go down.

> Cisco documentation presents the loopback interface as one that can never go down; however, administrative errors can disable the interface. Overall, it remains a better alternative than a physical interface.

Dynamic addressing   Dynamic addressing is an excellent solution in a number of installations, especially those that use modem-attached workstations from a remote location. The administrator can configure a pool of addresses that are assigned on a per-call basis rather than manually assigning a single IP address for each user. This greatly reduces the number of addresses that must be assigned and simplifies the administrative tasks. These assignments typically use DHCP, or Dynamic Host Configuration Protocol.

Configuring Dynamic Addressing

The commands to configure dynamic addressing are dependent upon the method used. Although DHCP is one option (used as an example in the following text), there are other methods, including proprietary ones.

Before we discuss incorporating a dynamic addressing solution, it is best to acknowledge the option of manually addressing the client. In Windows 95/98, this is accomplished by using the Dial-Up Connection Properties menu to access the TCP/IP Settings dialog box. This dialog box is shown in Figure 3.2. Note that you must select Specify an IP Address to manually enter a selection.

FIGURE 3.2   Manual IP address configuration in Windows 95/98

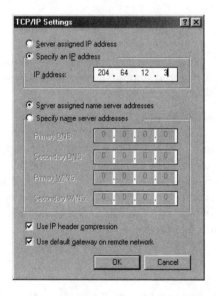

Windows will provide a warning if you attempt to use the Network Control Panel to configure the dial-up adapter, as shown in Figure 3.3. As shown, configuration parameters in properties will overwrite any custom parameters on the individual dial-up connection. Many users might connect to different locations with each requiring a different set of parameters—as such, the warning is well heeded and administrators will likely choose to configure all settings per connection.

FIGURE 3.3   Configuring a dial-up adapter from the Windows Control Panel

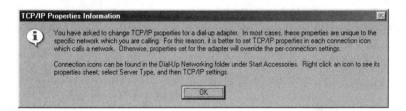

If you are configuring a router to provide the dial-up connection between the client and remote access server, you should use the standard Ethernet configuration commands. These entries, shown in Figure 3.4, include the IP address, subnet mask, default gateway, and name servers. Please note that although a static configuration is shown, the administrator could use DHCP.

FIGURE 3.4   Ethernet-based manual IP address configuration in Windows 95/98

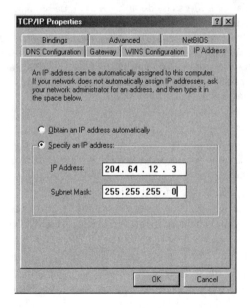

     The configuration dialog box is accessed through Control Panel ➢ Network ➢ TCP/IP ➢ Adapter.

On the router, the configuration is straightforward, but it is dependent upon the role of the router and the type of dynamic assignment desired. The `async dynamic address` command

enables the client to provide its address, but the `peer default ip address [ip-address | dhcp | pool` *poolname*`]` command is used more often. This command enables the administrator to select manual, DHCP, or pool-based address selection.

When selecting the DHCP option, the administrator must also configure the router for one of three choices:

- IP helper address
- IP DHCP server
- DHCP server on router

The IP helper address option is often found in router configurations, but without additional configuration, this option will forward broadcast traffic to the helper address. The *helper address* is the address of the server or group of servers that provide the required service—DHCP, in this example.

> It is important to remember that certain IP broadcast traffic will be forwarded to the helper address by default. This can be blocked to include only DHCP datagrams by using the `no ip forward-protocol udp` *udp-port-number* command. The following UDP (User Datagram Protocol) ports are enabled by default: 69 (TFTP), 53 (DNS), 37 (Time), 42 (nameserver), 49 (TACACS), 67 (BOOTP Client), 68 (BOOTP Server), 137 (NetBIOS WINS), and 138 (NetBIOS datagram). BOOTP (Bootstrap Protocol) was the predecessor to DHCP and shares the same UDP port numbers.

A newer command is `ip dhcp-server`, which the administrator can use to specify the address of the DHCP server.

In addition, some routers might also provide DHCP server functionality. This should be considered for smaller installations only; routers are best suited to provide routing. However, this feature might be ideal for small office/home office installations.

To configure DHCP services on the router, the administrator must first decide if they wish to use a DHCP database agent to help manage the lease process. Cisco calls this feature *conflict logging*.

If conflict logging is desired, the administrator must also configure an FTP or TFTP server, which is defined with the `ip dhcp database` command. If the administrator does not wish to implement conflict logging, the command `no ip dhcp conflict logging` must be used instead. Note that in some instances the administrator must exclude an address from the DHCP pool. To do this, they must use the `ip dhcp excluded-address low-address {high-address}` command.

An entire configuration file for DHCP services is shown here:

```
service dhcp
ip dhcp database ftp://dhcp:cisco@10.11.1.10/dhcp

ip dhcp pool 0
```

```
network 10.10.1.0 /24
default-router 10.10.1.1
domain-name foo.com
dns-server 10.2.20.51
netbios-name-server 10.2.20.51
```

The previous configuration example uses an FTP server at 10.11.1.10 to capture information regarding the DHCP leases. The pool is for 10.10.1.0/24 and a default gateway of 10.10.1.1. The domain is foo.com, and DNS and WINS services are provided by 10.2.20.51. The service dhcp command used here is optional; the service is available by default. The FTP server username is dhcp with a password of cisco in the previous output; however, this is not a very secure option.

Although this chapter focuses on Windows 95/98 configuration, readers should note that Windows NT and 2000 differ little in most regards. Figure 3.5 shows Windows 2000's dial-up networking configuration dialog box.

FIGURE 3.5   Windows 2000 dial-up networking

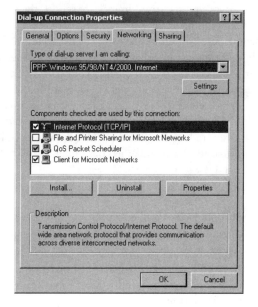

How DHCP Works

DHCP is an open standard that is based partly upon the BOOTP protocol specified in RFC 951 and RFC 1541. DHCP can be used by Unix, Macintosh, and Windows-based systems. However, the protocol did not attain mainstream, corporate recognition until the service was incorporated into Windows NT.

DHCP enables a host to learn its IP address dynamically. This process is termed a *lease* because the address assigned belongs to the host for an administratively defined time. On Windows implementations, this assignment is set for 72 hours by default.

   DHCP leases are discussed in the following section.

From a router perspective, DHCP requires one of two components: a DHCP server on the local subnet or a method of forwarding the broadcast across the router. DHCP lease requests are broadcasts, so the network designer would need a DHCP server present on each segment in the network. This clearly would not scale well and is impractical in most network designs, but it would provide addressing information to the clients.

The alternative is to provide a little help to DHCP. This is accomplished with the IP helper address, a statically defined address on each router interface that is connected to the local segment that needs the help. This segment, with the help of the helper address, will be able to get to the DHCP server. Broadcast requests for addresses are sent to the helper address as unicasts, thus significantly reducing overall broadcast traffic.

Most DHCP implementations, including Microsoft's, can provide a great deal of information to the client as well, including time servers, default gateways, and other address-based services.

When using the router as a DHCP server, there is generally less of a motivation to providing redundancy; whenever more than a handful of networks require addressing services, it is generally better to add a dedicated server. If the router is unavailable, it is unlikely that users will be concerned about the loss of a DHCP lease. If there are multiple networks, the likelihood of a single router point of failure is reduced, but there is also an increased load on the router from the number of leases that must be managed. When designing for DHCP, most architects and administrators consider the DHCP lease length.

DHCP Lease Length

The length of the DHCP lease governs the amount of time a host "owns" the address. To continue using the address, the host must renew with the server before the lease expires. Designers must consider the overhead of this renewal traffic and the impact of failed or unavailable DHCP servers. In general, long leases are appropriate for fixed environments, and short leases are applicable in more dynamic installations.

Consider a fully functioning network with 100 workstations and a lease length of five minutes. This is an extreme example (that no self-respecting engineer would install) because DHCP will send a renewal request at an interval equal to one-half the lease period. The overhead for just IP address leases would be 2,400 requests per hour, not including any DNS queries and the multiple packets involved in each request (see Figure 3.6). This is a high amount of overhead for information that should not change under normal circumstances.

In addition, when a lease expires, the host must release its IP address. Without a DHCP server, it will be unable to communicate on the network because it has no IP address. The alternative to a short lease is to make the lease very long. Consider the impact of a lease equal to 60 days. Should the hosts remain on a local subnet with very few changes, this would substantially reduce the volume of traffic. However, this would not be appropriate for a hotelling installation. *Hotelling* is a concept introduced years ago in which notebook users would check into a cubicle for a day or even a week. DHCP is a great solution for such an installation because the MAC addresses are constantly changing, but a long lease time would be inappropriate here. Consider a scenario in which each visitor connects once per quarter, or every 90 days. And, for this example, presume that there are 800 users of the service, and the pool is a standard Class C network of 254 host addresses. If the lease were long—90 days for this example—only the first 254 users would be able to obtain an address. Clearly, this is not appropriate for this type of installation, which is an important consideration for the network designer.

As mentioned earlier, the default DHCP lease renewal interval (on NT) is 72 hours. DHCP attempts to renew the lease after one-half the lease duration, or 36 hours in the case of default NT.

The default lease on Cisco IOS-based DHCP servers is 24 hours.

For reference, the mechanism by which DHCP obtains an address is illustrated in Figure 3.6. Note that DHCP uses a system of discovery to locate the DHCP server—a phase that uses the helper function. After the DHCP server is found, the offer is returned to the workstation, and the request is positively or negatively acknowledged. One way to remember the DHCP process is with the mnemonic DORA, which stands for Discover, Offer, Request, and Acknowledgment.

DHCP operates in similar fashion when served from the router: as noted previously, only the configuration process changes. While an interesting feature, the DHCP server on the router is not practical in most installations. The need to maintain a separate FTP server for the database usually leads the administrator to opt for a more scalable option that requires installing a dedicated server.

FIGURE 3.6   The DHCP process

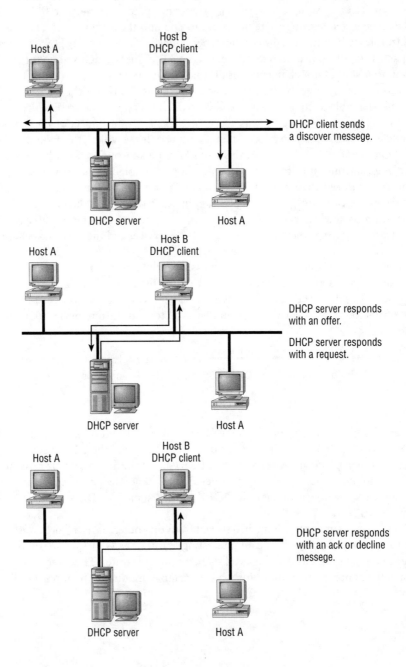

PAP and CHAP Authentication

One of the key benefits of PPP is the ability to add authentication services, which are provided by PAP or CHAP. Authentication adds substantially to the security of the network and should be used. Even though PAP is presented in this section, its use is discouraged and administrators should configure their networks for the more secure CHAP.

Password Authentication Protocol (PAP)

Password Authentication Protocol (PAP) provides basic security authentication for connections. The username and password information, however, are transmitted in clear-text, which can be intercepted by a hacker to compromise the network. Unfortunately, a few older systems support only PAP and not the more secure CHAP, which mandates PAP's usage in those cases.

PAP is defined in RFC 1334.

PAP operates by establishing a connection and then checking the username and password information. If the username and password information matches, an OK message is returned and the session is allowed to proceed. This is illustrated in Figure 3.7. Note that the username and password are transmitted in clear-text in PAP—a significant security risk.

PAP usernames and passwords are transmitted in clear-text, reducing the security benefits of the protocol. Use CHAP whenever possible.

FIGURE 3.7   PAP authentication

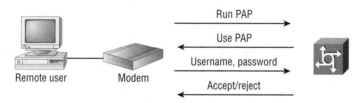

To configure PAP, the administrator needs to configure both the service and a database of usernames and passwords. The commands used to do this are shown here:

```
encapsulation ppp
ppp authentication {chap | chap pap | pap chap |
   pap} [if-needed] [list-name | default] [callin]
```

Usernames and passwords are added to the router with the `username` *name* `password` *secret* command.

There isn't much more to PAP—it works with a minimal amount of configuration, in large part due to its lack of security. Readers should be familiar with the existence of the protocol and know that it should not be used in current designs.

Challenge Handshake Authentication Protocol (CHAP)

The *Challenge Handshake Authentication Protocol (CHAP)* is significantly more secure than PAP. This is because of the mechanism used to transfer the username and password: CHAP protects against playback hacking (resending the packet as part of an attack) by using a hash value that is valid only for that transaction. When the attacker captures the CHAP session and replays that dialog in an attempt to access the network, the hash method will prevent the connection. The password is also hidden from the attacker; it is never sent over the circuit.

The hash value used in CHAP is derived from the Message Digest type 5 (MD5) algorithm, which takes a message of arbitrary length and produces as output a 128-bit message digest of the input. The message digest's strength comes from being nonreversible, and it is computationally infeasible to produce two messages having the same message digest. The MD5 algorithm is defined in RFC 1321.

The MD5 hash shown in Figure 3.8 is valid for a relatively brief time, and no unencrypted information is sent over the link. This data might allow a hacker to impersonate the authentic user.

FIGURE 3.8   CHAP authentication

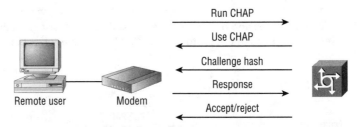

The commands to configure CHAP are similar to those for PAP. Instead of selecting pap in the **ppp authentication** command, the administrator uses the **chap** keyword. Notice, from the following configuration snippet, that two additional options are also available: **chap pap** and **pap chap**. These keywords provide the administrator with a means of selecting both protocols, and they are attempted in order; thus, **chap pap** tries to authenticate via the CHAP protocol first. Typically, this configuration option is used only during a transition because security would be compromised if PAP were permitted. The following commands are used to enable PPP, a requirement for CHAP, and to configure the router for CHAP authentication:

```
encapsulation ppp
ppp authentication {chap | chap pap | pap chap |
    pap} [if-needed] [list-name | default] [callin]
```

The additional commands that you see are used for external user authentication and one-way authentication. These are beyond the scope of this book but they are included for completeness.

Usernames and passwords are added to the router with the `username` *name* `password` *secret* command.

In Windows networking, the administrator is given the choice of whether to require password encryption, as shown in Figure 3.9. Note that this Require Encrypted Password check box is not selected, meaning that the user or administrator has chosen not to require encrypted passwords.

FIGURE 3.9   Windows 95/98 password encryption

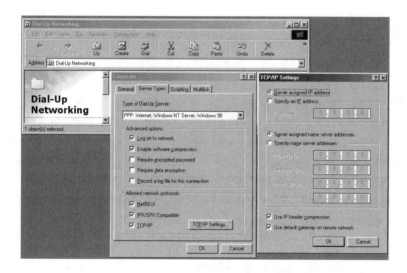

This configuration will work so long as PAP is not the only selected authentication method on the access server. The Windows client will attempt to connect with MS-CHAP, a Microsoft proprietary version of the CHAP protocol. If the check box is selected, meaning the password must be encrypted, either PAP or CHAP will be used, depending on the configuration of the server; if the server is not set to require CHAP, the client can fall back to a PAP, non-encrypted password.

PPP Callback

Security in PPP can be further augmented with the use of *PPP callback*, which instructs the access server to disconnect the incoming connection after successful authentication and reestablish the connection via an outbound call. This security feature requires that the caller be in a single physical location and diminishes the impact of a compromised username and password. The service can also be used to control costs because all connections appear to be from the remote access server—allowing volume-based discounts.

PPP callback is documented in RFC 1570.

Clearly, this solution is not well suited to mobile users; for example, callback to a hotel room would require repeated configuration and a mechanism to deal with extensions. Some callback solutions enable the remote user to enter the callback number—a solution that removes the physical location restrictions and enhances mobility.

    Cisco's callback feature does not permit remote users to dynamically enter the callback number.

Consider the security provided by a callback configuration:

- The remote client (user) must connect into the remote access server.
- By using an authentication protocol, such as CHAP, the user must authenticate.
- If authentication is successful, the session will terminate and the remote access server will call the remote client back. If the authentication fails, the connection will terminate.
- Upon callback, the client and server can again perform password verification.

Clearly, these extra steps could enhance security.

To configure callback, the administrator needs to use the ppp callback accept command on the router interface that receives the initial inbound call and ppp callback request on the interface that is making the initial outbound call.

    PPP callback will not make repeated retries to establish a return connection. This means that a busy signal or other impediment will require the client side to re-request the session.

 Real World Scenario

Configuring PPP Callback

For the following scenario, we set up a spoke router that needs to call into a hub router. The configuration must also allow the hub router to call the spoke router back on a predefined phone number after authentication. This situation has two benefits. One is added security, because the hub router calls Spoke1 back on a predefined number. The other benefit is that it is cheaper for the hub router to call Spoke1 because of discounts negotiated by the company for long-distance calls from the hub site.

As a backup, we configured a callback from a spoke router to the hub router, where each router is a Cisco 2600 series router and has a USR (US Robotics) modem attached to the aux port. We'll allow the Spoke1 router to call into the hub router, authenticate, and let the hub router call the Spoke1 router back on a predefined number.

Here are the relevant commands we used to get things started:

```
Hub#config title
Hub(config)#username Spoke1 password sybex
Hub(config)#chat script Dialout ABORT ERROR ABORT BUSY "" "AT" OK "ATDT \T" TIME-
OUT 45 CONNECT \c
Hub(config)#modemcap entry USR_MODEM:MSC=&F1S0=1
Hub(config)#dialer-list 1 protocol ip permit
Hub(config)#line aux 0
Hub(config-line)#modem inout
Hub(config-line)#modem autoconfigure type USR_MODEM
Hub(config-line)#script dialer Dialout
Hub(config-line)#speed 115200
Hub(config-line)#transport input all
Hub(config-line)#stopbits 1
Hub(config-line)#flowcontrol hardware
Hub(config-line)#exec-timeout 0 0
Hub(config-line)#exit
Hub(config)#interface async65
Hub(config-if)#ip address 192.168.190.1 255.255.255.0
Hub(config-if)#encapsulation ppp
Hub(config-if)#dialer in-band
Hub(config-if)#dialer-group 1
Hub(config-if)#async default routing
Hub(config-if)#async mode dedicated
Hub(config-if)#ppp authentication chap
Hub(config-if)#^Z
Hub#
Spoke1#config title
Spoke1(config)#username Hub password sybex
Spoke1(config)#chat script Dialout ABORT ERROR ABORT BUSY "" "AT" OK "ATDT \T"
TIMEOUT 45 CONNECT \c
Spoke1(config)#modemcap entry USR_MODEM:MSC=&F1S0=1
Spoke1(config)#dialer-list 1 protocol ip permit
Spoke1(config)#line aux 0
Spoke1(config-line)#modem inout
```

```
Spoke1(config-line)#modem autoconfigure type USR_MODEM
Spoke1(config-line)#script dialer Dialout
Spoke1(config-line)#speed 115200
Spoke1(config-line)#transport input all
Spoke1(config-line)#stopbits 1
Spoke1(config-line)#flowcontrol hardware
Spoke1(config-line)#exec-timeout 0 0
Spoke1(config-line)#exit
Spoke1(config)#interface async65
Spoke1(config-if)#ip address 192.168.190.2 255.255.255.0
Spoke1(config-if)#encapsulation ppp
Spoke1(config-if)#dialer in-band
Spoke1(config-if)#dialer-group 1
Spoke1(config-if)#async default routing
Spoke1(config-if)#async mode dedicated
Spoke1(config-if)#ppp authentication chap
Spoke1(config-if)#^Z
Spoke1#
```

There are some things we need to point out before continuing. We created a custom modem-cap entry for our USR modem instead of using the built-in modemcap entry. We also omitted the dialer map statements, which we will discuss in greater detail later. Finally, because both sides need to dial out, we configured a chat script required to successfully dial out.

Next we configured the routers, one as the client and one as the server, for callback. The configuration is slightly different between the client and server callback routers. The Spoke1 router will be the callback client, and the Hub router will be the callback server. We will use the dialer map command on the spoke router just as you might expect, but on the Hub router we need to add a class parameter to the dialer map command for callback purposes.

Please note that map-class configurations are beyond the scope of the exam and this book, and you need not be too concerned at this point about the minutia. However, the syntax is fairly straightforward. We recommend that you focus on the material for the exam at this point, and, after you've passed, refer to the Cisco website or practice in your lab environment with the following commands. Here is the configuration for each router:

```
Spoke1#config t
Spoke1(config)#interface async65
Spoke1(config-if)#dialer map ip 192.168.190.1 name Hub  broadcast 5551211
Spoke1(config-if)#ppp callback request
Spoke1(config-if)#^Z
```

```
Spoke1#
Hub#config t
Hub(config)#map-class dialer Spoke1_Auth
Hub(config-map-class)#dialer callback username
Hub(config-map-class)#exit
Hub(config)#interface async65
Hub(config-if)#dialer map ip 192.168.190.2 name Spoke1  broadcast 5551212 class
Spoke1_Auth
Hub(config-if)#ppp callback accept
Hub(config-if)#^Z
Hub#
```

When the spoke initiates a call to the hub router, the hub router will authenticate the spoke router, and the spoke router will tell the hub router it would like to use callback. Then, the hub router will drop the line and call back the spoke router on the number specified in the `dialer map` command. When the spoke router gets the call, it will authenticate again before starting the PPP negotiation process.

Notice that we did not specify any dynamic routing protocols over this link. Doing so would make this configuration complex and is beyond the scope of this Study Guide. As noted before, map-class and chat scripts are also beyond the scope of this book, but we wanted to give you a taste of the possibilities when configuring Cisco IOS.

PPP Compression and Multilink

It seems that there is never enough bandwidth for current user demand. However, PPP compression and multilink can provide a means of increasing the throughput between different locations.

Compression uses representation to remove bytes from the data stream. For example, if the word *the* is represented by an @ sign, the protocol could save 2 characters per instance. Repeated hundreds of times for different strings, it is possible to save substantial amounts of bandwidth, which will improve performance. The overhead incurred with most compression is minor compared to the resultant savings.

Multilink works differently from compression. *Compression* uses the current connection and squeezes additional information across the link. *Multilink* takes the standard data stream and bonds multiple connections to increase the amount of bandwidth available to the application. With multilink, two or more circuits can be made to appear as a single large pipe. This is more expensive than compression because each location requires two or more analog phone lines or ISDN circuits. This option is better when more bandwidth is required but higher-bandwidth technologies are not available. Multilink ultimately improves throughput and reduces latency. Compression and multilink can be combined to further improve throughput.

Compression Configuration

Compression is available in the IOS software on virtually every Cisco router. However, despite its benefits, software-based compression places a significant load on the router's processor. Therefore, administrators must weigh the benefits of compression against the potential performance degradation that could result. In addition, monitoring the router's CPU is required, that is, ensuring that the utilization of the CPU does not exceed 65 percent. You can determine the CPU utilization by viewing it with the `show process cpu` command. This command will show you a one-minute and five-minute CPU utilization trend, as shown next, where the router is running consistently at three percent utilization.

```
Router1#show process cpu
CPU utilization for five seconds: 3%/3%; one minute: 3%; five minutes: 3%
```

To configure compression, use the following commands:

```
encapsulation ppp
compress [predictor | stac | mppc [ignore-pfc]]
```

Note that both sides of the serial link need to be configured for the same compression method; different compression protocols are not compatible with each other. Designers should also consider the type of data that will be used when configuring compression:

Predictor   The predictor option provides a useful benefit in that compressed data will not be *recompressed*—a process that typically increases the transmitted size and adds substantial delay. This is a good choice for a mixture of compressed and uncompressed data that will traverse the link. Predictor can be more memory intensive than other choices, but it does not burden the router's CPU substantially.

Stac   Most significantly, the Stac compression option is the only supported algorithm for the CBOS-based router platforms, including the Cisco 700 series. As with other compression mechanisms, Stac substitutes repetitive data sequences with brief, summarized values, which are decoded on the other end. The specific compression algorithm is called LZW, or Lempel-Ziv-Welch, the names of the creators.

MPPC   Microsoft Point-to-Point Compression is used when receiving compressed data from Windows clients. With this option, all data is compressed.

In addition, a fourth compression type is available to the designer: TCP header compression. Invoked with the `ip tcp header-compression` command, TCP header compression does exactly that—it compresses only the TCP header information (20 bytes). The specifics of TCP header compression, which is not unique to PPP, are documented in RFC 1144. This type of compression reduces the number of bytes required for each TCP packet and provides this reduction with a minimum amount of overhead. TCP header compression does not impact UDP or Internet Control Message Protocol (ICMP) packets.

Administrators wishing to offload the route processor from the burdens of compression computations might wish to use the Cisco 7500 series router with the compression service adapter. When this card is present, the router will use the hardware-based compression that is running on this card. If the router contains VIP2 cards, the compression process can be *distributed*, which will move the overhead of compression away from the central processor. Interface functions on the card will be affected, however. Without VIP2 technology or the compression service adapter, the router will default to software-based compression.

Other Cisco routers support the use of hardware-assisted compression. The 2600, 3700, and 3660 series routers support the use of a compression advanced integration module (AIM) to offload compression duties from the CPU. Also, the 3620/40 routers support a network module that offloads PPP and Frame Relay (FRF.9) compression.

Compression is generally avoided beyond the 2Mbps level, and ideally, it is used only for links below 128Kbps. Review your requirements carefully before selecting the type of compression. If traffic is truly that high, it might be a short time before additional capacity is necessary anyway.

Multilink Configuration

Like compression, multilink is fairly easy to configure. Figure 3.10 illustrates the desired configuration. Users or administrators simply configure the modem to be used and the phone number to be dialed. Multilink services require two or more modems and two or more phone lines on the client side, which are bonded together into a single logical connection.

For further reference, the multilink PPP (MPPP) RFC is 1990.

FIGURE 3.10   Multilink installation

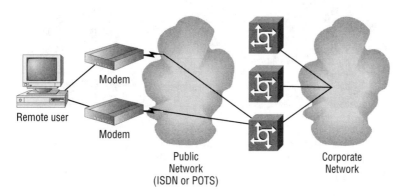

The commands for configuring asynchronous multilink or ISDN multilink differ little, and the primary commands need to include only the following:

```
encapsulation ppp
ppp multilink
```

Without multilink support, each individual ISDN B channel per interface remains isolated. Modems (async connections) can also be used for multilink, and the Multilink Protocol (MP) standard is supported in Windows 95/98. The configuration is fairly straightforward; the user or administrator defines the second access number under the Multilink tab, as shown in Figure 3.11.

Another multilink option is available on Cisco routers and access servers: *Multichassis Multilink Protocol (MMP)*. This proprietary protocol enables the various bonded sessions to terminate on different access servers, as shown in Figure 3.12.

FIGURE 3.11   Windows 95/98 multilink

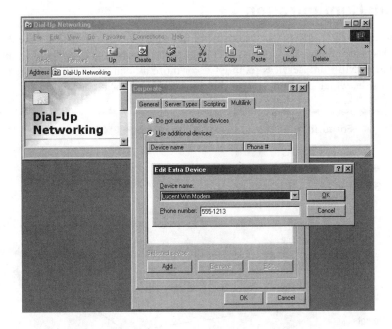

The benefit of this configuration is that single points of failure at the concentration point can be removed and port utilization can be optimized. MMP is an interesting subject but is beyond the scope of this Study Guide.

FIGURE 3.12   Multichassis Multilink Protocol

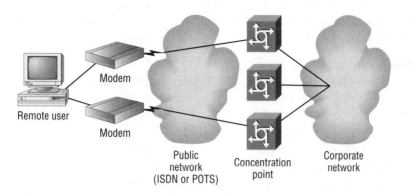

Modem

Remote user

Modem

Public
network
(ISDN or POTS)

Concentration
point

Corporate
network

> It is recommended that all PPP connections use authentication—PAP or CHAP.
> If authentication is not used, the telecommunications vendor will need to pass
> caller ID information for some services.

Verifying and Troubleshooting PPP

As with most troubleshooting on Cisco routers, administrators have a wide range of show and debug commands available to resolve problems that can occur with the Point-to-Point Protocol. Using standard troubleshooting methodologies, the administrator should be able to isolate physical problems quickly and then use these tools to locate and resolve logical issues.

Ideally, designers and administrators unfamiliar with PPP will need to implement a simple configuration before adding additional features such as authentication and multilink bonding. However, one or both of these services might be required as part of the initial installation. The debug and show commands will quickly help isolate the various issues.

This section focuses on the three most common debug commands:

- debug ppp authentication
- debug ppp negotiation
- debug ppp packet

The *debug ppp authentication* Command

Authentication failures can make a perfectly functional link appear faulty, and given the ease with which one can mis-enter a password or username, it is one of the most common issues. The debug ppp authentication command is useful for resolving these problems.

Examine the following output from the debug session. The ISDN BRI attempted to connect, but the challenge failed and the link was disconnected immediately. The second packet attempted to restore the link (`response id 8`) and also failed. This type of output points to either a username or password problem—in this case the password was incorrect.

```
Router#debug ppp authentication
01:54:14: %LINK-3-UPDOWN: Interface BRIO:1, changed state to up.
01:54:14: BRO:1 PPP: Treating connection as a callout
01:54:14: BRO:1 PPP: Phase is AUTHENTICATING, by both
01:54:14: BRO:1 CHAP: O CHALLENGE id 7 len 27 from "Router"
01:54:14: BRO:1 CHAP: I CHALLENGE id 7 len 24 from "Top"
01:54:14: BRO:1 CHAP: O RESPONSE id 7 len 27 from "Router"
01:54:14: BRO:1 CHAP: I FAILURE id 7 len 25 msg is "MD/DES
compare failed"
01:54:15: %ISDN-6-DISCONNECT: Interface BRIO:1
disconnected from 18008358661 , call lasted 1 seconds
01:54:15: %LINK-3-UPDOWN: Interface BRIO:1, changed state to down.
01:54:18: %LINK-3-UPDOWN: Interface BRIO:1, changed state to up.
01:54:18: BRO:1 PPP: Treating connection as a callout
01:54:18: BRO:1 PPP: Phase is AUTHENTICATING, by both
01:54:18: BRO:1 CHAP: O CHALLENGE id 8 len 27 from "Router"
01:54:18: BRO:1 CHAP: I CHALLENGE id 8 len 24 from "Top"
01:54:18: BRO:1 CHAP: O RESPONSE id 8 len 27 from "Router"
01:54:18: BRO:1 CHAP: I FAILURE id 8 len 25 msg is "MD/DES
compare failed"
01:54:19: %ISDN-6-DISCONNECT: Interface BRIO:1 disconnected
from 18008358661 , call lasted 1 seconds
01:54:19: %LINK-3-UPDOWN: Interface BRIO:1, changed state to down.
01:54:22: %LINK-3-UPDOWN: Interface BRIO:1, changed state to up.
```

The `debug ppp authentication` command is most helpful in troubleshooting password problems.

As shown, the message I FAILURE id 8 len 25 msg is "MD/DEScompare failedîl in trou≈∏p is a clear indication that the administrator should look at the password settings.

The *debug ppp negotiation* Command

The `debug ppp negotiation` command is useful for two reasons. First, it can enhance the troubleshooting process on PPP links. Second, it provides a wonderful summary of how PPP works, including LCP and the higher protocols. The upper protocols consist of IPCP (IP) and CDPCP (CDP), among others.

The following output shows the messages that might appear when using the debug ppp negotiation command:

```
Router#debug ppp negotiation
PPP protocol negotiation debugging is on
Router#ping 10.1.1.1
Type escape sequence to abort.
Sending 5, 100-byte ICMP Echos to 10.1.1.1, timeout is 2
seconds:
00:22:28: %LINK-3-UPDOWN: Interface BRIO:1, changed state to up
00:22:28: BRO:1 PPP: Treating connection as a callout
00:22:28: BRO:1 PPP: Phase is ESTABLISHING, Active Open
00:22:28: BRO:1 LCP: O CONFREQ [Closed] id 3 len 10
00:22:28: BRO:1 LCP: MagicNumber 0x50239604
(0x050650239604)
00:22:28: BRO:1 LCP: I CONFREQ [REQsent] id 13 len 10
00:22:28: BRO:1 LCP: MagicNumber 0x5023961F
(0x05065023961F)
00:22:28: BRO:1 LCP: O CONFACK [REQsent] id 13 len 10
00:22:28: BRO:1 LCP: MagicNumber 0x5.023961F
(0x05065023961F)
00:22:28: BRO:1 LCP: I CONFACK [ACKsent] id 3 len 10
00:22:28: BRO:1 LCP: MagicNumber 0x50239604
(0x050650239604)
00:22:28: BRO:1 LCP: State is Open
00:22:28: BRO:1 PPP: Phase is UP
00:22:28: BRO:1 CDPCP: O CONFREQ [Closed] id 3 len 4
00:22:28: BRO:1 IPCP: O CONFREQ [Closed] id 3 len 10
00:22:28: BRO:1 IPCP: Address 10.1.1.2 (0x03060A010102)
00:22:28: BRO:1 CDPCP: I CONFREQ [REQsent] id 3 len 4
00:22:28: BRO:1 CDPCP: O CONFACK [REQsent] id 3 len 4
00:22:28: BRO:1 IPCP: I CONFREQ [REQsent] id 3 len 10
00:22:28: BRO:1 IPCP: Address 10.1.1.1 (0x03060A010101)
00:22:28: BRO:1 IPCP: O CONFACK [REQsent] id 3 len 10
00:22:28: BRO:1 IPCP: Address 10.1.1.1 (0x03060A010101)
00:22:28: BRO:1 CDPCP: I CONFACK [ACKsent] id 3 len 4
00:22:28: BRO:1 CDPCP: State is Open
00:22:28: BRO:1 IPCP: I CONFACK [ACKsent] id 3 len 10
00:22:28: BRO:1 IPCP: Address 10.1.1.2 (0x03060A010102)
00:22:28: BRO:1 IPCP: State is Open
00:22:28: BRO IPCP: Install route to 10.1.1.1
```

```
Router#.!!!
Success rate is 60 percent (3/5), round-trip min/avg/max =
32/38/48 ms
00:22:29: %LINEPROTO-5-UPDOWN: Line protocol on Interface
BRIO:1, changed state to up
00:22:29: %LINK-3-UPDOWN: Interface BRIO:2, changed state to up
00:22:29: BRO:2 PPP: Treating connection as a callin
00:22:29: BRO:2 PPP: Phase is ESTABLISHING, Passive Open
00:22:29: BRO:2 LCP: State is Listen
00:22:30: BRO:2 LCP: I CONFREQ [Listen] id 3 len 10
00:22:30: BRO:2 LCP: MagicNumber 0x50239CC8
(0x050650239CC8)
00:22:30: BRO:2 LCP: O CONFREQ [Listen] id 3 len 10
00:22:30: BRO:2 LCP: MagicNumber 0x50239CDA
(0x050650239CDA)
00:22:30: BRO:2 LCP: O CONFACK [Listen] id 3 len 10
00:22:30: BRO:2 LCP: MagicNumber 0x50239CC8
(0x050650239CC8)
00:22:30: BRO:2 LCP: I CONFACK [ACKsent] id 3 len 10
00:22:30: BRO:2 LCP: MagicNumber 0x50239CDA
(0x050650239CDA) 00:22:30: BRO:2 LCP: State is Open
00:22:30: BRO:2 PPP: Phase is UP
00:22:30: BRO:2 CDPCP: O CONFREQ [Closed] id 3 len 4
00:22:30: BRO:2 IPCP: O CONFREQ [Closed] id 3 len 10
00:22:30: BRO:2 IPCP: Address 10.1.1.2 (0x03060A010102)
00:22:30: BRO:2 CDPCP: I CONFREQ [REQsent] id 3 len 4
00:22:30: BRO:2 CDPCP: O CONFACK [REQsent] id 3 len 4
00:22:30: BRO:2 IPCP: I CONFREQ [REQsent] id 3 len 10
00:22:30: BRO:2 IPCP: Address 10.1.1.1 (0x03060A010101)
00:22:30: BRO:2 IPCP: O CONFACK [REQsent] id 3 len 10
00:22:30: BRO:2 IPCP: Address 10.1.1.1 (0x03060A010101)
00:22:30: BRO:2 CDPCP: I CONFACK [ACKsent] id 3 len 4
00:22:30: BRO:2 CDPCP: State is Open
00:22:30: BRO:2 IPCP: I CONFACK [ACKsent] id 3 len 10
00:22:30: BRO:2 IPCP: Address 10.1.1.2 (0x03060A010102)
00:22:30: BRO:2 IPCP: State is Open
00:22:31: %LINEPROTO-5-UPDOWN: Line protocol on Interface
BRIO:2, changed state to up
00:22:32: BRO:1 LCP: O ECHOREQ [Open] id 12 len 12 magic
0x5020C645
```

```
00:22:32: BR0:1 LCP: echo_cnt 1, sent id 12, line up
00:22:32: BR0:1 PPP: I pkt type 0xC021, datagramsize 16
00:22:32: BR0:1 LCP: I ECHOREP [Open] id 12 len 12 magic
0x5020C654
00:22:32: BR0:1 LCP: Received id 12, sent id 12, line up
00:22:32: BR0:2 LCP: O ECHOREQ [Open] id 12 len 12 magic
0x5020CD1B
00:22:32: BR0:2 LCP: echo_cnt 1, sent id 12, line up
00:22:32: BR0:2 PPP: I pkt type 0xC021, datagramsize 16
00:22:32: BR0:2 LCP: I ECHOREP [Open] id 12 len 12 magic
0x5020CD0D
00:22:32: BR0:2 LCP: Received id 12, sent id 12, line up
00:22:33: BR0:1 PPP: I pkt type 0xC021, datagramsize 16
00:22:33: BR0:1 LCP: I ECHOREQ [Open] id 12 len 12 magic
0x5020C654
00:22:33: BR0:1 LCP: O ECHOREP [Open] id 12 len 12 magic
0x5020C64500:21:23: BR0:2 PPP: I pkt type 0xC021, datagramsize 16
00:22:33: BR0:2 LCP: I ECHOREQ [Open] id 12 len 12 magic
0x5020CD0D
00:22:33: BR0:2 LCP: O ECHOREP [Open] id 12 len 12 magic
0x5020CD1B
00:22:34: BR0:2 PPP: I pkt type 0x0207, datagramsize 15
00:22:35: BR0:2 PPP: I pkt type 0x0207, datagramsize 312
00:24:28: %ISDN-6-DISCONNECT: Interface BRI0:1 disconnected
from 18008358661 To p, call lasted 120 seconds
00:24:28: %LINK-3-UPDOWN: Interface BRI0:1, changed state to down
00:24:10: %ISDN-6-DISCONNECT: Interface BRI0:2
disconnected from 8358663 , call lasted 120 seconds
00:24:28: %LINK-3-UPDOWN: Interface BRI0:2, changed state to down
00:24:29: %LINEPROTO-5-UPDOWN: Line protocol on Interface
BRI0:1, changed state to down
00:24:29: %LINEPROTO-5-UPDOWN: Line protocol on Interface
BRI0:2, changed state to down
```

Notice that in this output, the first two ICMP packets (pings) failed due to the delay in bringing up the ISDN BRI. Although faster than asynchronous connections, ISDN still introduces connection delay, which can impact user applications. In addition, the output from the `debug ppp negotiation` command shows the process by which a PPP session is activated.

This output does not use CHAP, compression, or multilink. Instead, as you can see, PPP starts and then LCP is activated. After this occurs, the NCP negotiations begin, starting with CDPCP and followed by IPCP. *Cisco Discovery Protocol (CDP)* is a proprietary advertisement protocol that sends router and switch information between Cisco devices. It operates over any physical media that supports sub-network access protocol (SNAP) (except ATM) and is independent of IP. The IP Control Protocol, IPCP, was started to transport the ICMP pings that were sent from the router.

Remember that PPP sessions must undergo a negotiation process and that the debug ppp negotiation command will display upper-level protocols such as IPCP, along with LCP and PPP.

The *debug ppp packet* Command

The debug ppp packet command reports real-time PPP packet flow, including the type of packet and the specific B channel used in the case of ISDN. Although this command generates a significant amount of output and could slow the access server, it is quite useful for locating errors that involve upper-layer protocols.

As with other debug *protocol* packet commands, the debug ppp packet command records each packet that moves through the router using PPP. As such, the administrator can monitor traffic flows as if they had a protocol analyzer attached to the interface. This might be useful for troubleshooting Application Layer problems, but a formal protocol analyzer is highly recommended. This output includes both CDP packets (shown with the CDPCP entries) and IP packets (showing proper configuration of IP on the link):

```
Router#debug ppp packet
PPP packet display debugging is on
Router#ping 10.1.1.1
Type escape sequence to abort.
Sending 5, 100-byte ICMP Echos to 10.1.1.1, timeout is 2
seconds:
00:24:49: %LINK-3-UPDOWN: Interface BRIO:1, changed state to up.
00:24:50: BRO:1 LCP: O CONFREQ [Closed] id 4 len 10
00:24:50: BRO:1 LCP: MagicNumber 0x5025BF23
(0x05065025BF23)
00:24:50: BRO:1 PPP: I pkt type 0xC021, datagramsize 14
00:24:50: BRO:1 PPP: I pkt type 0xC021, datagramsize 14
00:24:50: BRO:1 LCP: I CONFREQ [REQsent] id 14 len 10
00:24:50: BRO:1 LCP: MagicNumber 0x5025BF46
(0x05065025BF46)
00:24:50: BRO:1 LCP: O CONFACK [REQsent] id 14 len 10
00:24:50: BRO:1 LCP: MagicNumber 0x5025BF46
(0x05065025BF46)
00:24:50: BRO:1 LCP: I CONFACK [ACKsent] id 4 len 10
00:24:50: BRO:1 LCP: MagicNumber 0x5025BF23
(0x05065025BF23)
00:24:50: BRO:1 PPP: I pkt type 0x8207, datagramsize 8
```

```
00:24:50: BR0:1 PPP: I pkt type 0x8021, datagramsize 14
00:24:50: BR0:1 CDPCP: O CONFREQ [Closed] id 4 len 4
00:24:50: BR0:1 PPP: I pkt type 0x8207, datagramsize 8
00:24:50: BR0:1 IPCP: O CONFREQ [Closed] id 4 len 10
00:24:50: BR0:1 IPCP: Address 10.1.1.2 (0x03060A010102)
00:24:50: BR0:1 CDPCP: I CONFREQ [REQsent] id 4 len 4
00:24:50: BR0:1 CDPCP: O CONFACK [REQ.!!!
Success rate is 60 percent (3/5), round-trip min/avg/max =
36/41/52 ms
Router#sent] id 4 len 4
00:24:50: BR0:1 PPP: I pkt type 0x8021, datagramsize 14
00:24:50: BR0:1 IPCP: I CONFREQ [REQsent] id 4 len 10
00:24:50: BR0:1 IPCP: Address 10.1.1.1 (0x03060A010101)
00:24:50: BR0:1 IPCP: O CONFACK [REQsent] id 4 len 10
00:24:50: BR0:1 IPCP: Address 10.1.1.1 (0x03060A010101)
00:24:50: BR0:1 CDPCP: I CONFACK [ACKsent] id 4 len 4
00:24:50: BR0:1 IPCP: I CONFACK [ACKsent] id 4 len 10
00:24:50: BR0:1 IPCP: Address 10.1.1.2 (0x03060A010102)
00:24:51: BR0:1 PPP: O pkt type 0x0021, datagramsize 104
00:24:51: %LINEPROTO-5-UPDOWN: Line protocol on Interface
BRI0:1, changed state to up
00:24:51: BR0:1 PPP: O pkt type 0x0207, datagramsize 323
00:24:51: %LINK-3-UPDOWN: Interface BRI0:2, changed state to up
00:24:51: BR0:2 PPP: I pkt type 0xC021, datagramsize 14
00:24:51: BR0:2 LCP: I CONFREQ [Listen] id 4 len 10
00:24:51: BR0:2 LCP: MagicNumber 0x5025C5EF
(0x05065025C5EF)
00:24:51: BR0:2 LCP: O CONFREQ [Listen] id 4 len 10 00:24:51: BR0:2 LCP:
MagicNumber 0x5025C605
(0x05065025C605)
00:24:51: BR0:2 LCP: O CONFACK [Listen] id 4 len 10
00:24:51: BR0:2 LCP: MagicNumber 0x5025C5EF
(0x05065025C5EF)
00:24:51: BR0:2 PPP: I pkt type 0xC021, datagramsize 14
00:24:51: BR0:2 LCP: I CONFACK [ACKsent] id 4 len 10
00:24:51: BR0:2 LCP: MagicNumber 0x5025C605
(0x05065025C605)
00:24:51: BR0:2 PPP: I pkt type 0x8207, datagramsize 8
00:24:51: BR0:2 PPP: I pkt type 0x8021, datagramsize 14
00:24:51: BR0:2 CDPCP: O CONFREQ [Closed] id 4 len 4
00:24:51: BR0:2 IPCP: O CONFREQ [Closed] id 4 len 10
```

```
00:24:51: BR0:2 IPCP: Address 10.1.1.2 (0x03060A010102)
00:24:51: BR0:2 CDPCP: I CONFREQ [REQsent] id 4 len 4
00:24:51: BR0:2 CDPCP: O CONFACK [REQsent] id 4 len 4
00:24:51: BR0:2 PPP: I pkt type 0x8207, datagramsize 8
00:24:51: BR0:2 IPCP: I CONFREQ [REQsent] id 4 len 10
00:24:51: BR0:2 IPCP: Address 10.1.1.1 (0x03060A010101)
00:24:51: BR0:2 PPP: I pkt type 0x8021, datagramsize 14
00:24:51: BR0:2 IPCP: O CONFACK [REQsent] id 4 len 10
00:24:51: BR0:2 IPCP: Address 10.1.1.1 (0x03060A010101)
00:24:51: BR0:2 CDPCP: I CONFACK [ACKsent] id 4 len 4
00:24:51: BR0:2 IPCP: I CONFACK [ACKsent] id 4 len 10
00:24:51: BR0:2 IPCP: Address 10.1.1.2 (0x03060A010102)
00:24:52: BR0:1 LCP: O ECHOREQ [Open] id 1 len 12 magic
0x5025BF23
00:24:52: BR0:1 LCP: echo_cnt 1, sent id 1, line up
00:24:52: BR0:1 PPP: I pkt type 0xC021, datagramsize 16
00:24:52: BR0:1 LCP: I ECHOREP [Open] id 1 len 12 magic
0x5025BF46
00:24:52: BR0:1 LCP: Received id 1, sent id 1, line up
00:24:52: BR0:2 LCP: O ECHOREQ [Open] id 1 len 12 magic
0x5025C605
00:24:52: BR0:2 LCP: echo_cnt 1, sent id 1, line up
00:24:52: BR0:2 PPP: I pkt type 0xC021, datagramsize 16 00:24:52: BR0:2 LCP: I
ECHOREP [Open] id 1 len 12 magic
0x5025C5EF
00:24:52: BR0:2 LCP: Received id 1, sent id 1, line up
00:24:52: %LINEPROTO-5-UPDOWN: Line protocol on Interface
BRIO:2, changed state to up
00:24:52: BR0:1 PPP: O pkt type 0x0207, datagramsize 323
00:24:52: BR0:2 PPP: I pkt type 0x0207, datagramsize 312
00:24:53: BR0:1 PPP: O pkt type 0x0021, datagramsize 104
00:24:53: BR0:2 PPP: I pkt type 0x0021, datagramsize 104
00:24:53: BR0:1 PPP: O pkt type 0x0021, datagramsize 104
00:24:53: BR0:2 PPP: I pkt type 0x0021, datagramsize 104
00:24:53: BR0:1 PPP: O pkt type 0x0021, datagramsize 104
00:24:53: BR0:2 PPP: I pkt type 0x0021, datagramsize 104
00:24:53: BR0:1 PPP: I pkt type 0xC021, datagramsize 16
00:24:53: BR0:1 LCP: I ECHOREQ [Open] id 1 len 12 magic
0x5025BF46
00:24:53: BR0:1 LCP: O ECHOREP [Open] id 1 len 12 magic
0x5025BF23
```

```
00:24:53: BR0:2 PPP: I pkt type 0xC021, datagramsize 16
00:24:53: BR0:2 LCP: I ECHOREQ [Open] id 1 len 12 magic
0x5025C5EF
00:24:53: BR0:2 LCP: O ECHOREP [Open] id 1 len 12 magic
0x5025C605
Router#
00:25:02: BR0:1 LCP: O ECHOREQ [Open] id 2 len 12 magic
0x5025BF23
00:25:02: BR0:1 LCP: echo_cnt 1, sent id 2, line up
00:25:02: BR0:1 PPP: I pkt type 0xC021, datagramsize 16
00:25:02: BR0:1 LCP: I ECHOREP [Open] id 2 len 12 magic
0x5025BF46
00:25:02: BR0:1 LCP: Received id 2, sent id 2, line up
00:25:02: BR0:2 LCP: O ECHOREQ [Open] id 2 len 12 magic
0x5025C605
00:25:02: BR0:2 LCP: echo_cnt 1, sent id 2, line up
00:25:02: BR0:2 PPP: I pkt type 0xC021, datagramsize 16
00:25:02: BR0:2 LCP: I ECHOREP [Open] id 2 len 12 magic
0x5025C5EF
00:25:02: BR0:2 LCP: Received id 2, sent id 2, line up
00:25:03: BR0:1 PPP: I pkt type 0xC021, datagramsize 16
00:25:03: BR0:1 LCP: I ECHOREQ [Open] id 2 len 12 magic
0x5025BF46
00:25:03: BR0:1 LCP: O ECHOREP [Open] id 2 len 12 magic
0x5025BF23
00:25:03: BR0:2 PPP: I pkt type 0xC021, datagramsize 16
00:25:03: BR0:2 LCP: I ECHOREQ [Open] id 2 len 12 magic
0x5025C5EF
00:25:03: BR0:2 LCP: O ECHOREP [Open] id 2 len 12 magic
0x5025C605
```

The debug ppp packet command is most helpful in locating upper-layer protocol errors. It filters out non-PPP output, resulting in a cleaner debug output than a regular debug ip packet command. Note that the magic numbers referred to in the previous output are used to thwart playback attacks by maintaining a form of state for the session.

Summary

PPP is a versatile protocol that provides a designer with many options when deploying it in the network. Through the use of interactive PPP, you can provide flexibility to dial-in users using asynchronous interfaces. If you are looking for a more secure dial-in environment, you can configure an asynchronous interface to run in dedicated PPP mode. Another option for the security conscious is to utilize PPP callback for enhanced security.

Addressing can be configured by using static IP addresses, but for greater flexibility we suggest using DHCP or address pools to automatically assign IP addressing. User authentication can be accomplished by using Password Authentication Protocol (PAP) or its more secure cousin, Challenge Handshake Authentication Protocol (CHAP).

Compression and multilink are two PPP options that a network designer can use to increase traffic flow on a connection. They can be used separately or together for even greater throughput.

When trouble occurs with an asynchronous connection, Cisco IOS offers a variety of troubleshooting commands to assist the administrator in narrowing down the problem. These commands can be used to show the PPP negotiation process, PPP authentication process, or each PPP packet as it traverses an interface.

Exam Essentials

Know how to set up PPP on an interface and know what LCP and NCP are used for.   To configure PPP encapsulation on an interface, use the `encapsulation ppp` command. LCP is used for PPP link control, including circuit testing and authentication. NCP is used to negotiate which upper-layer protocols will run over a connection and negotiates their addressing.

Understand how to set up an interface to allow multiple protocols and how to restrict the method of access to a single protocol.   An interface can be set up with the command `async mode interactive` to enable a user to choose between SLIP and PPP encapsulation. The administrator can restrict the user from changing the encapsulation by using the `async mode dedicated` command. By using the `autoselect` command to sense the desired protocol, the router can automatically configure the interface.

Know the three methods to give an interface an IP address.   You can use static IP addressing, which requires more administrator overhead; IP unnumbered, which has troubleshooting problems; or dynamic IP address allocation using DHCP or IP address pools.

Be able to give a general overview of how DHCP works.   The DHCP client uses a broadcast packet to communicate with a DHCP server. A negotiation process determines an IP address lease. After half of the lease time has expired, the DHCP client will attempt to renew the lease.

Understand the differences between the two PPP authentication protocols and when to use them.   You should understand how the PAP and CHAP protocols work and why CHAP is the better protocol to use. CHAP never sends the username and password over the link, whereas PAP sends both in clear-text. Security can be compromised with PAP, but sometimes legacy systems require its use.

Know the commands to use when configuring compression and multilink PPP (MPPP).   Use the `compress [predictor | stac | mppc [ignore-pfc]]` command to configure compression on a link, making sure to use the same method on each end of a connection. You can bond multiple channels into a single connection for greater speed by using the ppp multilink command. Compression and multilink can be used together or separately to enhance connection throughput.

Know the PPP troubleshooting commands and how to spot a problem.   You can use the debug ppp authentication, debug ppp negotiation, and debug ppp packet commands to determine the cause of a remote access problem.

Key Terms

Before you take the exam, be certain you are familiar with the following terms:

Address field	Information field
bit stuffing	lease
Challenge Handshake Authentication Protocol (CHAP)	Link Control Protocol (LCP)
checksum	Multichassis Multilink Protocol (MMP)
Cisco Discovery Protocol (CDP)	multilink
compression	Network Control Protocols (NCPs)
conflict logging	Password Authentication Protocol (PAP)
Control field	PPP callback
distributed	Protocol field
Frame Check Sequence field	recompressed
helper address	Request For Comments (RFCs)
hotelling	

Written Lab

1. As the network designer for your company, you've been asked to present a brief remote access solution. The document need not concern itself with specific hardware, but it does need to focus on scalability, security, and availability. All of the users will be mobile, frequently operating from hotels. Two future locations will use ISDN for large file transfers, and all users require both IP and IPX support. Based on this chapter, please write a succinct overview of your solution.

2. The command to configure the router to act as a DHCP server is _____.

3. What command is used to enable PPP encapsulation?

4. To define a logical grouping of DHCP parameters, the administrator would use what command?

5. The administrator does not have an FTP or TFTP server available for the DHCP process. What command is required?

6. Microsoft Windows clients use which compression method?

7. Rather than sending the password, CHAP sends a ____ across the link.

8. The default lease on Cisco IOS-based DHCP servers is _____.

9. The default DHCP lease on Windows NT servers is _____.

10. Using an Ethernet or loopback interface IP address to define the serial IP address is called _____.

Hands-on Lab

In this section, you will perform one lab that requires a router with a serial and Ethernet interface and a single client that is attached to the Ethernet segment. This client should be configured for DHCP address assignment.

Lab 3.1: PPP and DHCP Configuration

1. Configure the router for an Ethernet interface address of 10.1.1.1/24.

    ```
    interface e0
    ip address 10.1.1.1 255.255.255.0
    ```

2. Configure a serial interface on the router for PPP encapsulation and an IP address of 10.2.2.1/30.

    ```
    interface s0
    ip address 10.2.2.1 255.255.255.252
    encapsulation ppp
    ```

3. Create a DHCP pool for the Ethernet interface with the following parameters. The domain is called company.com, and the default router is the Ethernet interface configured in step 1. No FTP or TFTP server is available. The WINS server is at 10.20.2.10, and the DNS server is at 10.20.2.11.

    ```
    service dhcp
    no ip dhcp conflict logging
    ```

```
ip dhcp excluded-address 10.1.1.1

ip dhcp pool 0
network 10.1.1.0 /24
 default-router 10.1.1.1
domain-name company.com
 dns-server 10.20.2.11
 netbios-name-server 10.20.2.10
```

Review Questions

1. PPP improved upon SLIP by doing which of the following?
   - **A.** Allowing the transport of only IP packets across Ethernet segments
   - **B.** Allowing the transport of mostprotocols across serial segments
   - **C.** Adding support for compression
   - **D.** Adding support for AppleTalk to IP conversion

2. PPP uses which two protocols?
   - **A.** LCP and NCP
   - **B.** SLIP and SPX
   - **C.** EIGRP and RIP
   - **D.** LLC and IP

3. Which of the following compression methods can be used? (Select all that apply.)
   - **A.** Software
   - **B.** Hardware
   - **C.** Server
   - **D.** Distributed

4. Which of the following is the command to use CHAP authentication?
   - **A.** `ppp authentication protocol chap`
   - **B.** `authentication chap`
   - **C.** `ppp authentication chap`
   - **D.** `chap authentication`

5. The `async mode dedicated` command configures which of the following?
   - **A.** The port is locked to a single IP address.
   - **B.** The port is locked to a single encapsulation, such as PPP or SLIP.
   - **C.** The access server can terminate only asynchronous sessions.
   - **D.** The session is encrypted.

6. Does the use of PPP require the administrator to use static IP addressing?
   - **A.** No.
   - **B.** Yes, unless CHAP is also used.
   - **C.** Yes, unless PAP is also used.
   - **D.** Yes, unless the `ppp dynamic` command is used.

7. What is the best choice for compression when the remote users will connect with Windows stations?

   A. Stac

   B. Predictor

   C. MPPC

   D. TCP

8. Which of the following is the best choice for compression when data is both precompressed and uncompressed?

   A. Stac

   B. Predictor

   C. MPPC

   D. TCP

9. The Cisco 700 router supports which of the following compression methods?

   A. Stac

   B. Predictor

   C. MPPC

   D. All of the above

10. Will the TCP header compression mechanism also compress UDP headers?

   A. Yes.

   B. No.

   C. Yes, but only with DHCP enabled.

   D. Yes, but only with DHCP disabled.

11. Does CHAP require the use of PPP?

   A. Yes, CHAP is a subprotocol of PPP.

   B. No, only PAP requires PPP.

   C. No, CHAP will work with any IP supported transport.

   D. No, CHAP requires only PAP.

12. Which command would be used to troubleshoot a suspected CHAP authentication problem?

   A. `debug ppp authentication`

   B. `debug chap protocol`

   C. `debug ppp chap protocol`

   D. None of the above

13. As a general guideline, at what point should compression no longer be used?

    A. 56Kbps

    B. 128Kbps

    C. 256Kbps

    D. 2Mbps

14. What option is used when configuring a Windows 95/98 client for manual IP addressing on a dial-up adapter?

    A. Control Panel, Network, Dial-up Adapter, TCP/IP Address

    B. Control Panel, Network, Ethernet, TCP/IP Address

    C. Dial-up Networking, Properties for the Connections, Server Type, TCP/IP Settings

    D. The command `ifconfig -dial0 ip_address`

15. To configure an IP address for an Ethernet interface in Windows 95/98, the administrator would use which of the following?

    A. Control Panel, Network, Dial-up Adapter, TCP/IP Address

    B. Control Panel, Network, Ethernet, TCP/IP Address

    C. Dial-up Networking, Properties for the Connections, Server Type, TCP/IP Settings

    D. The command `ifconfig -hme0 ip_address`

16. When using DHCP for address assignment, what must the router be configured with? (Select all that apply.)

    A. An IP helper address

    B. An unnumbered interface

    C. A router configuration that provides DHCP services

    D. Header compression

17. To use a static pool of addresses for IP address assignment, the administrator would use which of the following commands?

    A. `peer default ip address pool` *poolname*

    B. `peer default ip address dhcp`

    C. `async ip address pool poolname`

    D. `async ip address dhcp`

18. Must compression and multilink PPP be used together?

    A. Yes, administrators must configure the two to work together.

    B. Yes, compression requires multilink, but multilink does not require compression.

    C. Yes, multilink requires compression, but compression does not require multilink services.

    D. No.

19. Is MMP an open standard for multilink bonding?

   A. Yes. It is defined in RFC 2101.

   B. Yes. However, MP is not an open standard.

   C. Yes. However, it is not part of the PPP standard.

   D. No. It is a Cisco protocol.

20. While troubleshooting a PPP session, the debug output reports CDPCP packets but no IPCP packets. What is the most likely meaning of this? (Select two.)

   A. IP is not configured for the link.

   B. CDP has been disabled.

   C. IP is not functioning on the link.

   D. IP is functioning on the link, but with TCP header compression.

Answers to Written Lab

1. It is proposed that the XYZ company use PPP for their remote access solution. This implementation should include CHAP, which is more secure than PAP; however, given the remote nature of the users, PPP callback should not be used. In the future, PPP multilink might be required for the ISDN connections, but this is not critical to this recommendation. Universal support and flexibility make PPP better suited than SLIP—especially considering the IPX requirement.

2. `service dhcp`

3. `encapsulation ppp`

4. `ip dhcp pool`

5. `no ip dhcp conflict logging`

6. MPPC, or Microsoft Point-to-Point Compression

7. Password hash

8. 24 hours

9. 72 hours

10. IP unnumbered

Answers to Review Questions

1. B. Point-to-Point Protocol provides support for virtually all protocols (IP, IPX, AT), whereas SLIP is limited to IP only.

2. A. Unfortunately, this is a strict memorization question; however, *SLIP and SPX* and *EIGRP and RIP* should be easy to eliminate. *LLC and IP* can also be eliminated because it infers a requirement for IP to support PPP.

3. A, B, D. Again, this is a memorization question, but *server compression* sounds awkward, which might help you eliminate it as an option.

4. C. This question might be answered by the process of elimination—CHAP requires PPP, so the answer should include the ppp command. The two options including ppp are very similar, but the first is noticeably verbose and incorrect, considering *protocol* is already part of PPP.

5. C. As noted in the text, dedicated async mode instructs the port to terminate only async connections.

6. A. DHCP and other dynamic address assignment methods are available with PPP.

7. C. MPPC is the only option presented that is found in Windows software.

8. B. The predictor compression method examines the data flow for compressibility and does not try to recompress already compressed data.

9. A. Remember that the Cisco 700 does not run the full Cisco IOS and supports only Stac compression.

10. B. TCP header compression is based on the characteristics of the TCP header itself. UDP headers are different in format and protocol number.

11. A. This should have been easy. CHAP and PAP both require the use of PPP. This is one of few questions that uses the word *require* and is also true.

12. A. Unfortunately, this is another case of needing to memorize the command. Remembering that CHAP is a function of PPP can help.

13. D. There are two reasons for this recommendation: first, the performance hit is quite high as bandwidth increases, and second, generally, there is no benefit to compression on E-1 or T-1 links. Note that this is a Cisco recommendation, and nothing prevents the use of compression on higher-bandwidth circuits. Note also that while 2Mbps is the upper limit for compression, many administrators opt to not use compression beyond the 128Kbps point.

14. C. If you're a Windows user, this was probably an easy question. The key is to remember that the dial-up adapter is different from the other network adapters. Unix administrators can use this tip also; however, it might be best to remember the steps.

15. B.   Ah, a trick question. Remember that non-dial-up adapters are configured from the Control Panel and that this question is concerned with the Ethernet interface.

16. A, C.   Of the choices provided, the router must have an IP helper address or a DHCP server configuration for the network to use DHCP for address assignment. The unlisted option of having a DHCP server on the subnet would not require a configuration setting on the router.

17. A.   It would be nice to provide a cute and simple way to remember this; however, the command is a tad awkward. Of these choices, the best solution is deduction—address assignment is not specific to async interfaces, and the use of the word *pool* in the question should negate the second choice.

18. D.   A common mistake is the belief that compression and multilink (MP or MMP) must be used together. The two are completely unrelated, and, in fact, it is usually best to choose one or the other. They can be used concurrently, however.

19. D.   Remember that MP is an open standard limited to a single pair of devices, whereas MMP is a Cisco protocol for bonding to multiple destination switches.

20. A, C.   Consider the parameters of the question. CDP packets are present, so it wasn't disabled. The IP header would still exist with TCP header compression. CDP is protocol independent, so IP need not be present. A routing configuration error or other problem could prevent the transmission of IP packets.

Chapter 4

Using Microsoft Windows 95/98/2000/XP

EXAM TOPICS COVERED IN THIS CHAPTER INCLUDE:

✓ **Connect to the central site with Microsoft Windows.**

We have elected to retain this chapter for the third revision of the text because the exam might incorporate questions related to the material. Based on the most recent information, this is admittedly unlikely. You should be confident that cursory retention of the material is all that might be needed for real-world and examination success. The chapter focuses on Windows 95/98 because of Cisco's focus on these versions. Please note that Windows XP and Windows 2000 incorporate processes and protocols that are similar to these earlier versions, and this chapter can provide benefit and understanding in that context.

Any text on remote access would be remiss if it did not include a section on the world's most popular desktop operating system. It would be difficult to find a remote access solution that does not require support for Windows. You might question the dedication of an entire chapter in a present-day remote access text to the consumer-oriented platforms of Windows 95 and 98, especially when Microsoft no longer supports Windows 95 and will retire Windows 98 in 2004. However, Cisco still requires an understanding of Windows dial-up networking. Fortunately, older versions parallel the modern versions of the operating system, and, as such, this chapter also provides a foundation for using Windows XP and 2000.

This chapter focuses on the configuration and support issues that surround this popular client software. Particular attention should be paid to the protocols that are supported and the configuration steps that are required on the client.

Reasons to Use Dial-Up Networking

Fortunately, not only is configuring and using dial-up networking in Windows 95/98 simple, but it also provides a broad base of services for remote users. These services include the following:

Automatic connection to websites   Once configured, the operating system will automatically establish a dial-up connection to connect with a remote web server. If a user simply types a URL into Microsoft Internet Explorer, the modem will dial the Internet Service Provider (ISP) and request the web page.

E-mail   Mobile clients can connect to Microsoft Exchange or another e-mail service in the office. This provides an efficient way to communicate with colleagues.

File synchronization   Remote users can obtain file updates and post their files on a server in the office for local users. Although Microsoft provides the My Briefcase application for this purpose, Symantec's pcAnywhere and other such programs might be desired by more demanding users.

Remote control   One alternative to high-bandwidth applications is remote control. Remote control software does exactly what it sounds like it does: keystrokes and mouse movements are sent to the host, and the host returns the image to the remote user, enabling the user to control the host. This solution enables only the screen images to be transferred, which can greatly reduce the required bandwidth for supporting the application.

Consider the following: a remote user on a dial-up connection needs to access a database, and this access will result in 10MB of data being transferred. When using remote control, only the screen data will be sent for the session; with compression, this means that possibly less than 2MB of data will be sent. Clearly, this bandwidth savings can be substantial. Note that remote control solutions must be connected to access data—unlike remote node solutions, which use the remote user's processor for local applications and data, and uses the modem as a slower network link). Also, the bandwidth savings can differ significantly depending on the data demands of the application; in this context, remote control utilizes remote node solutions for transport, but the connection must be maintained for the duration of the remote control session. Windows XP includes a terminal server option.

Effectively, anything that a user can accomplish in the office is possible to accomplish remotely with dial-up networking. Unfortunately, the significantly lower bandwidth of dial-up connections can make this impractical, depending on the application.

Configuring Dial-Up Networking with Windows 95/98

Dial-up networking in Windows 95/98 is extremely popular, perhaps for no other reason than approximately 100 million clients have Microsoft's operating system installed worldwide. From a client's perspective, the cost and effort needed to connect to the office remotely requires little more than a phone line and modem.

As you will see in this chapter, configuring and administrating a single Windows workstation for dial-up networking is very simple. Unfortunately, administering dial-up networking for thousands of remote users is not as simple, and there are few existing tools that make this task easier.

Microsoft Windows 95/98 supports remote dial-up networking with the protocols that provide transport for NetBIOS:

- NetBEUI
- IPX
- IP

Supporting these protocols is logical because of Windows networking's historical dependency upon the NetBIOS protocol and the name services that it provides—this changed in Windows 2000 and XP. It is possible to add other protocols with third-party transport, but most designers find IP support to be sufficient, and they configure the client for PPP services.

See Chapter 3 for more information about the Point-to-Point Protocol.

Configuring a Dial-Up Connection Client

The configuration of a Windows client for dial-up networking is a relatively painless process, although many configuration options are available, and good planning will greatly simplify an enterprise-level deployment.

By default, the Windows 95/98 installation includes the basic files for installing and configuring a network connection. It is always a good idea, though, to have the original installation CD-ROM available because the setup program might need additional files to complete the installation. In addition, the latest service packs and updates should be installed—service packs contain many updates and problem fixes called *patches*. In general, the installation of patches is a benign event; however, before performing the upgrade, it is best to back up critical files and review the appropriateness of the patch. For multiple node upgrades, it is best to test the patch before you deploy it.

Check the Windows website at www.microsoft.com for the latest patches, service packs, and tips for configuring dial-up networking.

Although many tools are available for installing and configuring dial-up networking, this text focuses on the basic installation—PPP and TCP/IP protocols; however, multilink connections and scripting are also presented.

The screen captures in this chapter, unless otherwise noted, are from Windows 98 Second Edition. The screens from other versions of Windows might differ slightly.

Dial-Up Networking Application

To start configuring a dial-up connection, choose Start ➤ Programs ➤ Accessories ➤ Communications ➤ Dial-Up Networking. This opens a dialog box similar to the one shown in Figure 4.1.

FIGURE 4.1   The Windows Dial-Up Networking dialog box

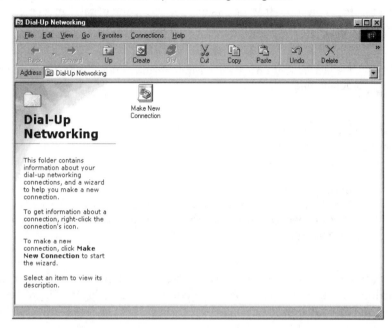

On the system shown here, this is the first dial-up connection, so Windows provides only a Make New Connection icon. Clicking this icon brings up the Dial-Up Networking Wizard. If other connections were available, the user or administrator could select them to initiate a call or to go into an already established connection in order to reconfigure options.

Make New Connection Wizard

After you select the Make New Connection icon, Windows begins the Make New Connection Wizard. The first dialog box of this wizard is shown in Figure 4.2.

FIGURE 4.2   Making a new connection

In this dialog box, you type a name for the connection and set the kind of modem that you will be using for the connection. If Windows did not detect and install a modem in the Select a Device box, you need to correct this before continuing.

For instructions on installing a modem in Windows, please refer to the product documentation.

Note that in Figure 4.2, the Lucent Win Modem has been automatically selected, and the user has been prompted to provide a name for the connection.

Check the hardware compatibility list (HCL) to verify that your equipment is certified to operate in the Windows environment. This information is found on the Microsoft website—www.microsoft.com, http://www.microsoft.com/whdc/hcl/search.mspx

By default, Windows inserts the name My Connection; however, you should change this to a more descriptive name for the particular connection you are setting up. Figure 4.3 shows the Make New Connection dialog box.

FIGURE 4.3   Changing the dial-up name

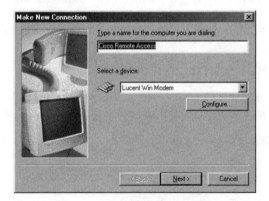

When you are finished renaming the connection and selecting the appropriate modem, click the Next button. The next dialog box (see Figure 4.4) enables you to define the phone number that will be called. The default area code is the area code defined when the modem was first installed. The Country or Region Code drop-down list is used to define what digits will precede the area code. For example, if you were making a call to somewhere in the United Kingdom, you would define it by selecting country code 44 for the connection.

FIGURE 4.4 Defining the phone number

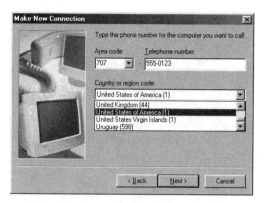

When you are finished, click Next. Windows then provides a confirmation similar to the one shown in Figure 4.5. An icon is placed in the Dial-Up Networking folder as well.

FIGURE 4.5 A successful connection defined

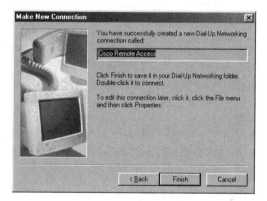

Connection Properties

After this initial phase is completed, you have the opportunity to select the icon and attempt a connection with the defaults, or you can right-click the icon to select the properties of the connection. Select the option you wish to edit, and the connection properties dialog box (shown in Figure 4.6) appears. Note that there are four tabs: General, Server Types, Scripting, and Multilink.

FIGURE 4.6   Connection properties dialog box

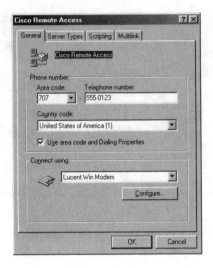

It is important to understand how to select and configure the properties on each of the four tabs.

General Tab

The General tab displays the initial configuration information, including the name, phone number, country code, and modem that will be used. This tab is shown in Figure 4.6.

Server Types Tab

You will find that the Server Types tab is the most important for remote access configuration. This tab addresses protocols, encapsulations, addressing, compression, and encryption. You need to match these settings to those on a Cisco remote access device in order to establish an efficient connection.

As shown in Figure 4.7, the first option asks you to specify the type of dial-up server. There are five options (although the drop-down list shown in this figure has room to show only four). The types of servers are as follows:

- CSLIP: Unix Connection with IP Header Compression
- NRN: NetWare Connect Version 1.0 and 1.1
- PPP: Internet, Windows NT Server, Windows 98
- SLIP: Unix Connection
- Windows for Workgroups and Windows NT 3.1

FIGURE 4.7   The Windows dial-up networking server types

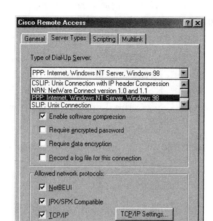

You will learn more about each of these server types next.

Note that the server types described here are not servers in the traditional sense; they are daemons or descriptions of protocols.

It is important to understand the distinctions between each of these server types:

CSLIP: Unix Connection with IP Header Compression   This server type is seldom used for the reason indicated in Chapter 3: SLIP (Serial Line Internet Protocol) is rarely used due to its sole support for IP. Legacy Unix servers, however, might still require this option. CSLIP stands for Compressed Serial Line Internet Protocol. This option supports only IP and does not support software compression, encrypted passwords, or data compression.

NRN: NetWare Connection Version 1.0 and 1.1   Just as SLIP and CSLIP will support only IP, the NRN connection will support only IPX/SPX. This option is provided for legacy installations of NetWare, but most environments have migrated away from this platform.

PPP: Internet, Windows NT Server, Windows 98   PPP is not only the default dial-up server type, it is also the most recommended. As shown in Figure 4.7, it supports all protocols and features.

PPP is described in detail in Chapter 3.

SLIP: Unix Connection   As with CSLIP, SLIP supports only IP connections and does not provide advanced features. Although PPP is both recommended and popular, a significant number of installations support only SLIP. Migration from SLIP to PPP is highly recommended because of PPP's multiprotocol support.

Windows for Workgroups and Windows NT 3.1   This server type supports only NetBEUI and its upper-layer protocol, NetBIOS. NetBEUI does not support routing, however. It is a simple protocol and negates the need for addressing. NetBEUI might provide the best performance for a single connection, but it cannot scale and, given the demands on the network, it is probably best to use PPP.

The remainder of this section focuses on the rest of the options on the Server Types tab for a PPP server type.

Advanced Options

Microsoft considers optional functions to be advanced options. These options include settings to control compression and authentication protocols.

Under Advanced Options, five choices can be made by the user or administrator. Figure 4.8 shows the default configuration for a PPP connection with the NetBEUI and IPX/SPX options unselected.

To improve performance, disable the NetBEUI and IPX/SPX Compatible network protocols unless they are required.

FIGURE 4.8   Configuring PPP

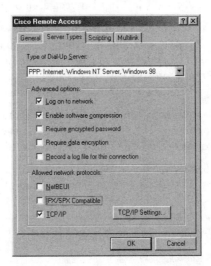

The five Advanced Option choices you can select are as follows:

Log On to Network   If you are connecting to an NT domain, you use this option to establish a network connection and to attempt to log into the domain. Leave this option unselected to improve performance on networks where this service is not required.

Enable Software Compression   Software-based compression is different from the modem-based compression features that were presented in Chapter 2. By selecting this option, you can improve throughput by enabling compression, but this depends on the type of data and equipment you use. By compressing with software, you are substituting a repetitious series of characters to reduce the amount of bandwidth required. When decompressing, the compressed data stream is translated back into an uncompressed form.

Require Encrypted Password   By selecting the Require Encrypted Password check box, you are precluding the use of clear-text authentication. Microsoft supports several encrypted password options, including Shiva Password Authentication Protocol (SPAP), Data Encryption Standard (DES), CHAP, and MS-CHAP. MS-CHAP is based on RSA MD4 (Message Digest type 4). On Windows NT, this is enhanced to MD5 with Service Pack 3 or greater, and is standard in newer versions of Windows.

Remember when choosing your password that passwords are generally case sensitive.

Require Data Encryption   By selecting this check box, you are making sure that information passing through your connection will be encrypted. Unlike data compression, encryption protects the contents of the data during transmission. Even though this option provides relatively weak encryption, you might want to use it when you are transmitting critical data. Note that your performance will suffer slightly with this option because the encryption is processed in software.

Record a Log File for This Connection   When you select this check box, a log file will be recorded. You might find that log files are useful for troubleshooting purposes, but most administrators find the lack of information provided by this output frustrating. The log file might help to augment the diagnostic process, however. When used with caution, the Cisco debug commands provide substantially better troubleshooting output.

Viewing a Log File

The output shown next provides an example of the log output. Note that the software automatically recovered from an error condition found when hanging up the modem via hardware command by lowering DTR (data terminal ready).

The log is a standard text file and it can be viewed by choosing Connection ➤ Advanced from the modem's properties dialog box and then clicking the View Log button in the dialog box that opens (see Figure 4.9).

FIGURE 4.9   The View Log option

Following is a sample log file that shows the preliminary handshake with the modem. This identifies the information file (INF) that is used, in addition to the status of connections, error control, compression, and hang-up characteristics. Note that in this case the modem did not respond to the lowering of DTR for the hang-up and was disconnected with software. This might indicate a configuration problem with the modem; however, it is benign in this case.

```
02-15-2000 22:36:33.15 - Lucent Win Modem in use.
02-15-2000 22:36:33.16 - Modem type: Lucent Win Modem
02-15-2000 22:36:33.16 - Modem inf path: LTMODEM.INF
02-15-2000 22:36:33.16 - Modem inf section: Modem_PNP_DSVD
02-15-2000 22:36:34.80 - 115200,N,8,1
02-15-2000 22:36:34.80 - 115200,N,8,1
02-15-2000 22:36:34.80 - Initializing modem.
02-15-2000 22:36:34.80 - Send: AT<cr>
02-15-2000 22:36:34.81 - Recv: AT<cr>
02-15-2000 22:36:34.81 - Recv: <cr><1f>OK<cr><1f>
02-15-2000 22:36:34.81 - Interpreted response: Ok
02-15-2000 22:36:34.81 - Send: AT &F E0 &C1 &D2 V1   S0=0\V1<cr>
02-15-2000 22:36:34.85 - Recv: AT &F E0 &C1 &D2 V1 S0=0\V1<cr>
02-15-2000 22:36:34.85 - Recv: <cr><1f>OK<cr><1f>
```

```
02-15-2000 22:36:34.85 - Interpreted response: Ok
02-15-2000 22:36:34.85 - Send: ATS7=60S30=0L0M1\N3%C1&K3B0B15B2N1\J1X4<cr>
02-15-2000 22:36:34.86 - Recv: <cr><1f>OK<cr><1f>
02-15-2000 22:36:34.86 - Interpreted response: Ok
02-15-2000 22:36:34.86 - Dialing.
02-15-2000 22:36:34.86 - Send: ATDT;<cr>
02-15-2000 22:36:37.38 - Recv: <cr><1f>OK<cr><1f>
02-15-2000 22:36:37.38 - Interpreted response: Ok
02-15-2000 22:36:37.38 - Dialing.
02-15-2000 22:36:37.38 - Send: ATDT#######<cr>
02-15-2000 22:37:10.81 - Recv: <cr><1f>CONNECT 26400 V42bis<cr><1f>
02-15-2000 22:37:10.81 - Interpreted response: Connect
02-15-2000 22:37:10.81 - Connection established at 26400bps.
02-15-2000 22:37:10.81 - Error-control on.
02-15-2000 22:37:10.81 - Data compression on.
02-15-2000 22:37:44.27 - Hanging up the modem.
02-15-2000 22:37:44.27 - Hardware hangup by lowering DTR.
02-15-2000 22:37:45.47 - WARNING: The modem did not respond to lowering DTR.
Trying software hangup...
02-15-2000 22:37:45.47 - Send: +++
02-15-2000 22:37:45.55 - Recv: <cr><1f>OK<cr><1f>
02-15-2000 22:37:45.55 - Interpreted response: Ok
02-15-2000 22:37:45.55 - Send: ATH E1<cr>
02-15-2000 22:37:45.63 - Recv: <cr><1f>OK<cr><1f>
02-15-2000 22:37:45.63 - Interpreted response: Ok
02-15-2000 22:37:45.63 - 115200,N,8,1
02-15-2000 22:37:46.69 - Session Statistics:
02-15-2000 22:37:46.69 -                 Reads : 811 bytes
02-15-2000 22:37:46.69 -                 Writes: 2991 bytes
02-15-2000 22:37:46.69 - Lucent Win Modem closed.
```

Allowed Network Protocols

The Allowed Network Protocols section of the Server Types tab enables eligible protocols to be included or omitted from the dial-up networking connection. All three—NetBEUI, IPX, and IP—are allowed in Figure 4.8 because PPP was selected. The TCP/IP Settings button enables the user or administrator to choose DHCP-assigned IP address information (the default), or to enter static entries.

Scripting Tab

Scripts enable the administrator or user to automate functions, including login or program execution. A parallel of a script is a to-do list for getting ready in the morning—get up, brush teeth, get dressed, and so forth. Scripts should be approached with care because they are not stored in a secure manner and therefore can present a security risk.

To select a script, type the script name in the File Name text box (see Figure 4.10). The Step through Script option (grayed out in this figure because a script file was not defined) can be useful for timing a script or for general debugging, and the Start Terminal Screen Minimized option can be used to hide the script's execution from being displayed to the user.

FIGURE 4.10   The Scripting tab

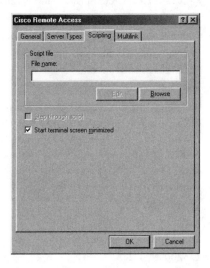

Multilink Tab

You learned about multilink services and the Multilink Protocol (MP) in Chapter 3. Multilink provides the ability to create a single logical connection through two or more physical modems, which can provide greater aggregate bandwidth for a remote user. Note that Microsoft's multilink feature does not support the Cisco proprietary Multilink Multipoint Protocol (MPP), only the standards-based MP. Users or administrators need only provide the phone number to configure the service, as shown in Figure 4.11. The Edit Extra Device dialog box shown in Figure 4.11 is provided when the user selects Use Additional Devices and clicks the Add button.

Figure 4.11 shows a Windows 98 screen. In Windows 2000, Microsoft changed the dialog boxes such that you must have installed and configured multiple modems for the option to appear.

FIGURE 4.11   The Multilink tab

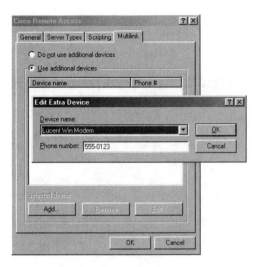

Setting Additional Configuration Options

This section addresses two of the most common optional configuration options that administrators and users select in dial-up networking:

- Lock DTE speed
- Launch terminal windows

The first, locking DTE (Data Terminal Equipment) speed, is predominately used for troubleshooting or for improving performance on degraded circuits—circuits that are impaired due to line conditions. This option is becoming less significant as phone line quality and termination equipment improve. The second option, launching terminal windows, is usually used for third-party authentication; however, it can also be used for manual control of the session. Unlike the previous options, both of these selections are grouped with the modem controls as opposed to the networking configuration options. This is due to their relationship with the Physical and Data Link Layers—DTE speed and a terminal window are both independent of the Network Layer protocol in use.

Lock DTE Speed

At times the user might want to lock the DTE speed o complete a connection. Locking the DTE speed can provide better performance on degraded lines if the speed is locked to a value lower than would otherwise be possible—a result of fewer retransmissions to cope with the errors. For most connections, this step is unnecessary.

To lock the DTE speed, select the Only Connect at This Speed option in the Modem Properties dialog box, as shown in Figure 4.12. Recall that this is DTE-to-DCE speed, and as such, it should relate to the capacity of the DCE device, as defined in Chapter 2.

FIGURE 4.12 Locking the DTE speed

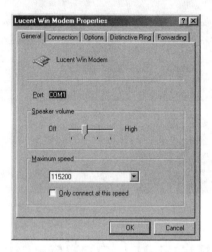

Launch Terminal Windows

On the Modem Properties Options tab, the user is offered the option of launching a terminal window either before or after the connection is made. The option of opening a terminal window after the connection is made is frequently necessary for hard authentication options such as SecureID. This tab is shown in Figure 4.13.

FIGURE 4.13 Launching a terminal window

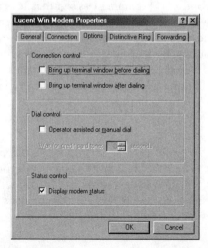

Typically, the terminal window is launched with a *challenge* sent from the SecureID or a similar third-party product. The challenge is a dynamically created value that is entered into a physical calculator programmed to generate the proper response. This response is valid only for the duration of the challenge—typically a minute—and it is a single-use password. These security solutions require physical possession of the token, or password generator, and the pin number that allows access. This security model is sometimes referred to as "something you have and something you know." Bank ATM cards use a similar principle.

Verifying a Dial-Up Connection

Dial-up connections work without a significant amount of troubleshooting under most circumstances. When they don't, Windows generally provides an indication of the error and a recommended course of action, as shown in Figure 4.14. This screen shows error 680, which means that there was no dial tone.

On the access server, the administrator can choose to use the `show line` command to view the status of the connection. Unfortunately, this requires that much of the connection is already established—a presumption that does not always coincide with troubleshooting.

FIGURE 4.14   Dial-up networking error

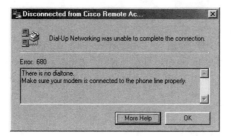

Summary

Remote access solutions provide connectivity beyond the local area network. In prior chapters, you read about solutions that use Cisco routers to communicate to other Cisco routers. This chapter differs in that it is completely focused on a non-Cisco technology, Microsoft Windows, the leading desktop operating system in use today. Although the current versions of Windows (XP and Windows 2000) are not covered in the chapter, the Cisco position to focus only on Windows 95/98 is not completely without merit. While outdated and no longer supported, Windows 95/98 shares many comparable traits with its offspring, and learning the old operating system can provide a solid foundation for newer implementations. Having said that, Cisco should update their exam materials to reflect shipping versions of software, and readers will need to augment this chapter's material, which focuses on the exam, with study and practice on newer versions in order to transition to real-world practical usage.

Windows dial-up networking interoperates with Cisco remote access solutions via each of the three Layer 2 and Layer 3 protocols offered by Microsoft. These are TCP/IP, which is actually IP; IPX, the Novell networking protocol; and NetBEUI. NetBEUI is a bridged protocol and technically operates at Layer 2. The most common of these in production networks is IP.

At the Data Link Layer, Microsoft installations are typically configured with PPP. This is the most common implementation with Cisco solutions and is the most important to understand.

For some reason, Cisco stresses knowing the method used in configuring the dial-up networking options within the Windows operating system. Microsoft places these options (unlike most other network settings) under the Accessories option, and not the Control Panel or Network icons. This is very important to know for successful implementation of the remote access solution; however, it would be fair to note that many users have already learned the quirks of Windows configuration and would therefore question Cisco's judgment in stressing a process that is more than seven years old. Suffice it to say that familiarity is important, and it would be prudent to focus on this if you are approaching the exam or practical usage without Microsoft experience.

There are other minor elements in Windows remote access that are valuable to know. Microsoft supports bonding and Multilink Protocol. Troubleshooting tools and terminal options are also available. Terminal windows are often used with third-party authentication solutions.

The use of Windows devices directly attaching to Cisco routers or AS5000 series aggregation routers can be an efficient way to provide remote connectivity. As a final point, readers are cautioned on using this model to provide new remote access solutions. Although outside the scope of this chapter due to Cisco's focus and objectives, modern solutions would likely take advantage of VPN, DSL, cable modem, and other more economical, secure, and scalable solutions.

Exam Essentials

Know which Cisco remote access protocols Windows 95 supports.   Windows 95 supports IP, IPX, and NetBEUI protocols, which are also supported by Cisco remote access. The most common of these is IP.

Know the configuration settings location.   The dial-up networking options are located under Start ➢ Programs ➢ Accessories ➢ Communications ➢ Dial-Up Networking.

Understand that the Windows Control Panel is not used to configure a dial-up networking session.   These options are controlled under Programs.

Realize that each dial-up networking session is started by a specific icon.   The dial-up networking icons are located in Start ➤ Programs ➤ Accessories ➤ Communications ➤ Dial-Up Networking, followed by the specific icon created for that connection.

Know how to use the terminal window option.   Remember that the terminal window can be used to add parameters to a dial-up session or to integrate with enhanced authentication products.

Key Terms

Before you take the exam, be certain you are familiar with the following terms:

challenge   scripts

patches

Written Lab

1. What dial-up networking protocol does not support routing?

2. What dial-up networking protocol is a proprietary version of CHAP?

3. What dial-up networking protocol would be best used with Novell networks?

4. What three protocols are supported for dial-up networking?

5. What do the three supported dial-up networking protocols have in common?

6. Does Windows 95/98 dial-up networking support SLIP?

7. Windows 95/98 dial-up networking provides for _____ and _____ IP addressing.

8. The logical linking of two or more physical connections is called _____.

9. Ethernet configuration is selected from the _____.

10. Dial-up networking configuration is selected from the _____.

Review Questions

1. Windows remote access connections support which of the following protocols? (Select all that apply.)

    A. IP

    B. IPX

    C. AppleTalk

    D. NetBEUI

    E. All of the above

2. The CSLIP server type supports which of the following?

    A. IP

    B. IPX

    C. NetBEUI

    D. All of the above

3. The Windows for Workgroups server type supports which of the following?

    A. IP

    B. IPX

    C. NetBEUI

    D. All of the above

4. The best reason to use PPP above all other server types is that it has

    A. Support for multiple protocols.

    B. Integrated 128-bit encryption.

    C. Enhanced AppleTalk support.

    D. None of the above.

5. To select an IP address for a dial-up network connection, the user would

    A. Use the network Control Panel.

    B. Select the icon from the Dial-up Networking folder.

    C. Either A or B.

    D. Neither A nor B.

6. To configure a network connection between a Novell NetWare network and a Windows dial-up client, the server type would be set to which of the following? (Select all that apply.)

    A. CSLIP

    B. SLIP

    C. PPP

    D. NRN

7. Which of the following would be a reason to launch a terminal window?

    A. To enable Cisco Discovery Protocol (CDP) packets on the link

    B. To set DTE speed after connection

    C. To use a third-party security solution

    D. When using dial-up DSL connections

8. Why might a user or administrator lock the DTE speed?

    A. To improve performance on degraded lines

    B. To alter the compression ratio

    C. To augment encryption on the line

    D. None of the above

9. To debug a script, the user or administrator might use which of the following?

    A. The `debug ppp script` command on the router or remote access device

    B. The protocol analyzer for the POTS product

    C. The Step through Script option

    D. The Windows 95/98 script debugger application

10. Does Microsoft support the Shiva Password Authentication Protocol (SPAP)?

    A. Yes.

    B. Yes, but only with EIGRP.

    C. No.

    D. Yes, but only with the Shiva add-in client.

11. The administrator might use which of the following to troubleshoot a script's execution?

    A. The Step through Script option

    B. A protocol analyzer

    C. The `debug script` command

    D. None of the above

12. Which of the following is true?

    A. Passwords can be case sensitive.

    B. PAP is less secure than CHAP.

    C. Microsoft supports the PPP protocol.

    D. All of the above.

13. To support only IPX, which of the following would the administrator select?

    A. PPP

    B. SLIP

    C. NRN

    D. None of the above

14. "Something you have" refers to which of the following?

    A. A security token

    B. A modem

    C. A router

    D. A computer

15. Which of the following protocols support NetBIOS?

    A. AppleTalk, IPX, and IP

    B. IPX, IP, and EIGRP

    C. IPX, IP, and NetBEUI

    D. AppleTalk, NetBEUI, and IP

16. Which of the following are services that can use dial-up networking?

    A. Electronic mail

    B. Remote control

    C. Automatic connections to websites

    D. All of the above

17. To correct problems with dial-up networking, which of the following might the administrator first install?

    A. Multilink services

    B. Compression services

    C. A service pack

    D. None of the above

18. To create a new dial-up configuration, which of the following would the administrator or user run?

    A. The Make New Connection Wizard

    B. The Windows Installer

    C. The Cisco DUN Setup Program

    D. None of the above

19. Which of the following is not true regarding NetBEUI?

    A. It is supported by Windows.

    B. NetBIOS can operate over the protocol.

    C. It is routable.

    D. It is only used for mainframe connections.

20. To improve performance on only remote IP sessions, which of the following should the administrator do?

    A. Disable compression

    B. Disable NetBEUI and IPX

    C. Disable multilink

    D. None of the above

Answers to Written Lab

1. NetBEUI/NetBIOS

2. MS-CHAP

3. IPX

4. IP, IPX, and NetBEUI

5. They all support NetBIOS.

6. Yes.

7. Static, dynamic

8. Bonding or multilink

9. The Network applet in the Control Panel

10. Dial-Up Networking folder

Answers to Review Questions

1. A, B, D. All protocols that support NetBIOS are allowed for remote dial-up networking. AppleTalk does not support NetBIOS.

2. A. Compressed SLIP supports only the IP protocol, just like SLIP.

3. C. Windows for Workgroups uses NetBEUI as the native transport for NetBIOS packets, which corresponds to this support.

4. A. Of the five server types, only PPP supports multiple protocols. It does not augment AppleTalk, nor does it include encryption.

5. B. The network Control Panel cannot be used for defining the IP address on a dial-up connection.

6. C, D. Both CSLIP and SLIP support IP only. This removes them from contention for IPX or Novell NetWare transport.

7. C. Launching a terminal window enables the user to key in a challenge/response password. The other options are nonsensical because they do not relate to the terminal window in any way.

8. A. On poor-quality lines, the DTE might try to establish higher than acceptable speeds. Locking the speed prevents overrunning the line and typically leads to better throughput because there are fewer dropped packets.

9. C. Although each of these choices, or a variation of them, could aid in debugging a script, only the Step through Script option is legitimate. The others are not available as presented.

10. A. Microsoft's dial-up networking supports SPAP, in addition to PAP and CHAP. No add-in client is needed, and EIGRP is not supported on Windows clients.

11. A. The Step through Script option will enable the administrator to find a faulty command in the script.

12. D. Each of these items is true.

13. C. Although you could select PPP and enable only IPX protocol support, the NRN option is the best answer because it supports only IPX.

14. A. A security token is something you have as part of the security solution.

15. C. Windows dial-up networking supports IPX, IP, and NetBEUI, which all provide support for NetBIOS.

16. D. Dial-up networking can provide all of the listed services.

17. C. Service packs, which include bug fixes, can correct problems with dial-up networking. Multilink and compression would not correct—and might compound—any problems.

18. A. The Make New Connection Wizard is used to define a new configuration.

19. C. NetBEUI contains no logical addressing information and is not routable.

20. B. Disabling NetBEUI and IPX can improve performance and reduce overhead. Multilink and compression can improve performance in some circumstances.

Integrated Services Digital Network (ISDN)

EXAM TOPICS COVERED IN THIS CHAPTER INCLUDE:

✓ Describe how different WAN technologies can be used to provide remote access to a network, including asynchronous dial-in, Frame Relay, ISDN, cable modem, and DSL.

✓ Explain the operation of remote network access control methods.

✓ Identify PPP components, and explain the use of PPP as an access and encapsulation method.

✓ Configure an ISDN solution for remote access.

✓ Plan a Cisco ISDN solution for remote access or primary link backup.

✓ Troubleshoot nonfunctional remote access systems.

Integrated Services Digital Network (ISDN) has gained quite a following over the past few years. It offers a switched high-speed data connection that you can also use to support voice, video, or fax calls, making it an excellent choice for small office/home office (SOHO) users. However, Digital Subscriber Line (DSL) will probably replace ISDN completely within the next few years because DSL is cheaper and faster—which means it must be better, right? Maybe. Just like ISDN, DSL can also provide data, voice, and fax services to end-users. Cable modems have also been around for a few years and provide a large amount of bandwidth for a neighborhood to access the Internet, but cable modems are really just composed of a large Thinnet network in which all your neighbors share the same bandwidth. Thinnet is the type of wiring used for 10Base2 Ethernet networks, which was popular before the 10-BaseT standard. It runs over a thin coaxial cable similar to RG-6 wiring used by cable providers, hence the term *Thinnet network*.

Now, you might be thinking, "Hey, I thought this was an ISDN chapter; what's with DSL taking over the discussion?" It is an ISDN chapter, and you do need to know about the topic. It won't be replaced overnight, and although DSL will probably replace it, it is possible that it won't. Remember about six or seven years ago when everyone was saying that ATM was going to take over the world? Pretty glad we didn't buy stock in that rumor. ATM is a contender, but the expense and difficult technical administration make it unpopular compared to Gigabit Ethernet for the LAN and to DSL for the WAN. In defense of ISDN, it does have a few benefits over DSL and cable modems that we describe in this chapter.

ISDN is still a good choice for WAN services because of its high speed (Cisco calls ISDN high speed). It can run anywhere from 56K to T-1 speeds (1.544Mbps). 128Kbps is the most common, though. Although 128Kbps is not high speed to most people, compared to a 33Kbps dial-up analog modem, it is.

Unlike a modem (which is analog), ISDN is digital from end to end. Analog modems translate from digital on the computer, to analog between modems, and then back to digital on the remote end. ISDN is more efficient and faster, and it also has a faster setup connection speed than an analog modem.

- In this chapter, you will learn about ISDN, beginning with the Physical Layer and working up. Topics covered in this chapter include ISDN device types, Layer 2 (Q.921) and Layer 3 (Q.931) specifications, ISDN reference points (R, S, T, U, and V), configuring dial backup and bandwidth on Demand configurations, and commonly used ISDN commands.

What Is Integrated Services Digital Network (ISDN)?

Integrated Services Digital Network (ISDN) has been under development for a couple of decades but has been hampered by the lack of applications that can use its speed. It wasn't until recently that telecommuting, video conferencing, and *small offices/home offices (SOHOs)* have needed the capabilities ISDN presented. Another factor slowing the development of ISDN was that it was somewhat proprietary in nature. However, this ended when National ISDN-1 became available in 1992. National ISDN-1 is a standard switch type used by ISDN providers. This standard enabled vendors to interoperate among devices.

Before getting into what ISDN is and does, you first need to understand how our traditional, or *plain old telephone service (POTS)*, operates. Typically, you pick up the telephone receiver, you dial the number, and the party answers at the other end. Your voice—which is an analog wave—is converted into a digital signal through a process called *Pulse Code Modulation (PCM)*. PCM samples your voice 8,000 times per second and converts the audio level into an 8-bit value. This 64Kbps channel, or *DS0*, is multiplexed with 23 other channels to form a T-1.

If you do the math, you'll notice that a T-1 is 1.544Mbps; however, 24 64Kbps is only 1.536Mbps. Where are the other 8Kbps? Before we answer that question, think of the purpose of a T-1. Each telephone call in the past required two copper wires to carry the voice traffic. A T-1 was originally designed to carry 24 individual voice calls on the same wire. Each voice call received its own channel. The underlying technique to carry all 24 channels on the same wire is called time division multiplexing (TDM). TDM breaks up the circuit into 24 separate channels and provides a distinct time slot for each.

Now back to the math. Each of the 24 channels is composed of 8 bits, for a total of 192 bits (8×24). According to the Nyquist theorem, we know that we need to sample at 8,000 times per second to replicate the human voice. Therefore, to produce all 24 channels, the entire 192 bits must be transmitted 8,000 times each second, for a subtotal of 1,536,000 bits per second, or 1.536Mbps $(8,000 \times 192)$.

Now for the missing 8Kbps. A single framing bit is added between each 24-channel frame. Therefore, an additional 8,000 framing bits are sent each second (remember the sampling rate for human voice), raising our total to 1,544,000 bits per second, or 1.544Mbps $(1,536,000 + 8,000)$. This number is the bit rate of the line itself, and the one you commonly see with reference to a T-1 circuit. Because 8,000 of the bits sent each second are used for framing and not data, however, the maximum data you could theoretically put on the wire is the smaller number: 1.536Mbps.

ISDN differs from POTS in a couple of ways. First, ISDN data starts off as digital signaling, so there is no analog-to-digital conversion. Second, call setup and teardown is accomplished through a dedicated 16Kbps channel also known as a D (data) channel. By using "out of band" signaling, you have the entire 64Kbps for data. This leaves one or two B (bearer) channels for your data or voice traffic that does not have an intrusion on the line for clocking or error control. ISDN then provides unadulterated bandwidth to end-users.

ISDN benefits include improved speed over an analog modem, fast call setup (one second or less, typically), and lower cost than a dedicated point-to-point circuit. DSLs and cable modems are replacing ISDN in some areas and will continue to do so as they fit the need for high-speed Internet access to the home. However, ISDN has some advantages over these newer, faster technologies. Here is a list of the advantages that ISDN can provide:

- Ability to dial into many locations simultaneously
- High-speed dial-up services for traveling telecommuters
- A fault-tolerant link for dedicated lines
- Remote SOHO connectivity
- Video conferencing

ISDN Line Options

ISDN is available in many configurations, or line options. In this section, you will learn about two of the most common: Basic Rate Interface (BRI) and Primary Rate Interface (PRI). These flavors of ISDN vary according to the type and number of channels that carry data. Each option has two or more DS0s, or *B (bearer) channels,* and a *D (data) channel.* ISDN is characterized by the presence of a D channel, which carries control and signaling information, freeing up the B channels exclusively for voice and data transport.

Each DS0 is capable of carrying 64,000 bits per second of either voice or data. Telephone companies (telcos) can provide ISDN on their current infrastructure with little additional work. Table 5.1 shows the relationship between the DS level, speed, designations, and number of DS0s per circuit. Only the DS1 level is associated with ISDN, which is the transport that a PRI circuit uses.

TABLE 5.1   North American Digital Hierarchy

Digital Signal Level	Speed	Designation	Channel(s)
DS0	64K	None	1
DS1	1.544Mbps	T-1	24
DS2	6.312Mbps	T-2	96
DS3	44.736Mbps	T-3	672
DS4	274.176Mbps	T-4	4,032

> Different standards, called Synchronous Optical Network (SONET) and Synchronous Digital Hierarchy (SDH), were developed for Fiber Optics Transmission Systems (FOTS). These standards are not covered in this book

Another ISDN element is the *Service Profile Identifier (SPID)*. A SPID identifies the characteristics of your ISDN line. SPIDs might or might not be needed, depending on the type of switch your service provider uses. ISDN National-1 and DMS-100 switches require a SPID for each B channel, whereas a SPID is optional with an AT&T 5ESS switch type. Please consult your ISDN provider if you are not sure whether you need a SPID. The format of a SPID is usually the 10-digit phone number, plus a prefix and possibly a suffix. For example, say that your telephone number is 949 555-1234. Now add a prefix of 01 and a suffix of 0100. This gives you a SPID of 0194955512340100.

To place an ISDN call, you will also need a *directory number*, or DN. A DN is the actual number you would call to reach that B channel. In the example, the DN would be 9495551234 or 5551231. Knowing the SPID, switch type, and DN will speed up the configuration of your router. Your service provider should provide you with this information. Other than the directory number, the rest might be automatically detected.

Basic Rate Interface (BRI)

A *Basic Rate Interface (BRI)* uses a single pair of copper wires to provide up to 192Kbps of bandwidth for both voice and data calls A BRI uses two 64Kbps B channels and one 16Kbps D channel. An additional 48Kbps are used for framing and synchronization.

To review the math, each B channel is 64Kbps, so that totals 128Kbps. Add the 16Kbps D channel, and the usable bandwidth for ISDN BRI is now at 144Kbps. Last, add the 48Kbps for framing and synchronization to get a total circuit speed of 192Kbps. Figure 5.1 shows the ISDN protocol layers.

FIGURE 5.1   ISDN protocol layers

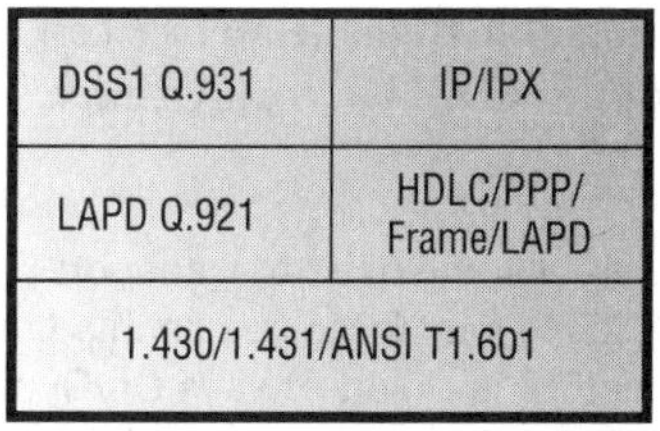

DSS1 Q.931	IP/IPX
LAPD Q.921	HDLC/PPP/ Frame/LAPD
1.430/1.431/ANSI T1.601	

Both the B and D channels share Layer 1. Layers 2 and 3 operate over the D channel, but the B channel operates in either an HDLC or PPP encapsulation mode. This architecture is used to encapsulate the upper-layer protocols instead of using Layer 2 and Layer 3 directly. LAPD is the framing protocol used for the D channel data. DSS1 (digital subscriber signaling system number 1) is the Layer 3 protocol for the D channel where Q.931 is used. B channels are used by the IP or IPX protocols for data transfer, and the D channel is used by dial-on-demand routing (DDR), which builds the connection over ISDN.

BRI Switch Options

Several BRI switch options are available for configuring your router. These switch types vary according to geographic location. The available switch types are shown in Table 5.2.

TABLE 5.2   ISDN BRI Switch Types

Switch Type	Typically Used
BASIC-1TR6	1TR6 switch type for Germany
BASIC-5ESS	AT&T 5ESS switch type for the U.S.
BASIC-DMS100	Northern DMS-100 switch type for the US
BASIC-NET3	NET3 switch type for the U.K. and most of Europe
BASIC-NI	National ISDN switch type for the US
BASIC-TS013	TS013 switch type for Australia
NTT	NTT switch type for Japan
VN3	VN3 and VN4 switch types for France
EZ-ISDN	North American ISDN standard service package

A benefit to using a BRI is being able to make a voice call while maintaining your Internet connection. This is a great solution for SOHO deployments.

The D channel can also be used to transport packet-switched data communications, such as X.25. In fact, Cisco has enabled this feature in version 12 of its IOS software. The feature is called Always On/Dynamic ISDN (AO/DI). Basically, it enables the low-bandwidth traffic to use the D channel and initiates a call by using one or two B channels if the traffic warrants. This feature will be most useful for point-of-sale applications but is not supported by all service providers.

Primary Rate Interface (PRI)

Most Internet service providers use *Primary Rate Interface (PRI)* ISDN to connect to the Public Switched Telephone Network (PTSN). A PRI enables service to analog modem users, digital modem users, and ISDN customers. The calls are routed to the appropriate modems after the access server receives the calling number's bearer capability. ISDN also provides a means to deliver Calling Line ID (CLID), as well as Called Number or Automatic Number Identification (ANI). These features can be used to determine the correct authentication server for this customer.

PRIs have the following capacities:

- A T-1–based PRI has twenty-three 64Kbps B channels and one 64Kbps D channel, which equals a bandwidth of 1.536Kbps. An 8Kbps channel for framing and synchronization is also used, resulting in a total bandwidth of 1.544Mbps for a U.S. T-1/PRI. The last T-1 channel is used as the D channel.

- An E-1–based PRI has thirty B channels and one 64Kbps D channel. An E-1 uses channel 15 for signaling (D channel). An E-1 has 2.048Mbps of total bandwidth.

PRI Switch Options

As with BRI, you have several switch types to select from. Check with your provider to configure the correct one. Otherwise, you might have to reboot your router for the switch type change to take effect.

Table 5.3 shows the typical available switch types used with PRI.

TABLE 5.3   PRI Switch Types

Switch Type	Typically Used
PRIMARY-5ESS	AT&T 5ESS switch type for the U.S.
PRIMARY-4ESS	AT&T 4ESS switch type for the U.S.
PRIMARY-DMS100	Northern DMS-100 switch type for the U.S.
PRIMARY-NET5	NET5 switch type for the U.K. and most of Europe
VN3	VN3 and VN4 switch types for France
PRIMARY-NTT	Japanese ISDN PRI switches
PRIMARY-NI	AT&T National ISDN switch type for the U.S.

T-1– and E-1–based PRIs use different linecoding and framing schemes. A T-1–based PRI uses binary 8-zero substitution (B8ZS) for encoding and Extended Super Frame (ESF) for framing. An E-1–based PRI uses High-Density Bipolar Order 3 (HDB3) for encoding and Cyclic Redundancy Check, level 4 (CRC-4) for framing.

ISDN Function Groups

The ISDN function groups represent the devices in an ISDN environment such as terminals, terminal adapters, network-termination devices and line-termination equipment. It is important to understand the different function groups when you design and troubleshoot your ISDN network. . Figure 5.2 shows the function groups and their placement in an ISDN network.

FIGURE 5.2 ISDN function groups

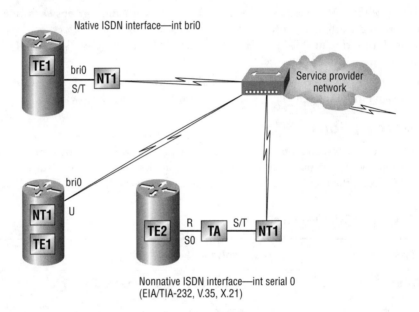

The following are definitions and examples of ISDN BRI function groups as they relate to Figure 5.2:

Terminal Equipment 1 (TE1)   A device that understands ISDN digital signaling techniques. Examples of TE1 devices are digital telephones, routers with ISDN interfaces, and digital facsimile equipment. TE1 devices are 4-wire (2 pair) and need to be 2-wire (1 pair) to communicate with an ISDN network. A TE1 will connect into a Network Termination type 1 (NT1) to connect the 4-wire subscriber wiring to the 2-wire local loop facility.

Terminal Equipment 2 (TE2)   Equipment that does not understand ISDN signaling standards. Examples of TE2 devices are analog telephones, X.25 interfaces, and serial interfaces on a router. A TE2 device needs to be converted to ISDN signaling, which is provided by a terminal adapter (TA). After that, it still needs to be converted to a 2-wire network with an NT1 device.

Network Termination type 1 (NT1)   This device is used to convert a 4-wire ISDN connection to the 2-wire ISDN used by the local loop facility. This device is primarily used in the United States, since European service providers retain ownership of this functionality.

Network Termination type 2 (NT2)   This device is used to direct traffic from ISDN devices (TEs) to an NT1. This is probably the most intelligent device in the ISDN network; it provides switching and concentrating and can sometimes even be a Private Branch Exchange (PBX).

Terminal Adapter (TA)   This device enables a TE2 device to communicate with the telco's network by providing any necessary protocol and interface conversion. In essence, a TA adapts the unipolar signal coming from a non-ISDN device into a bipolar signal used by the ISDN network.

Local Termination (LT)   This is the same device as an NT1, but located at the provider's site.

Exchange Termination (ET)   The connection to the ISDN switch, typically an ISDN line card. The ET forms the physical and logical boundary between the digital local loop and the carrier's switching office. It performs the same functions at the end office that the NT performs at the customer's premises. Both the LT and the ET together are typically referred to as the local exchange (LE).

ISDN Reference Points

A *reference point* defines a connection point between two functions; you can also refer to it as an interface, though it does not represent an actual physical interface. The reference point is where data is converted between device types. Figure 5.3 shows the reference points defined in an ISDN network.

FIGURE 5.3   ISDN reference points

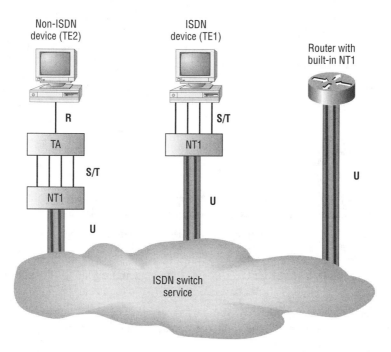

The reference points shown in Figure 5.3 are described in detail in the following list:

R reference point   This reference point defines the point between non-ISDN equipment and a TA. The R reference point enables a non-ISDN device to appear on the network as an ISDN device. Unlike the others, this is a nonstandardized reference because it is dependent on the TE2 equipment's interface.

S reference point   This is the point between the user terminals and NT2 or, in other words, between a TE1 or a TA and the Network Termination (which is either an NT1 or NT2).

T reference point   This reference point defines the point between NT1 and NT2 devices

S/T interface   As the name implies, the S/T interface combines both the S and T interfaces. This interface is governed by the ITU I.430 standard, which defines the connection as a 4-wire connection. The S/T interface is typically an RJ-45, with 8-pin cables using pins 3 and 6 to receive data and pins 4 and 5 to transmit data. Service providers in Europe use this interface to deliver ISDN BRI service.

The International Telecommunications Union (ITU) is a United Nations–sponsored organization formed in 1865 to promote worldwide communication systems compatibility. It has two groups, ITU-T and ITU-R. ITU-T deals with telecommunications, and ITU-R is responsible for radio communications. You can visit their website at www.itu.int for more information.

U reference point   This reference point is also known as a U (user) interface. This is a 2-wire connection between the NT1 and the telephone company (LE). Cisco routers are marked with an *X* if the interface is a U and with a crossed-out *X* if the interface is an S/T. This is an ANSI standard used in the U.S. but not in Europe.

V reference point   This reference point is the interface point in an ISDN environment between the line termination and the exchange termination.

ISDN Protocols

ISDN protocols define how information is transferred from one device to another in the network. The ITU-T has established three types of protocols to handle this information transfer:

- Protocols beginning with the letter *E* specify ISDN on the existing telephone network.

- Protocols beginning with the letter *I* specify concepts, terminology, and services.

- Protocols beginning with the letter *Q* specify switching and signaling. Two Q standards of interest are Q.921, which handles Layer 2, and Q.931, which deals with Layer 3 interfacing.

Spending some time reviewing the Q standards will help you use a couple of the IOS **debug** commands covered later in this chapter. As just stated, the ITU-T recommendations Q.921 and

Q.931 handle switching and signaling. Q.921 uses *Link Access Procedure, Data (LAPD)* to communicate with other ISDN devices across the D channel. LAPD's primary purpose is to transport signaling information.

LAPD Frames

While the ISDN protocols define the transfer of information, layer 2 and 3 functions are handled with LAPD. Understanding the information contained in this frame will help you understand Q.921 and Q.931 debug outputs. Remember that LAPD is the framing protocol used for D channel data and that the D channel is used to build connections to an ISDN link.

An *LAPD frame* has six parts to it: Flag, Address, Control, Information, CRC, and a final Flag. Figure 5.4 shows the LAPD frame and the fields within the frame.

FIGURE 5.4   Link Access Procedure, Data

Flag	Address	Control	Information	CRC	Flag

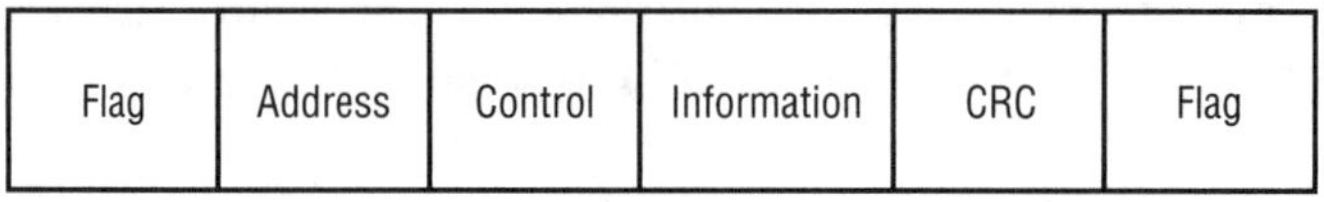

The following information describes the fields within the LAPD frame:

Flag   This one-octet field starts and ends the frame with a value of 7E (0111 1110). The LAPD Flag and Control fields are identical to those of HDLC.

Address   This field is two octets long and contains some important information. This field identifies the TE using this link and has four parts: Service Access Point Identifier (SAPI), Command/Response (C/R), Address Extension 0 (AE0), and Terminal Endpoint Identifier (TEI).

Service Access Point Identifier (SAPI)   This field is 6 bits long. Table 5.4 shows the SAPI values that can be used in an LAPD frame.

TABLE 5.4   SAPI Values

SAPI	Description
0	Call control procedures
1	Packet mode using Q.931 call procedures
16	Packet mode communications procedures
32–47	Reserved for national use

TABLE 5.4   SAPI Values *(continued)*

SAPI	Description
63	Management procedures
Others	Reserved for future use

Command/Response (C/R)   This is 1 bit long. This bit identifies the frame as either a command or a response. The user side always sends commands with this bit set to 0 and responds with it set to 1. The network side is the exact opposite, sending a command with this bit set to 1, or a 0 if it is responding.

Address Extension 0 (EA0 and EA1)   These are 1 bit long. Their value indicates whether the associated octet is the last in the Address field. Setting the value to 1 in the last bit of an address octet (the EA field) indicates to the receiving device that this is the last octet in the Address field.

Terminal Endpoint Identifier (TEI)   These values uniquely identify each TE on an ISDN S/T bus. A TEI can be either dynamically or statically assigned. Table 5.5 lists the values.

TABLE 5.5   Terminal Endpoint Identifier (TEI) Values

TEI	Description
0–63	Fixed TEI assignments
64–126	Dynamically assigned (assigned by the switch)
127	Broadcast to all devices

Control   This field has 11 available values, each one shown in Table 5.6, along with its application. You will see one of three types of information here: Information Transfer, Supervisory, or Unnumbered.

TABLE 5.6   Control Field Values

Format	Message Type	Control/Response
Information Transfer	I = Information	Control
Supervisory	RR = Receive Ready	Control/Response
Supervisory	RNR = Receive Not Ready	Control/Response

TABLE 5.6   Control Field Values *(continued)*

Format	Message Type	Control/Response
Supervisory	REJ = Reject	Control/Response
Unnumbered	SABME = Set Asynchronous Balanced Mode Extended	Control
Unnumbered	DM = Disconnected Mode	Response
Unnumbered	UI = Unnumbered Information	Control
Unnumbered	DISC = Disconnect	Control
Unnumbered	UA = Unnumbered Acknowledgment	Response
Unnumbered	FRMR = Frame Reject	Response
Unnumbered	XID = Exchange Identifier	Control/Response

Information   This field carries the Q.931 protocol data. Figure 5.5 illustrates how it is laid out. This is where the user data is carried.

FIGURE 5.5   Q.921/Q.931 Information field format

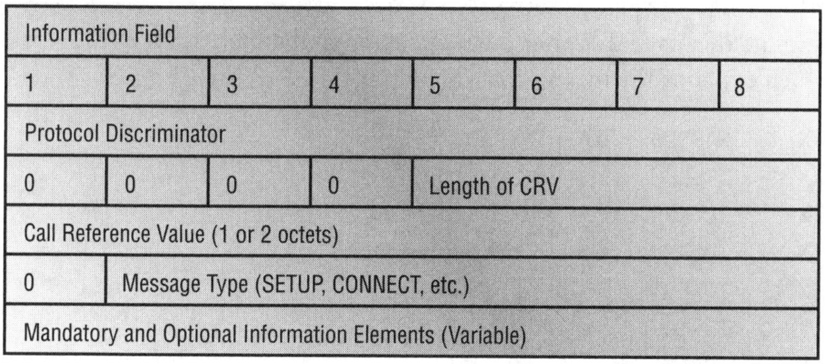

The following information describes the field format as shown in Figure 5.5.

Protocol Discriminator   One octet. Identifies the Layer 3 protocol.

Length   One octet. Indicates the length of the Call Reference Value (CRV).

Call Reference Value (CRV)   One or two octets. This value is assigned to each call at the beginning, is used to distinguish between other simultaneous calls, and is released after the call is torn down.

Message Type   One octet.

Mandatory and Optional Information Elements (variable length)   Options based on the message type.

CRC   Contains the cyclic redundancy check derived value from the Address, Control, and Information fields. This is also known as the Frame Check Sequence (FCS) field.

Layer 2 Negotiation

We need to have an understanding of the LAPD frame before we understand how Layer 2 negotiates. This will help help you identify where a potential or existing problem is occurring. One useful feature of Cisco equipment is that it includes good diagnostic tools for finding ISDN problems. Knowing which side of the ISDN connection does what will help you identify a problem and start corrective action.

The first part of the process is TEI assignment, which is accomplished by using this process:

1. The Terminal Endpoint (TE) and the network initially exchange Receive Ready (RR) frames, listening for an initiated connection.

2. The TE sends an Unnumbered Information (UI) frame with a SAPI of 63 (management procedure, query network) and TEI of 127 (broadcast).

3. The network assigns an available TEI (in the range 64–126).

4. The TE sends a Set Asynchronous Balanced Mode Extended (SABME) frame with a SAPI of 0 (call control, used to initiate a SETUP) and a TEI of the value assigned by the network.

5. The network responds with an Unnumbered Acknowledgment (UA); SAPI = 0, TEI = assigned.

As you examine this partial output from the command `debug isdn q921`, please refer to Table 5.7, which explains the meaning of the output.

```
ISDN BR0: TX ->   SABMEp sapi = 0   tei = 77
ISDN BR0: RX <-   IDCKRQ  ri = 0   ai = 127
ISDN BR0: TX ->   IDCKRP  ri = 44602  ai = 77
ISDN BR0: TX ->   IDCKRP  ri = 37339  ai = 78
ISDN BR0: RX <-   IDREM   ri = 0   ai = 77
ISDN BR0: TX ->   IDREQ   ri = 44940  ai = 127
ISDN BR0: RX <-   IDREM   ri = 0   ai = 78
ISDN BR0: TX ->   IDREQ   ri = 43085  ai = 127
ISDN BR0: TX ->   IDREQ   ri = 11550  ai = 127
ISDN BR0: RX <-   IDASSN  ri = 11550  ai = 79
```

```
ISDN BR0: TX ->  SABMEp sapi = 0  tei = 79
ISDN BR0: TX ->  IDREQ  ri = 65279  ai = 127
ISDN BR0: RX <-  UAf sapi = 0  tei = 79
ISDN BR0: TX ->  INFOc sapi = 0  tei = 79  ns = 0 _
nr = 0  i = 0x08007B3A0A30383335383636313031
ISDN BR0: RX <-  IDASSN  ri = 65279  ai = 80
ISDN BR0: TX ->  SABMEp sapi = 0  tei = 80
ISDN BR0: RX <-  INFOc sapi = 0  tei = 79  ns = 0  nr = 1  i = 0x08007B3B028181
ISDN BR0: TX ->  RRr sapi = 0  tei = 79  nr = 1
ISDN BR0: RX <-  UAf sapi = 0  tei = 80
ISDN BR0: TX ->  INFOc sapi = 0  tei = 80  ns = 0 _
nr = 0  i = 0x08007B3A0A30383335383636333031
ISDN BR0: RX <-  INFOc sapi = 0  tei = 80  ns = 0  nr = 1  i = 0x08007B3B028381
ISDN BR0: TX ->  RRr sapi = 0  tei = 80  nr = 1
```

TABLE 5.7 Debug ISDN Q.921 Details

Output	Meaning
ISDN BR0:	This is the interface.
TX ->	This router is sending this information.
RX <-	This router is receiving this information.
SABME	Indicates the Set Asynchronous Balanced Mode Extended command. This command places the recipient into modulo 128 multiple frame acknowledged operation. This command also indicates that all exception conditions have been cleared.
sapi	Identifies the service access point at which the Data Link Layer entity provides services to Layer 3 or to the management layer. A SAPI with the value 0 indicates it is a call control procedure.
IDCKRQ ri = 0 ai = 127	Indicates the Identity Check Request message type sent from the ISDN service provider on the network to the local router during the TEI check procedure. This message is sent in a UI command frame. The ri field is always 0. The ai field for this message contains either a specific TEI value for the local router to check or 127, which indicates that the local router should check all TEI values.

TABLE 5.7 Debug ISDN Q.921 Details *(continued)*

Output	Meaning
IDREM	This indicates the Identity Remove message type sent from the network to the user-side layer management entity during the TEI removal procedure. This message is sent in a UI command frame. The message includes a reference number that is always 0, because it is not responding to a request from the local router. It is sent twice by the network to prevent a lost message.
IDCKRP	Indicates the Identity Check Response message type sent from the local router to the ISDN service provider on the network during the TEI check procedure. This message is sent in a UI command frame in response to the IDCKRQ message
IDREQ	This indicates an Identity Request message sent from the local router to the network during the automatic TEI assignment.
UAf	This confirms that the network side has accepted the SABME command previously sent by the local router. The final bit is set to 1.
INFOc	This is an information command. It is used to transfer sequentially numbered frames containing Information Fields cap provided by Layer 3.
IDASSN	This indicates an Identity Assigned message type sent from the network's ISDN service provider to the local router during the automatic TEI assignment procedure.
RRx	This indicates Receive Ready. If $x = r$, it is responding to an INFOc. If $x = p$, the router is polling the network side. And $x = f$ means the network side has responded to the poll and the final bit is set.

Now what does everything in Table 5.7 mean? According to the output, the router attempts to establish a connection with the switch, using legacy TEI information that it has left over.

```
ISDN BR0: TX -> SABMEp sapi = 0  tei = 77
```

The service provider's switch disapproves of this and orders a check of the router's current TEIs with the IDCKRQ message. The ai of 127 (broadcast) simply tells the router that the switch would like for it to check all TEIs it currently has registered.

```
ISDN BR0: RX <-  IDCKRQ  ri = 0  ai = 127
```

The router promptly returns an IDCKRP message for each TEI it finds within itself. In this case, these are 77 and 78.

```
ISDN BR0: TX -> IDCKRP  ri = 44602  ai = 77
ISDN BR0: TX -> IDCKRP  ri = 37339  ai = 78
```

The switch does not want the router to continue using these TEIs, so it issues an IDREM message for each offending TEI. This tells the router to forget about these TEIs.

```
ISDN BR0: RX <- IDREM  ri = 0  ai = 77
```

The router quickly throws itself at the mercy of the switch by sending the IDREQ message with an ai of 127. Notice that the router is looking for two TEIs, one for each logical B channel interface within BRI0, but it has to issue four IDREQs to overcome the timeouts.

```
ISDN BR0: TX -> IDREQ  ri = 43085  ai = 127
ISDN BR0: TX -> IDREQ  ri = 11550  ai = 127
```

As soon as an IDASSN returns that matches the ri of one of the IDREQs,

```
ISDN BR0: RX <- IDASSN  ri = 11550  ai = 79
```

The router turns around and establishes service with a new SABME message, using the new TEI.

```
ISDN BR0: TX -> SABMEp sapi = 0  tei = 79
ISDN BR0: TX -> IDREQ  ri = 65279  ai = 127
```

Because the switch obviously approves of this TEI, it responds with the UA message the router was originally looking for.

```
ISDN BR0: RX <- UAf sapi = 0  tei = 79
```

After the UAs come in, the whole INFO/RR exchange for Layer 3 information begins for each TEI assigned.

```
ISDN BR0: TX -> INFOc sapi = 0  tei = 79  ns = 0  nr = 0  i =
    0x08007B3A0A30383335383636313031
ISDN BR0: TX -> RRr sapi = 0  tei = 79  nr = 1
```

This occurs for both the 79 and 80 TEIs.

ISDN Call Setup and Teardown

ISDN uses ITU-T Q.931 to establish and tear down calls. Call control and signaling information is carried over the D channel. Figure 5.6 shows the Q.931 procedures.

FIGURE 5.6   ISDN call setup and teardown

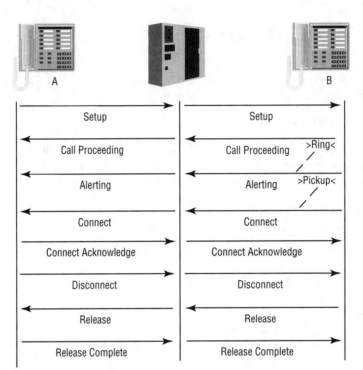

The process for ISDN call setup and teardown is as follows:

1. First, a SETUP message is sent from device A. The SETUP contains information necessary to make the call.

2. Next the switch sends a CALL PROCEEDING back to device A.

3. An ALERTING message is sent back when device B is contacted. You might hear the phone ring at this point.

4. CONNECT and CONNECT ACKNOWLEDGE messages are sent to indicate that the call has been accepted.

5. Call teardown starts when one of the users hangs up. Here device A hangs up, and a DISCONNECT message is sent to device B. The switch now disconnects B and sends a RELEASE to A. A RELEASE COMPLETE message confirms the process.

Using the `debug isdn q931` command, you get the following output.

```
ISDN BR0: TX ->  SETUP pd = 8  callref = 0x05 _
Bearer Capability i = 0x8890 Channel ID i = 0x83
        Keypad Facility i = '8358662'
ISDN BR0: RX <-  CALL_PROC pd = 8  callref = 0x85 _
Channel ID i = 0x89 Locking Shift to Codeset 5
        Codeset 5 IE 0x2A  i = 0x809402, '`=', 0x8307, _
'8358662', 0x8E0B, ' TELTONE 2 '
ISDN BR0: RX <-  CONNECT pd = 8  callref = 0x85
ISDN BR0: TX ->  CONNECT_ACK pd = 8  callref = 0x05
ISDN BR0: TX ->  DISCONNECT pd = 8  callref = 0x05 _
Cause i = 0x8090 - Normal call clearing
ISDN BR0: RX <-  RELEASE pd = 8  callref = 0x85
ISDN BR0: TX ->  RELEASE_COMP pd = 8  callref = 0x05
```

Table 5.8 describes the output from the Q.931 command.

TABLE 5.8   Debug ISDN Q.931 Details

Output	Meaning
TX ->	The message originating at the router.
RX <-	The message received from the network.
SETUP	Used to initiate a call. Either the network or the local router can send it.
pd = 8	Indicates the protocol discriminator. The protocol discriminator distinguishes messages for call control over the user-network ISDN interface from other ITU-T-defined messages, including other Q.931 messages.
Callref = 0x05	Indicates the number of calls the router has processed. It increments every time a call goes out or comes in.
Bearer Capability i = 0x8890	The bearer service requested by the router. 88 = ITU coding standard, unrestricted digital information 90 = Circuit mode, 64Kbps 21 = Layer 1, V.110/X.30 8F = Synchronous, no in-band negotiation, 56Kbps

TABLE 5.8   Debug ISDN Q.931 Details *(continued)*

Output	Meaning
Channel ID i = 0x83	The channel Identifier. It indicates which B channel to use. 83 = Use any channel. 89 = Use B1. 8A = Use B2.
Keypad facility	Also known as *Called Party Number.*
DISCONNECT pd = 8 callref = 0x05 Cause i = 0x8090 - Normal call clearing	The router is sending a DISCONNECT message to the network. The reason for this disconnect is Normal call clearing 0x80. See "ISDN Switch Types, Codes, and Values" on Cisco Connection Online (CCO) at www.cisco.com.

ISDN Configuration

To configure ISDN, you need to understand that there are both simple and complex configurations. Although you certainly can make more money by understanding the complex configurations, the simple ones are just as important. In this section, you will look at some benefits and drawbacks of two ISDN configuration types: PRI and BRI. In this section you will learn about the differences between the PRI and BRI interface configurations. First, though, you need to understand how the old and new ways differ.

 Real World Scenario

How to Order ISDN

Okay, we know this is a Remote Access Study Guide and you are probably getting ready for the test, but after you are certified (or certifiable,) you are the Cisco expert and should know the process of attaining as well as configuring the lines Here is what you do.

Who Do I Call?

The first step to getting your ISDN service up and running is to contact your local telephone company (service provider). The telephone numbers and web addresses for ordering ISDN service are provided at http://www.nationalisdncouncil.com.

What Do I Need to Tell the Telephone Company?

Ordering ISDN can be as easy as requesting basic phone service from the telephone company; most of the questions that the telephone company will ask you are the same in both cases. For example, because ISDN was designed to work over the existing wire, which supports your current telephone service, you will probably not have to specify any unique wiring changes or additions. However, some specialized capabilities of ISDN will require you to provide additional information related to your ISDN equipment selection. The best way to provide this additional information is through an ISDN Ordering Code (IOC), or as Cisco calls them, the capabilities package ordering codes, which should be identified in your ISDN equipment documentation. This will give you a set of standardized BRI line features that simplify the process of configuring an ISDN line that is connected to an NI1 switch. An example is the package R, which provides circuit-switched data on both B channels (no voice capabilities). Data capabilities include calling number identification. Cisco recommends this NI1 capability package for Cisco 801 and Cisco 802 routers.

What Does the Phone Company Need to Tell Me?

Most ISDN connections in North America require the use of one or more Service Profile Identifiers (SPIDs), which we discussed earlier in this chapter. SPIDs are numbers assigned only by North American telephone service providers. SPIDS identify the ISDN B channels. As stated earlier, the SPID format is generally an ISDN telephone number with several numbers added to it, for example, 40855512340101. Depending on the switch type that supports your ISDN BRI line, your ISDN line could be assigned none, one, or two SPIDs.

And that is it. The configuration of and use of this information is covered in the context of this Chapter.

Some of you might have grown up in a router world, where you used `dialer map` statements to configure a dial session. But the times they are a-changin', and actually for the better. By using a dialer profile, the basic configuration for a physical interface is entered under the actual interface, but the detailed configuration is placed under a virtual dialer interface. This is a really good feature if you have a PRI that receives and makes calls to and from different locations (with different subnets).

Using a Legacy Interface

To get your feet wet, let's start with a simple BRI configuration:

```
hostname R1
isdn switch-type basic-ni
!
```

```
interface BRI0
 ip address 10.1.1.3 255.255.255.0
 encapsulation ppp
 isdn spid1 91955512120100 5551212
 dialer map ip 10.1.1.1 name R2 555-1212
```

As you can see, the first statement defines the switch type. The BRI0 interface binds an IP address and sets up PPP as the encapsulation type. The last two lines identify the SPID and the `dialer map` command. These set the protocol with a next-hop address of `10./1.1.1`, identify the remote host as R2, and indicate that the dial string (telephone number) should be sent to the dialing device when it the device recognizes packets that have specified addresses matching the configured access lists.

Under the old legacy way, you could have a main IP address under the physical interface, along with several secondary addresses. This worked fine, but you ran into problems if you were using a routing protocol because the physical interface always uses its primary address when sending out packets.

Here is an example of a configuration using the old way. Notice the `dialer map` statements. This enabled an administrator to tell the router which number to dial based on the destination IP address in packets it received on one of the router's incoming interfaces. See for yourself:

```
hostname R1
!
interface Serial 0/0:23
 encapsulation ppp
 ip address 192.168.250.1 255.255.255.0
 ip address 192.168.251.1 255.255.255.0 secondary
 dialer map ip 192.168.250.2 name R2 555-1212
 dialer map ip 192.168.251.2 name R3 555-1234
router ospf 100
 network 192.168.250.1 0.0.0.0 area 0
 network 192.168.251.1 0.0.0.0 area 0
!
end

hostname R2
!
interface BRI0
 ip address 192.168.250.2 255.255.255.0
 encapsulation ppp
 isdn spid1 91955512120100 5551212
 isdn spid2 91955512130100 5551213
 dialer map ip 192.168.250.1 name R1 5551900
```

```
router ospf 100
 network 192.168.250.2 0.0.0.0 area 0
!
end

hostname R3
!
interface BRI0
 ip address 192.168.251.2 255.255.255.0
 encapsulation ppp
 isdn spid1 91955512230100 5551234
 isdn spid2 91955512350100 5551235
 dialer map ip 192.168.251.1 name R1 5551900
router ospf 100
 network 192.168.251.2 0.0.0.0 area 0
!
end
```

You need to look at several points in this configuration. Host R1 is using a PRI ISDN interface on Serial 0/0. The `secondary` command enables you to have a second route on the same interface. We cover the `Serial 0/0:23` command later in the chapter, but a quick explanation is that for ISDN, the D channel time slot, which is the :23 channel for channelized T-1. And last, we are using the dialer map to bind an IP address to a ISDN DN.

In these router configurations, both routers R2 and R3 will call into R1, but Open Shortest Path First OSPF will work only between R1 and R2, because R2 uses the primary address on R1 whereas R3 uses the secondary. This source IP address issue can be a real problem, but only if you are not aware of it. What is the solution to the primary IP address issue? Dialer interfaces.

Using a Dialer Interface

Using a dialer interface solves the primary IP address/secondary IP address problem because each interface can be assigned its own primary address. The `dialer map` command does not have to be used because each interface has its own IP address and dial number configured by using the `dialer string` command.

A virtual interface must be associated with a dialer pool. The dialer pool is a group of one or more physical interfaces in charge of placing calls. Here is an example of a configuration using dialer interfaces:

```
hostname R1
!
isdn switch-type basic-5ess
!
```

```
interface Ethernet0
 ip address 192.168.1.1 255.255.255.0
!
interface Serial0/0:23
 no ip address
 encapsulation ppp
 dialer pool-member 1 priority 100
!
interface Dialer1
 ip address 192.168.250.1 255.255.255.0
 encapsulation ppp
 dialer remote-name R2
 dialer idle-timeout 300
 dialer string 5551212
 dialer load-threshold 50 either
 dialer pool 1
 dialer-group 1
!
interface Dialer2
 ip address 192.168.251.1 255.255.255.0
 encapsulation ppp
 dialer remote-name R3
 dialer string 5551234
 dialer load-threshold 150 either
 dialer pool 1
 dialer-group 1
!
router ospf 100
 network 192.168.250.1 0.0.0.0 area 0
 network 192.168.251.1 0.0.0.0 area 0
!
dialer-list 1 protocol ip permit
!
end
```

Notice how the interface Dialer1 creates a virtual interface with the correct configuration—
ip address, encapsulation, and dialer string—the same items that were bound to the physical interface BRI0 in the first example. The interface Dialer carries a 1 as its index. The virtual Dialer
interface is then bound to a dialer string that references the ISDN DN. The dialer pool 1 is then
bound to the virtual Dialer to point to the physical interface that will be carrying out the dialing. The
index of the dialer pool 1 maps to the dialer pool-member 1—the physical interface of Serial 0/0.

The last configuration command worthy of noting is the `dialer-list 1 protocol ip permit`, which tells the router what traffic is interesting and to bring the connection up when interesting traffic is identified.

OSPF will work properly because the source address on both sides of the link matches the network statement. The source address of a packet originating at a router is the primary address on the outgoing interface. Dialer interfaces are easy to configure. For example:

```
router#config t
router(config)#interface dialer 2
router(config-if)#
```

Now the network administrator can create the configuration as you would under a physical interface. The physical PRI interface, Serial0/0:23, is designated as a member of a dialer pool using the `dialer pool-member` command.

Authentication

If you are using PPP encapsulation, you can also use authentication. *Authentication* enables you to verify who is connected to a service. Note that this is optional and not required in any ISDN configurations.

The two authentication choices are *Password Authentication Protocol (PAP)* and *Challenge Handshake Authentication Protocol (CHAP* CHAP is preferred over PAP because of its superior security features. CHAP and PAP are covered in greater detail in Chapter 3 of this book.

Password Authentication Protocol (PAP)

PAP uses a two-way handshake to establish the identity of the remote peer. This simple authentication protocol does not encrypt the username or password, making it somewhat insecure and subject to a playback attack. Because of this security problem, it is recommended that you use CHAP authentication instead.

After the PPP link establishment, the optional Authentication-Protocol Configuration Option packet is sent. An Authentication-Protocol Configuration Option packet for PAP has three fields: Type, Length, and Authentication-Protocol. The Type field is 8 bits long with a value of 3, Length is 8 bits long with a value of 4, and Authentication-Protocol is 16 bits long with a value of c023.

PAP Packets

A PAP packet has four fields carried one at a time in the PPP Information field: Code, Identifier, Length, and Data. The Code field is 8 bits long and can have one of three values:

- Authenticate-Authenticate-Ack
- Authenticate-Nak

The Identifier field is also 8 bits long and is used for matching authentication requests and replies. It changes every time an Authenticate-Request is sent. Length is a 16-bit field indicating the packet's length. The Data field varies in length and format, depending on the packet type: Request, Ack, or Nak.

Authenticate-Request Packets

An Authenticate-Request packet is sent by the calling party to the called party. The Data field has four fields:

Peer-ID Length   Eight bits long; indicates the length of the Peer-ID.

Peer-ID   Zero or more octets long; contains the username.

Passwd-Length   Eight bits long; indicates the length of the password.

Password   Zero or more octets long; contains the plain-text password.

The called end will respond with either an Authenticate-Ack (Type 2) or Authenticate-Nak (Type 3) packet. Both packets have two fields as data. One is Msg-Length (8 bits), and the other is Message (one or more octets).

The following output is from a debug ppp authentication command on a router that is authenticating by using PAP with PPP.

```
BRO/0:1 PPP: Phase is AUTHENTICATING, by the peer
BRO/0:1 PAP: O AUTH-REQ id 3 len 14 from "r3"
BRO/0:1 PAP: I AUTH-ACK id 3 len 5
```

You can follow this debug PPP authentication router output by referring to Figure 5.7.

FIGURE 5.7   PAP authentication

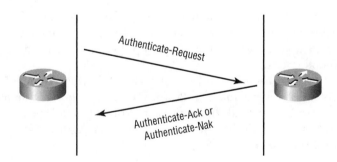

Configuring PAP authentication is a pretty straightforward process. Here is an example:

```
Router#config t
Router(config)#username todd password cisco
Router(config)#interface bri0
Router(config-if)#encapsulation ppp
```

```
Router(config-if)#ppp authentication pap
Router(config-if)#^Z
Router#
```

Challenge Handshake Authentication Protocol (CHAP)

CHAP is used to periodically verify the identity of the remote peer by using a three-way handshake. Normally this occurs immediately after the initial link establishment and before proceeding to the Network Layer phase. CHAP can also send a new challenge periodically to verify the remote node. All PPP authentications are optional. Both ends must be configured with the same authentication type if you are using authentication.

One CHAP packet is encapsulated in the Information field of a PPP packet, with the Type field set to 3, the Length field to 5, the Authentication-Protocol field to c223, and the algorithm to 5 (MD5). A CHAP Challenge packet is illustrated in Figure 5.8.

FIGURE 5.8   CHAP Challenge packet

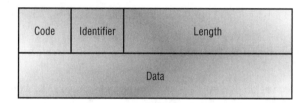

A CHAP packet consists of an 8-bit Code field, an 8-bit Identifier field, a 16-bit Length field, and a variable-length Data field. The Code field identifies the type of CHAP packet; there are four type options:

- Challenge
- Response
- Success
- Failure

The *Identifier* field contains an incrementally changing identifier, which the remote end copies into the response packet. Frequently changing the identifier provides protection against a playback attack. The *Length* field is 16 bits long and indicates the length of the CHAP packet including the Code, Identifier, Length, and Data fields. Octets outside the range will be ignored. The *Data* field is zero or more octets and is determined by the Code field.

Configuring CHAP authentication is a pretty straightforward process. Here is an example:

```
Router#config t
Router(config)#username todd password cisco
Router(config)#interface bri0
Router(config-if)#encapsulation ppp
```

```
Router(config-if)#ppp authentication chap
Router(config-if)#^Z
Router#
```

The username *name* password *password* command is used to configure authentication between two routers. The username is the hostname of the router you want to connect to. The passwords must be the same on each side for this to work. For example, if you had a corporate router with a hostname of Acmecorporate and a remote router with a hostname of Acmeremote, the configuration of the corporate router would look like this:

```
Acmecorporate(config)#username Acmeremote password sameone
```

The remote router's configuration would be this:

```
Acmeremote(config)#username Acmecorporate password sameone
```

The CHAP Authentication Process

The authentication process between two routers occurs as follows:

1. Challenger sends a Challenge (Type 1) packet to the remote end.
2. The remote end copies the identifier into a new packet and into a Response (Type 2) packet along with the hashed secret. The secret (the password) isn't transmitted, only the hashed value.
3. The Challenger receives the Response packet and checks the hashed secret against its hashed secret. If they match, it sends a Success (Type 3) packet back. Otherwise it'll send a Failure (Type 4) packet back.

Challenge and Response packets have the following fields:

Code   Eight bits; value of 1 for Challenge, or 2 for Response.

Identifier   Eight bits; must be changed every time a challenge is sent.

Value-Size   Eight bits; indicates the length of the Value field.

Value   Variable (8-bit minimum). The field is quite different depending on a Challenge or Response. The Challenge value contains the challenge and is a variable stream of octets. The Challenge value *must* be changed each time a Challenge is sent. The length of the Challenge value depends on the method used to generate the octets and is independent of the hash algorithm used.

The Response value is the one-way hashed response calculated over a stream of octets consisting of the Identifier, followed by (concatenated with) the "secret," followed by (concatenated with) the Challenge value. The length of the Response value depends on the hash algorithm used (16 octets for MD5).

Name   Variable (8-bit minimum); identifies the system transmitting the packet.

Success (3) and Failure (4) packets have these fields: CodeIdentifier (which is copied from Response), Length, and Message. The Message field is one or more octets long and contains information that is readable by humans. By using the debug ppp authentication command, you can see each step that is taken with the CHAP Challenge and Response fields.

```
BRO:1 PPP: Treating connection as a callout
BRO:1 PPP: Phase is AUTHENTICATING, by both
BRO:1 CHAP: O CHALLENGE id 1 len 23 from "r2"
BRO:1 CHAP: I CHALLENGE id 1 len 23 from "r3"
BRO:1 CHAP: O RESPONSE id 1 len 23 from "r2"
BRO:1 CHAP: I SUCCESS id 1 len 4
BRO:1 CHAP: I RESPONSE id 1 len 23 from "r3"
BRO:1 CHAP: O SUCCESS id 1 len 4
```

Figure 5.9 shows the CHAP authentication process.

FIGURE 5.9   CHAP authentication

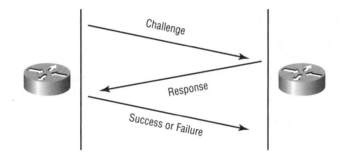

Dial-on-Demand Routing (DDR)

Dial-on-demand routing (DDR) enables two Cisco routers to use a dial-up connection on an as-needed basis and is usually used as a backup solution in case of WAN circuit failure. DDR is used only for low-volume, periodic network connections using either a PSTNasynchronous or ISDN link. This was designed to reduce WAN costs if you have to pay on a per-minute or per-packet basis.

Other terms you will undoubtedly run into are *Legacy DDR Spoke configuration* and *Legacy DDR Hub configuration*. The terms are pretty simple to understand. A spoke interface is any interface that calls or receives calls from exactly one other router. A hub, on the other hand, calls or receives calls from more than one other router. Both configurations are similar in theory except for the hub being configured to call multiple locations.

DDR works when a packet received on an interface meets the requirements of an administrator-defined access list, which defines interesting traffic. The following five steps give a basic description of how DDR works when an interesting packet is received in a router interface:

1. Route to the destination network is determined.
2. Interesting packets dictate a DDR call.
3. Dialer information is looked up.
4. Call is placed.
5. Connection is established.
6. Traffic is transmitted.
7. Call is terminated when no more interesting traffic is being transmitted over a link and the idle-timeout period ends.

Configuring DDR

To configure legacy DDR, you need to perform three tasks:

1. Define static routes, which define how to get to the remote networks and which interface to use to get there.
2. Specify the traffic that is considered interesting to the router.
3. Configure the dialer information that will be used to dial the interface to get to the remote network.

Configuring the Static Routes

To forward traffic across the ISDN link, you configure static routes in each of the routers. The suggested routing method is static routes. Keep the following in mind when creating static routes:

- All participating routers must have static routes defining all routes of known networks.
- Default routing can be used if the network is a stub network.

   An example of static routing with ISDN follows:

```
RouterA(config)#ip route 172.16.50.0 255.255.255.0 172.16.60.2
RouterA(config)#ip route 172.16.60.2 255.255.255.255 bri0
```

What this does is tell the router how to get to network 172.16.50.0, which is through 172.16.60.2. The second line tells the router how to get to host address 172.16.60.2 send traffic out the BRI0 interface.

Specifying Interesting Traffic

After setting the route tables in each router, you need to configure the router to determine what brings up the ISDN line. An administrator uses the dialer-list global configuration command to define what is interesting traffic.

The command to configure all IP traffic as interesting is shown next:

```
804A(config)#dialer-list 1 protocol ip permit
804A(config)#interface bri0
804A(config-if)#dialer-group 1
```

The `dialer-group` command associates a dialer-list to the BRI interface. Extended access lists can be used with the `dialer-list` command to define exactly which traffic is interesting. We'll cover that in a minute.

Configuring the Dialer Information

There are five steps in the configuration of dialer information:

1. Choose the interface.

2. Set the IP address.

3. Configure the encapsulation type.

4. Link interesting traffic to the interface.

5. Configure the number or numbers to dial.

Here is an example of how to configure the five steps:

```
804A#config t
804A(config)#interface bri0
804A(config-if)#ip address 172.16.60.1 255.255.255.0
804A(config-if)#no shutdown
804A(config-if)#encapsulation ppp
804A(config-if)#dialer-group 1
804A(config-if)#dialer string 8358662
```

Instead of the `dialer string` command, you can use a dialer map, which provides more security.

```
804A(config-if)#dialer map ip 172.16.60.2 name 804B 8358662
```

The `dialer map` command is used to configure the IP address of the next hop router, the name of the remote router for authentication, and the number to dial to get there. The name is usually the hostname of the remote router but must be the name used by the remote router to identify itself.

Take a look at the following configuration of an 804 router:

```
804B#show run
Building configuration...
Current configuration:
!
version 12.0
```

```
no service pad
service timestamps debug uptime
service timestamps log uptime
no service password-encryption
!
hostname 804B
!
ip subnet-zero
!
isdn switch-type basic-ni
!
interface Ethernet0
 ip address 172.16.50.10 255.255.255.0
 no ip directed-broadcast
!
interface BRI0
 ip address 172.16.60.2 255.255.255.0
 no ip directed-broadcast
 encapsulation ppp
 dialer idle-timeout 300
 dialer string 8358661
 dialer load-threshold 2 either
 dialer-group 1
 isdn switch-type basic-ni
 isdn spid1 0835866201 8358662
 isdn spid2 0835866401 8358664
 dialer hold-queue 75
 ppp multilink
!
ip classless
ip route 172.16.30.0 255.255.255.0 172.16.60.1
ip route 172.16.60.1 255.255.255.255 BRI0
!
dialer-list 1 protocol ip permit
!
```

The BRI interface is running the PPP encapsulation and has a timeout value of 300 seconds, which is discussed in the next section. The load-threshold command makes both BRI channels come up immediately (if you are paying for both, you want them both up all the time) and is used with multilink, which we discuss later in this section. The one thing you should really notice is the number in the `dialer-group 1` command. That number must match the number in the `dialer-list` command, which is used to define what is interesting traffic. The `dialer hold-queue 75` command tells the router that when it receives an interesting packet, it should queue up to 75 packets while it is waiting for the BRI to come up. If more than 75 packets are queued before the link comes up, the packets beyond the 75 will be dropped.

Using Optional Commands

You should configure two other commands on your BRI interface: `dialer load-threshold` and `dialer idle-timeout`. The `dialer load-threshold` command is used in conjunction with the `ppp multilink` command for multilink PPP (MPPP).

The `dialer load-threshold` command tells the BRI interface when to bring up the second B channel. The value specified is from 1–255, where 255 tells the BRI to bring up the second B channel only when the first channel is 100 percent loaded. The second option for that command is `in`, `out`, or `either`. This calculates the actual load on the interface either on outbound traffic, inbound traffic, or either inbound or outbound traffic. The default is outbound.

The `dialer idle-timeout` command specifies the number of seconds to wait for interesting traffic before a call is disconnected. The default is 120 seconds.

```
RouterA(config-if)#dialer load-threshold 127 either
RouterA(config-if)#dialer idle-timeout 180
```

The `dialer load-threshold 127` tells the BRI interface to bring up the second B channel if either the inbound or outbound traffic load is 50 percent. The `dialer idle-timeout 180` changes the default disconnect time from 120 to 180 seconds.

MPPP allows load balancing between two or more B channels on a BRI or PRI interface. It is non-vendor-specific and provides packet fragmentation and reassembly, along with sequencing and load calculating. Cisco's MPPP is based on RFC 1990, which is referred to as PPP Multilink Protocol (MP). The configuration would then look like this:

```
RouterA(config)#int BRI0
RouterA(config-if)#dialer load-threshold 127 either
RouterA(config-if)#dialer idle-timeout 180
RouterA(config-if)#ppp multilink
```

Not a tough configuration, but you should use it nonetheless. The `ppp multilink` command will fragment packets and send them over both lines, which provides a load balancing effect on the data being sent over the link. You can verify that the Multilink Protocol is working by using the `show ppp multilink` command.

Using DDR with Access Lists

You can use access lists to be more specific about what is interesting traffic. In the preceding examples, we set the dialer list to allow any IP traffic to bring up the line and keep it up. That is great if you are testing, but it can defeat the purpose of why you use a DDR line in the first place. You can use extended access lists to set the restriction, for example, to only e-mail or Telnet.

Here is an example of how you define the dialer list to use an extended access list:

```
804A(config)#dialer-list 1 protocol ip list 110
804A(config)#access-list 110 permit tcp any any eq smtp
804A(config)#access-list 110 permit tcp any any eq telnet
804A(config)#int bri0
804A(config-if)#dialer-group 1
```

In the previous example, you configure the `dialer-list` command to look at an IP extended access list. This doesn't have to be IP; it can be used with any protocol. Create your dialer list and then apply it to the BRI interface with the `dialer-group` command.

Verifying the ISDN Operation

The following commands can be used to verify legacy DDR and ISDN:

ping **and** *telnet*   These are great IP tools for any network. However, your interesting traffic must dictate that `ping` and `telnet` are acceptable as interesting traffic to bring up a link. After a link is up, you can ping or Telnet to your remote router regardless of your interesting traffic lists.

show dialer   This gives good diagnostic information about your dialer and shows the number of times the dialer string has been successfully connected, the idle-timeout values of each B channel, the length of the call, and the name of the router to which the interface is connected.

show isdn active   This shows the number called and whether a call is in progress.

show isdn status   A good command to use before you try to dial, this shows whether your SPIDs are valid and whether you are connected and communicating with Layers 1 through 3 to the provider's switch.

show ip route   A popular Cisco diagnostics command, this shows all routes that the router currently knows about.

debug isdn q921   This is used to see Layer 2 information only between the router and the service provider's ISDN switch.

debug isdn q931   This is like `debug isdn q921` but is used to see Layer 3 information, including call setup and teardown between the access-server and the provider's ISDN switch.

debug dialer   This gives you call setup and teardown activity from the dialer's standpoint.

isdn disconnect interface bri0   This clears the interface and drops the current connection if one exists. Performing a shutdown on the interface can give you the same results.

Dial Backup

Dial backup, dial-on-demand routing (DDR), and Bandwidth on Demand (BoD) all use the same basic interface configuration. Dial backup and BoD use the interface backup commands to determine if, when, and how long an interface is to be activated. DDR is used for a temporary dial-up connection from a branch or home office.

Time to do some design work: Using Figure 5.10, you'll design and configure both legacy and dialer interfaces. For the sake of this project, you'll assign some addresses to the interfaces on R2 and R3 in the figure. Add any additional configuration required to complete the project. The following list of addresses will give you a starting point. Here is a list of the addresses you'll use:

R2 - To0   172.16.2.0/24

R3 - E0/0   192.168.252.0/24

ISDN cloud   192.168.254.0/24

Frame cloud   192.168.123.0/24

FIGURE 5.10   Network diagram

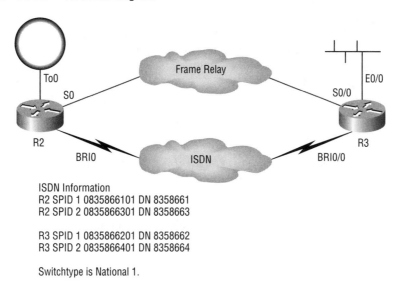

ISDN Information
R2 SPID 1 0835866101 DN 8358661
R2 SPID 2 0835866301 DN 8358663

R3 SPID 1 0835866201 DN 8358662
R3 SPID 2 0835866401 DN 8358664

Switchtype is National 1.

Setting Up Dial Backup

Your first project is setting up dial backup on the routers. You'll keep this fairly basic. R2 will call R3 when serial 0.202 goes down. The interesting traffic you'll designate is all IP. You will not use a routing protocol, so you'll have to use a floating static route. Typically, floating static routes are used with DDR because they can be set to a higher administrative distance than the routing protocol being used. This enables the router to automatically bring up the BRI line if the main serial line were to drop.

In the following configuration, you'll issue a show isdn status command on Router 2 to verify that the interface configuration is working correctly.

```
r2#show isdn status
The current ISDN Switchtype = basic-ni
ISDN BRI0 interface
    Layer 1 Status:
        ACTIVE
    Layer 2 Status:
        TEI = 100, State = MULTIPLE_FRAME_ESTABLISHED
        TEI = 101, State = MULTIPLE_FRAME_ESTABLISHED
    Spid Status:
        TEI 100, ces = 1, state = 5(init)
            spid1 configured, spid1 sent, spid1 valid
            Endpoint ID Info: epsf = 0, usid = 1, tid = 1
        TEI 101, ces = 2, state = 5(init)
            spid2 configured, spid2 sent, spid2 valid
            Endpoint ID Info: epsf = 0, usid = 3, tid = 1
    Layer 3 Status:
        0 Active Layer 3 Call(s)
    Activated dsl 0 CCBs = 1
        CCB: callid=0x0, sapi=0, ces=1, B-chan=0
    Total Allocated ISDN CCBs = 1
```

As you can see, Layers 1 and 2 are up, you are using TEI 100 and 101, and the SPIDs and DNs are valid. This is one of the most important commands you can use. If the SPIDs are invalid or the configuration is wrong, you will see it in the show isdn status command.

Now you'll issue the backup interface bri0 under serial 0.202. This tells the interface s0.202 to use interface BRI0 if the serial interface loses DCD (Data Carrier Detect), which means the link is down.

```
r2(config)#interface serial0.202
r2(config-subif)#backup interface bri0
r2(config-subif)#
%ISDN-6-LAYER2DOWN: Layer 2 for Interface BRI0, TEI 100 changed to down
%ISDN-6-LAYER2DOWN: Layer 2 for Interface BRI0, TEI 101 changed to down
%LINK-5-CHANGED: Interface BRI0, changed state to standby mode
```

```
%LINK-3-UPDOWN: Interface BRI0:1, changed state to down
%LINK-3-UPDOWN: Interface BRI0:2, changed state to down
```

As you can see, it places the main interface in Standby mode, effectively turning the interface down. This deactivates Layer 1 on the BRI0 interface. This can be verified by issuing a show ISDN status command at the router prompt.

r2#**show ISDN status**

```
The current ISDN Switchtype = basic-ni
ISDN BRI0 interface
    Layer 1 Status:
        DEACTIVATED
    Layer 2 Status:
        Layer 2 NOT Activated
    Spid Status:
        TEI Not Assigned,ces = 1, state = 1(terminal
        down)
            spid1 configured,spid1 NOT sent,spid1 NOT
            valid
        TEI Not Assigned,ces = 2, state = 1(terminal
        down)
            spid2 configured,spid2 NOT sent,spid2 NOT
            valid
    Layer 3 Status:
        0 Active Layer 3 Call(s)
    Activated dsl 0 CCBs = 0
    Total Allocated ISDN CCBs = 0
```

Using the physical BRI interface as a backup can cause problems because the BRI interface appears to be disconnected to the service provider. There is no way to verify that the ISDN BRI circuit is in proper working order unless you remove it as a backup interface. This is why it is best to use a dialer interface as the backup and not the physical ISDN BRI interface, which is illustrated later in the chapter.

Testing the Backup

After the configuration, it is important to test your backup link. You don't want to wait for an actual outage before discovering you have made a configuration mistake. You'll test the backup by disabling the connected serial interface on R2.

When the test is performed, it takes 11 seconds for the backup line to come out of Standby mode and another 4 seconds for Layers 1 and 2 to come up. The following router output shows this. Why would using a dialer interface save you 4 seconds in this scenario?

```
00:46:22: %LINEPROTO-5-UPDOWN: Line protocol on Interface Serial0, _ changed
    state to down
00:46:23: %LINK-3-UPDOWN: Interface Serial0, changed state to down
00:46:23: %FR-5-DLCICHANGE: Interface Serial0 - DLCI 202 state changed_ to
    DELETED
00:46:23: %FR-5-DLCICHANGE: Interface Serial0 - DLCI 100 state changed _to
    DELETED
00:46:23: %FR-5-DLCICHANGE: Interface Serial0 - DLCI 200 state changed _to
    DELETED
00:46:23: %LINEPROTO-5-UPDOWN: Line protocol on Interface Serial0.202, _ changed
    state to down
00:46:34: %LINK-3-UPDOWN: Interface BRI0:1, changed state to down
00:46:34: %LINK-3-UPDOWN: Interface BRI0:2, changed state to down
00:46:34: %LINK-3-UPDOWN: Interface BRI0, changed state to up
00:46:38: %ISDN-6-LAYER2UP: Layer 2 for Interface BR0, TEI 107 changed to up
00:46:38: %ISDN-6-LAYER2UP: Layer 2 for Interface BR0, TEI 108 changed to up
00:46:59: %LINK-3-UPDOWN: Interface BRI0:1, changed state to up
00:47:00: %LINEPROTO-5-UPDOWN: Line protocol on Interface BRI0:1, _ changed
    state to up
00:47:06: %ISDN-6-CONNECT: Interface BRI0:1 is now connected to 8358662
00:47:23: %LINEPROTO-5-UPDOWN: Line protocol on Interface Serial0, _ changed
    state to up
00:47:24: %LINK-3-UPDOWN: Interface Serial0, changed state to up
00:47:24: %FR-5-DLCICHANGE: Interface Serial0 - DLCI 202 state changed_ to
    ACTIVE
00:47:24: %LINEPROTO-5-UPDOWN: Line protocol on Interface Serial0.202_, changed
    state to up
00:48:24: %LINK-3-UPDOWN: Interface BRI0:1, changed state to down
00:48:24: %ISDN-6-DISCONNECT: Interface BRI0:1  disconnected from_ unknown, call
    lasted 85 seconds
00:48:24: %ISDN-6-LAYER2DOWN: Layer 2 for Interface BRI0, TEI 107_ changed to
    down
00:48:24: %ISDN-6-LAYER2DOWN: Layer 2 for Interface BRI0, TEI 108_ changed to
    down
00:48:24: %LINK-5-CHANGED: Interface BRI0, changed state to standby mode
00:48:24: %LINK-3-UPDOWN: Interface BRI0:1, changed state to down
00:48:24: %LINK-3-UPDOWN: Interface BRI0:2, changed state to down
00:48:25: %LINEPROTO-5-UPDOWN: Line protocol on Interface BRI0:1, _ changed
    state to down
```

You should also note in the preceding router output that the backup line dropped one minute after the primary link came up. Changing the delay between primary failure and activation of the backup line plus delay between primary recovery and deactivation of the backup line can be modified by using the backup delay 10 60 command. The first number (10) is how many seconds to wait before activating the backup interface, and the second number (60) is how many seconds to stay up once the primary line recovers.

As we stated earlier, it is best to use a *dialer profile,* or dialer interface, as the backup interface, so we will show you how this is done. Setting up a dialer profile requires two steps: configuring the primary interface and configuring the dialer interface. The primary interface needs only some basic information; for example, take a look at this configuration:

```
interface BRIO
 no ip address
 encapsulation ppp
 isdn spid1 0835866101 8358661
 isdn spid2 0835866301 8358663
 dialer pool-member 1
!
```

Basically, all we did was set up ISDN Layers 1 and 2, enable PPP encapsulation, and assign this interface to dialer pool 1—pretty simple so far.

The next step involves the dialer interface. A dialer interface is *virtual* meaning it is not a physical interface, and you add it by using the global command interface dialer 1. The connection-specific configuration commands are placed under this interface, including creation of the dialer pool, phone number to dial, remote device name, interesting traffic, authentication, and IP address information. Again, it's not that difficult. Take a look at this configuration:

```
interface Dialer1
 ip address 192.168.254.2 255.255.255.0
 encapsulation ppp
 dialer remote-name r3
 dialer string 8358662
 dialer pool 1
 dialer-group 1
 ppp authentication chap callin
```

Note that the callin option on the ppp authentication command indicates authentication on incoming (received) calls only.

You will notice that the dialer interface goes into Standby but the BRI interface doesn't. You can verify this by using the show ISDN status command:

```
r2#show isdn status
The current ISDN Switchtype = basic-ni
```

```
ISDN BRI0 interface
    Layer 1 Status:
        ACTIVE
    Layer 2 Status:
        TEI = 109, State = MULTIPLE_FRAME_ESTABLISHED
        TEI = 110, State = MULTIPLE_FRAME_ESTABLISHED
    Spid Status:
        TEI 109, ces = 1, state = 5(init)
            spid1 configured, spid1 sent, spid1 valid
            Endpoint ID Info: epsf = 0, usid = 1, tid = 1
        TEI 110, ces = 2, state = 5(init)
            spid2 configured, spid2 sent, spid2 valid
            Endpoint ID Info: epsf = 0, usid = 3, tid = 1
    Layer 3 Status:
        0 Active Layer 3 Call(s)
    Activated dsl 0 CCBs = 1
        CCB: callid=0x0, sapi=0, ces=1, B-chan=0
    Total Allocated ISDN CCBs = 1
```

The BRI interface is still active and not in Standby. This makes it easy to tell when there is a problem with the BRI circuit.

We will introduce a useful diagnostic command here: show dialer. This output gives you a lot of information, such as dial reason (what was the source and destination address of the packet that caused the call to be placed), whom you called or who called you, how long the interface has been up, how long it has been since it has seen interesting traffic, and how much more time remains until it hangs up.

```
r2#show dialer

BRI0 - dialer type = ISDN

Dial String      Successes    Failures     Last called    Last status
0 incoming call(s) have been screened.

BRI0:1 - dialer type = ISDN
Idle timer (120 secs), Fast idle timer (20 secs)
Wait for carrier (30 secs), Re-enable (15 secs)
Dialer state is data link layer up
Dial reason: ip (s=192.168.254.2, d=192.168.252.3)
Interface bound to profile Dialer1
Time until disconnect 105 secs
Current call connected 00:00:16
```

```
Connected to 8358662

Dialer1 - dialer type = DIALER PROFILE
Idle timer (120 secs), Fast idle timer (20 secs)
Wait for carrier (30 secs), Re-enable (15 secs)
Dialer state is data link layer up

Dial String  Successes Failures Last called  Last status
8358662      18        0        00:00:19     successful
```

The final configuration is shown next. R2 is set up to use a dialer interface; R3 is using the legacy configuration.

```
r2#show run
Building configuration...

Current configuration:
!
version 12.0
service timestamps log uptime
no service password-encryption
no service udp-small-servers
no service tcp-small-servers
!
hostname r2
!
enable password cisco
!
username r3 password 0 cisco
isdn switch-type basic-ni
!
interface Serial0
 no ip address
 encapsulation frame-relay
 no fair-queue
!
interface Serial0.202 point-to-point
 backup delay 10 60
 backup interface Dialer1
 ip address 172.16.34.2 255.255.255.0
 frame-relay interface-dlci 202
!
```

```
interface BRI0
 no ip address
 encapsulation ppp
 isdn switch-type basic-ni
 isdn spid1 0835866101 8358661
 isdn spid2 0835866301 8358663
 dialer pool-member 1
!
interface Dialer1
 ip address 192.168.254.2 255.255.255.0
 encapsulation ppp
 dialer remote-name r3
 dialer string 8358662
 dialer pool 1
 dialer-group 1
 ppp authentication chap
!
ip classless
ip route 0.0.0.0 0.0.0.0 172.16.34.3
ip route 0.0.0.0 0.0.0.0 192.168.254.3 210
!
dialer-list 1 protocol ip permit
!
end

r2#

r3#show run
Building configuration...

Current configuration:
!
version 12.0
service timestamps debug uptime
service timestamps log uptime
no service password-encryption
!
hostname r3
!
enable password cisco
!
```

```
username r2 password 0 cisco
ip subnet-zero
!
isdn switch-type basic-ni
!
interface FastEthernet0/0
 ip address 192.168.252.3 255.255.255.255
 no ip directed-broadcast
!
interface Serial0/0
 no ip address
 no ip directed-broadcast
 encapsulation frame-relay
 no ip mroute-cache
 frame-relay lmi-type cisco
!
interface Serial0/0.203 point-to-point
 ip address 172.16.34.3 255.255.255.0
 no ip directed-broadcast
 frame-relay interface-dlci 203
!
interface BRI0/0
 ip address 192.168.254.3 255.255.255.0
 no ip directed-broadcast
 encapsulation ppp
 dialer map ip 192.168.254.2 8358661
 dialer-group 1
 isdn switch-type basic-ni
 isdn spid1 0835866201 8358662
 isdn spid2 0835866401 8358664
 ppp authentication chap
 dialer hold-queue 75
!
ip classless
ip route 172.16.2.0 255.255.255.0 172.16.34.2
ip route 172.16.2.0 255.255.255.0 192.168.254.2 210
!
dialer-list 1 protocol ip permit
!
end
```

As you can see, the configuration is not that complex. Having a good working knowledge of this will help you solve many dial backup scenarios. Of course, you can make this as complex as you'd like; we kept this example fairly simple as an illustration.

The command `dialer-list` creates the interesting traffic. The command `dialer-group` assigns the dialer list to an interface. The numbers must match. In the previous example, both the dialer list and the dialer group are 1. The `dialer hold-queue` command creates a buffer for incoming interesting traffic that is waiting for the BRI to be dialed. The 75 means is that *if 75 interesting* packets arrive on queue before the interface comes up, the 76th and subsequent will be dropped until the line comes up and the queue gets some relief.

Bandwidth on Demand

What do you do if you have more traffic than bandwidth? Wouldn't it be great if you could pull your magic router wand out and make the traffic go faster? You can approximate this magic by using Bandwidth on Demand.

Bandwidth on Demand (BoD) is an interface-only command, meaning you cannot apply it to a subinterface. Here is the syntax to assign a backup load to an interface: `backup load {`*enable-threshold*` | never} {`*disable-load*` | never}`. The enable threshold load is the percentage of interface load where you want the additional bandwidth dialed up. The disable load is the percentage of interface load where you want the extra bandwidth dropped. At what point is the circuit congested enough to need extra bandwidth? Some people say 75 percent; yet others say queuing is needed. You will probably have to figure this out based on corporate policy, cost, sensitivity to slow responsiveness, and so on. Because BoD is a dial-up feature, you might incur additional long-distance costs, so be careful about setting your thresholds.

Configuring BoD is almost the same as configuring dial backup, except you're replacing the amount of backup delay with the amount of backup threshold. Here is an example:

```
Router#config t
Enter configuration commands, one per line.   End with CNTL/Z.
Router(config)#interface serial0
Router(config-if)#backup interface BRI0
```

This configuration sets the interface serial 0 to use interface BRI0 as a backup as the main interface goes down. The following configuration shows how to configure the backup delay and the backup load:

```
Router(config-if)#backup ?
  delay      Delays before backup line up or down transitions
  interface  Configure an interface as a backup
  load       Load thresholds for line up or down transitions
```

```
Router(config-if)#backup delay ?
  <0-4294967294>   Seconds
  never            Never activate the backup line

Router(config-if)#backup delay 10 ?
  <0-4294967294>   Seconds
  never            Never deactivate the backup line

Router(config-if)#backup delay 10 60
```

The previous configuration sets the backup delay to 10 seconds and 60 seconds. This means that the backup interface will not dial until serial 0 is down for 10 seconds, and it will drop the link after the serial link is back up for 60 seconds. The backup load command syntax is shown next:

```
Router(config-if)#backup load ?
  <0-100>   Percentage
  never     Never activate the backup line

Router(config-if)#backup load 75 ?
  <0-100>   Percentage
  never     Never deactivate the backup line

Router(config-if)#backup load 75 35
Router(config-if)#^Z
Router#
```

This command sets the router to dial the ISDN BRI0 interface if the bandwidth reaches a maximum of 75 percent and then to drop the link after the bandwidth is back at 35 percent. The interface configuration is shown next:

```
Router#show run
[output cut]
interface Serial0
 backup delay 10 60
 backup interface BRI0
 backup load 75 35
 ip address 10.53.69.69 255.255.255.0
 no ip directed-broadcast
--More-
```

Channelized T-1/E-1 (PRI)

Large businesses typically use point-to-point connections with DSU/CSUs to connect two sites. In turn, these are connected to low- and high-speed serial interfaces on routers—usually Cisco routers. The router backplane and the number of interfaces the router can handle determine how well it supports WAN connections. The Cisco 7000 series of routers supports the Fast Serial Interface Processor (FSIP), which provides either four or eight serial ports, permitting the four or eight point-to-point connections to remote offices. Other Cisco routers support the Multichannel Interface Processor (MIP), which furnishes support for two full T-1/E-1 ports in the 7000 series and one port in the 4000 series

ISDN T-1s, which are called Primary Rate Interfaces (PRIs), run at 1.544Mbps/ These use 24 channels in contrast to E-1s, which use 31 channels and run at 2.048Mbps. E-1 is mainly used in Europe, and both T-1 and E-1 are considered wide-area digital transmission schemes.

Each port in the MIP can support 24 DS0 channels of 64Kbps each when using a T-1 interface, and 31 DS0 channels when using an E-1 interface. The MIP refers to each serial interface as a channel-group; this enables each channel or DS0 to be configured individually. Each channel has the same characteristics and options as regular serial interfaces.

Configuring ISDN PRI

The serial links connect into either a private data network or a service provider's network. Both the line encoding and the framing must match the service provider's equipment. To configure a PRI on a serial link, you must supply the following information:

Channel type   Either T-1 or E-1.

Frame type   When using a T-1, this can be either D4, sometimes referred to as Super Frame, or Extended Super Frame (ESF). D4 is the original T-1 frame format and comprises one framing bit and a DS0 time slot for each channel on the line. ESF comprises 24 D4 frames. As each D4 frame contains a framing bit, an ESF has 24 framing bits that it uses for synchronization (6 bits), error checking (6-bit cyclic redundancy check), and diagnostic data channel (12 bits).

Linecode   This will be either alternate mark inversion (AMI) or binary 8-zero substitution (B8ZS). B8ZS is typically used in the U.S.; however, most legacy phone systems still use AMI.

Dynamic Multiple Encapsulation   Back in the old days, prior to Cisco IOS 12.1, the interface encapsulation that we used in the previous example—PPP and others such as Frame Relay, High-Level Data Link Control (HDLC), Link Access Procedure (LAP), and X.25—could support only one ISDN B-channel connection over the entire link, or as in the case of HDLC and PPP, the entire link needed to use the same encapsulation method. With the Dynamic Multiple Encapsulation feature, the ISDN B channel becomes a forwarding device, and the D channel is ignored, thereby allowing different encapsulation types and per-user configuration.

Which T-1 time slots to use   By using the `pri-group` command on your PRI interface, you can define which time slots will be controlled by the D channel (subchannel 23). You can also specify dedicated time slots on the same interface with the channel-group *number* time slot *range* command. This will assign the time slots in the *range* specified, to the subchannel group of *number*.

In the following example, we chose to configure Slot 1, Port 0 of the MIP card in a 7000 router, and we opted for ESF framing, with B8ZS line coding. Remember not to get confused with the channel-group and time slot numbering; the channel-group numbers range from 0 to 23, whereas the time slot values range from 1 to 24. Also remember that channel 15 on the E-1 and channel 23 on the T-1 are for the D channels. The command pri-group timeslots 12-24 indicates that the D channel will control time slots 11 through 23 on the PRI circuit. Channel group 1 has six time slots running at 64Kbps. We could choose up to 24 DS0s but purchased only six from our provider, with 12 through 24 being controlled with the PRI D channel. Here's the output:

```
Router#config t
Enter configuration commands, one per line.    End with CNTL/Z.
Router(config)#controller T1 1/0
Router(config-if)#framing esf
Router(config-if)#linecode b8zs
Router(config-if)#pri-group timeslots 12-24
Router(config-if)#channel-group 1 timeslots 1-6 speed 64
Router(config-if)#^Z
```

An IP address and the serial encapsulation method (HDLC is the default) then needs to be assigned to each interface, as shown in the following example:

```
Router#config t
Enter configuration commands, one per line. End with CNTL/Z.
Router(config)#interface serial1/0:23
Router(config-if)#encapsulation ppp
Router(config-if)#ip address 172.16.30.5 255.255.255.252
Router(config)#interface serial1/0:1
Router(config-if)#encapsulation hdlc
Router(config-if)#ip address 172.16.30.5 255.255.255.252
```

Output for the five other B channnels (serial/0-2-6) has been omitted to save space.

```
Router(config-if)#^Z
Router#
```

When connecting two MIP cards back-to-back, you must specify the clocking on one controller. This is done with the clock source internal command.

Configuring E-1

The E-1 configuration is similar to the T-1 configuration but has a few different parameters:

Framing The E-1 framing types available are crc4 and no-crc4, with australia as an option. The default is crc4, and it specifies CRC error checking, with no-crc4 specifying that CRC checking is (surprise!) disabled. The australia framing method is used when configuring an E-1 in (another surprise!) Australia.

Linecode This is either AMI or HDB3 when configuring an E-1, with HDB3 as the default.

In the following example, we specified Slot 0, Port 1 on our MIP card, using the crc4 framing type. The provider has defined HDB3 as the linecode (HDB3 is the default) to match the carrier's equipment. For an E-1 PRI circuit, the D channel is 15 so the command pri-group time-slots 1-16 will specify that channels 1 through 15 will be controlled by the D channel (subchannel 15). Again remember not to get confused with the channel-group and time slot numbering; the channel-group numbers range from 0 to 30 whereas the time slot values range from 1 to 31. Also remember that channel 15 on the E-1 and channel 23 on the T-1 are for the D channels. However, time slots 17 to 30 are for a dedicated connection with up to 30 available if purchased.

```
Router#config t
Enter configuration commands, one per line. End with CNTL/Z.
Router(config)#controller E1 1/0
Router(config-if)#framing crc4
Router(config-if)#linecode hdb3
Router(config-if)#pri-group timeslots 1-16
Router(config-if)#channel-group 1 timeslots 17-30 speed 64
Router(config-if)#^Z
Router#
```

You then need to specify the IP address and encapsulation methods used, just as in the T-1 example:

```
Router#config t
Enter configuration commands, one per line. End with CNTL/Z.
Router(config)#interface serial1/0:15
Router(config-if)#encapsulation ppp
Router(config-if)#ip address 172.16.30.5 255.255.255.252
Router(config)#interface serial1/0:1
```

```
Router(config-if)#encapsulation hdlc
Router(config-if)#ip address 172.16.30.5 255.255.255.252
Router(config-if)#^Z
Router#
```

Summary

ISDN is an old but still very viable networking standard that supports voice, data, and video. It is slowly being replaced by DSL and cable modems. Layer 2 is negotiated by using the ITU-T Q.921 standard, and Layer 3 is negotiated by using the Q.931 standard. The ISDN reference model is set up with function groups and reference points. The function groups classify each device in the ISDN network, and the reference points identify the connections and electrical characteristics between each function group. Many IOS debug and show commands are available to help you understand and troubleshoot ISDN connections.

The types of connections include dial backup, dial-on-demand routing (DDR), and Bandwidth on Demand (BoD). There are many ways to set up a connection from one device to another by using ISDN and analog links. The legacy method uses the physical interface to specify IP address, dialing properties, and authentication. Dialer profiles provide more flexibility when using dial backup and other dial-up connections. When using PPP authentication, both Password Authentication Protocol (PAP) and Challenge Handshake Authentication Protocol (CHAP) can be used. Some IOS debug and show commands are associated with PPP negotiation and authentication.

Exam Essentials

Know the types of ISDN.   ISDN comes in two flavors: BRI and PRI. The BRI is a standard that runs over a 192Kbps circuit, whereas a PRI can run over a T-1 (1.544Mbps) or E-1 (2.048Mbps) circuit. Know when to use a BRI and when to use a PRI. There are many PRI and BRI ISDN switch types supported, and you should know which ones require SPIDs and which do not.

Understand the ISDN function groups.   You need to know what function the groups NT1, NT2, TA, LT, ET, TE1 and TE2 provide in the ISDN network.

Know the ISDN reference points.   Identify the ISDN reference points of R, S, T, and U. Know where these reference points are in the ISDN network and between which function groups they are found.

Understand the two ITU-T Q standards used by ISDN.   The Q.921 standard is used to set up Layer 2 between the router and local switch, and the Q.931 standard is used to set up Layer 3. You need to know what these protocols' structures look like and what happens when a call is set up and when it is torn down. You should also be familiar with the debug isdn q921 and debug isdn q931 commands and what to look for in troubleshooting a problem.

Know how to set up dial-on-demand routing (DDR), dial backup, and Bandwidth on Demand (BoD) by using both legacy and dialer profiles. Dialer profiles are used when you need to set up a routing protocol over a dial-up connection; the legacy setup is used when a simple point-to-point connection is needed between two sites. You should know how to set up authentication and callback when security is needed on a dial-up connection. Multilink is also available when more bandwidth is needed on a connection.

Know how to set up a channelized interface. You should know how to set up a T-1 or E-1 controller for channelized operation. You need to know the different framing and linecoding options. The pri-group command is used when setting up a channelized interface to become an ISDN PRI. The channel-group is used when an interface or a portion of the interface is used for dedicated access.

Key Terms

Before you take the exam, be certain you are familiar with the following terms:

authentication	legacy DDR
B (bearer) channels	Link Access Procedure, Data (LAPD)
Bandwidth on Demand (BoD)	Password Authentication Protocol (PAP)
Basic Rate Interface (BRI)	plain old telephone service (POTS)
D (data) channel	Primary Rate Interface (PRI)
dial backup	Pulse Code Modulation (PCM)
dialer profile	reference point
dial-on-demand routing (DDR)	Service Profile Identifier (SPID)
DS0	small offices/home offices (SOHOs)
Integrated Services Digital Network (ISDN)	Thinnet network
LAPD frame	

Written Lab

In this written lab, you will write out the commands to configure a BRI interface.

1. Write the command to configure the basic-ni switch type on a BRI router.

2. Write the configuration of spid1 and spid2 on a BRI0 interface and make the IP address of the **172.16.60.1/24**. Use **0835866101** for SPID number 1 and use **8358661** for the DN. Use **0835866301** for SPID number 2 and use **8358663** for the DN.

3. Specify interesting traffic to bring up the ISDN link. Choose all IP traffic.

4. Under the BRI interface, add the command that matches the dialer-list number 1 and tells the BRI interface to be dialed if interesting traffic is found.

5. Configure the dialer information to dial 8358662.

6. Set the dialer load-threshold to bring up the second BRI at 50 percent bandwidth usage.

7. Set the BRI interface to fragment packets and load-balance over both BRI channels.

8. Set the BRI channel to drop the connection if no interesting traffic is sent for 240 seconds.

9. Set the hold queue for packets at 75 for when they are found interesting and need a place to wait for the ISDN link to come up.

10. Write the command that will verify the ISDN connection by showing you your interface's Layer 2 and 3 information as well as whether your SPIDs are valid.

Hands-on Labs

This section provides two hands-on labs that you can use to gain the experience needed to pass your Remote Access exam.

In the first lab, you will configure two ISDN routers called 804A and 804B to dial ISDN between the networks 172.16.30.0 and 172.16.50.0, using network 172.16.60.0 on the ISDN BRI interfaces when interesting traffic dictates a DDR link. The second lab will have you configure PRI at a corporate office and BRI at a remote branch office.

Lab 5.1: DDR

For this lab, use Figure 5.11 as a reference for the network you are configuring.

FIGURE 5.11 ISDN lab

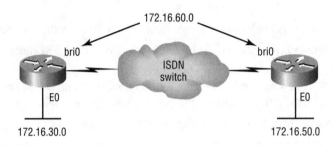

172.16.60.0

bri0   ISDN switch   bri0

E0   E0

172.16.30.0   172.16.50.0

1. Go to 804B and set the hostname and ISDN switch type.

```
Router#config t
Router(config)#hostname 804B
804B(config)#isdn switch-type basic-ni
```

2. Set the hostname and then the switch type on 804A at the interface level. (The point of these first two steps is to show that you can configure the switch type either through global configuration mode or at the interface level.)

```
Router#config t
Router(config)#hostname 804A
804A(config)#interface bri0
804A(config-if)#isdn switch-type basic-ni
```

3. On 804A, set the SPID numbers on BRI0 and make the IP address 171.16.60.1/24.

```
804A#config t
804A(config)#interface bri0
804A(config-if)#isdn spid 1 0835866101 8358661
804A(config-if)#isdn spid 2 0835866301 8358663
804A(config-if)#ip address 172.16.60.1 255.255.255.0
804A(config-if)#no shutdown
```

4. Set the SPIDs on 804B and make the IP address of the interface 172.16.60.2/24.

```
804B#config t
804B(config)#interface bri0
804B(config-if)#isdn spid 1 0835866201 8358662
804B(config-if)#isdn spid 2 0835866401 8358664
804B(config-if)#ip address 172.16.60.2 255.255.255.0
804B(config-if)#no shutdown
```

5. Create static routes on the routers to use the remote ISDN interface. Static routes are rec-ommended with ISDN DDR.

```
804A(config)#ip route 172.16.50.0 255.255.255.0 172.16.60.2
804A(config)#ip route 172.16.60.2 255.255.255.255 bri0

804B(config)#ip route 172.16.30.0 255.255.255.0 172.16.60.1
804B(config)#ip route 172.16.60.1 255.255.255.255 bri0
```

6. Specify interesting traffic to bring up the ISDN link. Choose all IP traffic. This is a global configuration mode command.

```
804A(config)#dialer-list 1 protocol ip permit

804B(config)#dialer-list 1 protocol ip permit
```

7. Under the BRI interface of both routers, add the command dialer-group 1, which matches the dialer-list number.

```
804A#config t
804A(config)#interface bri0
804A(config-if)#dialer-group 1

804B#config t
804B(config)#interface bri0
804B(config-if)#dialer-group 1
```

8. Configure the dialer information on both routers. This tells the BRI interface which number to dial when interesting traffic is found.

```
804A#config t
804A(config)#interface bri0
804A(config-if)#dialer string 8358662

804B#config t
804B(config)#interface bri0
804B(config-if)#dialer string 8358661
```

9. Set the dialer load-threshold and multilink commands, as well as the idle-timeout on both 804 routers.

```
804A#config t
804A(config)#interface bri0
804A(config-if)#dialer load-threshold 127 either
804A(config-if)#dialer idle-timeout 180
```

```
804A(config-if)#ppp multilink

804B#config t
804B(config)#interface bri0
804B(config-if)#dialer load-threshold 127 either
804B(config-if)#dialer idle-timeout 180
804B(config-if)#ppp multilink
```

These commands set the BRI interfaces to bring up the second B channel when the first B channel is at 50 percent capacity from either inbound or outbound traffic.

10. Set the hold queue for packets when they are found interesting and need a place to wait for the ISDN link to come up.

```
804A#config t
804A(config)#interface bri0
804B(config-if)#dialer hold-queue 75

804B#config t
804B(config)#interface bri0
804B(config-if)#dialer hold-queue 75
```

11. Verify the ISDN connection.

```
ping
telnet
show dialer
show isdn status
show ip route
```

Lab 5.2: Configuring PRI and BRI

This lab uses Figure 5.12 as a basis for configuring a PRI interface on a corporate router and BRI on a remote branch router.

FIGURE 5.12   PRI to BRI configuration

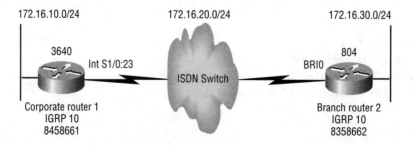

You'll start this lab by configuring the PRI interface on the corporate router.

1. Set the switch type on the router. Check with your provider to make sure you have the right switch type. Here is an example:

```
Router#config t
Router(config)#isdn switch-type primary-5ess
```

2. Create a hostname for the corporate office router and the username and password for the remote router. Remember, this is the remote router's hostname. The passwords must be set identically on each router.

```
Router#config t
Router(config)#hostname router1
router1(config)#username router2 password cisco
```

3. Create an access list to identify the interesting traffic you want to bring up on the ISDN link. At this point, keep it simple and use all IP traffic.

```
router1#config t
router1(config)#dialer-list 1 protocol ip permit
```

4. Create a static route to the remote network.

```
router1#config t
router1(config)#ip route 172.16.30.0 255.255.255.0 172.16.20.2
```

5. Configure the PRI (T-1) interface with a linecode of B8ZS and specify that the interface will click its transmitted data from a clock recovered from the lines receiving the data stream. Set the PRI framing as Extended Super Frame.

```
router1#config t
router1(config)#controller t1 0/1
router1(config-cont)#linecode b8zs
router1(config-cont)#clock source line
router1(config-cont)#framing esf
```

6. Enable the PRI on your T-1 interface with the channels you purchased. The following example uses all 24 channels.

```
router1#config t
router1(config)#controller t1 0/1
router1(config-cont)#pri-group timeslots 1-24
```

7. Configure the D channel to use PPP with CHAP authentication.

```
router1#config t
router1(config)#int serial 1/0:23
router1(config-if)#encapsulation ppp
router1(config-if)#ppp authentication chap
```

8. Add the IP address of the interface and add the command that will bring up the line when interesting traffic is found.

```
router1(config-if)#ip address 172.16.20.1 255.255.255.0
router1(config-if)#dialer-group 1
```

9. Configure the dialer idle-time.

```
router1(config-if)#dialer idle-timeout 180
```

10. Use a dialer map to set the number to dial.

```
router1#config t
router1(config)#dialer map ip 172.16.20.2 name router2 8358662
```

11. Use a passive interface on the D channel to stop routing updates.

```
router1(config)#router igrp 10
router1(config-router)#passive interface serial 1/0:23
router1(config-router)#redistribute static
```

12. Configure the BRI interface of the remote branch router. Start by setting the switch type.

```
Router#config t
Router(config)#isdn switch-type basic-5ess
```

13. Set the hostname of your router and set the username and password of the corporate office.

```
Router#config t
Router(config)#hostname router2
router2(config)#username router1 password cisco
```

14. Create an access list to specify all IP traffic as interesting.

```
router2#config t
router2(config)#dialer-list 1 protocol ip permit
```

15. Set the static routes.

```
router2#config t
router2(config)#ip route 172.16.10.0 255.255.255.0 172.16.20.1
```

16. Configure the BRI interface with PPP encapsulation and CHAP authentication.

```
router2(config)#interface bri0
router2(config-if)#encapsulation ppp
router2(config-if)#ppp authentication chap
```

17. Set the IP address of the interface, dialer-group, dialer idle-timeout, and dialer map statements.

```
router2(config-if)#ip address 172.16.20.2 255.255.255.0
router2(config-if)#no shutdown
router2(config-if)#dialer-group 1
router2(config-if)#dialer idle-timeout 180
router2(config-if)#dialer map ip 172.16.20.1 name router1 8358661
```

18. Set the passive interface so no updates bring up the ISDN link.

```
router2(config-if)#router igrp 10
router2(config-router)#passive interface bri0
router2(config-router)#redistribute static
```

19. Test the connection by pinging and Telnetting to the remote locations. Also, use the following commands:

```
show isdn status
show interface
debug q921
debug q931
```

Review Questions

1. What does an NT1 do?

   A. Converts non-ISDN devices into a compatible signal

   B. Acts as a point between an LE and TA that consolidates devices onto an ISDN line

   C. Connects a TE1 device to the ISDN network

   D. Converts the bipolar signal from the NT2 into a unipolar signal before sending it to the network

2. Which ISDN device refers to a non-ISDN device such as a POTS phone or fax machine?

   A. NT1

   B. NT2

   C. TA

   D. TE2

3. Which reference point is located between an NT1 and an NT2?

   A. R

   B. S

   C. T

   D. U

4. Which standard governs the S/T interface?

   A. ITU I.430

   B. ITU Q.931

   C. ITU I.225

   D. ITU E.911

5. Which commands are associated with dialer profiles? (Select all that apply.)

   A. `dialer string`

   B. `dialer pool-member`

   C. `dialer remote-name`

   D. `dialer map`

6. What TEI value is used as a broadcast?

   A. 0

   B. 127

   C. 64

   D. Z-1

7. Which ISDN call SETUP message might indicate a ring on the far end?

   A. ALERTING

   B. CONNECT

   C. CONNECT ACK

   D. CALL PROCEEDING

8. Which command must be used to configure a backup interface on the primary interface?

   A. `backup load`

   B. `backup delay`

   C. `backup interface`

   D. `delay interface`

9. Which ISDN switch type requires a Service Profile Identifier (SPID)?

   A. ntt

   B. basic-5ess

   C. basic-dms100

   D. basic-net3

10. An E-1-based PRI uses which bits to handle its in-band communication?

   A. E bit.

   B. There is no in-band signaling with an E-1.

   C. U bit.

   D. D channel.

11. What command do you use to display information about incoming and outgoing calls?

   A. `show calls`

   B. `debug call`

   C. `show dialer`

   D. `show inbound`

12. An invalid username and password pair supplied in a PAP packet will result in which type of message?

   A. Code 4, Authentication Mismatch

   B. Authenticate-Ack

   C. Authenticate-Fail

   D. Authenticate-Nak

13. Which of the following commands specify that any IP traffic over the interface causes an ISDN call to be initiated?

    A. `group dialer ip all`

    B. `dialer-list 1 protocol ip permit`

    C. `dialer-traffic ip`

    D. `dialer-list 1 protocol ip permit ip`

14. CHAP is identified by which Authentication-Protocol ID?

    A. 0xFFF

    B. 0xC223

    C. 0xEFF

    D. 0x89

15. What command is used to activate a backup interface when the load on the primary interface reaches 50 percent?

    A. `backup load 127`

    B. `backup delay 127`

    C. `backup load 50`

    D. `load-threshold 50`

16. Which command verifies ISDN Layer 3?

    A. `show isdn layer-3 status`

    B. `debug isdn q921`

    C. `show dialer`

    D. `show ip interface brief`

17. Which command is used to verify ISDN Layer 2?

    A. `show isdn status`

    B. `debug isdn q931`

    C. `show dialer`

    D. `show ip interface brief`

18. A Basic Rate Interface D channel does what? (Select all that apply.)

    A. Carries low bandwidth traffic

    B. Provides out-of-band signaling

    C. Determines which B channel to use

    D. Is a 20Kbps channel that provides out-of-band signaling

19. Which of the ISDN channels would be used for LAPD?

    A. B

    B. A

    C. C

    D. D

20. What is the channel configuration of a BRI?

    A. 1 B channel, 2 D channels

    B. 2 B channels, 1 D channel

    C. 23 B channels, 1 D channel

    D. 30 B channels, 1 D channel

Answers to Written Lab

1.

```
config t
isdn switch-type basic-ni
```

   or

```
config t
interface bri0
isdn switch-type basic-ni
```

2.

```
config t
interface bri0
isdn spid 1 0835866101 8358661
isdn spid 2 0835866301 8358663
ip address 172.16.60.1 255.255.255.0
no shut
```

3.

```
config t
dialer-list 1 protocol ip permit
```

4.

```
config t
interface bri0
dialer-group 1
```

5.

```
config t
interface bri0
dialer string 8358662
```

6.

```
config t
interface bri0
dialer load-threshold 127 either
```

7.

```
config t
int bri0
ppp multilink
```

8.

```
config t
interface bri0
dialer idle-timeout 240
```

9.

```
config t
int bri0
dialer hold-queue 75
```

10.

```
show isdn status
```

Answers to Review Questions

1. C. TE1 devices are 4-wire (2 pair) and need to be 2-wire (1 pair) to communicate with an ISDN network. A TE1 will connect into a Network Termination type 1 (NT1) to connect the 4-wire subscriber wiring to the 2-wire local loop facility.

2. D. A TE2 is a POTS telephone or fax machine. This device requires a TA to interface with the ISDN network.

3. C. The T reference point is between an NT1 and an NT2.

4. A. Physical interfaces on an ISDN device are governed by ITU standard I.430.

5. A, B, C. The only command not associated with dialer profiles is the `dialer map`.

6. B. The broadcast value TEI is 127, or all ones.

7. A. The ALERTING message is returned to indicate the call is proceeding.

8. C. You must use the `backup interface` command with the parameter of the interface that will be used to back up the configured interface.

9. C. National-1 and DMS-100 switches require a SPID for each B channel; a SPID is optional with an AT&T 5ESS.

10. B. A PRI and BRI do not use in-band signaling. Instead, this information is carried over the D channel.

11. C. Use the `show dialer` command to display information about inbound and outbound calls.

12. D. You will receive an Authenticate-Nak if the username/password pair is incorrect. You will receive an Authenticate-Ack if it is a good pair.

13. B. The `dialer-group` command is used to reference a dialer list. The `dialer-list protocol` command specifies an access list number or a protocol that defines interesting packets to trigger a call.

14. B. CHAP is identified as Authentication Protocol c223, which is carried in the Information field of a PPP frame

15. C. Use the `backup load` command to specify when to activate the backup interface when a certain load-threshold is exceeded.

16. C. The `show dialer` command will verify that ISDN Layer 3 is working. This is indicated by Success under Last Status.

17. A.   You can view Layer 1 and 2 information by using the show isdn status command. Layer 1 will be active, whereas Layer 2 will have valid TEIs.

18. A, B, C.   The D channel carries call setup and teardown information as well as low-bandwidth traffic. (This is a new option.) The D channel on a BRI is 16Kbps.

19. D.   D channel—16Kbps—is used for call setup, signaling, and call termination.

20. B.   A BRI is also known as a 2B+D, for 2 B channels and 1 D channel.

Chapter

6

Remote Access with Digital Subscriber Line

EXAM TOPICS COVERED IN THIS CHAPTER INCLUDE:

- ✓ Understand Digital Subscriber Line technologies
- ✓ Know the differences in Digital Subscriber Line technologies
- ✓ Know how to configure Digital Subscriber Line technologies
- ✓ Understand how to troubleshoot Digital Subscriber Line technologies

In this chapter we will examine the remote access technologies encompassed in Digital Subscriber Line (DSL) services. This set of newer remote connectivity access methods provides residential and business locations with high-speed, low-cost connections that can surpass T-1 in some instances. In addition to the basics of DSL, we will also compare the different flavors of the technology and the troubleshooting methodologies employed.

What is Digital Subscriber Line?

Digital Subscriber Line (DSL) is the result of demand for cheaper and higher bandwidth services over the already existing copper phone-line network. As with ISDN, there was, and is, a great deal of installed and widely available sub-Category 3 cable that, with a new encoding method, could provide high-bandwidth services.

Within this chapter the terms *DSL* and *xDSL* are used. By convention, both mean the same thing, although *xDSL* is a generic term that means all DSL technologies, including ADSL and HDSL. These variants of DSL are presented later in this chapter. *DSL* is typically used to describe the base technology.

However, this existing cable currently supports analog voice services, so the new technology, again like ISDN, needed to support legacy voice services in addition to providing the new data service. So, DSL is a voice and data service that supports multi-megabit data rates over the same cable that previously supported only voice.

The *Digital Subscriber Line Access Multiplexer (DSLAM)* provides the cornerstone of the DSL infrastructure. This device provides two important functions in the DSL network. First, it separates voice and data traffic from each line, and, second, it terminates each connection to the residence or business. Figure 6.1 illustrates a typical DSL residential installation with an access terminal (DSLAM) extending the link from the central office. Note that a remote access terminal is not required and that a 1-mile copper connection could extend directly from a central-office-located DSLAM.

FIGURE 6.1   xDSL installation

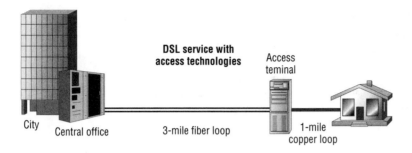

As an overview, DSL provides the following benefits:

- Voice and data services over the same copper pair
- Significantly greater bandwidth than ISDN or analog services over comparable physical media

Unfortunately, DSL also has some negatives, including these:

- Significant distance limitations at higher data rates
- Low tolerance for low-quality copper wiring
- Complex, labor-consuming installation procedures for some versions
- An inability to work with legacy line-conditioning equipment, including load coils

This chapter covers the flavors of DSL that are available to the administrator for remote access solutions, in addition to covering configuration and troubleshooting of this technology.

The Different Flavors of DSL

You learned in Chapter 5, "Integrated Services Digital Network (ISDN)," that there are a couple of different flavors to that technology—specifically BRI and PRI. We will discuss six different flavors of DSL in this chapter, although there are many more. These include:

- Asymmetric Digital Subscriber Line
- G.lite
- High Bit-Rate DSL
- Symmetric DSL

- ISDN DSL
- Very-High Data Rate DSL

The different flavors of DSL typically alter the bandwidth available and the range, or distance between the DSLAM and the end-point. There can be other differences as well, such as the need for a *splitter* to separate voice traffic from the circuit.

When discussing a DSL circuit without specifying the type of DSL being used, it is common to refer to xDSL.

Asymmetric Digital Subscriber Line

The most common DSL variant is *Asymmetric Digital Subscriber Line (ADSL)*, and this is often used for home and business users. It is called *asymmetric* because the bandwidth is not equal in the upstream and downstream directions. Upstream traffic is sent from the user, and downstream traffic is sent from the direction of the DSLAM.

This unequal traffic flow is well suited to Internet surfing and centralized data storage, as would be found in many tele-worker applications. For example, many users will download graphics, documents, and other large files from the remote network, while only sending small e-mail messages or requests for information. As such, the network needs to provide only a small amount of bandwidth to service these smaller datagrams from the user, and it is preferable to provide larger amounts of bandwidth to support the greater volume of data from the network.

 Real World Scenario

Oversubscription and Bandwidth Contention

A discussion of consumer DSL, of which ADSL is a common offering, necessitates a discussion of vendor claims regarding oversubscription and bandwidth contention. As you might know, oversubscription occurs when the network is provisioned with greater potential demand than could be serviced at any one time, under the reasonable assumption that use patterns and the quantity of bandwidth demanded will never be 100 percent.

This assumption is very reasonable in many networks. Consider your network for a moment. You might have 100 workstations connected to a switch with a single 100Mbps uplink to the core. If each of the 100 workstations is connected at 100Mbps, the network would be oversubscribed 100:1. Consumer DSL network vendors commonly oversubscribe at ratios between 3 and 10 to 1, or 10:1.

Let's suspend discussion of oversubscription for a moment and consider bandwidth contention. DSL providers will quickly point out that cable modem networks provide shared bandwidth from the head-end to a population of users. Think of this as shared Ethernet. They will then add that their DSL technology is more akin to switched Ethernet, where each user has no contention for bandwidth from their router to the DSLAM.

On the surface it would appear that DSL is the superior technology, as many networkers have migrated from the old shared network model to the superior switched network in Ethernet. The marketing folks for DSL providers enjoy that analogy and relish in users choosing the dedicated technology.

However, all is not as it appears. Although it is true that DSL dedicates bandwidth from the end-user to the head-end at the physical layer, we must return to oversubscription. I might have a dedicated 100Mbps Ethernet connection to my workstation, and Piper might have 100Mbps to her workstation, but if we have a single 100Mbps uplink from the switch to our resource, we could expect only 50 percent, or 50Mbps in this example, of throughput. So long as we have that consideration, shared bandwidth is always a factor, even if the hop from my router to the head-end is dedicated. As such, cable modem's shared technology (presented further in Chapter 7) is less of a concern than DSL providers would like.

ADSL requires the use of a splitter to isolate the voice traffic from the data stream on the copper pair.

Cisco contends that ADSL is best suited to video on demand and video conferencing; however, in practice we would recommend against this generalization. The asymmetric nature of ADSL is such that quality upstream video conferencing is unlikely if there is concurrent load. Because video conferencing is typically a bidirectional experience, it would be overgeneralizing to conclude that ADSL is the best solution. We justify their answer by simplifying the scope and comparing ADSL to ISDN, analog (POTS), and other remote access technologies. In this light, ADSL is the best solution. However, HDSL and other DSL flavors, discussed later, might be better for your installation.

G.lite

G.lite, which is sometimes called *splitterless DSL*, is quickly dethroning ADSL for the most common DSL variant, although technically it is only a subspecification of ADSL itself. As the *splitterless* nickname infers, this technology does not require a splitter to be installed at the customer location. In this splitterless installation, the provider isolates voice from data in the central office by controlling the frequency of the voice channel.

The advantage to this type of installation is significant. In a splitter (ADSL) type of deployment, the provider needs to visit the customer location and install a splitter on the line in addition to a second jack—one jack is for the DSL router, and the other is for the telephone. The cost of this is very high compared to the alternative of encoding the data and voice so the end-equipment can isolate the voice traffic where no splitter installation is required. G.lite installations can be completed at the central office, and the user can simply plug their router into the jack as they would a telephone.

G.lite is further described in ITU-T standard G.992.2.

High Bit-Rate DSL

High bit-rate DSL (HDSL) requires two pairs of copper for service, unlike most other DSL offerings. In exchange, it provides a T-1-like presence of 1.544Mbps in each direction. It is important to note that this service does not support analog voice.

Symmetric DSL

Symmetric DSL (SDSL) is a variant of HDSL; however, it runs over a single copper pair. HDSL requires two pairs of copper. The data rate is 1.544Mbps in each direction.

ISDN DSL

ISDN DSL (IDSL) provides up to 144Kbps of bandwidth, which is equal to the two B channels and one D channel of ISDN BRI by employing the same line coding (2B1Q) as ISDN. It is important to note that this flavor of DSL does not support analog voice service.

The primary reason for offering IDSL is that the range can be extended to cover virtually any existing copper path that is devoid of amplifiers or load coils—both of which can be used in very long analog connections. With repeaters, IDSL can extend to 45,000 feet.

Very-High Data Rate DSL

Very-high data rate DSL (VDSL), sometimes also called Very-high bit-rate DSL, is exactly that— a high bandwidth variant of DSL. Most implementations are capable of downstream bandwidths in excess of 50Mbps. Consider for a moment that most VDSL deployments are in residential settings, and that the service provides in essence a DS-3 worth of capacity, and you begin to appreciate the "very high" aspects indeed.

There are a few installations of VDSL available in large markets, including Denver and Phoenix in the United States. These services leverage VDSL to provide video, data, and voice services over the DSL circuit. With over 50Mbps, it is possible to provide four broadcast-quality video streams over the connection, while also supporting an always available Internet data path and analog voice services—a road to the fully converged network if you will.

Of course, you cannot get something for nothing, and VDSL is no exception. The significant downside to the technology is its limited range. Stated another way, ADSL technologies can frequently extend to over 18,000 feet, whereas VDSL is limited to 4,500 feet. The highest data rates are attainable at only 1,000 feet in most real-world settings.

The DSL types presented are summarized in Table 6.1.

TABLE 6.1   DSL Types

Type	Analog support	Downstream bandwidth	Upstream Bandwidth	Range
ADSL	Yes	Up to 9Mbps	Up to 640Kbps	Up to 18,000 feet
G.lite	Yes	Up to 1.5Mbps	Up to 512Kbps	Up to 18,000 feet
HDSL	No	1.544Mbps	1.544Mbps	Up to 12,000 feet
SDSL	No	1.544Mbps	1.544Mbps	Up to 10,000 feet
IDSL	No	144Kbps	144Kbps	Up to 45,000 feet
VDSL	Yes	Up to 52Mbps	Up to 2.3Mbps	Up to 4,500 feet

You might find that different vendors and sources document range and bandwidth figures that are not the same as those in Table 6.1. We have used the Cisco figures, which are sometimes over or under the values included in other specifications. The variances should not have a significant impact on the test or real-world deployment—for example, HDSL might have a range of 15,000 feet or 12,000 maximum, but wire condition, interference, and other factors can greatly influence this, and a real-world installation might operate correctly at only 7,000 feet. This chapter covers only DSL basics consistent with the examination.

Cisco DSL Routers

Cisco's product line for supporting DSL services is comprised of three classifications of equipment. The first is the focus of the Remote Access examination, which is primarily made up of the Cisco 800 series of routers and the SOHO (small office, home office) 70 series. The second is comprised of the xDSL modules for the branch and office routers, including the 2600 and 3600 series. And the third is the head-end DSLAM switches, including the Cisco 6260 IP DSL switch.

There could be a fourth Cisco DSL product category in their Linksys acquisition. The Linksys product line includes a wide range of solutions for the SOHO market and frequently integrates other functions such as print services and wireless networking.

For the SOHO environment and small remote office, Cisco provides their SOHO line of DSL routers in addition to the Cisco 800 series. Here is a list of the various DSL platforms in this category:

- Cisco 837 ADSL Broadband Router
- Cisco 836 ADSL over ISDN Broadband Router
- Cisco 828 G.SHDSL Router
- Cisco 827 ADSL Router
- Cisco 827 -4V ADSL Router
- Cisco 826 ADSL Router
- Cisco SOHO 78 G.SHDSL Router
- Cisco SOHO 77 ADSL Router
- Cisco SOHO 77 H ADSL Router
- Cisco SOHO 76 ADSL Router

There is not much to focus on in this list, other than noting the diversity within the Cisco 827 product line, which includes the 827-4V. This platform provides four voice ports in addition to ADSL support. The H variant of the 827 provides a four-port hub in addition to DSL termination.

For larger offices, Cisco provides DSL support on the 1700, 2600XM, and 3600 series routers via a WAN Interface Card (WIC). This allows for installation of other services, including network modules (NMs) for content delivery. Voice Interface Cards (VIC) can also terminate voice services on these platforms.

At the head-end, Cisco provides the following switches for terminating DSL connections:

- Cisco 6260 IP DSL Switch
- Cisco 6160 IP DSL Switch
- Cisco 6015 IP DSL Switch

These solutions are targeted toward servicing multi-tenant buildings, telecommunications service providers, and ISPs. The specifics of these platforms are well beyond the scope of the Remote Access examination.

Configuring DSL

The specific configuration settings for a DSL installation will depend on the type of router used and the features desired, but there are common elements.

The key element of a DSL installation is that the technology is fundamentally a physical transport of ATM cells. As such, we will configure a Cisco 3810 router to terminate multiple DSL connections (ADSL in this case). The head-end is a T-1 ATM connection (configuration of the DSLAM is beyond the scope of the test and this book, but functionally it is PVC configuration and other parameters—stated another way, it is not complicated). You might realize that the T-1 is a poor termination choice for ADSL services; however, for this application it is an appropriate solution. A DS-3 or other ATM connection could provide the termination just as well.

In addition to the typical configuration parameters you might include (such as routing, logging, security, and management), the DSL configuration requires very little additional configuration. In this excerpt, we configure the T-1 physical interface with Extended Super Frame and B8ZS encoding, in addition to setting it for ATM cells. The ATM interface has no configuration, but is subinterfaced for multiple connections (recall that this is a head-end, non-DSLAM connection). We configure a PVC with unspecified bit rate (UBR) ATM, and, as an extra service, we configure Operation, Administration, and Management (OAM) cells to the PVC. OAM provides link monitoring; if any part of the PVC fails, OAM will detect it and shut down the interface until corrected. We also specify AAL5SNAP, or AAL5 with SNAP headers, for the encapsulation type. So long as this matches on each side, there is no issue in most cases. For those not familiar with PVC configurations, interface ATM0.1 has a VPI (Virtual Path Identifier) of 5 and a VCI (Virtual Circuit Identifier) of 51.

```
!
controller T1 0
 framing esf
 linecode b8zs
 mode atm
 fdl both
 description T1 to DSL Cloud
!
interface ATM0
 description DSL Headend
 no ip address
 no ip directed-broadcast
!
interface ATM0.1 point-to-point
 description DSL link to Gryffendor
 ip address 10.1.1.25 255.255.255.252
 no ip directed-broadcast
 pvc 5/51
  ubr 1500
  oam-pvc manage
  oam retry 3 5 1
  encapsulation aal5snap
!
```

```
interface ATM0.2 point-to-point
 description DSL Link to Ravenclaw
 ip address 10.1.1.33 255.255.255.252
 no ip directed-broadcast
 pvc 4/51
  ubr 1500
  oam-pvc manage
  oam retry 3 5 1
  encapsulation aal5snap
 !
```

If there were only one PVC for this circuit, it would be acceptable to use the major interface and not a subinterface. However, if an installation *might* use more than one PVC in the future then the use of a subinterface is recommended.

Other routers might limit various options. The Cisco 827, for example, uses a Bridge-Group Virtual Interface (BVI), which is part of Integrated Routing and Bridging, or IRB. services for connectivity instead of routing in most installations. This bridging solution negates Layer 3 and leverages Network Address Translation (NAT) for those services that are Layer 3. The configuration is not DSL specific however, as the use of IRB is primarily used to negate the need for remote configuration; a standard router configuration file can service all endpoints because DHCP and NAT hide the Ethernet network, and the DSL side is assigned its address dynamically.

IRB, BVI, NAT, and DHCP in this context are beyond the scope of this chapter and of the exam. Chapter 10, "Network Address Translation (NAT) and Port Address Translation (PAT)," provides information regarding NAT, and Chapter 4 presents DHCP. If you are interested in learning more about the 827 router (a common remote DSL platform) and IRB/BVI, please refer to Cisco's documentation at http://www.cisco.com/en/US/customer/products/hw/routers/ps380/prod_release_note09186a008007e1fe.html.

Troubleshooting DSL

DSL is an ATM technology at its core, so troubleshooting DSL connections requires an understanding of ATM in addition to generic troubleshooting. Generic troubleshooting includes examination of the various layers, including physical connectivity, data link connectivity, and protocol configuration.

   In the following example, the DSL interface has received 1,714 frames with CRC errors, while the interface itself has reset three times. The IP address is confirmed to be correct, and the load does not appear to be problematic. Although the problem could be the ATM PVC configuration under different circumstances, in this case there is likely a line problem or an issue with the physical interface at the transmission end. Remember that ATM is a cell-based technology, and although beyond our scope here, each cell is 53 bytes long. Of this, with ATM Adaptation Layer 5, 48 bytes are for user data and 5 bytes of each cell are used for header information. A CRC error could occur if any one of the cells that made up a particular frame were damaged. With an average frame size of just over 100 bytes (159,780 bytes in 1,512 frames) it is apparent that the average frame is sent via three cells.

```
Router#show int atm0
ATM0 is up, line protocol is up
  Hardware is PQUICC_SAR (with Alcatel ADSL Module)
  Internet address is 10.1.1.1/24
  MTU 1500 bytes, sub MTU 1500, BW 640 Kbit, DLY 80 usec,
      reliability 40/255, txload 2/255, rxload 2/255
  Encapsulation ATM, loopback not set
  Keepalive not supported
  Encapsulation(s):AAL5, PVC mode
  10 maximum active VCs, 1 current VCCs
  VC idle disconnect time:300 seconds
  Last input 00:16:39, output 00:16:39, output hang never
  Last clearing of "show interface" counters never
  Input queue:0/75/0 (size/max/drops); Total output drops:0
  Queueing strategy:Per VC Queueing
  5 minute input rate 0 bits/sec, 0 packets/sec
  5 minute output rate 0 bits/sec, 0 packets/sec
     1512 packets input, 159780 bytes, 0 no buffer
     Received 0 broadcasts, 0 runts, 0 giants, 0 throttles
     0 input errors, 1714 CRC, 0 frame, 0 overrun, 0 ignored, 0 abort
     1426 packets output, 146282 bytes, 0 underruns
     0 output errors, 0 collisions, 3 interface resets
     0 output buffer failures, 0 output buffers swapped out
```

Summary

In this chapter, you learned that Digital Subscriber Line technology was developed to add functionality to the large existing copper cable plant installed for the analog phone system.

The service is built around ATM technology and provides a wide variety of flavors to offer different data rates and service distances. DSL variants range in bandwidth from 144Kbps to over 50Mbps.

Unlike other WAN technologies, many DSL flavors are asymmetric; that is, they provide different bandwidths in upstream and downstream directions.

We presented the configuration and troubleshooting elements of DSL, while noting that from the transport point of view DSL is examined the same as ATM. We also noted that DSL sometimes uses complex bridging and routing solutions to simplify larger deployments. DSL is a consumer service in many installations, and with over 28 million installations (as of late 2003) simple, repeatable deployments are crucial. To that end, we presented the primary feature of G.lite, or splitterless DSL.

Exam Essentials

Understand how DSL can fit into your remote access solutions.   DSL is well suited to remote workers and small branch offices for remote connectivity. It offers many of the same bandwidths as T-1 at lower prices, and, in some cases, its asymmetric offerings are perfect for high-demand users.

Know the differences in the various flavors of DSL.   The DSL service offerings are best considered in terms of bandwidth and analog voice support. G.lite is a splitterless offering that provides for analog voice without a splitter in the line. HDSL and SDSL provide symmetric bandwidth.

Be able to compare DSL to other remote access technologies.   HDSL and SDSL both provide bandwidths comparable to T-1 services. This can be very important for the administrator—for example, T-1 might not be available but HDSL is, and, ironically, HDSL might be cheaper. Other xDSL services can be replacements for Frame Relay or other access methods.

Understand the configuration of DSL services.   The key to configuring DSL services is to understand their relationship to ATM in the networking model. DSL commonly uses the same PVC configuration and other logical constructs.

Key Terms

Before you take the exam, be certain you are familiar with the following terms:

Asymmetric Digital Subscriber Line (ADSL)   ISDN DSL (IDSL)

Digital Subscriber Line (DSL)   splitter

Digital Subscriber Line Access Multiplexer (DSLAM)   splitterless

G.lite   Symmetric DSL (SDSL)

High bit-rate DSL (HDSL)   Very high bit-rate DSL (VDSL)

Written Lab

1. What command is used to configure ATM adaptation layer 5 with SNAP headers?
2. What feature would you use to configure more than one PVC for DSL services?
3. What command is used to enable PVC OAM services?
4. To configure a PVC for unspecified bit rate up to 1,500 bytes, what command is used?
5. What command would be used to define a VCI of 40 and a VPI of 2?
6. What show parameter would provide an indication of one ATM cell being damaged in transit?
7. How many cells are required for a single 64-byte frame?
8. What type of interface is used for DSL services on the Cisco 3810?
9. What command is used to configure the splitter in ADSL?
10. What command would display the type of DSL hardware and the number of bits input?

Hands-on Lab

Configure a Cisco router for DSL support by using the following parameters. Assume that the physical interface is already configured.

- AAL5SNAP
- VPI 2
- VCI 51
- Interface ATM 0
- IP address 10.1.1.1/24
- OAM PVC management

Review Questions

1. What is the primary advantage of IDSL?

   A. It provides the greatest amount of upstream bandwidth of the DSL variants.

   B. It provides greater range from the DSLAM than other DSL variants.

   C. It allows bursting for periods of heavy user demand.

   D. It has integrated support for redundant virtual paths.

2. What is the primary advantage of VDSL?

   A. It provides the greatest amount of upstream bandwidth of the DSL variants.

   B. It provides greater range from the DSLAM than other DSL variants.

   C. It is compatible with legacy ISDN systems.

   D. It has the greatest amount of downstream bandwidth.

3. What is the primary advantage of G.lite?

   A. It provides the greatest amount of downstream bandwidth of the DSL variants.

   B. It provides greater range from the DSLAM than other DSL variants.

   C. It does not require a splitter.

   D. It has integrated support for redundant virtual paths.

4. What is the primary characteristic of HDSL?

   A. It provides the greatest amount of upstream bandwidth of the DSL variants.

   B. It provides greater range from the DSLAM than other DSL variants.

   C. It provides symmetric bandwidth.

   D. It has integrated support for redundant virtual paths.

5. What is the primary disadvantage of ADSL?

   A. It requires a splitter for voice services.

   B. It provides greater range from the DSLAM than other DSL variants.

   C. It is compatible with legacy ISDN systems.

   D. It has integrated support for redundant virtual paths.

6. The asymmetric nature of ADSL is best suited for what type of user?

   A. Field offices with local servers and large backup requirements

   B. Remote users with little upstream traffic

   C. Mobile users

   D. Remote users with little downstream traffic

7. Which DSL variant is most like a T-1?

   A. VDSL

   B. HDSL

   C. IDSL

   D. ADSL

8. Which DSL variant is most like an ISDN BRI?

   A. VDSL

   B. HDSL

   C. IDSL

   D. ADSL

9. Which DSL variant is best for video conferencing?

   A. VDSL

   B. HDSL

   C. IDSL

   D. ADSL

10. Which DSL variant is best for users more than 20,000 feet from the DSLAM?

   A. VDSL

   B. HDSL

   C. IDSL

   D. ADSL

11. Which of the following is *not* true regarding DSL service offerings?

   A. DSL is a dedicated connection between the DSLAM and the terminating router.

   B. DSL is not oversubscribed in most consumer offerings.

   C. DSL is based on ATM.

   D. DSL can provide video, voice, and data services.

12. A background in what technology is helpful in troubleshooting DSL?

   A. ISDN

   B. Ethernet

   C. ATM

   D. Frame Relay

13. What DSL variant is best suited to broadcast television emulation?

    A. VDSL

    B. IDSL

    C. ADSL

    D. SDSL

14. Which DSL solution would be recommended for replacement of a T-1?

    A. VDSL

    B. ADSL

    C. SDSL

    D. IDSL

15. What is the maximum range of IDSL?

    A. 1,000 feet

    B. 3,000 feet

    C. 15,000 feet

    D. 45,000 feet

16. G.lite's advantage over standard ADSL is its splitterless installation. What is its downside?

    A. Range

    B. Reduced bandwidth

    C. Lack of voice support

    D. Cost

17. Which of the following best describes oversubscription?

    A. Burst provisioning

    B. The consolidation of many ports with a greater combined bandwidth than the egress port

    C. Cell header overhead

    D. Encapsulation

18. DSL provides a _____ connection.

    A. Shared

    B. Virtual

    C. Switched

    D. Wireless

19. An administrator needs to provide T-1 bandwidths over a single copper pair. Which DSL technology should be selected?

    A. IDSL

    B. SDSL

    C. HDSL

    D. G.lite

20. A splitter performs what function?

    A. Converts frames into cells

    B. Converts cells into frames

    C. Converts analog voice into IP datagrams

    D. Separates analog voice from the DSL data traffic

Answers to Written Lab

1. `encapsulation aal5snap`
2. `subinterfaces`
3. `oam-pvc manage`
4. `ubr 1500`
5. `pvc 2/40`
6. CRC
7. Two
8. ATM
9. None. The splitter is an external, pre-router device.
10. `show interface atm`

Answer to Hands-on Lab

```
interface ATM0
 ip address 10.1.1.1 255.255.255.0
 pvc 2/51
  ubr 1500
  oam-pvc manage
  oam retry 3 5 1
  encapsulation aal5snap
```

Answers to Review Questions

1. B.   IDSL allows for longer distances from the DSLAM than other DSL variants.

2. D.   VDSL can provide over 50Mbps of downstream bandwidth, depending on distance.

3. C.   G.lite does not require a splitter.

4. C.   HDSL provides equal amounts of bandwidth upstream and downstream.

5. A.   ADSL requires a splitter to be installed.

6. B.   ADSL is best suited for users who request large amounts of data and have little to upload.

7. B.   HDSL provides 1.544Mbps of bandwidth in each direction.

8. C.   IDSL provides 144Kbps of bandwidth in each direction, which is similar to the bandwidth provided by an ISDN BRI.

9. D.   ADSL is the best DSL technology for video conferencing, according to Cisco.

10. C.   IDSL can be theoretically extended to 45,000 feet with repeaters.

11. B.   DSL is commonly oversubscribed in consumer deployments.

12. C.   Because DSL is based on ATM technology, an understanding of ATM is most helpful.

13. A.   VDSL can provide 52Mbps of downstream bandwidth. This allows many video encoded data streams, which typically require less than 8Mbps each.

14. C.   SDSL is a single pair 1.544Mbps bidirectional solution.

15. D.   With repeaters, IDSL can reach up to 45,000 feet.

16. B.   Compared to splitter-based ADSL, G.lite has less available bandwidth in comparable installations as presented in Table 6.1.

17. B.   Oversubscription is the lack of available bandwidth to service full utilization of all user capacity at one time.

18. C.   DSL connections are considered switched as the circuit services a single endpoint, unlike cable modems wherein the link is shared.

19. B.   SDSL provides 1.544Mbps over a single pair. HDSL requires two or more pairs.

20. D.   Splitters perform a frequency-based separation of the analog voice traffic.

Chapter 7

Remote Access with Cable Modems and Virtual Private Networks

EXAM TOPICS COVERED IN THIS CHAPTER INCLUDE:

✓ Understand cable modem technologies

✓ Know how to configure cable modem technologies

✓ Understand how to troubleshoot cable modem technologies

✓ Understand VPN technologies including IPSec

✓ Know how to configure VPN technologies

In this chapter, we discuss two increasingly important technologies in remote access: cable modems and virtual private networks. Although Cisco has finally added these topics to the Remote Access exam, they have not attained the prominence that one might expect compared to legacy technologies such as ISDN. Cable modems, like DSL, provide high data rates at low cost, and don't suffer from the call setup and bonding issues that ISDN includes. In addition to providing an overview of cable modem and VPN technologies, this chapter also covers the configuration of IPSec, one of the most common VPN technologies.

What is a Cable Modem?

The *cable modem* is the industry's response to DSL and other broadband network services from competitors. It provides remote access connectivity by establishing a shared data channel across the existing cable television network. In fact, it is apt to call it a channel—the bandwidth provided to customers is actually taken from one of the 6MHz channels that would normally be used for a video feed such as CNN or ESPN.

This 6MHz channel (NTSC—the North American standard from the National Television System Committee) can provide up to 40Mbps of downstream (to the user) bandwidth and 12Mbps of upstream bandwidth. This bandwidth, as noted in Chapter 6, "Digital Subscriber Line (DSL)," is shared by all the customers within a specific area. As such, due to the normal installation and design model, in addition to bandwidth rate limiting by the provider, a typical user should expect less than 2Mbps downstream and 128Kbps to 256Kbps upstream. The typical cable modem installation is illustrated in Figure 7.1.

As shown, each home is connected to the COAX (coaxial cable) that is running through the neighborhood and providing video services. At the head-end, or cable service provider, this cable is connected to a Hybrid Fiber/COAX (HFC) device that might also provide the cable modem termination system (CMTS). This device is connected to the router that links to the Internet and to the video streams (greatly simplified in this figure). The CMTS is the electronic engine that processes cable modem feeds comparable to the DSLAM in DSL.

The installation at the home requires the installation of a filter to service all the televisions on the premises. An unfiltered connection is provided to the cable modem itself. Note that for customers without cable modems, the filter is typically placed in the street. In residences with cable data services the filter can be installed anywhere between the head-end and the televisions that will be using the cable signal. Many customers, as a result, never have to concern themselves with the filter, but it does complicate the installation of a cable modem, just as the splitter complicates DSL installations.

FIGURE 7.1 A cable modem installation

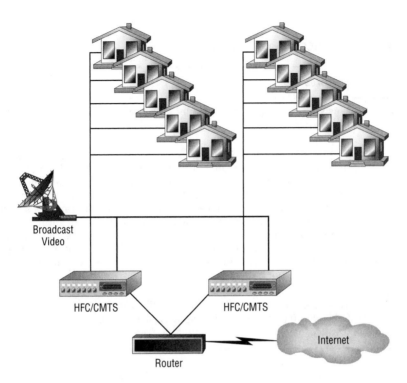

Note that cable modems have a perceived disadvantage of shared bandwidth for all users on a particular link—there are two distinct shared domains shown in Figure 7.1. As noted in Chapter 6, this is not a significant issue from a bandwidth perspective. It could be a security concern however, as data from one home is viewable from all other homes within that domain. This is addressed by the *Data Over Cable Service Interface Specification (DOCSIS)* ratified by CableLabs, a nonprofit organization composed of cable service providers in the Americas. DOCSIS is presented in the following section and it provides customer data protection over the shared medium.

The biggest advantage to cable modems is their capability to provide high per-user bandwidth over long distances, often significantly greater than DSL. Although the cable is capable of providing up to 40Mbps of downstream bandwidth, the network is provisioned so that each user can obtain only a predefined rate—typically less than 2Mbps. For consumer installations, this is sufficient and leads to a very economical solution. However, the provider could easily increase the bandwidth to an individual user, although they would need to have a dedicated COAX connection to attain the full capacity.

DOCSIS

The primary purpose of DOCSIS was to ensure interoperability between vendors' equipment. Different versions provide standards for security, encapsulation, management, QoS, and services. There are three versions of the DOCSIS specification. These are outlined in Table 7.1.

TABLE 7.1 The DOCSIS Specifications

Version	Features
DOCSIS 1.0	This was the original specification and provided for standardization between vendors.
DOCSIS 1.1	This version of DOCSIS is commonly used today, and provides basic quality of service and security functions. This is very important for most users, and cable networks leverage these features to protect user traffic in transit from being intercepted. Please note that this does not protect user machines from attack; the specifications are not firewalls, but rather a switched emulation over the shared infrastructure. The specification is backward compatible. DOCSIS 1.1 added voice and streaming services. This version also takes steps to prevent theft of service from the provider. In previous specifications, a user with cable service could remove the filter in the street and have data service for free.
DOCSIS 2.0	This emerging standard will provide six times the upstream capacity of DOCSIS 1.0 (three times the capacity of 1.1). The channel is increased to 6.4MHz for greater capacity and efficiency. It is also backward compatible.

DOCSIS specifies the connection between only the CMTS and the cable modem or cable modem router. The PC, network router(s), and other network elements are not involved.

Cisco's Cable Modem Product Line

As with the DSL product line, Cisco caters to the head-end and the remote installation. At the central office, Cisco provides the uBR10012 and uBR7100/7200 series Universal Broadband routers. The uBR10012 product combines the Cisco 10000 Edge Services Router with the uBR7200 product, which can support up to 8,000 terminations.

For remote installations, the product line contains two products: the uBR905 and the uBR925. Both support VPN tunnels (IPSec) and firewall services in addition to routing, but the uBR925 adds support for voice over the cable network and a USB port.

Unlike the DSL product line, Cisco does not currently support a cable modem interface for the higher-end routers, including the 1700, 2600XM, and the 3600 series. This will likely change in the future, but administrators should note that cable television is not as prevalent in business parks and commercial buildings as compared to residential settings.

Cisco Cable Manager

To help customers configure and monitor large cable modem infrastructures, Cisco has developed Cisco Cable Manager (CCM). This Solaris-based product is beyond the scope of the exam, but it provides a centralized interface for managing up to 100,000 devices, and it provides auto-topology and polling features.

Virtual Private Networks

You might be questioning the inclusion of a section on virtual private network (VPN) technologies in a chapter presenting cable modems. It is true that VPN is technology agnostic, and will operate over DSL, Frame Relay, or any other transport. However, cable modems and VPNs are both covered briefly on the Remote Access exam, and neither seems to warrant a chapter on its own. In addition, many cable modem installations for business customers leverage VPN tunnels to provide connectivity.

A *virtual private network* is a logical tunnel across a physical topology. This physical layer could be the Internet, or it could be a corporate network or other private network. The tunnel need not be encrypted to be private, but this is a method of providing privacy. In reality, however, so long as the data is not visible to non-recipients, the tunnel has a certain degree of protection. As such, VPNs are commonly thought of as IPSec, L2TP (Layer 2 Tunneling Protocol), SSL-VPN, and MPLS constructions, but Frame Relay and ATM PVCs, in addition to 802.1q and GRE (Generic Routing Encapsulation) can also be considered VPNs. This is discussed in greater detail later in the chapter.

By far the most common VPN technology deployed today is IPSec, or IP Security Protocol. Quickly gaining momentum is an alternative technology that has been used for years for Web-based security, Secure Sockets Layer (SSL).

IPSec

IPSec is a generic description of a set of protocols that establish the parameters and encryption for a tunnel between two end-points, but IPSec itself provides none of these functions. The standard is defined in RFCs 2401 through 2411 and in RFC 2451, and this is recommended reading for anyone supporting or installing a large-scale IPSec VPN. The elements that comprise many IPSec functions are outlined in Table 7.2.

TABLE 7.2 The Components of IPSec

Protocol or Function	Description
IKE	*Internet Key Exchange* is a general term used to define how keys are exchanged and tunnels are authenticated. It is defined in RFC 2409, which is recommended reading for anyone deploying IPSec VPNs.
3DES	Triple Data Encryption Standard performs three DES hash processes with three keys in sequence to encrypt data. DES, Data Encryption Standard, performs a single hash process.
AES	Advanced Encryption Standard will likely replace DES and 3DES because the processing power required for AES is significantly lower than that for 3DES.
AH	The *Authentication Header* option ensures authenticity and data integrity, but it does not encrypt the payload—thus the name reference to "authenticating the header." It is defined in RFC 2402.
Tunnel mode	*Tunnel mode* protects the entire IP packet, including the original header, and appends a new 20-byte IP header. Tunnel mode must be used for VPN applications involving hosts behind the IPSec peers, which is the most common configuration.
Transport mode	*Transport mode* protects only the IP payload via encryption, and the original header information is left unencrypted.
ESP	*Encapsulating Security Payload* protects the data within the datagram, but does nothing to the header. It is defined in RFC 2406 and is best remembered via the term *payload* in its title.

Because IPSec is the leading VPN technology, we will spend a moment discussing the configuration of this technology; however, please note that the current exam does not include configuration in scope.

Many configurations of IPSec have difficulties with Network Address Translation, presented in Chapter 11. A new feature, IPSec NAT Transparency, has been introduced with IOS version 12.2(13)T and should be evaluated for installations that require NAT and IPSec support.

The primary functions of IPSec address four key areas of concern for most data transmissions. These include the following:

- The confidential transmission of the data. This is provided by encryption of the payload as it crosses the network, and is important to prevent confidential data compromises.

- The integrity of the data. Receivers in IPSec can validate that the payload has not been altered in transmission.

- The authentication of the transmission source. IPSec receivers can authenticate the source of the packets to validate that they are from a trusted source.

- Protection from replay. The IPSec functions can support detection and rejection of packets that are replayed. This function is useful in preventing the retransmission of a packet containing a password for later authentication.

IPSec Configuration

Cisco could have made configuration of IPSec a little easier than they did, but unfortunately they didn't. This section defines a common IPSec configuration and illustrates some of the options available to the administrator, including the use of Data Encryption Standard (DES) or 3DES. The code sample in Table 7.3 is the basis for our configuration.

TABLE 7.3   Commands Used for IPSec

Command	Function
`crypto isakmp policy 10`	This creates an IKE process on the router. You must have an IOS version that supports the IPSec feature-set. The priority number can be anything from 1 to 10,000, and 1 is the highest priority. As with other elements, such as route maps, the convention is to start with 10 and increment by 10 to allow for future changes. You are now in ISAKMP policy configuration command mode.
`hash md 5`	This command specifies that you will use a preshared key and the MD5 hash algorithm for packet authentication. It is possible to configure a key dynamically using RSA public key signatures, but that requires a certificate server and other infrastructure.
`group 2`	This parameter is generally set to 2 to reflect the Diffie-Hellman group number to use for key negotiation. Group 1 uses a 768-bit key exchange, and group 2 uses 1,024 bits. A complete list of the group numbers and their related parameters is available at `http://www.cisco.com/en/US/customer/products/hw/vpndevc/ps2286/products_user_guide_chapter09186a008015d00c.html`.

TABLE 7.3   Commands Used for IPSec *(continued)*

Command	Function
lifetime *3600*	The lifetime parameter defines how long a security association will last. It is defined in seconds and can range from one minute to one day. A value of 3,600 seconds is equal to one hour. Longer lifetimes might compromise security but can reduce overhead.
crypto isakmp key *tyler* address *10.1.1.1*	This configuration command defines the key to be used and the IP address of the far-end Ethernet segment that services as the termination of the tunnel. In this instance, the key is tyler and the IP address is 10.1.1.1. This key will be defined on both routers, is case sensitive, and can be up to 128 characters long. Security can be enhanced by using longer keys with alphanumeric characters.
crypto IPSec transform-set *tunnel-A* *ah-md5-hmac esp-des*	This command defines the transforms that will be used. In this case, we are defining AH (MD5) and ESP (56-des), but other combinations might include specifying triple DES or LZS compression. Depending on the choices selected, the administrator can select up to three transforms. IOS will prevent incompatible values.
crypto map *map-A* local-address *Ethernet0*	Here we define a crypto map called map-A. It is bound to the Ethernet 0 interface; recall that we are going to create a tunnel from one Ethernet interface to another.
crypto map *map-A* 10 *ipsec-isakmp*	This command enters crypto map configuration mode with a map numbered 10. Again, this is a definable value.
set peer *10.1.1.1*	Here we set the peer by again defining the IP address of the remote. This is for the map and not the key, but it would be nice if Cisco would simplify this relationship.
set transform-set *tunnel-A*	This command links the map to the transform set previously defined.
match address *110*	This defines the ACL to be used in determining what traffic is encrypted. Please note that ACLs 100 through 102 are reserved for use by the DOCSIS configuration file and should not be used with cable modems.
interface Ethernet0	This selects the Ethernet interface.
ip address *10.1.2.1 255.255.255.0*	This defines the local IP address of 10.1.2.1/24.

T A B L E 7 . 3   Commands Used for IPSec *(continued)*

Command	Function
`interface cable-modem0`	This selects the cable modem interface.
`crypto map map-A`	This defines that crypto map map-A is to be used.
`access-list 110 permit ip 10.1.2.0 0.0.0.255 10.1.1.0 0.0.0.255`	This defines access list 110, which was assigned to tunnel-A. This defines that all traffic destined for 10.1.1/24 from 10.1.2/24 should be encrypted. Remember that this uses wildcard mask rules.

That's it. Of course, a real configuration would also need routing and other parameters to be defined. The cable modem would also require an IP address. The opposing router would require a comparable configuration as well to establish the tunnel.

Other VPN Technologies

As noted in the introduction to this chapter, VPNs can be composed of any tunneling technology to varying degrees. Some other VPN technologies include those outlined in Table 7.4.

T A B L E 7 . 4   VPN Technologies

Technology	Description
Generic Router Encapsulation (GRE)	GRE is not really a private technology because the data is not encrypted, but it is a tunneling technology, and the data contained within is somewhat transparent to the overall network. One common use of GRE is to tunnel IPX or other non-IP traffic over an IP-only backbone.
Virtual circuit (VC)	VCs can be permanent or switched, and are found in Frame Relay and ATM. Traffic within a VC is not encrypted, but could be considered a tunnel and can be marketed as a virtual private network.
802.1q in q	802.1q in q also lacks privacy because the data is not encrypted, but, like a virtual circuit, data that is tagged in one logical VLAN is private from other VLANs. The technology for q in q is the same as 802.1q itself, except for a second .q header being added. This second header is controlled by the service provider. One advantage to this model is that the original customer tag is not changed. For those familiar with ATM, an analogy is the virtual path identifier.

TABLE 7.4 VPN Technologies *(continued)*

Technology	Description
L2TP	Layer 2 Tunneling Protocol. This is an extension to PPP, discussed in Chapter 3, and allows for tunneling of packets independent of Layer 3.
Multi Protocol Label Switching (MPLS)	MPLS is quickly gaining as the standard service tagging model. Many service providers are converting their data networks to MPLS, which is simply a dynamic tag added to the front of the packet. Again, the data is not encrypted, but vendors are selling the service as a managed VPN. In reality, it has little functional difference when compared to other technologies, except for the significant benefit that it is transport agnostic. Most other technologies require a specific set of physical layer technologies. MPLS can also provide rapid fault-detection and correction compared to other technologies.
IPSec	IP Security is a set of protocols that encrypt and authenticate the integrity of the data between two points.
SSL	Secure Sockets Layer is a popular encryption technology used for many HTTP business transactions (HTTPS). However, the protocol is not limited to HTTP/HTTPS, and is now used for remote control and other remote access functions, and the protocol can be used for other services. The most significant advantage of SSL is that the client requires no preconfiguration and the network is transparent to the entire flow. Each end-station is responsible for encryption and decryption, and only the payload is protected.
Frame Relay and ATM	These PVC-based technologies can create private paths across the public network. Although not typically thought of in VPN concepts, they are rightfully included in the list.

Summary

In this chapter, we examined cable modem technology and presented VPN services, including IPSec. Cable modems offer the administrator an alternative low-cost technology for remote access, and they can provide longer-range connections than DSL. Although cable modems use a shared medium, the overall performance is comparable to the switched DSL in real-world deployments. The key to cable modem services is DOCSIS and the incorporated security and other services that this standard provides.

Most remote access users will map IPSec tunnels over the cable modem network to allow for corporate access. Although not the only VPN technology, IPSec is currently the most popular and provides for encrypted tunneling of IP data between locations. We also briefly noted a number of other tunneling technologies that provide solutions for remote access.

Exam Essentials

Understand how cable modems can be used as part of a remote access solution.   Be able to compare cable modem technologies to other remote access methods, including DSL. Also understand the internal characteristics of cable modem, including DOCSIS.

Understand VPN technologies such as IPSec.   Know the differences in various VPN technologies, including the modes of IPSec and its encryption benefits.

Know how to configure cable modems and IPSec.   Understand the protocols and relationships between IPSec components, including AH, ESP, and tunnel and transport mode. Knowing how to configure IPSec can help this, but is not required for the exam.

Key Terms

Before you take the exam, be certain you are familiar with the following terms:

Advanced Encryption Standard	Internet Key Exchange (IKE)
Authentication Header (AH)	IPSec
cable modem	transport mode
Data Encryption Standard	tunnel mode
Data Over Cable Service Interface Specification (DOCSIS)	virtual private network (VPN)
Encapsulating Security Payload (ESP)	

Written Lab

1. What command is used to relate an access list to a crypto map?

2. What access-list numbers should be not be used in DOCSIS deployments?

3. What command is used to relate a crypto map to an interface?

4. What number is recommended for the first entry of a numerically based router list, such as `crypto isakmp policy` or a `route-map`?

5. What is the maximum length of the `crypto isakmp key`?

6. The duration of a security association is defined with what command?

7. What parameter is used to configure Encapsulating Security Payload with Data Encryption Standard?

8. What mode is used to protect the entire IP packet, including the original IP header?

9. What is the mask used to define a /16 address block in an access list?

10. What is the benefit to longer `lifetime` values?

Hands-On Lab

We realize that some readers have a strong desire for elaborate labs that present every combination and syntax relating to the material in a chapter. This is a disservice in two contexts. The first is that the lab, and the chapter, should focus on the materials that you need to know. As such, this chapter does not list voltages, arcane technical specifications, and other minutiae.

The second is that no text can present every model and structure.

As such, this lab might appear very simple relative to IPSec, and you will note that it does not use a cable interface. IPSec is much more complex than this chapter presents, and we encourage readers to find other references for its configuration. In addition, Cisco is working on this portion of IOS with great speed, changing some commands and features. Complicated IPSec configurations would be quickly dated. The cable modem interface is not readily available—we assume that you have 2600 series routers for the labs, or some other small-scale serial/Ethernet device. This configuration is based on Ethernet. Don't worry—the only significant difference is the interface name. If you have a cable modem, substitute `interface cable 0` for the Ethernet interface.

Configure a pair of routers to run IPSec across an Ethernet link with the following parameters. Use Figure 7.2 as a guide.

- DES
- AH
- ESP
- A key value of `tyler`
- RIP version 1
- All traffic from nontransit Ethernet segment on Routers A and B should transit the tunnel. No other traffic should be encrypted.

FIGURE 7.2   IPSec lab

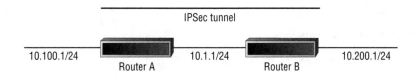

Review Questions

1. What is the primary advantage of cable modem technology?

   A. It provides high bandwidth at greater range than DSL.

   B. It can service ISDN terminations.

   C. It allows bursting for periods of heavy user demand.

   D. It has integrated support for redundant virtual paths.

2. What is IKE?

   A. Internal Krypto Enhancement

   B. Inter-Key Exchange

   C. Internet Key Exchange

   D. Internet Key Extensions

3. What service commonly has problems with IPSec VPN?

   A. ADSL

   B. Frame Relay

   C. NAT

   D. EIGRP

4. IPSec VPNs are not supported on _____.

   A. Cable modem links.

   B. ATM.

   C. DSL.

   D. IPSec is transport agnostic.

5. Which set of specifications define functions and interoperability between cable modem vendors?

   A. IPSec

   B. AH

   C. DOCSIS

   D. IKE

6. A possible disadvantage of cable modem networks is which of the following?

   A. Shared medium.

   B. Switched medium.

   C. There is no support for IPSec.

   D. There is no support for routing.

7. What mode is used in most VPN applications and protects the entire IP packet in IPSec?

   A. Tunnel mode

   B. ESP mode

   C. Transport mode

   D. 3DES mode

8. Remote control VPNs are increasingly supported with what technology?

   A. IPSec

   B. Frame Relay

   C. SSL

   D. MPLS

9. What is the benefit of AES over 3DES?

   A. AES encrypts the entire packet, and 3DES does not.

   B. AES requires less processing power than 3DES with comparable security.

   C. AES works with IPSec, whereas 3DES does not.

   D. AES supports SSL and not IPSec.

10. What problem can be experienced when running IOS 12.1(11) and NAT?

   A. IPSec might not work under specific configurations, such as AH.

   B. SSL will not work.

   C. DES cannot be used.

   D. IKE cannot be used.

11. What tool is available to administer cable modem networks?

   A. CiscoTools.

   B. Cisco Cable Manager.

   C. Cisco Cable Management Station.

   D. There is no tool for administration of cable modem networks.

12. How would an administrator terminate a cable modem connection to a Cisco 2600XM series router in a branch office?

    A. Install the cable modem network module.

    B. Install the cable modem WIC.

    C. Connect to an external cable modem via Ethernet.

    D. Purchase the Cisco 2695CM, which has a fixed configuration cable modem interface.

13. Which of the following is not a function of IPSec?

    A. Data encryption

    B. Replay protection

    C. Source authentication

    D. Compression

14. Downstream bandwidth of cable modem networks can reach up to what data rate?

    A. 2Mbps

    B. 10Mbps

    C. 40Mbps

    D. 100Mbps

15. A user should expect what download bandwidth on a cable modem network assuming standard provisioning and usage?

    A. 128Kbps

    B. 256Kbps

    C. 2Mbps

    D. 40Mbps

16. Bandwidth on a cable modem network is _____.

    A. Shared

    B. Switched

    C. Routed

    D. Tunneled

17. Encryption keys and tunnel authentication are addressed with what service?

    A. ESP

    B. AES

    C. IKE

    D. DOCSIS

18. The `set peer` command performs which of the following functions?

   A. Defines the address of the remote peer for the crypto map

   B. Defines the address of the remote peer for the tunnel termination

   C. Defines the address of a load balancing peer

   D. Defines the address of a local peer for the crypto map

19. The task of defining a peer for the encryption key is performed with which command if the key is `shaynatylereddie` and the remote peer is `10.1.1.1`? The local router is `10.2.1.1`.

   A. `crypto isakmp key shaynatylereddie address 10.1.1.1`

   B. `crypto isakmp key shaynatylereddie address-peer 10.1.1.1`

   C. `crypto isakmp key shaynatylereddie address-local 10.2.1.1 address-remote 10.1.1.1`

   D. `crypto isakmp key shaynatylereddie address 10.2.1.1`

20. The DOCSIS specification provides security and other services for which technology?

   A. DSL

   B. Cable modem

   C. SSL

   D. IPSec

Answers to Written Lab

1. `match address`

2. Access list 101 and 102 are reserved for DOCSIS configurations.

3. `crypto map map-A local-address Ethernet0`

4. The number 10 is recommended for the first entry, with incremental numbers increasing by 10.

5. 128 characters

6. `lifetime`

7. `esp-des`

8. Tunnel mode

9. `0.0.255.255`

10. It can reduce processor overhead on the routers.

Answer to Hands-on Lab

Router A

```
interface ethernet 0
  ip address 10.100.1.1 255.255.255.0
interface ethernet 1
  ip address 10.1.1.1 255.255.255.0
  crypto map map-a

router rip
  network 10.0.0.0

crypto isakmp policy 10
  hash md 5
  group 2
  lifetime 3600
crypto isakmp key tyler address 10.200.1.1
crypto ipsec transform-set tunnel-a ah-md5-hmac esp-des
crypto map map-a local-address ethernet0
crypto map map-a 10 ipsec-isakmp
  set peer 10.200.1.1
  set transform-set tunnel-a
  match address 110
access-list 110 permit ip 10.100.1.0 0.0.0.255 10.200.1.0 0.0.0.255
```

Router B

```
interface ethernet 0
  ip address 10.200.1.1 255.255.255.0
interface ethernet 1
  ip address 10.1.1.2 255.255.255.0
  crypto map map-a

router rip
  network 10.0.0.0
```

```
crypto isakmp policy 10
  hash md 5
  group 2
  lifetime 3600
crypto isakmp key tyler address 10.100.1.1
crypto ipsec transform-set tunnel-a ah-md5-hmac esp-des
crypto map map-a local-address ethernet0
crypto map map-a 10 ipsec-isakmp
  set peer 10.100.1.1
  set transform-set tunnel-a
  match address 110
access-list 110 permit ip 10.200.1.0 0.0.0.255 10.100.1.0 0.0.0.255
```

Please note that the right interface on Router B is Ethernet 0 in this configuration. The left interface is Ethernet 1 for convention.

Answers to Review Questions

1. A. Cable modems typically operate at distances greater than that available with DSL.

2. C. IKE stands for Internet Key Exchange, a mechanism for authenticating IPSec sessions.

3. C. Network Address Translation can fail in IPSec VPNs.

4. D. IPSec VPN tunnels operate over any physical layer medium.

5. C. The Data Over Cable Service Interface Specification defines cable modem services.

6. A. Users on cable modem networks share bandwidth with other users in the same neighborhood.

7. A. Tunnel mode protects the entire IP packet in IPSec by adding a new IP header to the packet. This is the most used mode for VPN applications.

8. C. SSL is a common VPN technology for Web-based remote access.

9. B. AES generally requires less processing power than 3DES.

10. A. IPSec NAT traversal resolves NAT/IPSec issues, but is not available until IOS 12.2(13)T.

11. B. Cisco Cable Manager is available to administer cable modem networks.

12. C. Cisco does not support direct termination of cable modem connections on the 2600XM.

13. D. IPSec does not compress data, but encrypts and authenticates data, in addition to preventing replay attacks.

14. C. The frequency used and encoding of cable modem networks allows for up to 40Mbps of downstream bandwidth.

15. C. Most networks provide up to 2Mbps per user on a cable modem network.

16. A. Users on cable modem networks share bandwidth with other users in the same neighborhood.

17. C. Internet Key Exchange provides key exchange and tunnel authentication services.

18. A. The `set peer` command defines the remote peer for the crypto map function.

19. A. The command `crypto isakmp key shaynatylereddie address 10.1.1.1` defines a key of `shaynatylereddie` with peer `10.1.1.1`.

20. B. DOCSIS is a cable modem specification.

Chapter

8

Frame Relay

EXAM TOPICS COVERED IN THIS CHAPTER INCLUDE:

- ✓ Describe how different WAN technologies can be used to provide remote access to a network, including asynchronous dial-in, Frame Relay, ISDN, cable modem, and DSL.

- ✓ Describe traffic control methods used to manage traffic flow on WAN links.

- ✓ Explain the operation of remote network access control methods.

- ✓ Identify PPP components, and explain the use of PPP as an access and encapsulation method.

- ✓ Configure Frame Relay operation and traffic control on WAN links.

- ✓ Design a Cisco Frame Relay infrastructure to provide access between remote network components.

- ✓ Troubleshoot nonfunctional remote access systems.

The use of *packet switching* protocols has become the most popular method for moving traffic across a wide area network (WAN). One particular packet switching protocol, Frame Relay, has become the dominant player in the packet switching market. Other methods of passing data between routers across the WAN include dedicated lines, time division multiplexing, ATM, ISDN, DSL, and others.

Because DSL is so much cheaper and faster than Frame Relay, it could eventually replace Frame Relay and ISDN as the dominant player in the WAN markets. As network sizes increase, you should pay particular attention to how DSL is playing a larger role in network deployment. However, DSL presently has too many distance limitations to completely replace Frame Relay anytime soon.

Understanding the theory and function of Frame Relay is important for numerous reasons. Not only is it still tested on Cisco's Remote Access exam, but when you get a Cisco-related job, you will most likely see quite a few networks that depend on Frame Relay. Mastery of the information covered in this chapter will enable you to gain an in-depth understanding of how and why you would implement Frame Relay on your internetwork. In this chapter we will go over what Frame Relay is, the components of Frame Relay, Frame Relay Configuration, and verifying that Frame Relay is running properly.

Understanding Frame Relay

Before we dive right into Frame Relay we need to have a better understanding of what Frame Relay is, how it is used, and how it came about.

What is Frame Relay?

Frame Relay is a telecommunications service designed for cost-efficient data transmission across a WAN. Frame Relay puts data in a variable-size unit called a *frame* and leaves any necessary error correction up to the endpoints. This provides for a high-speed, low-overhead, efficient network.

Frame Relay is a Layer 2 (Data Link Layer) connection-oriented protocol that creates virtual circuits (VCs)—usually Permanent Virtual Circuits (PVCs)—between two end devices such as routers, through a Frame Relay network. A Frame Relay *bearer service* was defined as a network service within the framework of ISDN. It was designed to be more efficient and faster than X.25. The major difference between Frame Relay and traditional ISDN is that in Frame Relay, the control information needed to keep the link synchronized is not in a separate channel as it is in ISDN, but instead is included with the data. This single stream of data provides for flow control, congestion control, and frame routing. Frame Relay is a form of packet switching, whereas ISDN is still considered circuit switching.

You should understand that the error and congestion control works only at the Data Link Layer and that Frame Relay also relies on upper-layer protocols and applications for error correction.

A Brief History of Frame Relay

Currently, Frame Relay is the most prevalent type of packet switching used in North America; however, Frame Relay's origin is very humble. Initially, Frame Relay was not even a standard unto itself; instead, it was an extension of the Integrated Services Digital Network (ISDN) standard. The International Telecommunications Union-Telecommunications, or ITU-T, (formerly known as the *Comité Consultatif International de Téléphonique et Télégraphique*, or CCITT) was the first to define the Frame Relay standard.

Many companies that saw the value of this technology quickly adopted the ITU-T standard for Frame Relay. After these companies showed interest, ITU-T and other organizations proceeded to develop the standard, but very slowly. Several corporations saw a need for a more rapid development and implementation of a Frame Relay standard. Four companies, Digital Equipment Corporation (DEC), Northern Telecom (Nortel), Cisco, and StrataCom, bound together to form the *Group of Four*. This group began developing Frame Relay technology more quickly, which enabled Frame Relay to work on disparate devices. In September 1990, the Group of Four published *Frame Relay Specifications with Extensions*. This group eventually became what is currently known as the *Frame Relay Forum*.

Frame Relay Virtual Circuits

As mentioned earlier, Frame Relay is a Layer 2 (Data Link Layer) connection-oriented protocol. After a connection has been established, end devices can transmit data across the network. This Layer 2 connection across the packet-switched network is called a *virtual circuit*.

The end devices (in this case, routers) will act as Data Terminal Equipment (DTE), and the Frame Relay switch will be the Data Communications Equipment (DCE). The difference between the two is that the DCE device will most likely be responsible for the clocking of the line and also initiates LMI messages, which we will discuss later in this chapter.

Two quick terms you will encounter later: *ingress* refers to Frame Relay frames from an access device toward the Frame Relay network, and *egress* refers to Frame Relay frames leaving a Frame Relay network toward the destination device.

From the point of view of the router, the virtual circuit is somewhat transparent. This means that the router sees the virtual circuit, but only up to the Frame Relay switch, which is where the term *locally significant* originates with regard to the DLCI. In other words, the router speaks LMI and understands what a DLCI is. This isn't all that transparent. The transparency comes in when you consider that the router uses the DLCI like a MAC address for the remote router to bind to the virtual circuit to the protocol address. The previous statement, however, is not a pure Frame Relay function. In pure Frame Relay terms, the router still has to know how to recognize the existence of the ingress Frame Relay switch. Even though the circuit might traverse many switches en route to its destination, the router simply sees its connection to the local Frame Relay switch, which again is part of the VC.

Figure 8.1 shows how routers see the Frame Relay network. In the figure, notice that Frame Relay is configured between the routers and the switching office.

FIGURE 8.1 Frame Relay operation

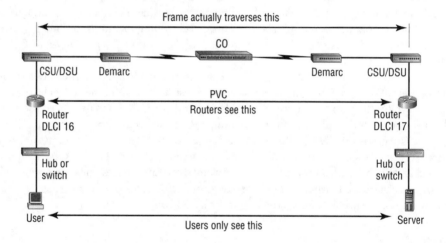

There are two ways for Frame Relay to establish this connectivity. Either you can set up a circuit that is enabled only when needed by using a Switched Virtual Circuit , or you can set up a dedicated circuit between the local router and remote router by using a Permanent Virtual Circuit. Each of these is discussed in more detail next.

Switched Virtual Circuits

Switched Virtual Circuits (SVCs) provide an economical way to connect to a Frame Relay network. An SVC is a type of circuit that is brought up only when there is data to send. These circuits provide temporary connectivity to the network on an as-needed basis. Switched Virtual Circuits are used with many technologies—for example, a standard telephone call.

It is rare to find a Frame Relay SVC connection, and indeed, you might never see one. Typically, PVCs are the only connections used with Frame Relay, although Cisco routers do support Frame Relay with SVCs.

Because they are rarely used, SVCs are not covered further in this book and are not on the Remote Access exam.

Permanent Virtual Circuits

Permanent Virtual Circuits (PVCs) are dedicated virtual paths through the Frame Relay network that are up and running 100 percent of the time (well, at least in theory!). Unlike an SVC, a PVC does not require the call establishment and call teardown phases. However, when the circuit initially comes up, some parameter negotiations do pass over the wire; these communications should occur only when the dedicated circuit goes down.

The two phases for PVCs are as follows:

Data exchange   Data is transmitted between two devices, and each device can transmit data as needed because it doesn't need to wait for a call to be established to do so. The data exchange can happen at any time because the virtual connection is permanent and always available.

Idle   The connection is still active, but data is not being transmitted. The idle time can be indefinite: the circuits will not time out. The idle time keeps the VC up and the line from timing out when no data is present. This is done by the transmission of idle frames, the sole purpose of which is to keep line synchronization in the absence of data.

PVCs have gained in popularity as the price for dedicated lines has decreased. They are the types of links that we configure later in this chapter.

Data Link Connection Identifier (DLCI)

Frame Relay provides statistical time-division multiplexing (Stat-TDM). Time division multiplexing (TDM) is like going to Disneyland. It's true. Remember how you have to stand in line to get into Space Mountain? Well, after you get to the loading area, you are placed in a section with rails that separate you from the other passengers. You can then get into only the one car that is in front of you and only when it is empty. Think of the holding area as the interface buffers of a router; the cars are the time slots on the circuit. When a time slot drives up, you can get in, but not before that, and not if someone is already in that slot.

Now Stat-TDM is an improvement over straight TDM. Stat-TDM enables you to jump into a different line if it is not in use and to get into any car. This is a first-come, first-served technology. Stat-TDM is used with Frame Relay to allow multiple logical data connections (virtual circuits) over a single physical link. Basically, these circuits give time slots to first-come, first-served and priority-based frames over the physical link. Going back to our analogy, you can think of Frame Relay as the capability to send multiple cars through space on one train, each car holding a different person.

So, how is each person (data) identified in the car (time slot)? How does the frame switch know where to send each frame? The answer to this is a *data link connection identifier (DLCI)*. Because Frame Relay is based on virtual circuits instead of physical ones, DLCIs are used to identify a virtual circuit and tie it to a physical circuit. This means each frame can be identified as it traverses the Frame Relay switch and is then sent to the routers at the remote ends.

DLCIs are considered only locally significant, which means that they see the entire virtual circuit but only up to the point of the Frame Relay switch. The provider is responsible for assigning DLCIs and their significance to the network.

DLCIs identify the logical virtual circuit between the Customer Premises Equipment (CPE) and the Frame Relay switch. The switch then maps the DLCIs between each pair of routers in order to create the PVC. The Frame Relay switch keeps a mapping table of DLCI numbers to outgoing ports; it uses this table to forward frames out ports on the switch. (More information about mapping follows in the next "DLCI Mapping" section.)

When configuring your Cisco router to participate in a Frame Relay network, you must configure a DLCI number for each connection. The Frame Relay provider supplies the DLCI numbers for your router. If a DLCI is not defined on the link, the switch will discard the frame.

Figure 8.2 shows an example of how DLCIs are assigned to offices in Chicago and Miami. The Chicago office will communicate through the Frame Relay switch to Miami by using DLCI 17. Miami will communicate to Chicago by using DLCI 16. Remember that the valid range of DLCIs is from 16 to 991.

FIGURE 8.2   Frame Relay PVC configuration

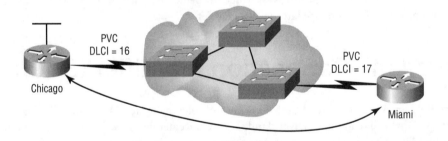

Some providers assign a DLCI in such a way that it appears that the DLCI is globally significant. For example, all circuits that terminate in Miami could be assigned the local DLCI 17 at each site. But remember that even though all of these DLCIs have the same number, they are not the same because DLCIs are typically only locally significant.

DCLI Mapping

There needs to be a way to link the Layer 2 identifiers (DLCI) to Layer 3 (network) addresses. *Mapping* provides a mechanism to link one or more network addresses to a DLCI. Remember that Frame Relay works only at the Data Link Layer (Layer 2 of the OSI model) and does not understand IP addressing. In fact, to communicate via IP (because it could just as easily be IPX and AppleTalk instead of IP), you need to convert the destination IP address to a destination DLCI (PVC) number. The frame switch uses only DLCI numbers to communicate, not IP addresses.

Mappings can be done either statically by an administrator or dynamically via the router. If you are mapping a static Network Layer address to a DLCI number, you use the `frame-relay map` command. It is necessary to create static mappings when the remote router does not support dynamic addressing or when you are using OSPF in some network configurations. It is also necessary even if you want to control broadcasts over your Frame Relay network.

To understand how to use static mappings, look at Figure 8.3. Figure 8.3 shows a corporate office in Chicago connected to two other sites, one in Miami and one in New York. The IP address of the serial interface in New York is 172.16.1.2/24, and the Miami serial interface is 172.17.1.3/24. It is important to note that the Miami location is a Cisco router, and the New York location is a non-Cisco router. A static mapping would have to be used for different Frame Relay encapsulation methods to run under the same physical serial interface, unless all routers used an open encapsulation type for interoperability, resulting in the ability to use dynamic mapping.

FIGURE 8.3   Configuring Frame Relay static mappings

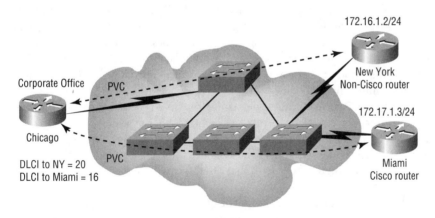

The following router output shows an example of how you would create static Frame Relay mappings on the Chicago router:

```
Router(config-if)#frame-relay map ip 172.16.1.2 20 broadcast ietf
Router(config-if)#frame-relay map ip 172.16.1.3 16 broadcast
```

The `frame-relay map` command maps the IP address of the remote location to a specific PVC or DLCI. The first map statement tells the Chicago router that if it has an IP packet with a destination IP address of 172.16.1.2, it should use PVC 20 to get there. Also, because the New York office is not a Cisco router (can you imagine that?), it should use the standard Internet Engineering Task Force (IETF) encapsulation method. We'll talk about encapsulation methods used with Frame Relay in a minute.

Because Miami is a Cisco router, no specification of encapsulation is necessary because Cisco is the default encapsulation method. The broadcast parameter at the end of each line specifies that broadcasts should be forwarded over the PVC because they are not forwarded by default. The `frame-relay map` command supports many Network Layer protocols including IP, Connectionless Network Services (CLNS), Digital Equipment Corporation's Networking architecture (DECnet), Xerox Network Services (XNS), and Virtual Integrated Network Service (Vines).

Dynamic addressing is turned on by default. It automatically maps Network Layer addresses to DLCI addresses rather well. *Inverse ARP (IARP)* is used to automatically map a DLCI to a network address (IP, IPX, and so on) without any user configuration. It provides Network Layer-to-DCLI-number translation and creates an entry in the DLCI mapping table. This table is used by the router to correctly route outgoing traffic. No map configuration is necessary for IARP to work.

Frame Relay Local Management Interface (LMI)

In 1990, the Group of Four developed extensions to the Frame Relay standard to help ease the management and configuration burden. One of these extensions was the *Local Management Interface (LMI)*. LMI provides for virtual circuit status messages and multicasting.

Cisco routers support three versions of the LMI standard: Cisco, ANSI, and ITU-T (Q.933a). LMI autosense, the automatic detection of the LMI type, was introduced in IOS version 11.2. LMI autosense determines the LMI type by rapidly trying each of them in order: ANSI, ITU-T (Q.933a), and then Cisco. If it cannot determine the LMI type within 60 seconds, it will terminate the autosense process and revert to the Cisco LMI type.

After LMI is established between the router and the switch, the next stage is DLCI determination and IARP. The router will query the switch, asking what the DLCI(s) is/are for this circuit. The router will configure itself with that DLCI(s) and query the switch to determine the status of the circuit.

This query is the first stage of discovery. The query that is sent includes the local router's network information. The remote router will record the network information and reply in kind. The local router will map the DLCI it learned from static or dynamic addressing to other network addresses it discovered from queries.

When an IARP is made, the router updates its map table with one of three possible LMI connection states:

Active   The connection is active, and the routers can exchange data through the PVC.

Inactive   The local connection to the Frame Relay switch is working, but the remote end of the PVC is not communicating to the Frame Relay switch.

Deleted   No LMI keepalive information from the switch to the router is being received for this PVC. This could be because no LMI is actually being exchanged or because the DLCI is not configured on the ingress switch.

Figure 8.4 shows that the Chicago office PVC to Miami is deleted because the Miami office is not receiving keepalives from the Frame Relay switch. Neither this inactive state nor this deleted state affect the other connections (PVCs) that Chicago might have to other locations.

FIGURE 8.4   LMI connection states

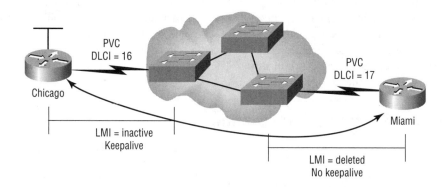

Configuring Frame Relay

The first step in configuring Frame Relay is to select the interface and then enable the Frame Relay encapsulation on the serial interface. You do this with the `encapsulation frame-relay` command. As you will notice in the following router configuration commands, there are two options: `cisco` and `ietf`.

```
Router#config t
Router(config)#interface serial 0
Router(config-if)#encapsulation frame-relay [cisco or ietf]
```

Cisco is the default encapsulation, which means that you have another Cisco router on the remote end with which your router will communicate. You will use the IETF encapsulation when communicating with a remote router that is not a Cisco device.

After you configure the encapsulation to the serial interface, you then need to add the Network Layer address, DLCI number, and LMI type. Cisco's capability to autosense the LMI type has greatly simplified configuration. The following router configuration shows the process of specifying the IP address and DLCI number, but not the LMI type because it is automatically detected:

```
Router(config-if)#ip address 172.16.10.1 255.255.255.0
Router(config-if)#frame-relay interface-dlci 16
Router(config-if)#no shutdown
```

Frame Relay Congestion Control

Frame Relay is optimized for speed and contains little error control. Frame Relay will discard errored frames and will not attempt to recover from the error either through retransmission or repair. Ideally, users can send as much data as they want across the network without interference. However, because user requests for bandwidth often outstrip the network's capability to provide bandwidth, a mechanism is needed to handle congestion in the frame switch.

In this section, you will learn about the factors that affect network performance, as well as methods for handling Frame Relay congestion. The two primary methods of congestion handling use Frame Relay switches and routers.

Factors Affecting Performance

Network performance at the router level is affected by three primary factors:

- Access rate
- Committed Information Rate (CIR)
- Bursting

Each of these has an effect on Frame Relay.

Access Rate

Access rate is the maximum speed at which data can be transferred to the Frame Relay network. This number denotes the actual line speed of the connection to the provider. In a dedicated circuit, you would consider this the actual data rate. However, in a Frame Relay network, this is considered the maximum data rate.

Committed Information Rate (CIR)

Committed Information Rate (CIR) is the rate at which the provider guarantees to deliver network traffic. The CIR is always less than or equal to the access rate. The CIR is advertised in Kbps and is actually averaged over a specified time period, referred to as *committed rate measurement interval* (T_c). This is what the cost of the Frame Relay connection is normally based upon.

Bursting

Bursting is one of the features that has made Frame Relay so popular. Bursting enables a user to transmit data faster than the CIR for a short period of time. Figure 8.5 shows the difference between the CIR and the access rate and how the burst traffic rate can increase beyond the CIR. The network controls this bursting capability, and it usually does not result in any additional fees on the user. There is a catch, though. Some burst traffic has the *Discard Eligibility (DE) bit* turned on, indicating excess traffic above CIR. If a Frame Relay switch becomes congested, traffic with the DE bit set (excess burst traffic) is the first to be dropped.

FIGURE 8.5 Frame Relay rates

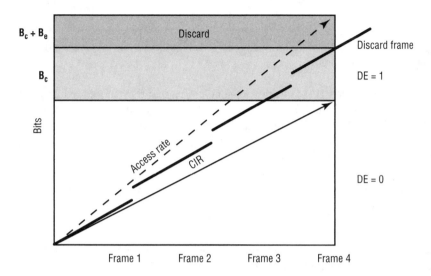

In Figure 8.5, you will see the following symbols: B_c, B_e, and T_c. Committed burst size (B_c) and excess burst size (B_e) are the two types of burst sizes. Each of these sizes is measured over the committed rate measurement interval (T_c). B_c is the maximum amount of data that the network can guarantee will be delivered during the time T_c. B_e is the amount of traffic by which the user can exceed the committed burst size.

For example, take a user who buys a Frame Relay circuit with the following characteristics:

- 1544Kbps access rate
- 256Kbps Committed Information Rate
- Four-second committed time interval

The user is guaranteed a CIR of 256Kbps over a four-second period. The user could transmit 256Kbps for four seconds, and the network would ensure delivery. The user could alternately send 1,024Kbps for one second, representing the committed burst. However, for the remaining three seconds, there would be no guarantee of delivery for the excess burst traffic.

Congestion Handling by Frame Relay Switches

A Frame Relay switch has a simple job: it forwards all the data that it can. If there is more data than bandwidth, the switch will first drop the data with the DE bit set and will then drop committed data if needed. In addition, the Frame Relay switch will also send out messages that congestion is occurring.

Backward Explicit Congestion Notification (BECN) and *Forward Explicit Congestion Notification (FECN)* are the primary notification mechanisms used for handling congestion on the Frame Relay switching internetwork. BECNs and FECNs both send notices that congestion is occurring. A BECN is transmitted in the direction from which the traffic came, and an FECN is transmitted in the direction in which the traffic is going.

> Under normal circumstances, only Frame Relay switches send BECN and FECN messages.

The end devices receive these notifications indicating that they should reduce the amount of traffic that they are sending. A Frame Relay switch does not enforce the reduction; it simply notifies the end devices. It is the responsibility of the end devices to reduce the traffic.

The congestion mechanisms are important to understand because congestion occurs frequently on Frame Relay networks. As providers attempt to maximize the use of their lines, they sell more bandwidth than they can actually provide. This is called *oversubscription*. Oversubscription is a growing trend, so you must be aware of the implications and effects of the resulting congestion.

> Some providers will attempt to sell you a zero CIR. Although inexpensive, you have no guarantee that mission-critical data (or any data, for that matter!) will get through.

Congestion Handling by Routers

The router can also play a part in determining which traffic is more or less important on the Frame Relay network. The Discard Eligibility list (frame-relay de-list global command) and Discard Eligibility group (frame-relay de-group interface command) give the router the capability to set the Discard Eligibility bit on a frame.

Consider a company that notices an increased number of dropped frames on the Frame Relay network. They determine that the primary cause is an increase in the amount of AppleTalk traffic across the Frame Relay network. The additional traffic has impaired the performance of mission-critical traffic.

To have the router turn on the DE bit for AppleTalk traffic, thereby dropping the noncritical AppleTalk traffic before any other traffic, use the frame-relay de-list command. Here is an example of how to configure a router to do this:

```
RouterA#config t
RouterA(config)#frame-relay de-list 1 protocol appletalk
RouterA(config)#interface serial0
RouterA(config-if)#frame-relay de-group 1 100
```

In this example, the frame-relay de-list command uses a list number of 1 and a protocol of AppleTalk. The list number of 1 is then applied to the interface connected to the Frame Relay network with the frame-relay de-group command for a specified DLCI, in this case 100.

The modified router configuration looks like this:

```
RouterA#show running-config
Building configuration...

Current configuration:
!
version 11.2
!
hostname RouterA
!
appletalk routing
frame-relay de-list 1 protocol appletalk
!
interface Serial0
 ip address 192.168.1.1 255.255.255.0
 encapsulation frame-relay
 appletalk address 8.202
 appletalk zone Sybex
 frame-relay de-group 1 100
 frame-relay map appletalk 8.201 100 broadcast
 frame-relay map ip 192.168.1.2 100 broadcast
!
end
RouterA#
```

The Frame Relay DE list will match AppleTalk frames. The `frame-relay de-group` command binds the DE list to the interface. In the event of congestion, these two packet types are much more likely to be dropped than mission-critical traffic. The 100 at the end of the `frame-relay de-group` command specifies to use the list on DLCI 100.

Point-to-Point and Multipoint Interfaces

At times it is useful to have a multipoint network, such as Frame Relay, behave as if each connection were a point-to-point link. The network example in Figure 8.6 has two connections from one location (multipoint); this type of setup can lead to network problems if not thoroughly understood. This multipoint configuration experiences problems primarily because of the way it handles routing updates. In distance-vector routing protocols, there is a mechanism known as *split horizon*. Split horizon states that it is never advantageous to send routing information back out on the interface through which that information was learned. Or, simply put, "Don't tell me what I told you." This is used to stop possible routing loop problems. Consider the split-horizon implication of Figure 8.6.

FIGURE 8.6   Split-horizon issues with Frame Relay

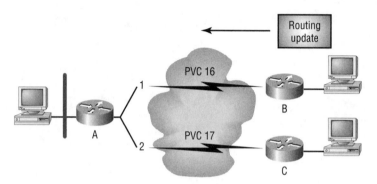

In this figure, Router B sends a routing update to Router A, telling it about its directly connected networks. Router A receives the routing information on its serial 0 interface and modifies its routing table. Router A does not send the routing information back out serial 0 because of split horizon. Because the routing information cannot be sent back out serial 0, Router C never learns the networks off Router B. The networks are unreachable from Router C because Router C has not heard of Router B's directly connected networks.

The problem in Figure 8.6 is that there is only one physical interface and there are two virtual circuits. The solution is to create a logical interface for each circuit, which solves the split horizon issues. A *subinterface* is a logical interface within the router that is mapped to a particular DLCI. When you set up subinterfaces, the interface previously configured for multipoint will now appear as two point-to-point interfaces to the router. This would change the previous example, as shown in Figure 8.7.

FIGURE 8.7   Split horizon issues with subinterfaces

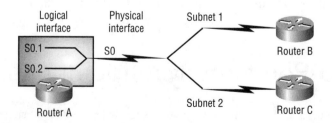

In this figure, Router A learns of Router B's networks on the Serial 0.1 subinterface. Without violating the split horizon rule, Router A can send all the network information out on subinterface Serial 0.2 to Router C.

To configure a subinterface on an interface, use the `interface` *type.subinterface-number* [`point-to-point` | `multipoint`] command. For illustration purposes, configure Router A with a subinterface; the router commands are shown next. Both types of subinterfaces that can be configured appear in this example: point-to-point and multipoint. Point-to-point is used when each PVC is a separate subnet. Multipoint is used when all PVCs use the same subnet.

Also notice in the following configuration that you can use any subinterface number, but for administration purposes the DLCI number can be used. The subinterface number is only locally significant.

```
RouterA(config)#interface serial0.?
  <0-4294967295>  Serial interface number
RouterA(config)#interface serial0.16 ?
  multipoint       Treat as a multipoint link
  point-to-point  Treat as a point-to-point link
RouterA(config)#interface serial0.16 point-to-point
RouterA(config-subif)#ip address 192.168.1.1 255.255.255.0
RouterA(config-subif)#frame-relay interface-dlci 16
RouterA(config-subif)#exit
RouterA(config)#interface serial0.17 multipoint
RouterA(config-subif)#ip address 192.168.2.2 255.255.255.0
RouterA(config-subif)#frame-relay map ip 192.168.2.1 17 broadcast
```

The configuration of Router A will now look like this:

```
RouterA#show running-config
Building configuration...
Current configuration:
!
version 11.3
!
hostname RouterA
!
interface Serial0
 no ip address
 encapsulation frame-relay
!
interface Serial0.16 point-to-point
 ip address 192.168.1.1 255.255.255.0
```

```
 frame-relay interface-dlci 16
!
interface Serial0.17 multipoint
 ip address 192.168.2.2 255.255.255.0
 frame-relay map ip 192.168.2.1 17 broadcast
!
end
RouterA#
```

This configuration specifies which DLCI is associated with which subinterface. This is necessary because the router has no way of determining which particular DLCI should be associated with which subinterface.

 Many people find the point-to-point subinterface configuration easier and less prone to routing errors than a physical multipoint configuration.

Verifying Frame Relay

It is just as important to be able to verify Frame Relay as it is to be able to understand how to configure it. In this section, you will learn about the various commands used to verify Frame Relay. These include the following:

- show interface
- show frame-relay pvc
- show frame-relay map
- clear frame-relay-inarp
- show frame-relay lmi
- debug frame-relay lmi

The *show interface* Command

The show interface command can be used with interface parameters, for example, show interface serial 0. This provides information pertaining to just serial 0. By itself, the show interface command provides information about all interfaces on the router.

The show interface command displays information regarding the encapsulation, Layer 1 and Layer 2 status, and the LMI DLCI. In the following code, the show interface serial 0 command is used. Notice the encapsulation is Frame Relay. The LMI information is shown as well.

```
Router#show interface serial0
Serial0 is up, line protocol is up
  Hardware is HD64570
  MTU 1500 bytes, BW 1544 Kbit,DLY 20000 usec,rely 255/255,load 1/255
  Encapsulation FRAME-RELAY,loopback not set,keepalive set(10 sec)
  LMI enq sent  0, LMI stat recvd 0, LMI upd recvd 0, DTE LMI down
  LMI enq recvd 0, LMI stat sent  0, LMI upd sent  0
  LMI DLCI 1023  LMI type is CISCO  frame relay DTE
  FR SVC disabled, LAPF state down
  Broadcast queue 0/64, broadcasts sent/dropped 0/0, interface broadcasts 0
  Last input never, output never, output hang never
  Last clearing of "show interface" counters never
  Queueing strategy: fifo
  Output queue 0/40, 0 drops; input queue 0/75, 0 drops
  5 minute input rate 0 bits/sec, 0 packets/sec
  5 minute output rate 0 bits/sec, 0 packets/sec
     0 packets input, 0 bytes, 0 no buffer
     Received 0 broadcasts, 0 runts, 0 giants, 0 throttles
     0 input errors, 0 CRC, 0 frame, 0 overrun, 0 ignored, 0 abort
     0 packets output, 0 bytes, 0 underruns
     0 output errors, 0 collisions, 19 interface resets
     0 output buffer failures, 0 output buffers swapped out
     0 carrier transitions
     DCD=down  DSR=down  DTR=down  RTS=down  CTS=down
Router#
```

Notice that the LMI counter information is shown, as well as the LMI type, which is Cisco by default. As you can see, this output shows both errors for the interface and the time that the interface counters were last cleared

The *show frame-relay pvc* Command

The show frame-relay pvc command displays the status of each configured connection as well as traffic statistics. As you'll notice in the following router output, if you type the command show frame-relay pvc, you'll see all the PVCs that are configured on your router and their status. You can also use a specific PVC number at the end of the command to see only that particular PVC information.

```
Router_A#show frame-relay pvc

PVC Statistics for interface Serial0 (Frame Relay DTE)

DLCI = 160, DLCI USAGE = LOCAL, PVC STATUS = ACTIVE, INTERFACE = Serial0

   input pkts 7     output pkts 13        in bytes 2252
   out bytes 1886   dropped pkts 0        in FECN pkts 0
   in BECN pkts 0   out FECN pkts 0       out BECN pkts 0
   in DE pkts 0     out DE pkts 0
   out bcast pkts 8 out bcast bytes 1366
   pvc create time 00:06:54, last time pvc status changed 00:03:17

DLCI = 17, DLCI USAGE = LOCAL, PVC STATUS = ACTIVE, INTERFACE = Serial0

   input pkts 1     output pkts 7         in bytes 30
   out bytes 832    dropped pkts 0        in FECN pkts 0
   in BECN pkts 0   out FECN pkts 0       out BECN pkts 0
   in DE pkts 0     out DE pkts 0
   out bcast pkts 7 out bcast bytes 832
   pvc create time 00:01:59, last time pvc status changed 00:00:49
Router_A#
```

As you can see, this command also shows you the number of BECN and FECN packets received on the router. Please note that the BECN and FECN statistics are per PVC, not across the entire router.

The *show frame-relay map* Command

You can see the current map entries and information about the connections by using the show frame-relay map command. This command shows the Network-Layer-to-DLCI mappings table in the router. An example output of this command is given here:

```
Router_A#show frame-relay map
Serial0 (up): ip 172.16.1.2 dlci 500(0x64,0x1840), dynamic,
              broadcast, status defined, active
Router_A#
```

LMI used IARP to determine the address of the remote router and created this dynamic mapping.

> If you want to clear the Network Layer-to-DLCI mappings on a router, you can use the command clear frame-relay-inarp, which clears dynamically created maps on the router.

The *show frame-relay lmi* Command

The show frame-relay lmi command shows you the LMI statistics for an interface. An example is provided here:

```
Router#show frame lmi
LMI Statistics for interface Serial0 (Frame Relay DTE) LMI TYPE = CISCO
  Invalid Unnumbered info 0          Invalid Prot Disc 0
  Invalid dummy Call Ref 0           Invalid Msg Type 0
  Invalid Status Message 0           Invalid Lock Shift 0
  Invalid Information ID 0           Invalid Report IE Len 0
  Invalid Report Request 0           Invalid Keep IE Len 0
  Num Status Enq. Sent 109087        Num Status msgs Rcvd 109087
  Num Update Status Rcvd 0           Num Status Timeouts 0
Router#
```

The important statistic to notice is the number of inquiries sent and received. This indicates the number of LMI status messages sent by the DTE device. The DCE sends a status message in return. Noticing this statistic enables you to see whether data is passing between the two devices.

The *debug frame-relay lmi* Command

The debug frame-relay lmi command is used to help you troubleshoot and verify Frame Relay connections. As you'll see in the router output shown next, the out parameter is an LMI status inquiry sent out from the router, and the (in) parameter is a reply from the Frame Relay switch:

```
Router#debug frame-relay lmi
Serial0(in): Status, myseq 128
RT IE 1, length 1, type 0
KA IE 3, length 2, yourseq 128, myseq 128
PVC IE 0x7, length 0x6, dlci 16, status 0x2, bw 0
Serial0(out): StEnq, myseq 128, yourseen 214, DTE up
datagramstart = 0x1959DF4, datagramsize = 13
FR encap = 0xFCF10309
```

```
00 75 01 01 01 03 02 C6 E5

Serial0(in): Status, myseq 129
RT IE 1, length 1, type 1
KA IE 3, length 2, yourseq 129, myseq 129
Serial0(out): StEnq, myseq 130, yourseen 129, DTE up
datagramstart = 0x1959DF4, datagramsize = 13
FR encap = 0xFCF10309
00 74 01 01 01 03 02 C9 E3
```

The type 1 is an LMI keepalive between the router to the Frame Relay switch every 10 seconds. This tells the router that the switch is still active and vice versa. The type 0 is an IARP exchanged between routers every 60 seconds. Now notice that when the type is 0, you have a full status message on your hands. When the type is 1, it is the standard status message, which is the heartbeat keepalive mentioned earlier. Remember that the DLCI is known. There is no IP address in this output. Therefore, this would be a poor excuse for an InARP reply (notice the *in* designation, corresponding to a reply). Furthermore, Status and StEnq messages go between the DTE and DCE only. These messages do not traverse the cloud, meaning they couldn't possibly have anything to do with InARP. Full status messages from the switch include all PVCs known by the switch. In this case, there's only one, DLCI = 16. The type 1 message will always have three lines, whereas the type 0 message will have four or more, assuming PVCs exist. You would see InARP messages coming in the exact same way you would see any other non-LMI frames coming in (such as, ICMP pings), by using the debug frame-relay packet command. Status indicators are pretty straightforward and adhere to the following rules:

0x0 (no bits turned on) means "inactive."

0x2 (second bit turned on) means "active."

0x3 means that the active DLCI cannot accept any more traffic without drops occurring—sort of a flow-control code (active bit [2nd] is on, but the first bit is also on as sort of an Receive Not Ready (RNR) bit because Cisco uses this bit even though the ITU-T indicates the first bit is reserved).

0x4 (third bit turned on) means "deleted."

Looking at our status, the DLCI 16, status 0x2 means the DLCI is active.

Frame Relay Switching

Routers are typically edge devices that connect your LANs to the Frame Relay network. However, you can use a router as part of the Frame Relay cloud or you can use it to create your own Frame Relay network. *Frame Relay switching* is the forwarding of Frame Relay frames based upon their DLCI assignments. You have seen how to configure a Frame Relay DTE device; now, let's look at how to configure a Frame Relay DCE switch. Routers are DTE devices by default; however, by changing the Frame Relay interface type to a DCE, you can provide switching of frames.

Compare Figure 8.8 to Figure 8.9. Both of these diagrams represent the same network. In Figure 8.8, you see the Frame Relay cloud without any detail. Each router on the right side will send traffic to the router on the left by using DLCI 100. Keep in mind that the DLCI is an identifier and that the DLCIs in this diagram could be the same or different and still communicate. The router on the left will use DLCIs 101 and 300 to reach each router on the right. This is the normal way that you should think about the frame cloud. It is typically not your concern what happens within the Frame Relay network. Figure 8.9 shows that this particular Frame Relay cloud is a single router configured as a switch.

FIGURE 8.8   Logical Frame Relay network

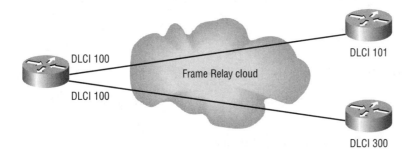

FIGURE 8.9   Physical Frame Relay network

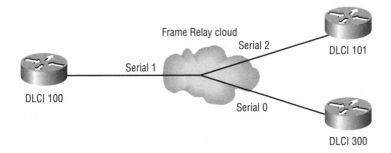

Frame Relay Switching Commands

The command used to enable Frame Relay switching on a Cisco router is as follows:

```
Router_A#config t
Router_A(config)#frame-relay switching
```

This command must come before any of the other Frame Relay switching–related commands can be executed, or these commands won't be allowed. When Frame Relay encapsulation is enabled on an interface, it defaults to DTE, so you will need to change it to DCE for Frame

Relay switching. For a Frame Relay serial connection to function, you must have a DTE at one end and a DCE at the other. You first configure the router with the following command:

```
Router_A(config)#interface serial0
Router_A(config-if)#frame-relay intf-type dce
```

 The clocking on a serial link is provided by the DCE device, which is determined by the type of cable connected to the serial interface. For a Frame Relay connection, the DCE status is configured, whereas serial DCE status is cabled. For Frame Relay, the DCE device is the one that provides LMI.

Because this interface is now functioning as the Frame Relay DCE device, you can change the LMI type from the default of Cisco with the following command:

```
Router_A(config-if)#frame-relay lmi-type ?
  cisco
  ansi
  q933a
Router_A(config-if)#frame-relay lmi-type
```

The next step in the configuration process is to create the proper DLCI forwarding rules. These rules dictate that when a frame enters a particular interface on a certain DLCI, it will be forwarded to another interface and DLCI. Let's look at such an example on interface serial 1:

```
Router_A#config t
Router_A(config)#interface serial 1
Router_A(config-if)#frame-relay route 100 interface Serial2 101
```

This command states that any frame received on interface serial 1, with DLCI 100, shall be forwarded to interface serial 2, with DLCI 101. You can view all the frame routing information with the show frame-relay route command. The following router output shows the settings of Router A:

```
Router_A#show frame-relay route
Input Intf    Input Dlci    Output Intf    Output Dlci    Status
Serial0       300           Serial1        200            active
Serial1       100           Serial2        101            active
Serial1       200           Serial0        300            active
Serial2       101           Serial1        100            active
Router_A#
```

The configuration of a router as a Frame Relay switch can be useful for a lab environment or even part of a production network.

Now, let's look at the configuration of the Frame Relay switch:

```
Router_A#show running-config
Building configuration...
Current configuration:
!
version 11.2
!
hostname Router_A
!
frame-relay switching
!
interface Serial0
 no ip address
 encapsulation frame-relay
 clockrate 56000
 frame-relay intf-type dce
 frame-relay route 300 interface Serial1 200
!
interface Serial1
 no ip address
 encapsulation frame-relay
 clockrate 56000
 frame-relay intf-type dce
 frame-relay route 100 interface Serial2 101
 frame-relay route 200 interface Serial0 300
!
interface Serial2
 no ip address
 encapsulation frame-relay
 clockrate 56000
 frame-relay intf-type dce
 frame-relay route 101 interface Serial1 100
!
end
Router_A#
```

Notice the global command `frame-relay switching` is at the top of the configuration. Also notice that both interfaces are configured with `frame-relay intf-type dce` commands. On the serial interfaces, you'll also see that the `clock rate` command is used to provide clocking for the line because the router serving as the Frame Relay switch is a DCE device on the physical interface.

Frame Relay Traffic Shaping

Traffic shaping on Frame Relay provides different capabilities, and because this information might be covered on the exam, it is important that you can describe each one. On production networks, this information can help you understand whether switch problems are occurring.

In this section, you will learn about traffic shaping techniques and when to use them. You'll then learn how to configure traffic shaping.

Using Traffic Shaping Techniques

The following list outlines traffic shaping techniques used with Frame Relay:

- To control the access rate transmitted on a Cisco router, you can configure a peak rate to limit outbound traffic to either the CIR or Excess Information Rate (EIR).

- You can configure BECN support on a per-VC basis, which will enable the router to then monitor BECNs and throttle traffic based on BECN-designated packets.

- Queuing can be used for support at the VC level. Priority, custom, and weighted-fair queuing can be used. This gives you more control over traffic flow on individual VCs.

It is also important to understand when you would use traffic shaping with Frame Relay. The following list explains this:

- Use traffic shaping when one site, such as the corporate office, has a higher speed line (for example, a T1), and the remote branches have slower lines (for example, 56Kbps). This connection would cause bottlenecks on each VC and would result in poor response times for time-sensitive traffic such as SNA and Telnet. This can cause packets to be dropped. By using traffic shaping at the corporate office, you can improve response on each VC.

- Traffic shaping is also helpful on a router with many subinterfaces. Because these subinterfaces will use traffic as fast as the physical link allows, you can use rate enforcement on the subinterface to match the CIR of the VC. This means you can preallocate bandwidth to each VC.

- Traffic shaping can be used to throttle back transmission on a Frame Relay network that is constantly congested. This can help prevent packet loss and is done on a per-VC basis.

- Traffic shaping is used effectively if you have multiple Network Layer protocols and want to queue each protocol to allocate bandwidth effectively. Since IOS version 11.2, queuing can be performed at the VC level.

Configuring Traffic Shaping

To configure Frame Relay traffic shaping, you must first enter the map class configuration mode so you can define a map class. You enter the map class with the global configuration command `map-class frame-relay` *name*. The *name* parameter is the name you use to apply to map class the VC where you want traffic shaping performed. The command looks like the following:

```
RouterA#config t
RouterA(config)#map-class frame-relay scott
RouterA(config-map-class)#
```

Notice that the `map-class frame-relay scott` command changes the prompt to `config-map-class`. This enables you to configure the parameters for your map class.

The map class is used to define the average and peak rates allowed in each VC associated with the map class. The map class mechanism enables you to specify that the router can dynamically fluctuate the rate at which it sends traffic, depending on the BECNs received. It also enables you to configure queuing on a per-VC basis.

To define the average and peak rate for links that are faster than the receiving link can handle, use the following command:

```
RouterA(config-map-class)#frame-relay traffic-rate average [peak]
```

The average parameter sets the average rate in bits per second, which is your CIR. Now, how do you calculate the peak value? First start with the EIRThe EIR is the average rate over which bits will be marked with DE and is given by the formula $EIR = B_e/T_c$, with B_e being excessive burst and T_c representing the committed rate measurement interval. The peak value is then calculated by taking the CIR plus EIR, or peak = CIR + EIR.

The peak parameter is optional. An example of a line is as follows:

```
RouterA(config-map-class)#frame-relay traffic-rate 9600 18000
```

To specify that the router should dynamically fluctuate the rate at which it is sending traffic depending on the number of BECNs received, use the following command:

```
RouterA(config-map-class)#frame-relay adaptive-shaping becn
```

To set bandwidth usage for protocols, you can configure traffic shaping to use queuing on a per-VC basis. To perform this function, use the following commands:

```
RouterA(config-map-class)#frame-relay custom-queue-list number
RouterA(config-map-class)#frame-relay priority-group number
```

You can use either command, depending on the type of queuing you are using. The `number` parameter at the end of the command is the queue list number. A detailed discussion of queuing is presented in the next chapter.

After the map class parameters are completed, you then need to configure the traffic shaping on the interface you want. The following commands are used to perform traffic shaping on an interface and to apply the map class and its parameters to a subinterface and, by association, its corresponding VC.

```
RouterA#config t
RouterA(config)#interface serial0
RouterA(config-if)#frame-relay traffic-shaping
RouterA(config-if)#interface serial0.16 point-to-point
RouterA(config-subif#frame-relay class scott
RouterA(config-subif)#frame-relay interface-dlci 16
```

You first must enable traffic shaping and per-VC queuing on the interface with the `frame-relay traffic-shaping` command. You can then go to the interface or subinterface and assign the map class by using the `frame-relay class` *name* command. The example just shown uses the name `scott` because that is the name of the map class defined in the earlier example.

After you have completed the configuration, use the `show running-config` and the `show frame-relay pvc` commands to verify the configuration.

 Real World Scenario

The Lowdown on Committed Information Rate (CIR)

We've talked formally about CIR—we even presented a calculation—but what does it really mean? As we have said, the acronym itself stands for Committed Information Rate, which really doesn't seem that difficult to understand. But there seems to be widespread misinterpretation of this concept, especially by some service providers, so let's attempt to figure the whole thing out.

We've discussed terms such as *burst rate* and phrases such as *bursting above your CIR*, but these can be pretty misleading. They were devised by network engineers who assumed—you know what that leads to—that we wouldn't understand hardcore network-engineering concepts, so they tried to put them in layman's terms and botched the whole thing up. In reality, you're always "bursting" to your line speed because Frame Relay is an HDLC protocol and there's no other way to make it work.

HDLC is a synchronous protocol (which means that the data is synchronized to a clock) that sends data with a standardized framing and checksum technique. When a frame is transmitted, the data must be contiguous; that is, there cannot be any holes or spaces between bytes of data. So if you're transmitting 500 bytes of data, you can't send 250 and then wait for a while and then send the rest. It has to go out as one big chunk. The Frame Relay expression *bursting over your CIR* comes into play because there is no way to slow down the data or to change the length of the chunk after you start transmitting; you just send until you are finished. If you happen to send too much data because your data chunk is larger than the allotment, you've bursted over your CIR.

So what is the big deal about CIR, then? And why, when you buy Frame Relay from a company like Qwest, do they quote you a CIR? CIR is the "worst-case" throughput that the Frame Relay network provider attempts to guarantee. It's like a restaurant guaranteeing that you'll always be able to eat a certain amount of food from its buffet. Like the restaurant, the Frame Relay network provider can't guarantee that you'll always be able to transmit at the CIR (take the case when everyone on the network happens to be transmitting at once), but they can guarantee it over a reasonable time span (usually over a span of seconds). Basically, the network backbone is engineered to handle reasonable loads—just like the number of lanes in a highway. Given a certain amount of traffic, the data should flow through the backbone without delay. At times, when unusually heavy traffic exists, you have what is called congestion.

Summary

Frame Relay is one of the most popular WAN protocols in the world. This technology will become even more critical as corporations stretch their networks globally and the Internet becomes more pervasive.

To become a successful CCNP, you need to understand the Frame Relay protocol. This technology makes up the majority of the world's nondedicated circuits and its importance cannot be underestimated.

Frame Relay is the distant cousin to X.25 without some of its overhead. It does provide congestion notification, which can be used with traffic shaping to help traffic response. Like X.25, Frame Relay provides for permanent and switched virtual circuits.

LMI is an extension to the Frame Relay protocol developed by the Frame Relay Forum and is used to provide management for virtual circuits. This makes the management of DLCI information easier for the network administrator.

Cisco provides for a mechanism to enable a multipoint interface such as Frame Relay to look like multiple virtual point-to-point or multipoint interfaces called subinterfaces. Point-to-point subinterfaces can be used to solve problems caused by distance-vector routing protocols running over multipoint interfaces.

Setting up a Cisco router as a Frame Relay switch is not something that you would do often, but it is a useful feature when you are working in a lab environment. There are many troubleshooting commands that can be used to verify the configuration of Frame Relay on a Cisco router. They can be used to see the DLCI-to-Network-Layer-address mapping and the current state of LMI on the router. Frame Relay is a technology used in many networks, and mastering its configuration and operation will take you far in your networking career.

Exam Essentials

Understand Frame Relay and its history.   Frame Relay is a streamlined version of X.25 without the windowing and retransmission capabilities. Frame Relay is a Layer 2 protocol that was defined as a network service for ISDN by the CCITT (now ITU-T). The Group of Four extended Frame Relay in 1990 to allow for a Local Management Interface (LMI) to assist in PVC management.

Understand the two types of virtual circuits (VCs).   Know what a Switched Virtual Circuit (SVC) is used for and what a Permanent Virtual Circuit (PVC) is used for. Understand why you would use one type over another.

Know what a DLCI is and how it is mapped to Network Layer protocols.   The data link connection identifier (DLCI) is used to identify a PVC in a Frame Relay network. The DLCI-to-Network-Layer mapping can be statically configured by an administrator using the frame-relay map command or can be dynamically set by using Inverse ARP (IARP).

Understand the Local Management Interface (LMI).   LMI was an extension to Frame Relay to manage the virtual circuits on a connection. LMI virtual circuit status messages provide communication and DLCI synchronization between Frame Relay DTE and DCE devices.

Know how to configure Frame Relay and what it uses for congestion control.   The encapsulation frame-relay command is used to configure an interface for Frame Relay operation. The frame-relay intf-type dce command is used to configure an interface for DCE operation, but by default the Frame Relay interface type is DTE. Frame Relay uses Backward Explicit Congestion Notification (BECN) and Forward Explicit Congestion Notification (FECN) messages to control congestion on a Frame Relay switch.

Understand the options for traffic shaping on a Frame Relay interface.   There are many options for traffic shaping to enable a Frame Relay network to operate more efficiently. You can have the router slow traffic on a VC in response to BECNs received. You can set up queuing on a per-VC basis and limit traffic going out of a VC. You need to know what the Committed Information Rate (CIR) and Excess Information Rate (EIR) are.

Know what Cisco IOS commands are used to verify and troubleshoot a Frame Relay connection.   The commands show interface, show frame-relay pvc, show frame-relay map, show frame-relay lmi, and debug frame-relay lmi are all used to see and verify the operation of Frame Relay. The command clear frame-relay-inarp is used to delete the dynamic PVC-to-Network-Layer addressing entries.

Key Terms

Before you take the exam, be certain you are familiar with the following terms:

access rate

Backward Explicit Congestion Notification (BECN)

bearer service

bursting

data link connection identifier (DLCI)

Discard Eligibility (DE) bit

Forward Explicit Congestion Notification (FECN)

frame

Frame Relay Forum

Frame Relay specifications with extensions

Frame Relay switching

Group of Four

Inverse ARP (IARP)

Local Management Interface (LMI)

oversubscription

packet switching

split horizon

subinterface

traffic shaping

virtual circuit

Written Lab

1. Write the command to see the encapsulation method on serial 0 of a Cisco router.
2. Write the command to configure serial 0 with Frame Relay encapsulation.
3. Write the command to configure a point-to-point subinterface number of 16 on serial 0.
4. Write the command to add the LMI type of ANSI to the subinterface 16.
5. Write the commands to configure the DLCI number for subinterface 16. Use PVC number 16.
6. Write the commands to configure the IPX protocol to be the first packets discarded in the frame switch if congestion occurs. Assign this to the subinterface 16 DLCI .
7. Write the command to make your router a Frame Relay switch.
8. Write the command to see the line, encapsulation, DLCI, and LMI information of the serial interface.
9. Write the command that will show you all the configured PVCs on your router.
10. Write the command that will show you the Network-Layer-protocol-address-to-PVC mappings.
11. Write the command to create a Frame Relay map class.
12. Write the command to define the average and peak rate for links that are faster than the receiving link can handle.

13. Write the command that specifies that the router should dynamically fluctuate the rate at which it is sending packets depending on the number of BECNs received.

14. Write the two commands that will enable the router to queue traffic on a per-VC basis.

15. Write the command to configure Frame Relay traffic shaping on an interface.

16. Write the command to configure a Frame Relay map class to an individual VC.

Hands-on Labs

In this section, you will perform two labs. These labs both require a minimum of three Cisco 2501 routers. Figure 8.10 provides you with a visual network layout for Labs 8.1 and 8.2.

FIGURE 8.10   Frame Relay lab

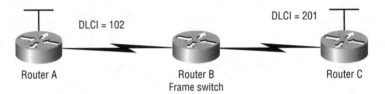

DLCI = 102

DLCI = 201

Router A

Router B
Frame switch

Router C

Lab 8.1: Configuring Frame Relay with Subinterfaces

1.   Set the hostname, `frame-relay switching` command, and the encapsulation of each serial interface on the Frame Relay switch.

```
Router#config t
Router(config)#hostname RouterB
RouterB(config)#frame-relay switching
RouterB(config)#interface serial0
RouterB(config-if)#encapsulation frame-relay
RouterB(config-if)#interface serial1
RouterB(config-if)#encapsulation frame-relay
```

2.   Configure the Frame Relay mappings on each interface. You do not have to have IP addresses on these interfaces because they are only switching one interface to another based on Frame Relay frames.

```
RouterB(config-if)#interface serial0
RouterB(config-if)#frame-relay intf-type dce
RouterB(config-if)#frame-relay route 102 interface Serial1 201
RouterB(config-if)#interface serial1
RouterB(config-if)#frame-relay intf-type dce
```

```
RouterB(config-if)#frame-relay route 201 interface Serial0 102
```

This is not as hard as it looks. The `frame-relay route` command just says that if you receive frames from PVC 102, send them out interface serial 1 by using PVC 201. The second mapping on serial 1 is just the opposite. Anything that comes in interface serial 1 with PVC 201 is routed out serial 0 by using DLCI 102.

3.   Configure Router A with a point-to-point subinterface.

```
Router#config t
Router(config)#hostname RouterA
RouterA(config)#interface serial0
RouterA(config-if)#encapsulation frame-relay
RouterA(config-if)#clock rate 64000
RouterA(config-if)#interface serial0.102 point-to-point
RouterA(config-subif)#ip address 172.16.10.1 255.255.255.0
RouterC(config-subif)#ipx network 10
RouterA(config-subif)#frame-relay interface-dlci 102
```

4.   Configure Router C with a point-to-point subinterface.

```
Router#config t
Router(config)#hostname RouterC
RouterC(config)#interface serial0
RouterC(config-if)#encapsulation frame-relay
RouterC(config-if)#clock rate 64000
RouterC(config-if)#interface serial0.201 point-to-point
RouterC(config-subif)#ip address 172.16.10.2 255.255.255.0
RouterC(config-subif)#ipx network 10
RouterC(config-subif)#frame-relay interface-dlci 201
```

5.   Verify your configurations by using the following commands.

```
RouterA>show frame ?
 ip      show frame relay IP statistics
 lmi     show frame relay lmi statistics
 map     Frame-Relay map table
 pvc     show frame relay pvc statistics
 route   show frame relay route
 traffic Frame-Relay protocol statistics
```

6.   Use ping and Telnet to verify connectivity.

Lab 8.2: Frame Relay Traffic Shaping

1. Create a map class named lab2 on Router A.

    ```
    RouterA#config t
    RouterA(config)#map-class frame-relay lab2
    RouterA(config-map-class)#
    ```

2. Define the average and peak rates for Router A's serial 0 subinterface. Because the sub-interface is the only link, set the CIR to 56K and the EIR to a full T1.

    ```
    RouterA(config-map-class)#frame-relay traffic-rate ?
      <600-45000000>  Committed Information Rate (CIR)
    RouterA(config-map-class)#frame-relay traffic-rate 56000 ?
      <0-45000000>  Peak rate (CIR + EIR)
      <cr>
    RouterA(config-map-class)#frame-relay traffic-rate 56000 1544000
    RouterA(config-map-class)#
    ```

3. Tell Router A to dynamically fluctuate the rate at which it is sending packets depending on the number of BECNs received.

    ```
    RouterA(config-map-class)#frame-relay adaptive-shaping becn
    ```

4. Assign priority queue 2 to be used with the map class.

    ```
    RouterA(config-map-class)#frame-relay custom-queue-list 2
    ```

5. Enable Frame Relay traffic shaping for serial 0.

    ```
    RouterA#config t
    RouterA(config)#interface serial0
    RouterA(config-if)#frame-relay traffic-shaping
    ```

6. Assign the Frame Relay map class lab2 to the subinterface.

    ```
    RouterA(config-if)#interface serial0.102 point-to-point
    RouterA(config-subif)#frame-relay class scott
    ```

7. Use the show running-config and the show frame-relay pvc commands to verify your configuration.

Review Questions

1. Which two Frame Relay encapsulation types are supported on Cisco routers?

   A. ANSI

   B. Q.933a

   C. Cisco

   D. IETF

   E. Shiva

2. Which three Frame Relay LMI types are supported on Cisco routers?

   A. ANSI

   B. Q.933a

   C. Cisco

   D. IETF

   E. Shiva

3. Your site has a T1 connection to the WAN. The streaming video application you are using periodically requires 100 percent utilization of the T1. Which technology would be best for this application in order to ensure that no video frames are lost?

   A. Frame Relay

   B. X.25

   C. Dedicated circuit

   D. POTS

   E. Not possible

4. Your site has a 256Kbps satellite link to the WAN. The circuit will be used by a variety of applications. The main concern is speed of delivery and cost. It is acceptable for some frames to be delayed and even retransmitted. Which technology would best suit this environment?

   A. Frame Relay

   B. X.25

   C. Dedicated circuit

   D. TDM circuit

   E. Not possible

5. A provider can sell more bandwidth than the actual Frame Relay network can supply. What is this called?

   A. Illegal

   B. Zero-sum multiplexing

   C. Frame stealing

   D. Oversubscription

   E. XOT

6. Frame Relay was first intended to work with what other protocol?

   A. SNA

   B. LAT

   C. TCP/IP

   D. X.25

   E. ISDN

7. What are the types of VCs used with Frame Relay? (Select all that apply.)

   A. DLCI

   B. PVC

   C. SVC

   D. LMI

8. What is used to identify the PVC in a Frame Relay network?

   A. LMI

   B. BECN

   C. DLCI

   D. FECN

9. Your Frame Relay circuit is installed on a full T1 (1,544Kbps). You were told that you would be guaranteed 256Kbps on the circuit. What is your access rate?

   A. Depends on the burst rate

   B. 256Kbps

   C. 512Kbps

   D. 1,544Kbps

   E. Not possible to determine from information

10. You have a CIR of 256K and you are told your committed rate measurement interval is 10 seconds. What is your burst-committed rate?

    A. 256Kbps

    B. 2,560Kbps

    C. 1,544Kbps

    D. 1,5440Kbps

    E. 10

11. Which of the following is a feature of LMI?

    A. Status inquiry

    B. BECN

    C. FECN

    D. Inverse ARP

    E. DE

12. Your central site has a single serial connection to the Frame Relay cloud. You have five virtual circuits from your central site to the remote sites. Your remote sites are not receiving routing updates. You suspect a problem with split horizon. What would be the best solution?

    A. Static routes

    B. Subinterfaces

    C. Disable split-horizon

    D. Route filtering

    E. Modify administrative distance

13. You wish to configure your router so that it forwards frames based on their DLCI. What is this known as?

    A. IP routing

    B. Frame routing

    C. Impossible

    D. Frame switching

    E. Frame tagging

14. For which of the following OSI layers is Frame Relay defined?

    A. Physical

    B. Data Link

    C. Network

    D. Transport

    E. Session

15. What single bit field, when set to 1 by a router, indicates that congestion was experienced in the network in the direction opposite of the frame transmission from source to destination?

     A. DLCI

     B. BECN

     C. FECN

     D. LMI

16. What is used to tell a receiving router that the path the frame just traversed is congested?

     A. DLCI

     B. BECN

     C. FECN

     D. LMI

17. If you wanted to create a map class named bob, what command would you need to use?

     A. RouterA# `frame-relay map-class bob`

     B. RouterA(config-if)#`frame-relay map-class bob`

     C. RouterA(config-if)#`map-class frame-relay bob`

     D. RouterA(config)#`map-class frame-relay bob`

18. What command allows traffic shaping on a Cisco Frame Relay link?

     A. RouterA(config-if)#`frame-relay class name`

     B. RouterA(config)#`frame-relay class name`

     C. RouterA(config)#`frame-relay traffic-shaping`

     D. RouterA(config-if)#`frame-relay traffic-shaping`

19. After an interface is configured to allow traffic shaping, what command places the map class on the actual VC?

     A. RouterA(config-subif)#`frame-relay class name`

     B. RouterA(config)#`frame-relay class name`

     C. RouterA(config)#`frame-relay traffic-shaping`

     D. RouterA(config-if)#`frame-relay traffic-shaping`

20. What is the solution of multipoint links and distance-vector routing protocols?

     A. Frame Relay

     B. ATM

     C. ISDN

     D. PPP

     E. Subinterfaces

Answers to Written Lab

1.

```
show interface s0
```

2.

```
config t
interface serial0
encapsulation frame-relay
```

3.

```
config t
interface serial0.16 point-to-point
```

4.

```
config t
interface serial0.16 point-to-point
frame-relay lmi-type ansi
```

5.

```
config t
interface serial0.16 point-to-point
frame-relay interface-dlci 16
```

6.

```
config t
frame-relay de-list 1 protocol ipx
interface serial0.16 point-to-point
frame-relay de-group 1 100
```

7.

```
config t
frame-relay switching
```

8.

```
Show interface
```

9.

```
show frame-relay pvc
show running-config
```

10.

```
show frame-relay map
```

11.

```
map-class frame-relay name
```

12.

```
frame relay traffic-rate average [peak]
```

13.

```
frame-relay adaptive-shaping becn
```

14.

```
frame-relay custom-queue-list number
frame-relay priority-group number
```

15.

```
config t
interface serial0
frame-relay traffic-shaping
```

16.

```
interface serial0.16 point-to-point
frame-relay class name
```

Answer to Review Questions

1. C, D. Cisco is the default Frame Relay encapsulation type. Internet Engineering Task Force (IETF) is used to communicate between routers from different vendors.

2. A, B, C. The three LMI types supported are ANSI, Q933a, and Cisco. Cisco is the default LMI type.

3. C. Although it might be possible to get Frame Relay to deliver the video, the best way to guarantee 100 percent of the bandwidth, with no drops, is a dedicated circuit.

4. A. When cost is a concern, packet switching technology is the solution. Both X.25 and Frame Relay are inexpensive, but Frame Relay is faster.

5. D. Oversubscription is what happens when the combined Committed Information Rate exceeds the backbone capabilities.

6. E. Frame Relay was first fleshed out in an ISDN RFC.

7. B, C. The two types of VCs used with Frame Relay are Permanent Virtual Circuits and Switched Virtual Circuits. Permanent Virtual Circuits are most frequently used.

8. C. Each PVC in the cloud is identified by its DLCI address.

9. D. The access rate is the actual line speed of the circuit.

10. B. The burst-committed rate is the CIR multiplied by the measurement interval. In this case, it is 256Kbps multiplied by 10 seconds.

11. A. Local Management Interface provides for DLCI status inquiry. Inverse ARP provides a mechanism to map DLCIs to IP addresses.

12. B. Most IP routing protocols support disabling split horizon; however, Internet Packet Exchange (IPX), Routing Information Protocol (RIP) and Apple Routing Table Maintenance Protocol (RTMP) do not. Static routes are popular, but choosing them is an inflexible solution. Subinterfaces are the most popular and the best solution.

13. D. Cisco routers can be configured as Frame Relay switches.

14. B. Frame Relay is defined only at the Data Link Layer of the OSI model.

15. B. Backward Explicit Congestion Notification (BECN) is used to tell a transmitting router to slow down its transfer rate.

16. C. Forward Explicit Congestion Notification (FECN) is used to tell a receiving router that the frame switch is congested.

17. D. To create a map class, use the global `map-class frame-relay` *name* command.

18. D. The interface command `frame-relay traffic-shaping` is used to enable an interface to accept map class parameters.

19. A. The command `frame-relay class name` sets the map class on a subinterface. The `frame-relay traffic-shaping` command must first be enabled on the interface.

20. E. Subinterfaces will automatically fix spit-horizon issues associated with distance-vector routing protocols.

Chapter

9

Queuing and Compression

EXAM TOPICS COVERED IN THIS CHAPTER INCLUDE:

✓ Determine why queuing is enabled, identify alternative queuing protocols that Cisco products support, and determine the best queuing method to implement.

✓ Specify the commands to configure queuing.

✓ Specify the commands and procedures used to verify proper queuing configuration.

✓ Specify the commands and procedures used to effectively select and implement compression.

✓ Describe traffic control methods used to manage traffic flow on WAN links.

✓ Plan traffic shaping to meet required quality of service on access links.

✓ Troubleshoot traffic control problems on a WAN link.

This chapter teaches you how to use both queuing and compression to help maintain a healthy network, which is important because user data consists of many types of data packets roaming the internetwork, hungering for and consuming bandwidth. *Queuing* is the act of sequencing packets for servicing—similar to a line at an amusement park with a 'FastPass' or 'go to the front' ability. Compression is the ability to communicate a piece of information with fewer bits, typically by removing repetitions within the data.

As a network administrator, you can help save precious bandwidth on WAN links, the largest bottlenecks in today's networks. With Gigabit Ethernet running the core backbones and 10-gigabit Ethernet networks just now being deployed, a 1.544Mbps T-1 link is painfully slow. By implementing both queuing and compression techniques, you can help save bandwidth and get the most for your money.

In addition, this chapter teaches you the three queuing techniques available on the Cisco router: Weighted Fair Queuing, priority queuing, and custom queuing. You will learn when to use each type, as well as how to configure each type on your router. We also present an overview of newer queuing and policing technologies, including Low Latency Queuing (LLQ), Class-Based Weighted Fair Queuing (CBWFQ), and Committed Access Rate (CAR).

Finally, this chapter provides the information you need to both understand and configure the types of compression on Cisco routers. The types of compression techniques covered in this chapter include header, payload, and link compression.

Queuing

When a packet arrives on a router's interface, a protocol-independent switching process handles it. The router then switches the traffic to the outgoing interface buffer. An example of a protocol-independent switching process is first-in, first-out (FIFO), which is the original algorithm for packet transmission. FIFO was the default for all routers until Weighted Fair Queuing (WFQ) was developed. The problem with FIFO is that transmission occurs in the same order as messages are received. If an application, such as Voice over IP (VoIP) required traffic to be reordered, the network engineer needed to establish a queuing policy other than FIFO queuing.

Cisco IOS software offers three queuing options as an alternative to FIFO queuing:

Weighted fair queuing (WFQ) prioritizes interactive traffic over file transfers to ensure satisfactory response time for common user applications.

Priority queuing ensures timely delivery of a specific protocol or type of traffic that is transmitted before all others.

Custom queuing establishes bandwidth allocations for each type of traffic.

We discuss these three queuing options in detail in the "IOS Queuing Options" section later in this chapter.

Traffic Prioritization

Packet prioritization has become more important because many types of data traffic need to share a data path through the network, often congesting WAN links. If the WAN link is not congested, you don't need to implement traffic prioritization, although it might be appropriate to add more bandwidth in certain situations.

Prioritization of traffic will be required on your network if you have, for example, a mixture of file transfer, transaction-based, and desktop video conferencing. Prioritization is most effective on WAN links where the combination of bursty traffic and relatively lower data rates can cause temporary congestion. This is typically necessary only on WAN links slower than T-1/E-1. However, prioritization can also be used across OC (Optical Carrier)-12 and OC-48 links, because at times tests can be run to saturate these links, but you might still want voice and video to have a priority.

Queuing Policy

Queuing policies help network managers provide users with a high level of service across a WAN link, as well as control WAN costs. Typically, the corporate goal is to deploy and maintain a single enterprise network even though the network supports disparate applications, organizations, technologies, and user expectations. Consequently, network managers are concerned about providing all users with an appropriate level of service while continuing to support mission-critical applications and having the ability to integrate new technologies at the same time.

Figure 9.1 shows a serial interface that is congested and needs queuing implemented. It is important to remember that you need to implement queuing only on interfaces that experience congestion.

FIGURE 9.1   Queuing policy

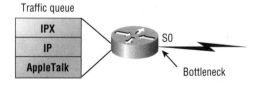

The network administrator should understand the delicate balance between meeting the business requirements of users and controlling WAN costs. Queuing enables network administrators to effectively manage network resources.

IOS Queuing Options

As we have said, if your serial links are not congested, you do not need to implement queuing. However, if the load exceeds the transmission rate for small periods of time, you can use a Cisco IOS queuing option to help the congestion on a serial link.

To effectively configure queuing on a serial link, you must understand the types of queuing available. If you choose the wrong type of queuing, you can do more harm on the link than helping. Also, this is not a one-time analysis of traffic patterns. You must constantly repeat your analysis of your serial link congestion to make sure you have implemented the queuing strategy correctly.

Figure 9.2 shows the queuing options available from Cisco.

FIGURE 9.2   Queuing options

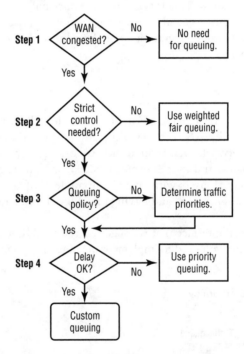

The following steps and Figure 9.2 describe the analysis you should make when deciding on a queuing policy:

1. Determine whether the WAN is congested.

2. Decide whether strict control over traffic prioritization is necessary and whether automatic configuration is acceptable.

3. Establish a queuing policy.

4. Determine whether any of the traffic types you identified in your traffic pattern analysis can tolerate a delay.

Weighted Fair Queuing

Weighted fair queuing (WFQ) provides equal amounts of bandwidth to each conversation that traverses the interface. WFQ uses a process that refers to the timestamp found on the last bit of a packet as it enters the queue.

Assigning Priorities

WFQ assigns a high priority to all low-volume traffic. Figure 9.3 demonstrates how the timing mechanism for priority assignment occurs. The algorithm determines which frames belong to either a high-volume or low-volume conversation and forwards the low-volume packets from the queue first. Through this timing convention, remaining packets can be assigned an exiting priority.

In Figure 9.3, packets are labeled A through F. As depicted in the diagram, Packet A will be forwarded first because it's part of a low-volume conversation, even though the last bit of session B will arrive before the last bit of the packets associated with Packet A did. The remaining packets are divided between the two high-traffic conversations, with their timestamps determining the order in which they will exit the queue.

FIGURE 9.3   Priority assignment using WFQ

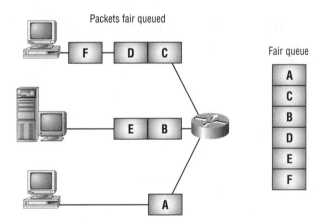

• Conversations are assigned a channel.

• Sorts the queue by order of the last bit crossing its channel

Assigning Conversations

We've discussed how priority is assigned to a packet or conversation, but it's also important to understand the type of information that the processor needs to associate a group of packets with an established conversation.

The most common elements used to establish a conversation are as follows:

- Source and destination IP addresses
- MAC addresses
- Port numbers
- Type of service
- DLCI number assigned to an interface

Say a router has two active conversations, one a large FTP transfer and the other an HTTP session. The router, using some or all of the factors just listed to determine which conversation a packet belongs to, will allocate equal amounts of bandwidth to each conversation. Each of the two conversations receives half of the available bandwidth.

Configuring Weighted Fair Queuing

You're now ready to learn how to configure WFQ. For all interfaces having a line speed equal to or lower than 2.048Mbps (E-1 speed), WFQ is on by default. Here's an example of how WFQ is configured on an interface. You can use the fair-queue command to alter the default settings:

```
Router_C#config t
Enter configuration commands, one per line. End with CNTL/Z.
Router_C(config)#interface serial0
Router_C(config-if)#fair-queue 96
Router_C(config-if)#^Z
Router_C#
```

To understand what was configured, look at the syntax of the command:

fair-queue [*congestive-discard-threshold* [*dynamic-queues* [*reservable-queues*]]]

congestive-discard-threshold This value specifies the number of messages allowed in each queue. The default is 64 messages, with a range 16–4,096. When a conversation reaches this threshold, new message packets will be dropped.

dynamic-queues Dynamic queues are exactly that—queues established dynamically to handle conversations that don't have special requirements. The valid values for this parameter are 16, 32, 64, 128, 256, 512, 1024, 2048, and 4096, with the default value being 256 – ISDN BRI has a default of 16.

reservable-queues This parameter defines the number of queues established to handle special conversations. The available range is from 0 to 1,000. The default is 0. These queues are for interfaces that use Resource Reservation Protocol (RSVP).

Verifying Weighted Fair Queuing

Now that WFQ is configured on the router's serial 0 interface, let's see what it's doing. To verify the configuration and operation of the queuing system, you can issue the following two commands:

```
show queueing [fair | priority | custom]
show queue [interface-type interface-number]
```

 When you use the show commands, note that *queuing* is misspelled. It has that extra *e*.

Results from these commands on Router C can be seen next. Since WFQ is the only type of queuing that's been enabled on this router, it isn't necessary to issue the optional commands of `fair`, `custom`, or `priority`.

```
Router_C#show queueing
Current fair queue configuration:

Interface  Discard     Dynamic       Reserved
           threshold   queue count   queue count
Serial0    96          256           0
Serial1    64          256           0


Current priority queue configuration:
Current custom queue configuration:
Current RED queue configuration:
Router_C#
```

This command shows that WFQ is enabled on both serial interfaces and that the discard threshold for serial 0 was changed from 64 to 96. There's a maximum of 256 dynamic queues for both interfaces—the default value. The lines following the interface information are empty because their corresponding queuing algorithms haven't been configured yet.

The next command displays more detailed information pertaining to the specified interface:

```
Router_C#show queue serial0
 Input queue: 0/75/0 (size/max/drops); Total output drops: 0
 Queueing strategy: weighted fair
 Output queue: 0/1000/96/0 (size/max total/threshold/drops)
   Conversations 0/1/256 (active/max active/max total)
   Reserved Conversations 0/0 (allocated/max allocated)
```

This command will show the input queue information, which is the current size of the queue, the maximum size of the queue, and the number of conversations that have been dropped. The queuing strategy is defined as `weighted fair`, or WFQ. The output queue (usually the one with the most activity) defines the current size, maximum total number of output queue entries, number of conversations per queue, and number of conversations dropped. The conversations section represents the number of conversations in the queue. The `active` number describes the number of current active conversations. The `max active` keeps a record of the maximum number of active conversations at any one time, and finally, `max total` gives the total number of all conversations possible within the queue. Reserved queues are also displayed with the current number allocated and maximum number of allocated queues.

Priority Queuing

Unlike Weighted Fair Queuing, which occurs on a session basis, *priority queuing* occurs on a packet-by-packet basis and is ideal in network environments that carry time-sensitive traffic. When congestion occurs on low-speed interfaces, priority queuing guarantees that traffic assigned a high priority will be sent first. On the negative side, if the queue for high-priority traffic is always full and monopolizing bandwidth, packets in the other queues will be severely delayed or dropped.

Assigning Priorities

Priority queuing uses the packet header information consisting of either the TCP port or the protocol as a classification mechanism. When a packet enters the router, it's compared against a list that will assign a priority to it and forward it to the corresponding queue.

Priority queuing can assign a packet to one of four priorities: high, medium, normal, and low, with a separate dispatching algorithm to manage the traffic in all four. Figure 9.4 shows how these queues are serviced—you can see that the algorithm starts with the high-priority queue processing all the data there. When that queue is empty, the dispatching algorithm moves down to the medium-priority queue, and so on down the priority chain, performing a cascade check of each queue before moving on. So if the algorithm finds packets in a higher-priority queue, it will process them first before moving on. This is where problems can develop; packets in the lower-priority queues could be totally neglected in favor of the higher-priority ones if they're continually busy with the arrival of new packets.

FIGURE 9.4 Using priority queuing

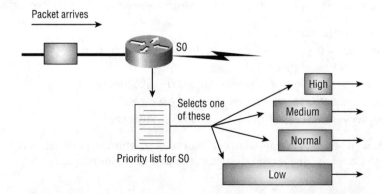

Configuring Priority Queuing

Implementing priority queuing on an interface requires three steps:

1. Create a priority list that the processor will use to determine packet priority.
2. Adjust the size of the queues if desired.
3. Apply the priority list to the desired interfaces.

Let's go over how to build a priority list by using the following commands:

```
priority-list list-number protocol protocol-name] {high | medium | normal |
low}} queue-keyword keyword-value
priority-list list-number interface interface-type {high | medium | normal | low}
```

The *list-number* parameter identifies the specific priority list, and the valid values are 1 through 16. The protocol parameter directs the router to assign packets to the appropriate queue based on the protocol, and *protocol-name* defines which protocol to match. The *queue-keyword* and *keyword-value* parameters enable packets to be classified by their byte count, access list, protocol port number, or name and fragmentation. With the interface parameter, any traffic coming from the interface is assigned to the specified queue. Next, after specifying the protocol or interface, the type of queue needs to be defined—high, medium, normal, or low.

```
priority-list list-number default queue-number
```

The same priority-list command can be used to configure a default queue for traffic that doesn't match the protocols or interfaces defined in the priority list.

```
priority-list list-number queue-limit [high-limit [medium-limit [normal-limit
[low-limit]]]])
```

The queue-limit parameter is used to specify the maximum number of packets allowed in each of the priority queues. The configuration of the queue size must be handled carefully, because if a packet is forwarded to the appropriate queue but the queue is full, the packet will be discarded—even if bandwidth is available. This means that enabling priority queuing on an interface can be useless (even destructive) if queues aren't accurately configured to respond to actual network needs. It's important to make the queues large enough to accommodate congestion so that the influx of packets can be accepted and stored until they can be forwarded.

After creating the priority list, you can apply that list to an interface in interface configuration mode with the following command:

```
priority-group list
```

The *list* parameter is the priority list number, from 1 to 16, to use on this interface. After the list is applied to the interface, it is implicitly applied to outbound traffic. All packets will be checked against the priority list before entering their corresponding queue. The ones that don't match will be placed in the default queue. Here's an example:

```
Router_C#config t
Enter configuration commands, one per line. End with CNTL/Z.
```

```
Router_C(config)#priority-list 1 protocol ip high gt 1000
Router_C(config)#priority-list 1 protocol ip low lt 256
Router_C(config)#priority-list 1 protocol ip normal
Router_C(config)#priority-list 1 interface serial 1 normal
Router_C(config)#priority-list 1 interface ethernet 0 high
Router_C(config)#priority-list 1 default normal
Router_C(config)#priority-list 1 queue-limit 40 80 120 160
Router_C(config)#interface serial 0
Router_C(config-if)#priority-group 1
Router_C(config-if)#^Z
Router_C#
```

The first line of the priority list assigns high priority to all IP traffic with a packet size greater than (gt) 1,000 bytes. The second line assigns low priority to IP traffic with a packet size less than (lt) 256bytes. The third line assigns all remaining IP traffic to the normal queue. The fourth line assigns all incoming traffic on serial 1 to the normal queue also. All incoming traffic on Ethernet 0 is assigned a high priority, and any remaining traffic will be assigned normal priority. The size of each queue is defined by the queue-limit parameter, and the numbers follow the order of high, medium, normal, and low queue sizes.

Following is an example of what the interface configuration looks like. The priority list has been assigned to the interface with the priority-group command. You can see the final form of the applied priority list in the following configuration snippet:

```
!
interface Serial0
 ip address 172.16.40.6 255.255.255.252
 priority-group 1
!
priority-list 1 protocol ip high gt 1000
priority-list 1 protocol ip low lt 256
priority-list 1 protocol ip normal
priority-list 1 interface Serial1 normal
priority-list 1 interface Ethernet0 high
priority-list 1 queue-limit 40 80 120 160
```

As with access control lists, the order of a matching packet is important. A 1,500-byte packet on Serial 0 would match the first and fourth lines, but would only be queued by the first instruction, placing it in the high-priority queue.

Verifying Priority Queuing

To make sure the queuing configuration is working and configured properly, you can use the same command used to verify WFQ with the added option for priority queuing.

The following command output summarizes the preceding configured priority list:

```
Router_C#show queueing priority
Current priority queue configuration:

List  Queue Args
1    high  protocol ip gt 1000
1    low   protocol ip lt 256
1    normal protocol ip
1    normal interface Serial1
1    high interface Ethernet0
1    high limit 40
1    medium limit 80
1    normal limit 120
1    low limit 160
Router_C#
```

Custom Queuing

Custom queuing functions on the concept of sharing bandwidth among traffic types. Instead of assigning a priority classification to a specific traffic or packet type, custom queuing forwards traffic in the different queues by using the FIFO method within each queue. Custom queuing offers the ability to customize the amount of actual bandwidth that a specified traffic type uses.

While remaining within the limits of the physical line's capacity, virtual pipes are configured through the custom queuing option. Varying amounts of the total bandwidth are reserved for various specific traffic types, and if the bandwidth isn't being fully utilized by its assigned traffic type, other types can borrow its bandwidth. The configured limits go into effect during high levels of utilization or when congestion on the line causes different traffic types to compete for bandwidth.

Figure 9.5 shows each queue being processed, one after the other. After this begins, the algorithm checks the first queue, processes the data within it, and then moves to the next—if it comes across an empty one, it will simply move on to the next one without hesitating. Each queue's byte count specifies the amount of data that will be forwarded from that queue, which directs the algorithm to move to the next queue after it has been reached. Custom queuing permits a maximum of 16 configurable queues. The system queue is for network specific traffic, including system datagrams such as SNMP and routing updates.

FIGURE 9.5   Custom queuing algorithm

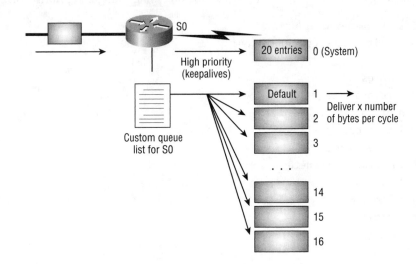

Figure 9.6 shows how the bandwidth allocation via custom queuing looks relative to the physical connection. Using the frame size of the protocols and configuring the byte count for each queue will configure appropriate bandwidth allocations for each traffic type. In other words, when a particular queue is being processed, packets are sent until the number of bytes sent exceeds the queue byte count defined.

FIGURE 9.6   Bandwidth allocation using custom queuing

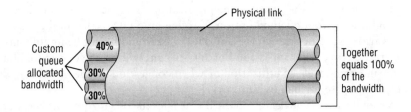

Configuring Custom Queuing

Configuring custom queuing is similar to configuring priority queuing, but instead of completing three tasks, you must complete five. As with priority queuing, you have to configure a list to separate types of incoming traffic into their desired queues. After that, you must configure a default queue for the traffic that will be unassigned to any of the other queues. After the specific and default queues are defined, you can adjust the capacity or size of each queue or just stick with the default settings.

When that's complete, specify the transfer rate, or byte count, for each queue. This is important—the byte count determines the percentage of bandwidth reserved for a specified queue, with a default of 1,500 bytes as the denominator. After these parameters are set, apply them to an interface.

The commands used to configure the queuing list, default queue, queue size, and transmit rate follow:

```
queue-list list-number default queue-number
queue-list list-number interface interface-type interface-number queue-number
queue-list list-number lowest-custom queue-number
queue-list list-number protocol protocol-name queue-number queue-keyword
keyword-value
queue-list]list-number queue [queue-number byte-count byte-count-number | limit
limit-number]
queue-list list-number stun [queue-number | address STUN-group-number]
```

The syntax can be presented in many ways to configure the desired command. The *list-number* is a value from 1 to 16 and associates the list with the given number. The following are available options:

default designates a custom queue for packets that do not match another queue-list.

interface assigns incoming packets on the specified interface to a custom queue. When the interface option is specified, you must supply the *interface-type* and *interface-number* as well. The *interface-type* is the type of physical interface, and *interface-number* is the interface's physical port.

lowest-custom specifies the lowest queue number considered a custom queue.

protocol indicates that the packets are to be sent to the custom queue if they are of the protocol specified. The protocol option also requires additional information. Obviously, the *protocol-name* must be specified. In Table 9.1, a sample of available protocol names is listed, but available protocols are dependent upon the feature set and version of IOS. After the *protocol-name*, you might supply the *keyword-value* to refine the protocols and port numbers used for filtering.

queue allows for specific queue parameters to be configured. The parameters for the queue are discussed later in this section.

stun establishes queuing priority for STUN packets.

TABLE 9.1   Sample of Available Protocol Names

Protocol Name	Description
aarp	AppleTalk ARP
apollo	Apollo
appletalk	AppleTalk

TABLE 9.1   Sample of Available Protocol Names *(continued)*

Protocol Name	Description
arp	IP ARP
bridge	Bridging
bstun	Block Serial Tunnel
cdp	Cisco Discovery Protocol
compressedtcp	Compressed TCP
decnet	DECnet
decnet_node	DECnet Node
decnet_router-l1	DECnet Router L1
decnet_router-l2	DECnet Router L2
dlsw	DLSw+
ip	IP
llc2	LLC2

Table 9.2 lists the available keyword values.

TABLE 9.2   Available Keyword Values

Keyword Value	Description
fragments	Prioritize IP fragments
gt	Greater than specified value
list	Access list
lt	Less than specified value
tcp	TCP packets
udp	UDP packets

To define the operational parameters for the custom queues, you use the `queue` option. After specifying the *queue-number*, you're given two parameters to configure:

`limit` enables you to change the number of packets allowed in the queue. The range is from 0 to 32,767, with the default being 20.

`byte-count` specifies the average number of bytes forwarded from each queue during a queue cycle.

Configuring Byte Count

Configure the byte-count queues carefully, because if the setting is too high, the algorithm will take longer than necessary to move from one queue to the next. This is not a problem while the processor empties the queue, but if it takes the processor too long to get back to other queues, they could fill up and start to drop packets.

This is why it's important to understand how to configure the bandwidth percentage relationship by using the `byte-count` command. Because frame sizes vary from protocol to protocol, you'll need to know the average frame sizes of the protocols using the custom queued interface to define the byte count efficiently. You can do this by using simple math.

Suppose you have a router that uses IP, IPX, and SNA as its protocols. Let's arbitrarily assign frame sizes, realizing that the values aren't the real ones. Assign a frame size of 800 bytes to IP, 1,000 bytes to IPX, and 1,500 bytes to SNA. You calculate a simple ratio by taking the highest frame value and dividing it by the frame size of each protocol:

IP = 1,500/800 = 1.875
IPX = 1,500/1,000 = 1.5
SNA = 1,500/1,500 = 1.0

These values equal your frame size ratios. To assign correct bandwidth percentages, multiply each ratio by the bandwidth percentage you want to assign to that protocol. For example, assign 40 percent to IP, 30 percent to IPX, and 30 percent to SNA:

IP = 1.875 * (0.4) = 0.75
IPX = 1.5 * (0.3) = 0.45
SNA = 1 * (0.3) = 0.30

These values now need to be normalized by dividing the results by the smallest value:

IP = 0.75/0.3 = 2.5
IPX = 0.45/0.3 = 1.5
SNA = 0.3/0.3 = 1

Custom queuing will send only complete frames. As the ratios are fractions, you must round them up to the nearest integer values that maintain the same ratio. To arrive at the nearest integer value, multiply the original ratios by a common number that will cause the ratios to become integers. In this case, you can multiply everything by 2 and get the resulting ratio of 5:3:2. What does this mean? Well, five frames of IP, three frames of IPX, and two frames of SNA will be sent. Because of the protocols' varying frame size, the bandwidth percentage works out just the way you calculated:

IP = 5 frames 800 bytes = 4,000 bytes
IPX = 3 frames 1,000 bytes = 3,000 bytes
SNA = 2 frames 1,500 bytes = 3,000 bytes

Total bandwidth is 10,000 bytes. Percentages are verified by dividing the protocol rate by the total. After doing the math, you verify that IP = 40 percent, IPX = 30 percent, and SNA = 30 percent.

Now that the byte count is calculated (4,000, 3,000, and 3,000), you can apply the results in the `queue-list` command. The custom queuing algorithm will forward 4,000 bytes worth of IP packets, move to the IPX queue and forward 3,000 bytes, and then go to the SNA queue and forward 3,000 bytes.

 The following queue list does not follow the IP, IPX, and SNA example we've been discussing.

See the following example on how to configure and apply custom queuing lists:

```
Router_B#config t
Enter configuration commands, one per line. End with CNTL/Z.
Router_B(config)#queue-list 1 interface Ethernet0 1
Router_B(config)#queue-list 1 protocol ip 2 tcp 23
Router_B(config)#queue-list 1 protocol ip 3 tcp 80
Router_B(config)#queue-list 1 protocol ip 4 udp snmp
Router_B(config)#queue-list 1 protocol ip 5
Router_B(config)#queue-list 1 default 6
Router_B(config)#queue-list 1 queue 1 limit 40
Router_B(config)#queue-list 1 queue 5 byte-count 4000
Router_B(config)#queue-list 1 queue 4 byte-count 500
Router_B(config)#queue-list 1 queue 3 byte-count 4000
Router_B(config)#queue-list 1 queue 2 byte-count 1000
Router_B(config)#interface serial0
Router_B(config-if)#custom-queue-list 1Router_B(config-if)#^Z
Router_B#
```

After analyzing the list, you can see that six queues were configured. The first one was configured to handle incoming traffic from interface Ethernet 0, and the second is reserved for Telnet traffic. Queue number 3 is for WWW traffic, and the fourth is configured to handle SNMP traffic. The fifth queue will handle all other IP traffic, while queue number 6 is set up as the default queue where all unspecified traffic will go. A limit of 40 packets was placed on queue 1 (from the default of 20), and the byte count was changed from the default value of 1,500 for queues 2, 3, 4, and 5. Finally, after the queue list was created, it was applied to interface serial 0.

Here is what the configuration looks like:

```
!
interface Serial0
 ip address 10.1.1.1
 255.255.255.0
 custom-queue-list 1
!
```

```
queue-list 1 protocol ip 2 tcp telnet
queue-list 1 protocol ip 3 tcp www
queue-list 1 protocol ip 4 udp snmp
queue-list 1 protocol ip 5
queue-list 1 default 6
queue-list 1 interface Ethernet0 1
queue-list 1 queue 1 limit 40
queue-list 1 queue 2 byte-count 1000
queue-list 1 queue 3 byte-count 4000
queue-list 1 queue 4 byte-count 500
queue-list 1 queue 5 byte-count 4000
```

As with the other queuing algorithms, you need to verify both the configuration and the status of custom queuing. Issuing the same command as before, except this time substituting `custom` for `priority`, produces the following output:

```
Router_B#show queueing custom
Current custom queue configuration:

List  Queue Args
1     6     default
1     1     interface Ethernet0
1     2     protocol ip      tcp port telnet
1     3     protocol ip      tcp port www
1     4     protocol ip      udp port snmp
1     5     protocol ip
1     1     limit 40
1     2     byte-count 1000
1     3     byte-count 4000
1     4     byte-count 500
1     5     byte-count 4000
Router_B#
```

This output information gives you a breakdown of the custom queue lists configured on the device, detailing queue assignments and any limits or byte counts assigned to each custom queue.

The Real Use of Queuing

As with most things in networking, queuing is a trade-off technology that can provide significant benefit or detriment to the administrator. As a result, when coupled with the implementation and management overhead involved, most networks forgo queuing and quality of service in favor of other techniques. The most common of these is bandwidth.

The reality is that bandwidth can be used as a QoS mechanism; however, it will not prioritize a filled queue, which is the point where queuing takes over. This can greatly degrade voice services (VoIP), but can also be a factor when the link is presented with a significant amount of additional data. This can occur under parallel link failure, wherein two paths are reduced to one, presumably with a resulting 50 percent loss of total bandwidth.

QoS and queuing can provide a mechanism to protect traffic under this model, and might be a good augmentation to bandwidth services in your network. The challenge is how to categorize and prioritize traffic—identification of traffic flows, the amount of bandwidth required, the amount available, the benefit to the firm, and the ability to categorize are all considerations for the designer to evaluate. NetFlow, a Cisco IOS feature that can audit network traffic, and Network-Based Application Recognition (NBAR), can help in this process, but NetFlow requires a good amount of storage and manual evaluation, and NBAR is not recommended for high-capacity links because of its processor demands.

In addition, you will likely find infighting as a result of your decisions; a group with its traffic prioritized as bronze will commonly buck and question why an application was rated above it at gold. Obtaining early sign-off can greatly reduce this contention.

Another queuing option available to the administrator is in-band prioritization. This does not help user traffic, but can insulate the network from large-scale denial of service attacks. In this model, queue priority is given to Telnet, Secure Shell (SSH), and TFTP (Trivial FTP) so that these ports are available to the network administrator when the network is under heavy load. This load might be due to user traffic or an attack such as Code Red or Nimda. The caution is that processor load and other factors might be saturated to negate this protection, and, of course, users will still lose their applications under attack.

Cisco's Newer Queuing Technologies

Because of their notable absence in the topics covered by the Remote Access examination, we only briefly cover some of the newer queuing management technologies in this section. Queue control has become a more important issue in remote access networking with the proliferation of voice services and other real-time protocols. As these protocols suffer from congestion and low bandwidth, they are strong candidates for quality of service (QoS), of which queuing is a part.

Remember that queuing is intended to manage the transmission of packets held in the router's buffer. Unlike voice, data networks buffer packets during periods of congestion.

Although we could discuss a wide number of queuing options, three key methods are gaining prominence in the market: Low Latency Queuing, Class-Based Weighted Fair Queuing, and Committed Access Rate.

Low Latency Queuing

Low latency queuing (LLQ) is actually a strict priority queue within Class-Based Weighted Fair Queuing (CBWFQ), discussed in the next section. LLQ is Cisco's solution for voice and other very small packets that require real-time processing. LLQ operates by prioritizing key packets to the front of the queue. Because these packets are small by nature, there is little risk of queue starvation or other problems. However, administrators should evaluate the demands of other traffic within the network.

Class-Based Weighted Fair Queuing

Class-Based Weighted Fair Queuing (CBWFQ) builds upon WFQ by adding the concept of traffic classes. Classes can be defined by a tag within the frame such as Type of Service (TOS) or Differentiated ServicesCode Point (DSCP). These tags are added by the end station or the access router and used to forward packets through the network core without each router reexamining the packet to determine that datagram's priority. We are not defining the methodology used but simply the fact that you can use this information for CBWFQ.

Common implementations of CBWFQ establish three or four classes of application services, typically described as gold, silver, bronze, and other. This categorization does not include network traffic, such as routing updates, which should always have priority over user application traffic. Although some users will take exception to their traffic being described as a low priority, the network administrator needs to constrain the total number of classes to keep administration manageable and negate a situation in which bandwidth is being managed to the bit via QoS policy.

One of the strongest benefits to CBWFQ is the ability to define a specific amount of bandwidth to an application. For example, Financial Information Exchange (FIX) is a common financial systems protocol that might warrant special attention. Perhaps this application requires a guaranteed 256Kbps to prevent application failure on a T-1 link. CBWFQ can provide this guarantee, and, perhaps more importantly, will allow the application to use more than the 256Kbps if bandwidth is available. This is different from CAR, discussed in the next section, which establishes a hard limit on the bandwidth available to a specific protocol. Please note that by default you cannot allocate more than 75 percent of the link's total bandwidth for management by CBWFQ.

With regards to traffic classes, the model is fairly straightforward. When congestion occurs, the queue will process packets in the gold class before those in the silver class within the constraints of Weighted Fair Queuing. As such, the administrator is defining that the queue should be fair to all applications, but that gold traffic is the most important. This will lead to the managed unfairness that is the basis for all QoS policies—under congestion, the network will have to discard something to stay within the available resources.

ToS and DSCP are not commonly accepted from end-nodes because many applications and some operating systems will automatically tag all packets for the highest priority. It is recommended that you configure your edge routers to ignore the end station and tag based on address or port information.

Committed Access Rate

Committed Access Rate (CAR) is an older bandwidth and policing system; however, it is commonly used in concert with bandwidth management. As noted before, like CBWFQ, committed access rate can specify a bandwidth guarantee to an application. However, CAR also specifies a hard upper limit to that application as well. This can be very useful when wanting to reserve bandwidth for bursty applications. One example of this would be file transfer with Common Internet File System (CIFS) and other protocols on a circuit with web traffic. An administrator might wish to use CAR to allocate 128Kbps for HTTP/web traffic, which would have the same impact as saying all traffic on a T-1 except HTTP/web has over 1,400Kbps available. The advantage is that an administrator need not define each of the other applications to implement this solution.

CAR has some benefits. However, in many enterprises with a QoS strategy, CBWFQ is leading the way, and administrators are opting to protect important applications with the newer technique. You should evaluate CAR and CBWFQ for your specific environment.

Compression

The Cisco IOS provides congestion control on WAN links by adding compression on serial interfaces. This can ease the WAN bandwidth bottleneck problems by using less bandwidth on the link. Along with using the different queuing methods we discussed earlier in this chapter, one of the more effective methods of WAN optimization is compression of the data traveling across the WAN link.

Software compression can significantly affect router CPU performance, and the Cisco rule of thumb is that the router's CPU load must not exceed 65 percent when running software compression. If it does exceed this limit, it would be better to disable any compression running.

Cisco equipment supports the following types of compression:

- Header compression
- Payload compression
- Link compression
- Microsoft Point-to-Point Compression (MPPC)

By default, Cisco routers transmit data across serial links in an uncompressed format, but by using Cisco serial compression techniques, you can make more efficient use of your available bandwidth. It's true that any compression method will cause overhead on the router's CPU, but the benefits of compression on slower links can outweigh that disadvantage.

Figure 9.7 shows the three types of compression used in a Cisco internetworking environment.

FIGURE 9.7 Cisco serial compression methods

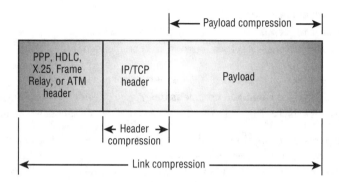

The compression methods are as follows:

TCP header compression Cisco uses the Van Jacobson algorithm to compress the headers of IP packets before sending them out onto WAN links.

Payload compression This approach compresses the data but leaves the header intact. Because the packet's header isn't changed, it can be switched through a network. This method is the one generally used for switching services such as X.25, Switched Multimegabit Data Service (SMDS), Frame Relay, and ATM.

Link compression This method is a combination of both header and payload compression, and the data will be encapsulated in either PPP or LAPB. Because of this encapsulation, link compression allows for transport protocol independence.|

Microsoft Point-to-Point Compression (MPPC) protocol This is defined in RFC 2118 and enables Cisco routers to exchange compressed data with Microsoft clients. You would configure MPPC when exchanging data with a host using MPPC across a WAN link. The MPPC is not discussed further in this section.

The Cisco compression methods are discussed in more detail next.

TCP Header Compression

TCP header compression as defined in RFC 1144 compresses only the protocol headers, not the packet data. TCP header compression lowers the overhead generated by the disproportionately large TCP/IP headers as they are transmitted across the WAN.

It is important to realize that the Layer 2 header is not touched, and only the headers at Layers 3 and 4 are compressed. This enables the Layer 2 header to direct that packet across a WAN link.

You would use the header compression on a network with small packets and a few bytes of data such as Telnet. Cisco's header compression supports X.25, Frame Relay, and dial-on-demand WAN link protocols. Because of processing overhead, header compression is generally used at lower speeds, such as 64Kbps links.

TCP header compression is achieved by using the `ip tcp header-compression` command:

```
Router(config)#interface serial0
Router(config-if)#ip tcp ?
  compression-connections  Maximum number of compressed
connections
  header-compression        Enable TCP header compression
Router(config-if)#ip tcp header-compression ?
  passive  Compress only for destinations which send compressed headers
```

The `passive` parameter is optional and is used to instruct the router to compress the headers of outbound TCP traffic if the other side is also sending compressed TCP headers. If you don't include the `passive` argument, all TCP traffic will use compressed TCP headers.

Payload Compression

Payload compression, also known as *per-virtual-circuit compression*, compresses only the payload, or data portion, of the packet. The header of the packet is not touched.

Link Compression

Link compression, also known as *per-interface compression*, compresses both the header and payload section of a data stream. Unlike header compression, link compression is protocol independent.

The link compression algorithm uses *Stac* or *Predictor* to compress the traffic in another link layer such as PPP or LAPB, ensuring error correction and packet sequencing. Cisco proprietary HDLC protocol is capable of using Stac compression only.

Predictor Use this approach to solve bottleneck problems caused by a heavy load on the router. The Predictor algorithm learns data patterns and "predicts" the next character by using an index to look up a sequence in a compression dictionary. This is sometimes referred to as *lossless* because no data will be lost during the compression and decompression process.

Stac This method is best used when bottlenecks are related to bandwidth issues. It searches the input data stream for redundant strings and replaces them with a token that is shorter than the original redundant data string.

If the data flow traverses a point-to-point connection, use link compression. In a link compression environment, the complete packet is compressed and the switching information in the header is not available for WAN switching networks. Typical examples are leased lines or ISDN.

If you use payload compression you should not use header compression. This is redundant and you should configure payload compression only.

In the following example, we turned on LAPB encapsulation with Predictor compression and set the Maximum Transmission Unit (MTU) and the LAPB N1 parameters:

```
Router#config t
Enter configuration commands, one per line. End with CNTL/Z.
Router(config)#interface serial0
Router(config-if)#encapsulation lapb
Router(config-if)#compress ?
predictor   predictor compression type
stac        stac compression algorithm
Router(config-if)#compress predictor
Router(config-if)#mtu 1510
Router(config-if)#lapb n1 12096
```

The LAPB N1 represents the number of bits in an LAPB frame, which holds an X.25 packet. It is set to eight times the MTU size, plus any overhead when using LAPB over leased lines. For instance, the N1 is specified at 12,080 (that is, $1,510 \times 8$) plus 16 bits for protocol overhead. The LAPB N1 parameter can cause major problems if it's not configured correctly and most often should be left at its default value. Even so, it can be really valuable if you need to set the MTU size.

Compression Considerations

You need to keep a few considerations in mind when selecting and implementing a compression method:

Modem compression   Modems can compress data up to four times smaller than its original size. There are different types of modem compression techniques, so make sure you understand that modem compression and router software compression are not compatible. However, the modems at both ends of the connection will try to negotiate the best compression method to use. If compression is being done at the modem, do not configure the router to also run compression.

Encrypted data   Compression happens at the Data Link Layer (Layer 2), and encryption functions at the Network Layer (Layer 3), although the payload is also encrypted, which includes Layer 7. After the application encrypts the data, the data is then sent to the router, which provides compression. The problem is that encrypted data typically does not have repetitive patterns, so the data will not compress. The router will spend a lot a processor time to determine the traffic is not compressible. So, if data is encrypted, do not attempt to compress it by using a Layer 2 compression algorithm.

CPU cycles versus memory   The amount of memory that a router must have varies according to the protocol being compressed, the compression algorithm, and the number of configured interfaces on the router. Memory requirements will be higher for Predictor than for Stac, but Stac is typically more processor intensive.

Viewing Compression Information

To view information about the status of compression on the router, use the `show compress` command. The following is a sample of the output from this command:

```
Router2#show compress
 Serial1
  uncompressed bytes xmt/rcv 82951/85400
  1 min avg ratio xmt/rcv 0.798/0.827
  5 min avg ratio xmt/rcv 0.789/0.834
  10 min avg ratio xmt/rcv 0.779/0.847
  no bufs xmt 0 no bufs rcv 0
  restarts 0
      Additional Stacker Stats:
      Transmit bytes: Uncompressed = 27044 Compressed =        66749
      Received bytes: Compressed = 76758 Uncompressed = 0
```

This command shows the uncompressed byte count of compressed data transmitted and received as well as the ratio of data throughput gained or lost in the compression routine in the last 1, 5, and 10 minutes. If the restarts are more than 0, the compression routine detected that the dictionaries were out of sync and restarted building the compression dictionary. Using this command, you will be able to see if compression is making a difference for the type of traffic being compressed.

Summary

Queuing is an important technology when using WAN links. As the speed of LAN interfaces increases more and more, data will be expected to traverse WAN links. Congestion is inevitable, so to ensure that important data gets through, a queuing mechanism is necessary. There are many queuing options available when using Cisco IOS.

Weighted Fair Queuing is the default technique when using interfaces of 2.048Mbps or slower. WFQ will track conversations and enable lower-bandwidth conversations to take priority over higher-bandwidth conversations. This feature can be tuned to allow tracking of more conversations.

Priority queuing is used to classify traffic into four queues of high, medium, normal, and low. Each queue is serviced sequentially, and the traffic is forwarded from the higher-level queues before the router services the lower-level queues. The lower-level queues might not be serviced for quite some time if there is a large amount of higher priority traffic.

Custom queuing can allocate a certain percentage of the total bandwidth available on the interface. There are 16 queues available, which can hold a certain type of traffic, and each queue can be allocated a specific amount of bandwidth. Custom queuing does not suffer from queue starvation as priority queuing can.

To alleviate congestion on WAN links, compression can be configured on the interface. The types of compression algorithms are Stac, Predictor, and MPPC. MPPC is used primarily for Windows clients, whereas Stac and Predictor can be used on many types of WAN technologies. TCP header compression is the simplest compression technique. Payload compression compresses the payload portion of the packet and does not alter the Layer 2 or Layer 3 header information. The link compression algorithm uses Stac or Predictor to compress the traffic and then encapsulates the compressed traffic in another link layer such as PPP or LAPB to ensure error correction and packet sequencing.

Various techniques can ensure that the queuing and compression technologies are working correctly. The `show queue` command is used to see queuing on the interface, and the `show queueing [priority | custom | fair]` command is used to display the queuing technique configured on the router. For compression, the `show compress` command is used to see how well the compression process is compressing traffic and whether problems might occur with the compression process.

Exam Essentials

Understand the queuing technologies available in Cisco IOS.   You should know that there is Weighted Fair Queuing, priority queuing, and custom queuing. Each has its strengths and weaknesses, but Weighted Fair Queuing is the default technique used for 2.048Mbps or slower interfaces. WFQ can be tuned with the `fair-queue` command to enable more conversations to be tracked per interface.

Know how to configure priority queuing and when it is best used.   Picking the proper queuing mechanism is very important, and Priority Queuing is ideal if you want to ensure that certain traffic gets priority over other traffic. A priority queue is set up with the `priority-list` command and is applied to the interface with the `priority-group` command.

Know how to configure custom queuing and when it is best used.   Custom Queuing is a technique that enables the WAN designer to allocate a certain amount of bandwidth to different traffic types. There are 16 queues that can be set up to contain certain types of traffic, and each of these queues can be allocated a specific amount of bandwidth. A custom queue is configured with the `queue-list` command and is applied to the interface with the `custom-queue-list` command.

Understand compression techniques and algorithms and when to use them.   You should know that the compression techniques are TCP header compression, payload compression, link compression, and MPPC compression. TCP header compression is used on point-to-point links and when smaller TCP packets, such as Telnet traffic, are being sent over the link. Payload compression can be used on links other than point-to-point and is used to compress the data portion of the packet; it will not alter the Layer 2 and Layer 3 headers. Link compression is used only on point-to-point links but is protocol independent. It will compress the whole packet and encapsulate that packet in another protocol to ensure reliability and sequencing. MPPC is used when the Cisco device needs to talk to Windows-based clients.

Know the troubleshooting commands used for queuing and compression. The commands to show queuing are show queue and show queueing [fair | priority | custom]. These can be used to display queuing on the device and the counters involved. The compression troubleshooting command is show compress, which can be used to view the compression efficiency and status.

Key Terms

Before you take the exam, be certain you are familiar with the following terms:

CAR	payload compression
CBWFQ	Predictor
custom queuing	priority queuing
encryption	queuing
link compression	Stac
LLQ	TCP header compression
lossless	Weighted Fair Queuing

Written Lab

1. What command would you use to view the custom queues configured on your router?

2. What type of compression leaves the data intact, compressing only the header information?

3. What command do you use to see queue information related only to serial 0?

4. How do you change the number of trackable conversations available to WFQ from the default of 64 to 96?

5. What type of compression compresses both the header and payload section of a data stream and is also called per-interface compression?

6. What priority queue command takes all packets received on Ethernet 0 and places them in a high queue?

7. What type of compression compresses only the data portion of the packet?

8. What command would you use to assign a custom queue for Telnet to queue 2?

9. What type of queuing function is based on the concept of sharing bandwidth among traffic types?

10. How do you assign a high-priority list to all IP traffic with a packet size greater than 1,000?

Hands-on Lab

Use the network diagram in Figure 9.8 to complete the tasks in this lab.

FIGURE 9.8   Network diagram for lab

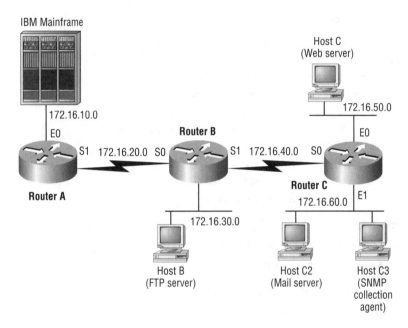

Lab 9.1: Queuing

1. Configure the queuing algorithm that will give the SNA traffic from the IBM mainframe the highest priority across the 172.16.20.0 network. Apply queuing to the appropriate router and interface. Here is how you would perform this on Router A:

```
RouterA#config t
RouterA(config)#priority-list 1 interface ethernet0 high
RouterA(config)#interface serial1
RouterA(config-if)#priority-group 1
```

2. Configure the queuing algorithm that will give precedence to WWW traffic over file transfer sessions. Apply the queuing to the appropriate router and interface(s). Here is how you would configure this on Router B:

```
RouterB#config t
RouterB(config)#interface serial0
RouterB(config-if)#fair-queue
RouterB(config-if)#interface serial1
RouterB(config-if)#fair-queue
```

3. Configure the correct queuing algorithm that will allocate 50 percent of the bandwidth to WWW traffic, 25 percent to Simple Mail Transport Protocol (SMTP), and 25 percent to FTP. For this example, use the following frame size information:

    WWW = 500 bytes

    SMTP = 300 bytes

    FTP = 200 bytes

    Here is how you would configure this on Router C:

```
RouterC#config t
RouterC(config)#queue-list 1 protocol ip 1 tcp www
RouterC(config)#queue-list 1 protocol ip 2 tcp smtp
RouterC(config)#queue-list 1 protocol ip 3 udp ftp
RouterC(config)#queue-list 1 queue 1 byte-count 6000
RouterC(config)#queue-list 1 queue 2 byte-count 3000
RouterC(config)#queue-list 1 queue 3 byte-count 3000
RouterC(config)#interface serial0
RouterC(config-if)#custom-queue-list 1
```

4. Show the details of all the queuing that was configured in the preceding tasks.

    On Router A, use the following command:

```
RouterA#show queueing priority
```

    On Router B, use the following commands:

```
RouterB#show queueing fair
RouterB#show queue serial 0
RouterB#show queue serial 1
```

    On Router C, use the following command:

```
RouterC#show queueing custom
```

Review Questions

1. What is the correct syntax for implementing Weighted Fair Queuing?

  A. `weighted-fair queue`

  B. `fair-queue`

  C. `queue-fair`

  D. None of the above

2. To which type of traffic does Weighted Fair Queuing assign the highest priority?

  A. SNA

  B. IPX

  C. High-volume

  D. Low-volume

3. When should Weighted Fair Queuing be used?

  A. To provide priority to interactive traffic

  B. To provide priority to file transfers

  C. To allow all traffic to be forwarded

  D. A and C

  E. A and B

4. Where is the most effective place to implement queuing?

  A. High-speed LAN links

  B. T-1/E-1 links only

  C. Any WAN link whose capacity is 2Mbps or slower

  D. All interfaces

5. When should priority queuing be used?

  A. When traffic has a hierarchical order of importance

  B. When delay doesn't matter

  C. When all traffic must be forwarded

  D. None of the above

6. Which one of the following steps is *not* part of configuring priority queuing?

  A. Configuring a default queue

  B. Configuring a priority list

  C. Configuring the queue transfer rate

  D. Assigning the priority list to an interface

7. How many queues are defined by priority queuing?

    A. 1–16

    B. Limited by the amount of memory available

    C. 4

    D. 1–10

8. When should custom queuing be used?

    A. When traffic has a hierarchical order of importance

    B. To overcome the possible problem that is introduced with priority queuing

    C. When trying to provide bandwidth-sharing for all traffic

    D. When delay is not important

9. Which step is *not* part of configuring custom queuing?

    A. Defining the custom queuing filter

    B. Assigning a default queue

    C. Configuring the transfer rate per queue

    D. Assigning a priority queue list to the interface

10. What is accomplished by configuring the byte count for a queue?

    A. Allocating a percentage of the total bandwidth to defined queues

    B. Setting the size of the queue

    C. Setting the amount of data that will be processed before moving to the next queue

    D. A and C

11. Which of the following options best describes Weighted Fair Queuing?

    A. Queues based on the source and destination of packets

    B. Shares bandwidth among all traffic types, giving priority to low-volume traffic

    C. Shares bandwidth among high-priority traffic only

    D. Queues using FIFO

12. Which option best describes priority queuing?

    A. Processes all queues in a round-robin fashion

    B. Queues based on the destination address of the packet

    C. Queues based on the traffic type; processes all queues equally

    D. Queues based on the traffic type; will always process the highest-priority traffic first

13. Which option best describes custom queuing?

   A. Queues based on traffic type; processes all queues equally

   B. Queues based on traffic type; always processes the high-priority traffic first

   C. Queues based on bandwidth allocation

   D. Processes packets based on the source address

14. What is accomplished by the following configuration?

```
Router_C(config)#priority-list 1 protocol ip low lt 256
Router_C(config)#interface serial 0
Router_C(config-if)#priority-group 1
Router_C(config-if)#^Z
Router_C#
```

   A. IP is held to a packet size of less than 256.

   B. Priority list 1 is applied to serial interface 0 and permits packet sizes less than 256.

   C. IP packets with sizes less than 256 are assigned to the low-priority queue, and the list is applied to serial interface 0.

   D. All packets are blocked if less than 256 bytes.

15. Which of the following is *not* used to establish a conversation for Weighted Fair Queuing?

   A. Source address

   B. Destination address

   C. Packet size

   D. Port number

16. Why is queue size important when configuring queuing?

   A. If the queue is full, the packet will be discarded.

   B. If the queue is full, the interface will become congested.

   C. If the queue is full, the algorithm halts and allows FIFO queuing.

   D. None of the above.

17. Which of the following commands should be used to assign all traffic from serial interface 1 to queue 1?

   A. `Router_B(config-if)#queue 1`

   B. `Router_B(config-if)#priority-list 1 interface Serial 1 1`

   C. `Router_B(config-if)#queue-list 1 interface Serial1 1`

   D. `Router_B(config-if)#queue-list 1 queue-number 1`

18. How many separate priority lists can be written for priority queuing?

     A. 4

     B. 8

     C. 12

     D. 16

19. Which algorithm does custom queuing use within each defined queue to forward packets?

     A. Priority

     B. Weighted fair

     C. FIFO

     D. None of the above

20. When should the default byte count for custom queuing be changed?

     A. When available bandwidth needs to be allocated as a percentage of the total bandwidth.

     B. When the application uses larger packet sizes.

     C. It should never be changed from the default setting.

     D. To utilize all available bandwidth.

Answers to Written Lab

1. `show queueing custom`
2. Header compression
3. `show queue serial0`
4. `fair-queue 96`
5. Link compression
6. `priority-list 1 interface ethernet 0 high`
7. Payload compression
8. `queue-list 1 protocol ip 2 tcp 23`
9. Custom queuing
10. `priority-list 1 protocol ip high gt 1000`

Answers to Review Questions

1. B. From a serial interface, use the command `fair-queue` to change the defaults of Weighted Fair Queuing (WFQ).

2. D. Low-volume traffic has priority in a WFQ environment. This stops a large file transfer from monopolizing the line.

3. A. WFQ is used to forward low-bandwidth traffic before file transfer traffic.

4. C. Typically, queuing should be implemented on slow serial links that experience only temporary congestion.

5. A. Priority queuing is used when you have a hierarchical order of importance that you want to implement on your serial link.

6. C. You do not configure the queue transfer rate with priority queuing.

7. C. When you initiate priority queuing, you define four queues.

8. B. When priority queuing does not meet an application congestion issue, custom queuing should be used.

9. D. A priority queue list has nothing to do with custom queuing.

10. D. By configuring the byte count for a queue, you allocate a percentage of the bandwidth to individual queues and set the amount of data that is processed for each queue.

11. B. WFQ was designed to stop large file transfers from hogging the bandwidth of a serial link.

12. D. The highest-priority queues, based on the different types of traffic, will always be processed first.

13. A. Unlike priority queuing, custom queuing processes all queues equally. However, the administrator bases the queues on traffic types.

14. C. A priority queue list was created and assigned to serial 0, which assigns any packet smaller than 256 bytes to a low-priority queue.

15. C. Source and destination address, as well as port number, are used to establish a conversation for WFQ.

16. A. If the queue becomes full, the packets will be discarded.

17. C. To assign packets received on an interface to a custom queue, use the `queue-list [#] [int] [queue]` command.

18. D.   You can have up to 16 priority lists configured on a router.

19. C.   Custom queuing uses a first-in, first-out queuing algorithm within each queue.

20. A.   You should change the byte count with custom queuing when you need to allocate a percentage of the bandwidth.

Chapter

10

Network Address Translation (NAT) and Port Address Translation (PAT)

EXAM TOPICS COVERED IN THIS CHAPTER INCLUDE:

- ✓ Describe the process of Network Address Translation (NAT).
- ✓ Configure Network Address Translation (NAT).
- ✓ Troubleshoot nonfunctional remote access systems.

As the Internet grows and individuals increasingly need more than one IP address to use for Internet access from their home and office PCs, their phones (voice over IP), their office's network printers, and many other network devices, the number of available IP addresses is diminishing. To add insult to injury, the early designers of TCP/IP—back when the Internet project was being created by the Advanced Research Projects Agency (ARPA)—never anticipated the explosion of users from private industry that has occurred.

ARPA's goal was to design a protocol that could connect all the United States Defense Department's major data systems and enable them to talk to one another. The ARPA designers created not only a protocol that would enable all the Defense Department's data systems to communicate with one another, but one that the entire world now relies on to communicate over the Internet.

Unfortunately, because of the unexpected popularity of this protocol, the distribution of IP addresses was inadequately planned. As a result, many IP addresses are unusable, and many are placed in networks that will never use all the addresses assigned to them. For example, every organization with a Class A network, which provides 16,777,214 addresses per Class A assignment, would find it difficult to use more than half of the addresses available, and those that are not used are wasted.

All the Class A and Class B addresses are already assigned to organizations. There are 65,534 Class B addresses available in each Class B address range. If a new organization needs more than one Class C address range, which provides only 254 addresses, they must get another Class C address range.

IP version 6 will eventually alleviate IP addressing problems because it increases the address space from 32 bits to 128 bits, but its adoption has been slow because of the problems associated with infrastructure and application support. Outside the United States, IPv6 is being paid more attention because less IPv4 address space is available. Specifically, Japan has implemented a large-scale IPv6 network because of the number of addresses needed and the availability of IPv6 address space.

This chapter introduces you to Network Address Translation (NAT) and Port Address Translation (PAT). Cisco routers and internal route processors use these two protocols to allow the use of a limited number of registered IP addresses by a large number of users and devices. As you progress through the chapter, you will learn the differences between NAT and PAT, as well as their operational boundaries, how to configure them, and how to troubleshoot problems associated with these two protocols.

Understanding Network Address Translation (NAT)

Before exploring the details of *Network Address Translation (NAT)* operations, configuration, and troubleshooting, it is important to thoroughly understand what it is, the terminology associated with it, its advantages and disadvantages, and the traffic types it supports. NAT is a protocol that maps an inside IP address used in the local, or inside, network environment to the outside network environment and vice versa. There are many reasons for using NAT in your network environment. Some of the benefits you will receive from NAT include the following:

- Enabling a private IP network to use nonregistered IP addresses to access an outside network such as the Internet

- Providing the ability to reuse assigned IP addresses that are already in use on the Internet

- Providing Internet connectivity in networks where there are not enough individual Internet-registered IP addresses

- Appropriately translating the addresses in two merged intranets such as two merged companies

- Translating internal IP addresses assigned by old Internet Service Providers (ISPs) to a new ISP's newly assigned addresses without manually configuring the local network interfaces

NAT Terminology

Before continuing with this chapter, you should be familiar with the following Cisco terms:

Inside network   The *inside network* is the set of network addresses that is subject to translation. The IP addresses used within the network are invalid on an outside network, such as the Internet or the network's ISP. Often, the IP addresses used in the inside network are obsolete, or an IP address is allocated in a range specified by RFC 1918 or RFC 3330 (which reserves certain IP addresses for internal use only) and is not Internet routable.

Outside network   The *outside network* is not affiliated with or owned by the inside network organization (keep in mind we are referring to a network—not network addresses). This can be the network of another company when two companies merge, but typically is the network of an ISP. The addresses used on this network are legally registered and Internet-routable IP addresses.

Inside local IP address   The *inside local IP address* is the IP address assigned to an interface in the inside network. This address can be illegal to use on the Internet or can be an address defined by RFC 1918 as unusable on the Internet. In both cases, this address is not globally routable. If the address is globally routable, it can be assigned to another organization and cannot be used on the Internet.

Inside global IP address   The *inside global IP address* is the IP address of an inside host as it appears to the outside network. This is the "translated IP address." Addresses can be allocated from a globally unique address space, typically provided by the ISP (if the enterprise is connected to the global Internet).

Outside local IP address   The *outside local IP address* is the IP address of an outside host as it appears to the inside network. These addresses can be allocated from the RFC 1918 space if desired.

Outside global IP address   The *outside global IP address* is the configured IP address assigned to a host in the outside network.

Simple translation entry   A *simple translation entry* is an entry in the NAT table that results when the NAT router matches an illegal inside IP address to a globally routable IP address that is legally registered for Internet use.

Extended translation entry   An *extended translation entry* is a translation entry that maps one IP address and port pair to another.

How NAT Works

NAT is configured on the router or route processor closest to the border of a stub domain (a LAN that uses IP addresses—either registered or unregistered for internal use), between the inside network (local network) and the outside network (public network such as an ISP or the Internet). The outside network can also be another company, such as when two networks merge after an acquisition.

An illustration of NAT is shown in Figure 10.1. You should note that the router separates the inside and outside networks. NAT translates the inside local addresses into the globally unique inside global IP address, enabling data to flow into the outside network.

FIGURE 10.1   The NAT router on the border of an inside network and an outside network such as the Internet

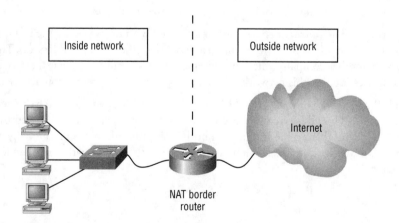

Inside network

Outside network

Internet

NAT border router

NAT takes advantage of there being relatively few network users using the outside network at any given time. NAT does this by using process switching to change the source address on the outbound packets, directing them to the appropriate router. This enables fewer IP addresses to be used than the number of hosts in the inside network. Before the implementation of NAT on all Cisco enterprise routers, the only way to implement these features was to use pass-through firewall gateways.

NAT was first implemented in Cisco's IOS release 11.2 and spelled out in RFC 1631.

Advantages of NAT

There are many advantages of using NAT. Some of the more important benefits include the following:

- NAT enables you to incrementally increase or decrease registered IP addresses without changes to hosts, switches, or routers within the network. (The exception to this is the NAT border routers that connect the inside and outside networks.)

- NAT can be used either statically or dynamically:

  - Static translation occurs when you manually configure an address translation table with IP addresses. A specific address on the inside of the network uses a specific outside IP address, manually configured by the network administrator, to access the outside network. The network administrator could also translate an inside IP address and port pair to an outside IP address and port pair.

  - Dynamic mappings enable the administrator to configure one or more pools of outside IP addresses on the NAT border router. The addresses in the pools can be used by nodes on the inside network to access nodes on the outside network. This enables multiple internal hosts to utilize a single pool of IP addresses.

- NAT can allow the sharing of packet processing among multiple servers by using the Transmission Control Protocol (TCP) load distribution feature. NAT load distribution can be accomplished by using one individual global address mapped to multiple local server addresses. This round-robin approach is used on the router distributing incoming connections across the servers.

There is no limit to the number of NAT sessions that can be used on a router or route processor. The limit is placed on the amount of DRAM the router contains. The DRAM must store the configurable NAT pools and handle each translation. Each NAT translation uses approximately 160 bytes, which translates into about 1.53MB for 10,000 translations. This is far more translations than the average router needs to provide.

- If your internal addresses must change because you have changed your ISP or have merged with another company that is using the same address space, you can use NAT to translate the addresses from one network to the other.

Disadvantages of NAT

Now that you know about the advantages of using NAT, you should learn about the disadvantages as well. The following is a list of some of the disadvantages of using NAT compared to using individually configured, registered IP addresses on each network host:

- NAT increases latency (delay). Delays are introduced into the switching path due to the processor overhead needed to translate each IP address contained in the packet headers. The router's CPU must be used to process every packet to decide whether the router needs to translate and change the IP header. Some Application Layer protocols supported, such as DNS, have IP addresses in their payload that must be translated also. This adds to the increased delay.

- NAT hides end-to-end IP addresses that render some applications unusable. Some applications that use the host IP address inside the payload of the packet will break when NAT translates the IP addresses across the NAT border router.

- Because NAT changes the IP address, there is a loss of IP end-to-end traceability. The multiple packet-address changes confuse IP tracing utilities. This provides one advantage from a security standpoint: it eliminates some of a hacker's ability to identify a packet's source.

- NAT also makes troubleshooting or tracking down where malicious traffic is coming from more troublesome. Because the traffic could be coming from a single user who is using different IP addresses depending on when the traffic passes through the NAT router, accountability becomes much more difficult.

NAT Traffic Types

NAT supports many traffic types. The Remote Access exam includes questions on both the supported and unsupported types. Let's take a look at these types now.

Supported Traffic Types

NAT supports the following traffic types:

- TCP traffic that does not carry source and destination addresses in an application stream
- UDP traffic that does not carry source and destination addresses in an application stream
- Hypertext Transfer Protocol (HTTP)
- Trivial File Transfer Protocol (TFTP)
- File Transfer Protocol (FTP PORT and PASV commands)
- Archie, which provides lists of anonymous FTP archives
- Finger, a software tool for determining whether a person has an account at a particular Internet site
- Network Time Protocol (NTP)
- Network File System (NFS)
- rlogin, rsh, rcp (TCP, Telnet, and Unix entities to ensure the reliable delivery of data)

NAT supported protocols that carry the IP address in the application stream such as:

- Internet Control Message Protocol (ICMP)
- NetBIOS over TCP (datagram, name, and session services)
- Progressive Networks's RealAudio
- CUseeMe Networks CUseeMe
- Xing Technology's StreamWorks
- DNS "A" and "PTR" queries
- H.323 in IOS versions 12.0(1)/12.0(1)T or later
- Microsoft's NetMeeting (IOS versions 12.0(1)/12.0(1)T or later)
- VDOnet's VDOLive – IOS versions 11.3(4)/11.3(4)T or later
- Microsoft's VXtreme – IOS versions 11.3(4)/11.3(4)T or later
- IP Multicast – IOS version 12.0(1)T or later, source address translation only
- Point to Point Tunneling Protocol (PPTP) support with Port Address Translation (IOS version 12.1(2)T or later)
- Skinny Client Control Protocol, IP Phone to Cisco CallManager (IOS version 12.1(5)T or later)

Unsupported Traffic Types

NAT does not support some traffic types, including the following:

- Routing table updates
- DNS zone transfers
- BOOTP and DHCP
- Talk
- Ntalk
- Simple Network Management Protocol (SNMP)
- NetShow

Performing NAT Operations

Understanding how NAT functions when it is configured a certain way will aid you in your configuration decisions. This section covers NAT's operations when NAT is configured to provide the following functions:

- Translating inside local addresses
- Overloading inside global addresses
- Using TCP load distribution
- Overlapping networks

Translating Inside Local Addresses

NAT operates on a router and usually connects two networks. NAT translates the local nonunique IP addresses into legal, registered Internet addresses before forwarding packets from the local network to the Internet or another outside network. To do this, NAT uses a six-step process, as shown in Figure 10.2.

FIGURE 10.2   The process of translating inside local addresses

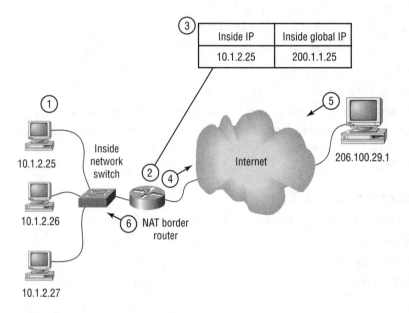

The six-step process, as Figure 10.2 shows, is as follows:

1.   User 10.1.2.25 sends a packet and attempts to open a connection to 206.100.29.1.

2.   When the first packet arrives at the NAT border router, the router checks to see whether there is an entry for the local address that matches a global address in the NAT table.

3.   If a match is found in the NAT table, the process continues to step 4. If a match is not found, the NAT router uses what is called a simple entry from its pool of global addresses. A simple entry occurs when the NAT router matches a local IP address (such as the one currently being used) to a global IP address. In this example, the NAT router will match the address of 10.1.2.25 to 200.1.1.25.

4.   The NAT border router then replaces the local address of 10.1.2.25 (listed as the packet's source address) with 200.1.1.25. This makes the destination host believe that the sending device's IP address is 200.1.1.25.

5.   When the host on the Internet using the IP address 206.100.29.1 replies, it uses the NAT router–assigned IP address of 200.1.1.25 as the destination address.

6.   When the NAT border router receives the reply from 206.100.29.1 with the packet destined for 200.1.1.25, the NAT border router checks its NAT table again. The NAT table shows that the local address of 10.1.2.25 should receive the packet destined for 200.1.1.25 and replaces the destination address with the internal interface's IP address.

Steps 2 through 6 are repeated for each individual packet.

Overloading Inside Global Addresses

You can conserve addresses in the inside global address pool by enabling the router to use one global address for many local addresses. When NAT overloading is enabled, the router maintains higher-level (Layer 4) protocol information in the NAT table for TCP and UDP port numbers to translate the global address back to the correct inside local address. When multiple local addresses map to one global address, NAT uses the TCP or UDP port number of each inside host to make unique, distinguishable outside network addresses.

Figure 10.3 shows the NAT operation when one inside global address represents multiple inside local addresses. The TCP port number is the portion of the global IP network address that differentiates between the two inside local addresses on the network.

FIGURE 10.3   NAT overloading inside global addresses

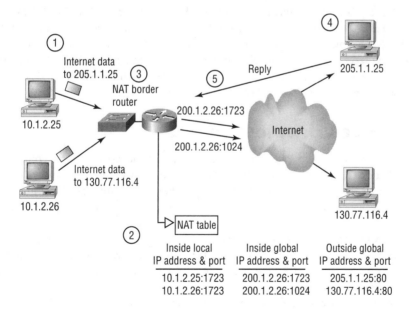

When the router processes multiple nonroutable inside IP addresses to one globally routable global IP address, it performs the following steps to overload inside global addresses:

1.   The host at the inside IP address of 10.1.2.25 opens a connection to a host at IP address 205.1.1.25 on an outside network.

2. The first packet that the NAT border router receives from the host at 10.1.2.25 causes the router to check its NAT table. Because no translation entry exists, the router determines that address 10.1.2.25 must be translated and configures a translation to the inside global address of 200.1.2.25. If overloading is enabled and another translation is active, the router reuses the global IP address from that translation and saves enough information to translate returning packets back. This type of entry is called an extended entry.

3. The router replaces the inside local source address of 10.1.2.25 with the selected globally routable address and a unique port number and forwards the packet. In this example, the source address is now shown as 200.1.2.26:1723 in the NAT table.

4. The host at 205.1.1.25 receives the packet and responds to the host at 10.1.2.25 by using the inside global IP address and port in the source address field of the packet received (200.1.2.26:1723).

5. The NAT border router receives the packet from 205.1.1.25. It then performs a NAT table lookup, using the inside global address and port, with the outside address and outside port number. The router then translates the address back to the destination address of 10.1.2.25. The NAT border router then forwards the packet to the host using the IP address of 10.1.2.25 on the inside network.

Steps 2 through 5 are continued for all subsequent communications until the connection is closed.

Both the host at IP address 205.1.1.25 and the host at IP address 130.77.116.4 think they are talking to a single host at IP address 200.1.2.26. They are actually talking to different hosts, with the port number being the difference that the NAT border router uses to forward the packets to the correct host on the local inside network. In fact, with the port addressing scheme, you use could allow approximately 4,000 hosts to share the same inside global IP address by using the many available TCP and UDP port numbers.

Using TCP Load Distribution

TCP load distribution is a dynamic form of destination IP address translation that can be configured for certain outside network traffic to be mapped to a valid inside network for IP traffic destined for more than one node. After a mapping scheme is created, destination IP addresses matching an access list are replaced with an address from a rotary pool on a round-robin basis.

When a new connection is established from the outside network to the inside network, all non-TCP traffic will be passed without being translated, unless another translation type is applied to the interfaces. Figure 10.4 demonstrates TCP load distribution, which is explained in further detail next.

Let's look at the process NAT uses to map one virtual host to several real hosts:

1. In Figure 10.4, the PC using global IP address 206.2.2.25 opens a TCP connection to a virtual host at 200.1.1.25.

FIGURE 10.4   TCP load distribution steps

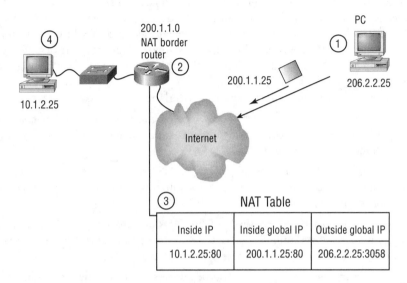

2. The NAT border router receives this new connection request and creates a new translation, which allocates the next real host of 10.1.2.25 for the inside local IP address and adds this information to the NAT table.

3. The NAT border router replaces the destination IP address with the selected real host IP address and then forwards the packet.

4. The real host at IP address 10.1.2.25 receives the packet and responds.

5. The NAT border router receives the packet and performs another NAT table lookup by using the inside local IP address and port number and the outside IP address and port number as the key. The NAT border router then translates the source address to the virtual host's address and forwards the packet.

6. The next connection request to that inside global IP address causes the NAT border router to allocate 10.1.2.26 for the inside local address.

Overlapping Networks

Let's say your network uses an IP addressing scheme that is valid and globally usable, but another company is using it or you are no longer authorized to use it. Now imagine your ISP thinks it has you locked in because it is providing your IP address scheme, and it suddenly doubles your prices. Rather than pay the higher prices, you shop for a new ISP with a different IP address range.

You finally find this terrific new ISP that is going to supply you with terrific Internet speeds at a third of the cost of your other ISP. Unfortunately, it is also going to supply you with a terrific new IP address scheme that you must apply to your network. Even in a midsize network, you would spend many hours changing your IP address scheme—and waiting for this would affect your users tremendously. The solution is to implement a *NAT overlapping address translation*.

In this section, you will learn how to translate IP addresses that are not legally usable on an outside network such as the Internet into the new officially assigned IP addresses from your ISP. For now, we cover only the steps NAT uses to translate overlapping addresses. We cover configuring overlapping address translation later in this chapter, in the section "Configuring NAT to Perform Overlapping Address Translation."

The following steps are used when translating overlapping addresses:

1. The host on the inside network tries to open a connection to a host on the outside network by using a fully qualified domain name by requesting a name-to-address lookup from an Internet Domain Name Server (DNS).

2. The NAT border router intercepts the Internet DNS's reply and begins the translation process with the returned address if there is an overlapping address that is residing illegally in the inside network.

3. To translate the returned address, the NAT border router creates a simple translation entry. This entry maps the overlapping legal outside address to an address from an outside local address pool of addresses legally usable on the outside network

4. The NAT border router replaces the source address with the new inside global address, replaces the destination address with the outside global address, and forwards the packet. This translation is for new outgoing traffic to the newly DNS-Learned IP Address.

5. The host on the outside network receives the packet and continues the conversation.

6. For each packet sent from the outside to the inside host, the router will perform a NAT table lookup, replace the inside global destination address with the inside local address, and replace the outside global source address with the outside local address. Conversely, for each packet sent from the inside to the outside host, the router will perform a NAT table lookup, replace the outside local destination address with the outside global address, and replace the inside local source address with the inside global address.

Configuring NAT

In this section, you will learn to configure NAT for the following situations:

- Static NAT
- Dynamic NAT
- Inside global address overloading
- TCP load distributiing
- Translating of overlapping addresses
- Verifying NAT's configuration
- Troubleshooting NAT
- Clearing NAT translation entries

Configuring Static NAT

Static NAT maps an illegal inside IP address to a legal global IP address so that the data can be sent through the Internet. Before trying to configure static NAT, IP routing should be enabled on your router, and the appropriate IP addresses and subnet masks should be configured on each interface.

Let's start the configuration process in global configuration mode, assuming that you have only one interface on the router connected to your inside network. In this example, the PC using the illegal inside IP address of 10.1.2.25 needs to access data on the Internet. When the NAT border router receives a packet going to the outside network from the IP address of 10.1.2.25, you will configure it to translate the source address to a legally usable address of 200.1.1.25. Do this by using the following command:

```
BorderRouter(config)#ip nat inside source static 10.1.2.25 200.1.1.25
```

To enable NAT, you must first select the interface that connects your inside network to the router or internal route processor. There is at least one interface on the router connected to the inside network and at least one interface connected to the outside network. You need to identify each and enable NAT on both with different commands. In this example, the router's inside network interface is Ethernet 0, and the outside interface is serial 0. To configure Ethernet 0 as a NAT inside interface, use the following steps from global configuration mode:

1. Enter the interface configuration mode, enable NAT, and identify whether you would like NAT to translate inside or outside addresses. In this example, you will have NAT translate inside addresses to outside addresses:

    ```
    BorderRouter(config)#interface ethernet0
    BorderRouter(config-if)#ip nat inside
    BorderRouter(config-if)#
    ```

2. Next, you will need to configure serial 0 as the interface connected to your outside network. From global configuration mode, use the following commands:

    ```
    BorderRouter(config)#interface serial0
    BorderRouter(config-if)#ip nat outside
    BorderRouter(config-if)#
    ```

3. You should see the following when displaying the router configuration. The IP addresses of 10.1.2.254 and 200.1.1.1 are the IP addresses configured on the physical interfaces on the router:

    ```
    !
    interface Ethernet0
      ip address 10.1.2.254 255.255.0.0
      ip nat inside
    !
    interface Serial0
      ip address 200.1.1.1 255.255.0.0
      ip nat outside
    ```

Configuring Dynamic NAT, Inside Global Address Overloading, and TCP Load Distribution

This section explains how to configure *dynamic NAT* using inside global address overloading as well as TCP load distribution.

Dynamic NAT maps an illegal inside IP address to any legally registered, globally routable IP address from an identified pool of addresses. Before trying to configure dynamic NAT, you should enable IP routing on your router and configure the appropriate IP addresses and subnet masks on each interface.

Again, let's start the configuration process in global configuration mode, assuming you have only one interface on the router connected to your inside network and one connected to your outside network. In this example, a PC using the illegal inside IP address of 10.1.2.25 needs to access data on the Internet. When the NAT border router receives a packet going to the outside network from IP address 10.1.2.25, the NAT border router will choose an available globally routable IP address from the address pool and translate the source IP address to the legally usable address of 200.1.1.26. Do this by following these steps:

1. NAT translations from the inside local network to the inside global network take place after routing. Therefore, any access lists or policy routing will have been applied before the translation occurs. You will create an access list to specify the IP addresses to translate. In this example, you have a rather large network using the 10.1.0.0/16 IP address range, so the following command will be used to create a standard IP access list that contains a wild-card mask for the last two octets:

   BorderRouter(config)#**access-list 2 permit 10.1.0.0 0.0.255.255**

2. Now that you have an access list, which defines that packets coming from 10.1.2.25 will be translated, you need to define the actual pool of addresses that are routable on the Internet. This is the range of legal IP addresses that your ISP allocated to you for your use. You might have been given only 254 IP addresses for your 1,000 PCs and servers in the network, but because all your PCs aren't on the Internet at any given time, this might be enough. If it isn't, you need to use another solution, such as configuring inside global address overloading. Before you begin configuring your pool of addresses, you need to decide on a name. In this case, you will call your address pool **InternetIPPool**. To define the 254 IP addresses your ISP gave you (200.1.1.1 to 200.1.1.254 with the subnet mask 255.255.255.0), use the following command:

   BorderRouter(config)# ip nat pool InternetIPPool 200.1.1.1 200.1.1.254 netmask 255.255.255.0

3. At this point, you need to associate access list 2 (which you created in step 1) with the IP NAT pool InternetIPPool you created in step 2. To do this, use the following command:

   BorderRouter(config)#ip nat inside source list 2 pool InternetIPPool

Additional Options of *ip nat pool*

The command ip nat pool has two other options. First, instead of using the netmask syntax, you can use the prefix-length command followed by the number of bits in the mask, which indicates how many bits are ones. In this case, 24 indicates your netmask. You can also use type rotary after the netmask to enable TCP load distribution. This indicates that the IP addresses in the pool are real inside hosts that can be used for TCP load distribution. Second, you can use the parameter match-host, which attempts to match the host portion of the IP address to be translated to the same host number in the translated IP address. This is useful for quickly finding which internal host a translated IP address belongs to, but you must have at least a one-to-one relationship between local and global addresses.

To configure the router to utilize individual TCP ports, thus enabling an IP address to be used more than once, add the parameter overload after the NAT pool name.

4. To enable NAT, you must first select the interface that connects your inside network to the router or internal route processor. To configure Ethernet 0 as a NAT inside interface, use the following commands from global configuration mode:

```
BorderRouter(config)#interface ethernet0
BorderRouter(config-if)#ip nat inside
BorderRouter(config-if)#
```

5. Next, you need to configure serial 0 as the NAT interface connected to your outside network. From global configuration mode, use the following commands:

```
BorderRouter(config)#interface serial0
BorderRouter(config-if)#ip nat outside
BorderRouter(config-if)#
```

There is another option when configuring dynamic NAT. You can use an interface instead of a pool of IP addresses. This is useful when you might not know the IP address of the outside interface—for example, when using DHCP on the outside interface. You still configure an access list that defines the traffic to NAT and defines which interfaces are inside and outside, but there is no ip nat pool command. In addition, the command to configure the NAT is slightly different: ip nat inside source list *list-number* interface *outside-interface* overload. The overload parameter is not required but is highly recommended because many inside hosts will be using the outside interfaces' IP address for their link to the outside network.

Configuring NAT to Perform Overlapping Address Translaton

Configuring NAT to perform overlapping address translation is similar to configuring dynamic NAT. The difference is that you must identify and apply a pool of addresses for the NAT border router interface connecting to the inside network interface, as well as a pool to allow for connection to the outside network.

You will start the NAT configuration process in global configuration mode. The pool of addresses used in the inside network is 10.1.2.1 to 10.1.2.254. On the outside interface, you will configure a smaller pool of addresses that are globally routable on the Internet, assuming not all 100 of your PCs will need to access the outside network at the same time. The pool of addresses you will configure will be 200.1.1.1 to 200.1.1.50. It is assumed that the NAT border router is configured with routing, and the interfaces are configured with the proper IP addresses. Again, assume that your inside network is connected to the Ethernet 0 interface on the router, and the serial 0 interface connects your NAT border router to the outside network.

To configure the NAT router to perform overlapping address translation, complete the following steps:

1. Define a standard IP access list for the IP addresses on the inside network, as discussed earlier in the "Configuring Dynamic NAT, Inside Global Address Overloading, and TCP Load Distribution" section. The access list needs to be configured to permit traffic on the inside network that needs to be translated by NAT:

```
BorderRouter(config)#access-list 2 permit 10.1.2.0 0.0.0.255
```

2. Define an IP NAT pool for the inside network addresses. The pool name will be called outsidepool, and the range of addresses is 192.168.1.1 to 192.168.1.253. The final syntax indicates the number of bits for the subnet mask. You can also use the command netmask 255.255.255.0 as shown in step 3, which also identifies a 24-bit subnet mask. The pool does not include address 192.168.1.254 because that is the NAT border router's inside interface IP address.

```
BorderRouter(config)#ip nat pool outsidepool  192.168.1.1 192.168.1.253
prefix-length 24
```

3. Define an IP NAT pool for the inside local network addresses. The pool name will be called insidepool, and the range of addresses is 200.1.1.1 to 200.1.1.50.

```
BorderRouter(config)#ip nat pool insidepool 200.1.1.1 200.1.1.50 netmask
255.255.255.0
```

4. Next, associate the previously created access list to the previously created inside NAT pool with the following command:

```
BorderRouter(config)#ip nat inside source list 2 pool insidepool
```

Again, you can use the overload command after the NAT pool name to reuse IP addresses in the pool.

5. Also, associate the same access list used in the previous command to the outside NAT pool with the following command:

   ```
   BorderRouter(config)# ip nat outside source list 2 pool outsidepool
   ```

6. For NAT to work, you must first configure the interface that connects your inside network to the router. To configure Ethernet 0 as the inside NAT interface, use the following commands from global configuration mode:

   ```
   BorderRouter(config)#interface e0
   BorderRouter(config-if)#ip nat inside
   BorderRouter(config-if)#
   ```

7. Next, you will need to enable NAT on the serial 0 interfaceconnected to your outside network. From global configuration mode, use the following commands:

   ```
   BorderRouter(config)#interface s0
   BorderRouter(config-if)#ip nat outside
   BorderRouter(config-if)#
   ```

The finished NAT router configuration follows:

```
ip nat pool insidepool200.1.1.1 200.1.1.50 netmask 255.255.255.0
ip nat pool outsidepool 192.168.1.1 192.168.1.253prefix-length 24
ip nat outside source list 2 pool outsidepool
ip nat inside source list 2 pool insidepool!
interface Serial0
 ip address 200.1.1.51 255.255.255.0
 ip nat outside
!
interface Ethernet0
 ip address 10.1.2.254 255.255.255.0
 ip nat inside
!
access-list 2 permit 10.1.2.0 0.0.0.255
```

Verifying NAT Configuration

To aid in verifying the configuration of NAT, you can use two specific commands. The show ip nat translation command shows the translations in the NAT table and the output in the following simple example:

```
BorderRouter(config)#show ip nat translation
Pro Inside global Inside local Outside local Outside global
--- 200.1.1.25     10.1.1.25    ---           ---
--- 200.1.1.26     10.1.1.26    ---           ---
```

You can use the same command with an additional parameter to get more information about each NAT table entry. The show ip nat translation verbose command displays more information about each NAT table entry, such as the time left until the entry in the NAT table expires, as shown here:

```
BorderRouter(config)#show ip nat translation verbose
Pro Inside global    Inside local Outside local    Outside global
--- 200.1.1.25    10.1.1.25    ---            ---
   create 00:05:01, use 00:00:00, left 23:12:40, flags: none
--- 200.1.1.26    10.1.1.26    ---            ---
   create 00:04:29, use 00:00:00, left 23:13:10, flags: none
```

The second command is used to display statistics and configuration information about NAT running on the router. The show ip nat statistics command displays information about the NAT table, as shown here:

```
BorderRouter(config)# show ip nat statistics
Total active translations:2(0 static, 2 dynamic,0 extended)
Outside interfaces: Loopback 0, Serial1
Inside interface: Serial0
Hits: 243 Misses: 2
Expired translations: 0
Dynamic mappings:
-- Inside Source
access-list 2 pool insidepool refcount 1
  pool insidepool: netmask 255.255.255.0
    start 200.1.1.1 end 200.1.1.4
    type generic,total address 5,allocated 2 (50%),misses 0
```

Troubleshooting NAT

Using the debug ip nat command can assist you when troubleshooting NAT problems. In the following output, you will notice that the source address 10.1.2.5 is sending a packet to the destination address 206.1.2.5. An -> indicates that a packet's source address was translated. An * indicates that a packet is traveling through the *fast path* or the hardware processing path. A packet in a conversation with another node will always first travel through a process-switched *slow path* or the software processing path. Additional packets used in that flow will go through the fast path if there is a cache entry for the source and destination address. Here is the output from the described scenario:

```
BorderRouter#debug ip nat
NAT: s=10.1.2.5->200.1.2.25, d=206.1.2.5 [0]
NAT: s=206.1.2.5, d=200.1.2.25->10.1.2.5 [0]
```

```
NAT: s=10.1.2.5->200.1.2.25, d=206.1.2.5 [1]
NAT: s=10.1.2.5->200.1.2.25, d=206.1.2.5 [2]
NAT: s=10.1.2.5->200.1.2.25, d=206.1.2.5 [3]
NAT*: s=206.1.2.5, d=200.1.2.25->10.1.2.5 [1]
NAT: s=206.1.2.5, d=200.1.2.25->10.1.2.5 [1]
NAT: s=10.1.2.5->200.1.2.25, d=206.1.2.5 [4]
NAT: s=10.1.2.5->200.1.2.25, d=206.1.2.5 [5]
NAT: s=10.1.2.5->200.1.2.25, d=206.1.2.5 [6]
NAT*: s=206.1.2.5, d=200.1.2.25->10.1.2.5 [2]
```

Two parameters can be used with the debug ip nat command: list and detailed. The value in brackets is the IP identification number. This information enables you to correlate these trace packets with other packet traces from sniffers used for troubleshooting in the network. (*Sniffers* are devices that can be used to look at the traffic flowing through the network.)

Clearing NAT Translation Entries

Occasionally, NAT is properly configured but translations are not occurring. Most of the time, clearing the NAT translations resolves the problem. Table 10.1 shows the available commands for clearing the NAT table.

T A B L E   1 0 . 1   Commands Available to Clear the NAT Table

Command	Meaning
clear ip nat translation *	Clears all NAT table entries
clear ip nat translation inside *global-ip*	Clears all inside NAT table simple translation entries
clear ip nat translation outside *local-ip*	Clears all outside NAT table simple translation entries
clear ip nat translation *protocol inside global-ip global-port local-ip local-port [outside local-ip local-port global-ip global-port]*	Clears all NAT table extended entries

Using Port Address Translation (PAT)

If you wish to enable address translation on the 700 series router, you use *Port Address Translation (PAT)*. PAT is a subset of NAT and is the only address translation feature on the Cisco 700 series of routers. PAT uses TCP ports to enable an entire network to use only one globally routable IP address in the network. PAT is similar to overloading with traditional NAT.

The Cisco 700 series routers with release 4 software and higher support PAT, which enables local hosts on an inside IP network to communicate to an outside IP network such as the Internet. Traffic destined for an outside IP address on the other side of a border router will have its source IP address translated before the packet is forwarded to the outside network. IP packets returning to the inside network will have their destination IP addresses translated back to the original source IP addresses on the inside network.

PAT conserves network addresses by enabling a single Internet-routable IP address to be assigned to an entire LAN. All WAN traffic is usually mapped to a single IP address, which is the ISDN-side IP address of the Cisco 700 series router. Because all the traffic on the outside network appears to come from the Cisco 700, the inside network appears invisible to the outside network or Internet.

You should configure a static IP address and port if remote users need to access a specific server on the inside network. PAT will allow packets with a specific well-known port number to get through, such as FTP or Telnet. This feature is known as a default port handler.

Disadvantages of PAT

Using PAT has some disadvantages because it takes away end-to-end reachability. These disadvantages are as follows:

- You cannot use ping from an outside host to a host in the private network.

- Telnet from an outside host to an inside host is not forwarded unless the Telnet port handler is configured.

- Only one FTP server and one Telnet server are supported on the inside network.

- Packets destined for the router itself and not an inside network IP address, such as DHCP, SNMP, PING, or TFTP, are not rejected or filtered by PAT.

- Because the 700 series is a low-end solution, if more than 12 PCs try to boot up simultaneously on the inside, one or more might get an error message about not being able to access the server.

- The PAT table is limited to 400 entries for the inside machines to share. If TCP translations are set up and the TCP timeouts are kept alive, no more than 400 machines can get to the outside world at any one time.

- The Cisco 700 series router with PAT enabled does not handle any fragmented FTP packets; this needs to be noted when troubleshooting.

- Some well-known ports cannot have port handlers defined. They include the following:
  - DHCP client ports used by the router for getting DHCP server responses
  - WINS NetBIOS ports used by the inside network clients operating Windows 95 PCs to get WINS information

Configuring PAT

The PAT feature enables local hosts with designated private IP addresses to communicate with the outside world. Basically, the router translates the source address of the IP header into a global, unique IP address before the packet is forwarded to the outside network. Likewise, IP packets returning will go through address translations again to the designated private IP addresses where the communication originated.

When PAT is enabled, RIP packet transmission is automatically disabled to prevent leaking private IP addresses to the outside network.

To enable PAT, the two commands that you need are as follows:

set ip pat on   This command enables PAT and must be configured before the `set ip pat porthandler` command can be used.

set ip pat porthandler   The port handler translates a public TCP or UDP port to a private IP address and port. When a packet is received from the outside, the router compares the port number with an internally configured port-handler list of up to 15 entries. If a port handler is defined for this port, it routes the packet to the appropriate port handler (internal IP address). If a default port handler is defined, it routes the packet there. The possible parameters are as follows.

> *default* enables the port handler for all well-known ports, except ports specifically assigned a handler.
>
> *telnet* enables the port handler for the Telnet protocol on port 23.
>
> *ftp* enables the port handler for File Transport Protocol (FTP) and uses TCP protocol port 21.
>
> *smtp* enables the port handler for Simple Mail Transfer Protocol (SMTP) and uses TCP protocol port 25.
>
> *wins* enables the port handler for NetBIOS session service on port 139.
>
> *http* enables the port handler for World Wide Web–HTTP service and secure-HTTP port 80 or 443.
>
> *off* disables a certain port handler.
>
> *port* configures a custom port handler for a port not normally considered a well-known port. Remember that only 15 port handlers can be configured at once.

All parameters are followed by the appropriate IP address.

**Real World Scenario**

Configuring a Typical Office with a 700 Series Router for Internet Access

Company XYZ has decided it is time to get into this Internet thingy. The company has determined that their employees need to have Internet access to do research and send e-mail to their suppliers and customers. There is an internal web server that outside clients and employees will need to access from the Internet. They have contracted with you to set up a low-cost solution that will enable them to have access to the Internet from an ISDN line.

You have come up with the following configuration, which enables IP unnumbered across the WAN connection, enabled DHCP server functionality, created a port handler for the internal web server at IP address 10.1.2.21, and enabled PAT on a Cisco 765 router. It will set the IP address on the router to 10.1.2.1 and then create a username, XYZ, which was supplied by the ISP. The following lists the entire configuration on a 765 router. The bold commands are those discussed in the previous section.

```
>set systemname XYZ
XYZ> set switch ni-1
XYZ> set 1 spid 80155511110101
XYZ> set 2 spid 80155522220101
XYZ> set 1 directory 5551111
XYZ> set 2 directory 5552222
XYZ> set dhcp server
XYZ> set dhcp address 10.1.2.2 100
XYZ> set dhcp netmask 255.255.255.0
XYZ> set dhcp gateway primary 10.1.2.1
XYZ> set dhcp dns primary 200.1.1.48
XYZ> set dhcp wins primary 200.1.1.49
XYZ> set dhcp domain mydomain
XYZ> cd lan
XYZ:LAN> set bridging off
XYZ:LAN> set ip routing on
XYZ:LAN> set ip address 10.1.2.1
XYZ:LAN> set ip netmask 255.255.255.0
XYZ:LAN> cd
XYZ> set user ISP
XYZ:ISP> set ppp clientname XYZ
XYZ:ISP> set ppp secret client
Enter new Password: sybex1
Re-Type new Password: sybex1
```

```
XYZ:ISP> set ppp password client
Enter new Password: sybex1
Re-Type new Password: sybex1
XYZ:ISP> set bridging off
XYZ:ISP> set ip routing on
XYZ:ISP> set ip rip update off
XYZ:ISP> set ip route destination 0.0.0.0/0 gateway 0.0.0.0
XYZ:ISP> set 1 number 18015553333
XYZ:ISP> set 2 number 18015553333
XYZ:ISP> set ip pat on
XYZ:ISP> set ip pat porthandler http 10.1.2.21XYZ:
ISP> set ppp address negotiation local on[
XYZ:ISP> set ppp authentication outgoing none
XYZ:ISP> set timeout 300
XYZ:ISP> set active
```

With this configuration, a router in XYZ's office will be able to dial up to the ISP and place their office on the Internet by using PAT through a single IP address. This will also allow outside clients and employees access to their web server by using the HTTP port handler.

Monitoring PAT

To monitor PAT and view the configuration settings, use the show ip pat command. When monitoring PAT, you can view the number of packets dropped, the timeouts, and the service or IP address using each individual TCP port. When you configure a Cisco 765 with the configuration shown in the real-world scenario, you should see output similar to the following example using the show ip pat command:

```
765:user1>show ip pat
Dropped - icmp 0, udp 0, tcp 0, map 0, frag 0
Timeout - udp 5 minutes, tcp 30 minutes
Port handlers [no default]:


Port    Handler        Service
-------------------------------------
21      Router         FTP
23      Router         TELNET
67      Router         DHCP Server
68      Router         DHCP Client
69      Router         TFTP
```

80	10.1.2.21	HTTP
161	Router	SNMP
162	Router	SNMP-TRAP
520	Router	RIP

Summary

As the Internet grows and companies need more and more IP addresses, the number of available IP addresses diminishes. This is one of the main reasons for the implementation of NAT and PAT—key technologies to overcoming the shortage of IP addresses. You need to understand how NAT and PAT operate and how to configure each of them.

These two protocols, which allow for specifically defined address translations, provide some other interesting uses as well. For instance, NAT and PAT enable private IP networks to use nonregistered IP addresses to access outside networks such as the Internet. They also provide the ability to reuse assigned IP addresses already in use on the Internet. In addition, they appropriately translate the addresses in two merged intranets, such as those of two merged companies. Finally, NAT and PAT translate internal IP addresses assigned by an old Internet Service Provider (ISP) to a new ISP's newly assigned addresses without manual configuration of all the local network interfaces.

There are some disadvantages to using NAT and PAT in a network. Specifically, they don't allow for a full end-to-end communication between two hosts. Some protocols carry IP address information in the payload of the packet that might not get translated by the border NAT router.

There are many IOS commands used specifically for troubleshooting NAT problems. The `show ip nat translations` command is one of the most useful, in addition to the `debug ip nat` feature. PAT also has its own troubleshooting commands; the `show ip pat` command is the most important.

Exam Essentials

Understand what NAT and PAT are and how to use them.   NAT is a technology, specified in RFC 1631, that is used to hide network addresses behind a single IP address or multiple IP addresses. A company can use IP addresses set aside by RFC 1918 on their internal networks and use single or multiple Internet-routable IP addresses to connect their company to the network. PAT is like using NAT through a single IP address.

Know the advantages of NAT and PAT.   The advantages of NAT and PAT are that they enable an entire network to hide behind IP addresses. They provide a certain level of security and enable a company to change ISPs quickly and painlessly. They also provide a primitive load-balancing mechanism between multiple hosts performing the same function.

Know the disadvantages of NAT and PAT.   One disadvantage of using NAT and PAT is that some protocols will not work because they carry IP address information in the payload of the packet. In addition, NAT and PAT do not provide end-to-end significance for the IP address. Cisco IOS will correct some of these problems with the most popular protocols, but it cannot cover them all. Finally, a significant delay occurs in translating IP addresses, which introduces latency in the communication path.

Understand how to configure NAT and PAT on a Cisco router.   One option when configuring NAT is to use dynamic NAT using a pool of IP addresses or through an interface. You can also reuse those IP addresses with the `overload` parameter. PAT uses only a single IP address. Another option is to configure a static translation from an outside IP address to an internal IP address. PAT can also be configured with static translations, but they are based on TCP and UDP port numbers and not IP addresses only.

Know the troubleshooting techniques for NAT and PAT.   The commands used to trouble-shoot NAT are `show ip nat translation` with the optional `verbose` parameter, and `debug ip nat`, which logs NAT events as they occur on the router. For PAT, the only command used to show troubleshooting information is the `show ip pat` command on the 700 series router.

Key Terms

Before you take the exam, be certain you are familiar with the following terms:

dynamic NAT	outside network
extended translation entry	outside global IP address
inside global IP address	outside local IP address
inside local IP address	Port Address Translation (PAT)
inside network	static NAT
NAT overlapping address translation	TCP load distribution
Network Address Translation (NAT)	

Written Lab

1.   Which command enables PAT on a 700 series router?
2.   Which command displays IP NAT debugging information?
3.   Which command enables IP NAT on an interface connected to an outside network?
4.   Which command enables you to view NAT statistics?

5. Which command enables you to view the current NAT translation table information?

6. Which command enables you to view the current PAT monitoring information?

7. Which command disables IP NAT debugging?

8. Which command deletes all NAT table entries?

9. Which command enables IP NAT to use the IP address on an interface while reusing the interface for multiple translations on a Cisco router?

10. Access lists are created with what command?

Hands-on Lab

In this hands-on lab, you will configure NAT on a router by using another router to loop your packets back. This step-by-step lab exercise enables you to configure a simulated NAT environment using two IOS-based routers.

Lab 10.1: Static NAT

You will configure an inside PC with the nonroutable inside IP address of `10.1.2.200` to have a static outside address of `200.1.1.200`. To do this, complete the following steps:

1. Enter global configuration mode on the branch office router and configure the router with the following information to create a static mapping of the outside IP address to the inside IP address:

    `ip nat inside source static` *200.1.1.200 10.1.2.200*

2. Enter interface configuration mode for the inside interface. In this example, use Ethernet 0 as the inside interface. To do this, use the following command:

    `interface ethernet0`

3. Next, you need to simulate your inside network. Enter loopback 1 configuration mode with the following command:

    `interface loopback 1`

4. Configure the IP address of the loopback 1 interface with the following command:

    `ip address 200.1.1.200 255.255.255.0`

5. Enable NAT on the inside interface (`loopback1`) with the following command:

    `ip nat inside`

6. Enter the configuration mode for the outside interface. In this example, use the serial 0 interface as your outside network interface by using the following command:

`interface serial 0`

7. Enable NAT on the outside interface by using the following command:

`ip nat outside`

8. Exit interface configuration mode.

9. On another router connected to the outside interface serial 0, create a static IP route that will route your packets back to the router you just configured. To do this, use the following command:

`ip route 10.1.1.1 255.255.255.255 10.1.2.200`

This will enable any packets, such as those created with a ping, to route back to the interface on the originally configured router simulating your NAT environment. You can enable debugging on the originally created router to view the processing of the packets. To do this, use the `debug ip nat` command.

Review Questions

1. Which of the following NAT table entries indicates the translation of a static inside IP address to a globally routable address?

   A. Simple translation entry

   B. Extended translation entry

   C. Global translation entry

   D. Inside translation entry

2. Which of the following best describes an inside network?

   A. The network of another company

   B. The set of networks that are subject to IP translation

   C. The side of the network using global addresses

   D. The Internet

3. NAT cannot do which of the following?

   A. Enable a private network using unregistered IP addresses to access another outside network.

   B. Provide the ability to reuse addresses already in use on the Internet.

   C. Replace the functions provided by a DHCP server.

   D. Provide IP address translation for merged internetworks.

4. A Class A IP address range can provide a maximum of how many individual hosts with unique IP addresses on the inside network?

   A. 254

   B. 16,777,214

   C. 255

   D. None of the above

5. Which of the following is a function that NAT and PAT are designed to address?

   A. Assigning a DHCP address

   B. Assigning an IP address to a border router

   C. Translating nonroutable IP addresses to legal routable addresses

   D. Resolving IP addresses to fully qualified domain names

6. Which of the following describes the router that should be configured with NAT? (Select all that apply)

   A. A spoke router on a hub-and-spoke network

   B. The router that is the demarcation point between the inside network and the outside network

   C. The local bridging router between two subnets

   D. The router closest to the border of a stub domain

7. Which of the following types of NAT configurations would you implement if you were mapping all your inside IP addresses to one globally routable address?

   A. TCP load distribution

   B. Static NAT

   C. One-on-one mapping

   D. Overloading

8. Which of the following traffic types is not supported by NAT?

   A. File Transfer Protocol (FTP)

   B. Network Time Protocol (NTP)

   C. Telnet

   D. SNMP

   E. Internet Control Message Protocol (ICMP)

   F. Trivial File Transfer Protocol (TFTP)

   G. All of the above

9. Approximately how much DRAM on the NAT border router is used for each NAT translation?

   A. 160 bytes

   B. 100KB

   C. 1MB

   D. 64KB

10. Which parameter used with the `set ip porthandler` command configures all well-known TCP ports except for the ports specifically assigned?

   A. `all`

   B. `enable`

   C. Do not use a parameter.

   D. `default`

11. In which of the following router configuration modes should you use the command `ip nat inside source static 10.2.2.6 200.4.4.7`?

    A. Global configuration mode

    B. Interface configuration mode

    C. User exec mode

    D. Any of the above

12. The command `ip nat inside source static 10.1.3.2 200.4.2.5` is an example of which type of NAT translation?

    A. Static NAT

    B. Dynamic NAT

    C. Overlapping NAT

    D. Port mapping

13. Which of the following commands can be used to verify the NAT configuration? (Choose the two best answers.)

    A. `show ip nat statistics`

    B. `show ip nat configuration`

    C. `show ip nat all`

    D. `show ip nat translations`

14. Which of the following protocols can be enabled on a Cisco 765 router? (Select all that apply.)

    A. NAT only

    B. PAT only

    C. Both NAT and PAT

    D. None of the above

15. NAT is used to translate which types of protocol addresses?

    A. IP

    B. IPX

    C. AppleTalk

    D. IP and IPX

16. Which of the following commands can be used to monitor PAT?

    A. `show ip pat`

    B. `show ip pat statistics verbose`

    C. `show ip pat all`

    D. `show ip pat configuration`

17. Which of the following defines the NAT protocol?

   A. RFC 1911

   B. IEEE 802.11

   C. RFC 1631

   D. ANSI X311

18. In a routing table, what does the *S* mean?

   A. Dynamically defined

   B. Directly connected

   C. Statically defined

   D. Sending packets

19. Which of the following traffic types is supported by NAT?

   A. Routing table updates

   B. BOOTP

   C. SNMP

   D. DNS zone transfers

   E. None of the above

20. Which of the following is not a disadvantage of using NAT?

   A. Delay in switching paths.

   B. All IP address translation pools can be changed only on the NAT border router.

   C. Hidden end-to-end IP addresses from applications.

   D. Loss of traceability.

   E. None of the above.

Answers to Written Lab

1. `set ip pat on`
2. `debug ip nat`
3. `ip nat outside`
4. `show ip nat statistics`
5. `show ip nat translations`
6. `show ip pat`
7. `no debug ip nat`
8. `clear ip nat translation *`
9. `ip nat inside source list` *list-number* `interface` *interface-number* `overload`
10. *access-list*

Answers to Review Questions

1. **A.** The simple translation entry indicates the translation of a static inside IP address to a globally routable IP address.

2. **B.** The inside network is a network in which addresses need to be translated before entering an outside network such as the Internet.

3. **C.** NAT will support certain DHCP server traffic but does not replace any functions of a DHCP server.

4. **B.** A Class A network can provide up to 16,777,214 unique IP addresses for individual hosts.

5. **C.** NAT and PAT provide functions that enable a nonroutable IP address to be translated into a routable IP address. Some of NAT's and PAT's functions allow for fewer routable addresses than there are nonroutable addresses.

6. **B, D.** The router that is closest to the edge of the network and that separates the inside network and the outside network is the router that should be configured with NAT or PAT.

7. **D.** By enabling NAT overloading and using port information to differentiate, you can map more than one inside IP address to a single IP address.

8. **D.** SNMP is the only traffic type listed that is not supported by NAT.

9. **A.** The NAT border router uses about 160 bytes per translation. This means that about 10,000 translations, far more than the average router should need to translate, will use about 1.6MB of DRAM.

10. **D.** The `set ip porthandler default` command configures all well-known TCP ports except for the ports specifically assigned a handler.

11. **A.** IP NAT configuration additions and change commands are configured in the global configuration mode. The `ip nat inside` or `ip nat outside` commands enable NAT on the interface they are applied on the router.

12. **A.** The `ip nat inside source static 10.1.3.2 200.4.2.5` command is an example of a manually configured static NAT table entry.

13. **A, D.** The three commands that can be used to verify the NAT configuration are `show ip nat translations`, `show ip nat translations verbose`, and `show ip nat statistics`.

14. **B.** The Cisco IOS for the 765 uses a `set/clear` command set typically found in switches and does not support NAT. PAT is the only address translation protocol supported by the Cisco 700 series of routers.

15. **A.** NAT translates only IP addresses. It does not support IPX or AppleTalk.

16. **A.** The command `show ip pat` displays the statistical and configuration information for PAT.

17. C.   The NAT protocol is defined in the Internet standard RFC 1631 document titled "The IP Network Address Translator (NAT)."

18. C.   Statically defined routes are identified in the routing table with an *S*.

19. E.   None of the listed traffic types is supported by NAT.

20. B.   The ability to change the global IP address pool on only the NAT border router is a great feature, not a disadvantage. This enables the address pool to be changed without any manual configuration of any other host on the inside network.

Chapter

11

Centralized Security in Remote Access Networks

EXAM TOPICS COVERED IN THIS CHAPTER INCLUDE:

✓ Know the security features of CiscoSecure and the operation of a CiscoSecure server.

✓ Understand the commands and procedures used to configure routers to access a CiscoSecure server and to use AAA.

✓ Know the commands used to configure AAA on a router to control access from remote access clients.

Remote access encompasses two elements. The first is the communications channel between two points, or the connection. The second is access control, or determining who or what can access the network and its data.

These concepts are known as *authentication, authorization, and accounting (AAA)*. AAA is Cisco's way of explaining the access control components and processes, and it is the topic of this chapter.

This book has covered many of the fundamental elements of authentication and authorization—particularly in the context of Challenge Handshake Authentication Protocol, or CHAP (see Chapter 3, "Point-to-Point Protocol"). This chapter explores these concepts further, but the discussion focuses more on the theoretical concepts of security and Cisco's preferred implementation of each of these concepts. AAA services are essential to providing centralized access control services, which is a recurrent theme in this chapter and most Cisco security implementations.

Security Terminology

Many of the terms presented in the other chapters of this book are familiar or easily interpreted from the context. This chapter's terms differ slightly because they might not be as familiar. Treat this list as a high-level introduction to these security components, but realize that more detail will be provided throughout the chapter:

Authentication   The *authentication* function answers the fundamental question: who is the user? By performing this function, you ensure that unwanted intruders will be denied access to the network while other users will permitted. The user's identity can then be used to determine access permissions and to provide an audit trail of activity.

Authorization   The *authorization* function often works in concert with authentication. It provides a means for defining which network services will be available to the authenticated user.

Accounting   *Accounting* is an optional function in AAA; however, it is responsible for the auditing process, which can greatly enhance the security of the network. Accounting can also log the activities of the user, including the time that they start and stop their connection.

RADIUS   *Remote Access Dial-In User Service (RADIUS)* is a protocol that is used to communicate between the remote access device and an authentication server. Sometimes an authentication server running RADIUS will be called a *RADIUS server*.

TACACS+   *Enhanced Terminal Access Controller Access Control System (TACACS+)* is a protocol similar to RADIUS. Sometimes the server is called a *T-plus* or *T+ server*.

Security server   A *security server* runs the protocol, TACACS+ or RADIUS, that is used to provide AAA services. It should be secured and redundant—especially if it provides business-critical access control. CiscoSecure is Cisco's version of this type of server and is available on Windows NT and Unix.

Cisco Access Control Solutions

Consider your home or apartment for a moment. It contains all your property, and theoretically, it is a private space for you and your family. Most likely, the door has a lock of some kind that restricts entry and, with the use of a key, only you and other authorized persons will be able to enter.

In this example, the door is very much like the remote access device in the network. It provides a gateway between the outside world and the home—in this case, the corporate network. The electronic door also has a key of sorts—frequently a username and password. *Access control* defines the manner in which these metaphorical keys are allocated and used; also, it defines what each person who enters the system can do.

Cisco access control solutions are used to implement the security policies of the network—specifically, the remote access connectivity. These solutions are targeted for a wide variety of platforms and functions. You will find Cisco access solutions for several platforms, including Windows NT and Unix.

Consider the following components used in remote access:

Clients   In Cisco access control, a client is typically a remote user using a dial-in connection, like the one that would be found on an asynchronous or an ISDN connection. These clients can use different forms of security and authentication, including CHAP and PAP (discussed in Chapter 3), or they can use remote client software, such as CiscoRemote. In addition, hardware-based tokens can be used to increase security—the tokens do this by calculating the proper response to a one-time challenge from the access server.

RADIUS and token-based authentication usually require the use of PAP, which passes the password in clear-text and is less secure than CHAP.

Access servers   Clients connect to *access servers*, which provide the far end of a connection as viewed from the remote user's perspective. Stated another way, the access server is the front door to the network for remote users. The Cisco IOS and other software, including Cisco Broadband Operating System (CBOS), can provide varying degrees of security, including dialer profiles, access control lists (ACLs), and encryption.

To communicate between security servers and access servers, new protocols were developed, including TACACS+, RADIUS, and Kerberos.

Security servers   Security servers provide a centralized means of controlling policy and storing account information. This can greatly simplify administration—similar to the way Domain Name Server (DNS) eases name-to-address resolution. Recall that before DNS, each workstation was populated with a hosts file, which had to be modified for each change. DNS enabled hosts to query a single server for the resolution. Security servers operate in much the same manner—rather than storing usernames and passwords on each router, they can be stored on the server and queried by the network device when needed. Cisco's security server offering is called CiscoSecure, and it operates on Unix and Windows NT platforms. CiscoSecure is discussed later in this section.

Protocols for centralized authentication   CHAP and PAP were designed for use on serial connections, making them unsuitable for Ethernet and other LAN technologies.

CiscoSecure

The CiscoSecure product is Cisco's security server solution. The product incorporates many services, including TACACS+ and RADIUS servers, as well as logging functionality.

CiscoSecure uses Web-based interfaces and Java to provide multiple administrators with access to the server. Though the product supports both Internet Explorer and Netscape, it ships with a Netscape FastTrack Server, and some administrators find it to be more reliable with the Netscape client. CiscoSecure also relies on a relational database to manage accounts and store information—currently it supports the Oracle and Sybase database platforms.

For enhanced security, administrators can choose to use *one-time challenge tokens*. These tokens provide for the use of a different password for each login—a tactic that prevents session replay and other techniques that would otherwise compromise security. Token cards from CRYPTOCard, Enigma Logic, and Security Dynamics Technologies are supported with CiscoSecure.

Real World Scenario

CiscoSecure's Response to Brute Force and Denial-of-Service Attacks

The CiscoSecure product, like other such products, has the capability to disable accounts automatically in response to brute force attacks. This is accomplished by *intruder detection*, in which the software assumes that the party is an intruder after a certain number of failed logins. A *brute force attack* is one in which the attacker bombards the system with login attempts. Ultimately, such an attack can lead to access—especially when passwords and account information are relatively simple. By detecting such an attack, products can disable the account before it is compromised. Frequently, such logic is limited to the number of attempts per unit of time, however. For example, a brute force rule might allow five bad login attempts per hour before locking the account for a day, or it might detect three bad passwords and then lock the account until the administrator releases it.

Unfortunately, most solutions to a brute force attack lead to another type of attack: denial-of-service. A *denial-of-service attack* usually does not lead to the access of private information; rather, as the name suggests, it prevents legitimate users from obtaining that data or using the resource. Administrators must balance the impact of brute-force compromises against the potential of blocking access to legitimate users as a result of this protection. As with most products, including CiscoSecure and others, the responsibility to balance access control with access is placed on the administrator.

Authentication, Authorization, and Accounting

Regarded as distinct elements, authentication, authorization, and accounting (AAA) all work cooperatively to establish and enforce a security model. This model is the result of a *security policy*, which should define an overall set of standards that will be used by the organization to secure and protect its assets. This policy can include definitions of access rights that will be assigned to different groups and the protocols that will be used for various functions. For example, one policy statement might include that TACACS+ is the sole protocol used and that SSH, a secure tool used for administration, is preferred over Telnet.

It is important to understand how authentication, authorization, and accounting work together to promote and support a security model. In this chapter, you will learn about how AAA works, as well as how AAA functions in Cisco's router access modes. AAA services are the basic tenet of Cisco remote access solutions, and, although their presentation has been left to the end of the book, you should find that the Physical and Network Layers supplement these concepts well. This includes physical security, the use of access lists, static or authenticated IP routing, and other security techniques.

How AAA Works

It is important to remember that AAA is simply a grouping of three security functions—authentication, authorization, and accounting. Most texts examine each component as an isolated process, and, although this is perhaps more accurate, here they have been placed into a three-step process to better communicate the interactions between each service. For example, it is perfectly valid to use only authentication and authorization while omitting accounting, but if you do so, administrators will lose the auditing benefits that are provided by the auditing service.

Step 1: Authentication

Authentication is the first facet of the three security elements, and it provides a basis for the remaining two components. Authentication provides the "who" in the AAA model. Like journalists who ask themselves the questions they must answer to make their story good (Who?, What?, Where?, When?, and How?), administrators need to ask who is involved in their system; it is one of the fundamental pieces of information they need to set up their system. Unfortunately, in computing, as in noncomputing situations, it can be fairly simple to lie about one's identity.

To facilitate the authentication process, most systems require both a username and a password—it is hoped the password will be maintained in confidence in order to preclude the potential of compromise. By requiring two elements of identity, the computer-based system doubles the likelihood that the user is accurately identified.

However, it is possible to obtain, lie about, or guess both pieces of information. The likelihood of accurate authentication is stronger if a physical element is added. In noncomputing situations, this might include a passport or driver's license, whereas in the computer world it might include a token-based device. As presented in the CiscoSecure section of this chapter, there are many products that can provide this service as a software receiver of the physical code card data.

Step 2: Authorization

After the identity of the user has been established, a decision must be made regarding what rights that user can exercise. This is called *authorization*, and is assigned by the administrator based on the requirements and business policies of the organization. An example of authorization would include permissions to access a remote access device or the ability to print a file. Because authentication and authorization are so involved and dependent on each other, they are regarded as a single security component in most environments.

Step 3: Accounting

Whereas authentication and authorization work to prevent unauthorized access, *accounting* provides a means of verifying that only authorized users obtain access. In addition, accounting is used to audit the actions of an authorized user.

An accounting record relies on the authenticity of the authentication process—a fraudulent user might provide a valid login, but the accounting feature provides the audit trail required to assess the damage. This log provides a record of when an activity occurred and what action was performed—connecting to a router, for example.

Router Access Modes

A Cisco router can be accessed by using one of two access modes. These are broadly categorized as character mode and packet mode. In essence, the difference between these modes can be best understood by looking at the commands that configure character and packet modes. You should understand the difference in the modes and use this section as an introduction to the configuration command syntax.

Character-Mode Connections

Character-mode connections describe character-based access, including access via the VTY, TTY, AUX (auxiliary), and CON (console) ports. Although such access might be through a packet-based network—Telnet, for example—the connection is still viewed as being character based. The AAA commands that configure character-mode access are as follows:

- `login`
- `exec`
- `nasi`
- `connection`
- `arap`
- `enable`
- `command`

Character-mode access usually includes connections only to the router or network device. Table 11.1 includes explanations of these commands.

TABLE 11.1   Character-Mode Authentication and Authorization Commands

Command	Description
`aaa authentication enable default tacacs+ enable`	Uses TACACS+ to determine whether the user can access enabled mode. If TACACS+ is unavailable, the local enable password will be used.
`aaa authorization exec tacacs+ local`	Determines whether the user is allowed access to the EXEC shell. This example provides for TACACS+ authentication, and should TACACS+ fail, it permits authorization via the local database. The local database is populated with the username command.
`aaa authorization command` *n* `tacacs+ local`	Runs authorization for all commands at privilege level *N* (a number between 0 and 15). Every line entered by a user can be controlled and authorized by TACACS+, although performance can suffer.
`username` *user* `password` *password*	Creates or adds to the local database with a username of *user* and the password of *password*. This database is stored in the router's configuration file in NVRAM (nonvolatile random access memory), and it can be accessed upon authentication failure depending on configuration.

Packet-Mode Connections

Packet-mode connections include most dial-up connections, including the following:

- `async`
- `group-async`
- `serial`
- `ISDN BRI`
- `ISDN PRI`

Packet-mode connections typically secure connections that pass traffic through the network device. You use the ppp, `network`, and `arap` AAA commands to control packet-mode connections. Table 11.2 offers a list with explanations of these commands.

These sections do not provide a complete breakdown of all possible commands, but instead introduce the more common commands. Please refer to the documentation specific to your version of the IOS for a current listing of all commands and options, or use the incorporated Help function.

TABLE 11.2   Packet-Mode Authentication Commands

Command	Description
aaa authentication ppp user if-needed tacacs+	AAA is used for PPP packet-mode challenges. The list user is used first, and if unsuccessful, TACACS+ will be used.
aaa authorization network tacacs+ if-authenticated	TACACS+ is used to determine whether the user is permitted to make packet-mode connections if the user is authenticated.
interface async16 ppp authentication chap user	This is a new command for this chapter in that it associates an AAA function with an interface. Specifically, line async16 is instructed to use the list user for CHAP authentication. Note that an AAA server (RADIUS, and so on) is not used.

AAA Configuration

Although AAA was designed to centralize access control, it still requires configuration on each and every network device. Fortunately, after AAA is configured, there are few instances when the administrator will need to alter its configuration—for example, when the encryption key is changed. Aside from such minor alterations, all changes, including those for user accounts, are invoked at the security server. This configuration process lets the router or access device know about the type of security to be used, the location of the security server, and the passwords or other information needed to facilitate communications.

In addition to these configuration commands, the administrator must establish network-level connectivity between the access device and the security server. This might require access-list modification or route entries.

Table 11.3 outlines some of the AAA commands, including those for authentication and accounting. The configurations that relate to these commands are shown later in this section.

TABLE 11.3   Overview of AAA Commands and Configuration

Command	Description
`aaa new-model`	Enables AAA services on the router. new-model reflects changes from the initial implementation, which is no longer supported. In the absence of other AAA commands, the local database will be used for username and password. If no database is present and no other AAA method is specified will lock out the router.
`aaa authentication login default tacacs+ enable`	Configures TACACS+ to be the default method used for login-level access. If TACACS+ is unavailable, use the local enable password.
`aaa authentication enable default tacacs+ enable`	Configures TACACS+ to be the default method used for enable-level access. If TACACS+ is unavailable, use the local enable password.
`aaa accounting exec start-stop tacacs+`	Configures the accounting process, logging the start and stop times of each exec session access.
`tacacs-server host 10.1.98.36`	Specifies the IP address of the TACACS+ server. The `single-connection` parameter can be used to improve performance by maintaining a single TCP session as opposed to starting a separate session for each authentication.
`tacacs-server key tjelkprp`	Specifies the encryption key to be used for communications between the router and TACACS+ server.

Authentication Configuration

Authentication is configured differently on Cisco routers and switches; however, the general parameters are similar. In broad terms, the administrator must first instruct the device to use an authentication protocol and then provide the IP address for communications to the security server.

Router Configuration

The following is extracted from the full configuration file of the router to highlight the commands used for AAA configuration:

```
aaa new-model
aaa authentication login default tacacs+ enable
aaa authentication enable default tacacs+ enable
aaa accounting exec start-stop tacacs+
tacacs-server host 10.1.98.36
tacacs-server host 10.1.5.36
tacacs-server key tjelkprp
```

The preceding output is an example of a typical router configuration. This output starts the AAA service, establishes authentication services for both the login and enable processes, and audits the start and end times of each access. The two TACACS+ servers noted here are defined, and the preshared key is assigned.

In this example (which uses TACACS+), the aaa authentication command is used to define the type of authentication protocol. The enable keyword at the end of the two authentication commands allows the local enable secret password (use of the enable password would be used if the secret is not defined, but this is not recommended from a security perspective) to be used if network connectivity is lost between the security server and router; however, this also can be considered a security risk. This risk is minor, considering that the attacker would have to physically access the router or compromise the internal network sufficiently to change routes or block packets. Here, the tacacs-server command is being used to define the IP address of each TACACS+ server. In this example, the server key is being used to provide basic security over the communications link to the security server. Note that this configuration includes an aaa accounting command, which instructs the router to log the start and stop times of an exec session to the TACACS+ server.

NOTE   Each of these commands is documented at the end of the chapter.

Catalyst Switch Configuration

On the Cisco Catalyst series switch platform running Catalyst Operating System (CatOS), the authentication commands present themselves differently, but the resulting behavior is the same. The following configuration, like the router configuration, uses TACACS+ for login and enable (privileged) mode:

```
#tacacs+
set tacacs server 10.1.98.36 primary
set tacacs server 10.1.5.36
set tacacs attempts 3
```

```
set tacacs directedrequest disable
set tacacs key tjelkprp
set tacacs timeout 5
set authentication login tacacs enable
set authentication login local enable
set authentication enable tacacs enable
set authentication enable local enable
```

Again, this configuration file is an excerpt from the Catalyst switch configuration file—displayed with the show config command. There are two TACACS+ servers defined; however, notice that one is defined as primary. On the router, the first server listed is defaulted to primary, but the switch allows for the primary's configuration by using the primary keyword. Don't be too concerned with understanding the switch configuration—the test focus only on the router-based commands. The configuration is provided here so readers who have not previously experienced Catalyst commands can become familiar with them. The remainder of this chapter focuses only on the router commands.

The switch commands in this chapter are based on version 4.5.5 of the Catalyst code. There might be minor differences with other versions. show config or write terminal are often used to show the configuration information.

Authorization Configuration

Authorization defines the network services that are available to an individual or group. It provides an easy means of allowing privileged-mode (enable-mode) access while restricting the commands that can be executed. For example, you might want to isolate most enable commands to a single administrator or manager, while allowing operators to perform limited diagnostic functions. More experienced operators would be granted higher levels of authorization—for example, they might be permitted to shut down an interface. The unrestricted enable-mode administrator would be required for additional functions.

Use care in restricting administrative rights to the router. Although this is a helpful option when allocating rights to vendors and other parties, too restrictive a policy will lead to the distribution of the unrestricted account information, which can create a larger security risk.

A Sample TACACS+ Configuration File

The easiest way to understand the authorization function is to examine a configuration file that controls authorized services. Look at the following sample configuration file that controls authorized services:

```
#TACACS+ V2.1 configuration file
#created 5/14/03
#edited 8/26/03
#
#If user doesn't appear in the config file user/etc/password
default authentication = file /etc/passwd
accounting file = /home1/logs/tacacs+.accounting
#Must be same as router IOS "tacacs-server key"
key = tjelkprp
#
user=netops {
   member=operator
   login=cleartext dilbert
}
user=rpadjen {
   # Robert Padjen
   default service=permit
   login=cleartext yummy
}
group=operator {
   name="Network Operator"
   cmd=debug {
      permit .*
   }
   cmd=write {
      permit terminal
   }
   cmd=clear {
      permit .*
   }
   cmd=show {
   #permit show commands
```

```
        permit .*
    }
}

user=shayna {
    # Shayna Padjen
    member=operator_plus
    login=cleartext flatshoe
}
group=operator_plus {
    name="Network Operator Plus"
    cmd=debug {
        permit .*
    }
    cmd=write {
        permit terminal
    }
    cmd=clear {
        permit .*
    }
        #permit show commands
    cmd=show {
        permit .*
    }
    cmd=configure {
        permit terminal
    }
    cmd=interface {
        permit .*
    }
    cmd=shutdown {
        permit .*
    }
    cmd=no {
        permit shutdown
    }
}
```

This file establishes a number of user accounts and authorization rights. The first group, operator, is provided with basic diagnostic and administrative functions, while the operator_plus group is enhanced with shutdown, interface, and configure commands. All commands are available to one administrator. Note that Shayna is a member of operator_plus, and Rob is allowed full access.

Pay particular attention to a few additional items about this specific configuration file. First, the passwords are in clear-text—meaning that anyone with access to the server can obtain them. Most configuration files are encrypted. Second, observe that restrictions can be quite granular and could include functions such as ping while blocking extended ping.

> Please refer to the documentation that accompanies your server for syntax and configuration instructions specific to your installation.

Authorization Commands

Recall that authorization is the AAA process responsible for granting permission to access particular components in the network. The administrator will need to define these permissions based on corporate policy and user privileges. It is important to note that although a TACACS+ file was included in the previous section to illustrate authentication, the actual authorization controls were not included.

The commands associated with authorization include parameters for the protocols that are to be used and the method used for authorization. These commands are used after the authentication phase of AAA, and they are described in Table 11.4.

TABLE 11.4   AAA Authorization Commands

Command	Description
aaa authorization network *method*	Performs authorization security on all network services, including SLIP, PPP, and ARAP, using the method specified by the *method* parameter. The method could be TACACS+, RADIUS, local, and so on.
aaa authorization exec *method*	Authorizes the EXEC process with the specified AAA method.
aaa authorization commands level *15 method*	Authorizes all EXEC commands used at the specified level (0–15) by using the specified method. In this example, this is level 15, which is regarded as full authorization and normally associated with enable mode.
aaa authorization config-commands	Uses AAA authorization for configuration mode commands.
aaa authorization reverse-access *method*	Uses AAA authorization specified by the *method* parameter for reverse Telnet connections.

TABLE 11.4 AAA Authorization Commands *(continued)*

Command	Description
aaa authorization **function** *if-authenticated*	Permits the user to use the requested function only if the user is authenticated.
aaa authorization function *local*	Uses the local database for authorization for the specified function. This database is stored on the router's configuration in NVRAM.
aaa authorization function *radius*	Uses RADIUS for authorization of the specified function.
aaa authorization function *tacacs+*	Uses TACACS+ for authorization of the specified function.

Accounting Configuration

The accounting function records who did what and for how long. Because of this, it relies upon the authentication process to provide part of the audit trail. For this reason, it is recommended that accounts be established with easily identified usernames—typically a last-name, first-initial configuration. This information is coupled with six accounting types, as described in Table 11.5.

TABLE 11.5 AAA Accounting Types

Accounting Type	Function
Command	Documents the commands submitted by the user and the privilege level associated with them
Connection	Provides auditing of all outbound connections
EXEC	Logs user EXEC terminal sessions
Network	Audits all PPP, SLIP and ARAP session traffic counts, including number of packets and total bytes
System	Records system level events
Resource	Provides information regarding connections that have failed, enabling the administrator to evaluate user attempts

The configuration of accounting is fairly simple, but there are a few choices that should be considered. Table 11.6 provides a subset of the more common commands. Administrators will need to balance the desire to obtain complete accounting records against the overhead incurred. In Table 11.6, there is a function that is being accounted for, which includes commands, connections, system events, and so on. There is a method used to account for those functions, which includes start-stop, stop-only and wait-start, and the server type to send this information to.

TABLE 11.6 AAA Accounting Commands

Command	Description
aaa accounting command *level method server*	Audits all commands at a specified level by using the specified method (the options being start-stop, stop-only and wait-start). Sends this information to the server type (TACACS+ or RADIUS) specified.
aaa accounting connection *method server*	Audits all outbound connections (including Telnet and rlogin) to the specified server type by using the specified method.
aaa accounting exec *method server*	Audits the EXEC process with the specified method to the specified server type.
aaa accounting network *method server*	Audits network service requests (including SLIP, PPP, and ARAP requests) to the specified server type by using the specified method.
aaa accounting system *method server*	Audits system-level events by using the specified method to the specified server type. This includes reload, for example. Because a router reload is one of the ultimate denial-of-service attacks, it would be useful to know what user identification was used to issue the command.
aaa accounting *function start-stop server*	Documents the start and stop of a particular type of session specified by the *function* parameter to the specified server type. Audit information is sent in the background, negating any delay for the user.
aaa accounting *function stop-only server*	Sends a stop accounting notice at the end of a user process specified by the *function* parameter to the specified server type.

TABLE 11.6   AAA Accounting Commands *(continued)*

Command	Description
aaa accounting *function wait-start server*	Similar to aaa accounting start-stop, this command documents the start of a particular type of session specified by the *function* parameter to the specified server type. However, the user is not permitted to continue until the accounting server acknowledges the log entry. This can delay user access.
aaa accounting *function method {tacacs+	radius}*	Enables accounting information to be sent to the TACACS+ or RADIUS accounting server for the specified *function* by using the specified method.

One area in which accounting transcends security is charge-back. If accurate start and stop times are recorded, a company could charge users for their time on the system to offset the cost. Internet Service Providers (ISPs) have long considered this as an alternative to the flat-rate model currently found in the United States.

Virtual Profiles

Virtual profiles and virtual templates provide ways to apply centralized, user-specific parameters to multiple access servers and their physical interfaces. This can greatly reduce the impact of changes to widely distributed access points.

As suggested by the name, there is a difference between a virtual profile and the element it replaces—the dialer profile. Dialer profiles maintain information on a single access server for specific users. The virtual profile adds the following:

- User-specific configurations served from the AAA server

- An open methodology for defining both standards-based and vendor-specific parameters

After the user authenticates the system, a virtual template is applied to the virtual access interface. User parameters are then obtained from the AAA server (security server) and applied to the virtual access interface. This solution allows for better scalability and easier administration than would be allowed with standard dialer profiles. As a result, the virtual profile is actually a combination of the physical interface, generic information stored in a virtual template on the access server, and user-specific parameters stored on the security server.

If you want to expand your understanding of virtual profiles and their usage, refer to the Cisco website (www.cisco.com).

Summary

To have a complete security policy in place, authorization, authentication, and accounting (AAA) must be implemented on a network. AAA not only allows full control over dial-up connections, but login and exec access to devices. Tracking and auditing is accomplished through the accounting services in AAA.

CiscoSecure is software that allows for centralized control over access to every device in your network. It will run on Windows NT and Unix and provides RADIUS as well as TACACS+ authentication, authorization, and accounting services.

The two access modes, which are controlled by AAA, are character- and packet-mode connections. Character-mode connections usually terminate at the access server or router, and packet-mode connections are those that pass traffic through an access server or router.

Configuration of AAA services for Cisco devices has many facets. The administrator must first configure how to authenticate users and then define which services those users will be allowed to access. The optional accounting feature can be used to audit the user's activity on the system.

The use of a virtual template is a technology that enables the security server to supply the access server with user-specific dialer profile information. Instead of each access server containing user-specific dialer profile information, this information is kept on the security server and downloaded to the access server when the user is authenticated.

Exam Essentials

Understand the components of AAA. You should know that AAA is the acronym for authentication, authorization, and accounting. Authentication is used to verify a user's authenticity, usually with a username and password. Authorization is used to determine which services are available to a verified user. Accounting is used to audit the user's activity on the system to provide tracking.

Know the services provided by CiscoSecure. The CiscoSecure software runs on Windows NT and Unix and provides a Java-based web client for configuration. The software provides RADIUS and TACACS+ services for authentication, authorization, and accounting. The software can store and retrieve user information with outside databases, including Oracle and Sybase.

Understand the functions provided by each AAA component, including the six accounting types. In addition to the AAA functions of authorizing and authenticating a user for access to various functions in the router, the accounting function can audit commands, connections, EXEC, network, system, and resources.

Know how to configure AAA services for Cisco IOS.   AAA has been updated since its initial inception; the command `aaa new-model` is used so the user can utilize the new AAA commands. There are many AAA commands used to configure authentication, authorization, and accounting on a Cisco device. Each service command begins with the `aaa` prefix. You don't need to know the AAA commands for Cisco Catalyst series switches, but they are included in this chapter for completeness.

Understand the differences between packet- and character-mode services.   Packet-mode services are typically dial-up connections, including asynchronous and ISDN access. Character-based services are connections such as login, exec, NASI, and commands. Most of these services terminate at the access device, which is typical of character-mode services.

Know that `aaa new-model` requires additional commands to configure correctly.   Invoking the `aaa new-model` command with no other parameters will lock the administrator out of the router.

Key Terms

Before you take the exam, be certain you are familiar with the following terms:

access control	denial-of-service attack
access servers	Enhanced Terminal Access Controller Access Control System (TACACS+)
accounting	intruder detection
authentication	one-time challenge tokens
authentication, authorization, and accounting (AAA)	packet-mode connections
authorization	Remote Access Dial-In User Service (RADIUS)
brute force attack	security policy
character-mode connections	security server

Written Lab

1. What command starts the AAA process on a Cisco IOS device?
2. What is the command to define the IP address 192.168.72.5 as the TACACS+ server?

3. Write the command used to specify the TACACS+ shared encryption key by using password as the key.

4. What is the command to define the use of RADIUS for accounting exec mode services using stop times only?

5. To make certain that each exec session is logged to the RADIUS server with a start time, what command would the administrator use?

6. It is important to audit significant events in the network to the TACACS+ server, including the reload command. To configure this, which command would the administrator use?

7. What command would the administrator use to create a local database entry for George with the password curious?

8. What command(s) would be used to define a TACACS+ server at address 192.168.2.1 and a standby server of 192.168.90.1?

9. Question 5 asked for the RADIUS command to configure wait-start accounting. How would you alter this command to use TACACS+?

10. What parameters and sequence would be used to configure the access server for RADIUS? If RADIUS fails, what command would be used (using TACACS+) for enable mode authentication?

Hands-on Lab

In this lab, you will configure AAA services by using TACACS+. You do not need an actual TACACS+ server, although it might be helpful to configure that portion of the connection.

Configuring TACACS+

Configure the router to perform the following authentication, authorization, and accounting against your TACACS+ server. Accounting should be configured so that all session starts are logged to the server before the user can continue. Use the shared key of class and an IP address of 192.168.1.1 for the server unless otherwise instructed. Audit outbound Telnet sessions as well.

```
aaa new-model
aaa accounting exec wait-start tacacs+
aaa accounting connection start-stop tacacs+
aaa authentication enable default tacacs+ enable
aaa authentication login default tacacs+ enable
aaa authorization tacacs+
tacacs-server host 192.168.1.1
tacacs-server key class
```

Review Questions

1. What component of AAA is responsible for tracking the time that a user disconnected from the system?

   A. Authentication

   B. Authorization

   C. Accounting

   D. Auditing

2. The administrator wishes to restrict access to commands even if the user is in enable mode. Is this possible?

   A. This is possible.

   B. This is possible; however, the user must not be given the enable password.

   C. This is possible; however, each router must be configured with the restriction command locally.

   D. This is not possible.

3. The administrator enters the aaa new-model command without entering any other parameters and writes it to memory before terminating the session. The next login will do which of the following?

   A. Be successful as the router will not prompt for a username

   B. Fail, because there is no local database and no security server option

   C. Fail, but login will be possible using the default cisco/cisco account

   D. Be successful, but there will be an additional prompt for username, which the administrator will have to dismiss before continuing

4. What component of AAA is responsible for determining the identity of a user?

   A. Authentication

   B. Authorization

   C. Accounting

   D. Auditing

5. Login and enable are associated with which of the following?

   A. Packet mode

   B. Character mode

   C. Binary mode

   D. Hex mode

6. CiscoSecure provides which of the following?

   A. RADIUS and TACACS+ servers

   B. A Web-based management console

   C. A centralized, relational, database-based access management system

   D. All of the above

7. Authorization requires information from which AAA component?

   A. Authentication

   B. Accounting

   C. Auditing

   D. Access

8. Which of the following is an advantage of using a security server?

   A. All user and password information is propagated to every access server and router automatically.

   B. Security information can be stored in a central location, similar to the way DNS stores host names centrally.

   C. Users must first authenticate to the security server and then to the access device—this adds an extra authentication step that results in a more secure system.

   D. None of the above.

9. Which of the following is a method of scaling and simplifying the distribution of user-specific configuration information?

   A. Virtual parameters

   B. Virtual routing

   C. Parameter servicing

   D. Virtual profiles

10. What command is used to log the beginning and end of a user exec session to a TACACS+ server?

   A. `aaa tacacs+ accounting exec begin-end`

   B. `aaa exec auditing tacacs+ start-stop`

   C. `aaa accounting exec start-stop tacacs+`

   D. `accounting ppp start-stop tacacs+`

11. What is the command to define the shared secret encryption key for connections with a TACACS+ server?

    A. `aaa tacacs-server key` **key**

    B. `aaa server-key tacacs` **key**

    C. `tacacs-server key` **key**

    D. `aaa shared-secret tacacs` **key**

12. Which AAA component might be used to establish a charge-back system?

    A. Authorization

    B. Accounting

    C. Administration

    D. Authentication

13. Which of the following is not true regarding CiscoSecure?

    A. The server runs on Windows NT or Unix.

    B. Profiles are stored in a relational database, such as Oracle or Sybase.

    C. Clients must run Windows NT.

    D. It supports TACACS+ and RADIUS.

14. The implementation of intrusion detection can lead to which of the following?

    A. Improved security with service impacting risk

    B. The potential for an attacker to use the function for a denial-of-service attack

    C. Simplified administration

    D. Improved security from required token-based authentication

15. The wait-start parameter on the `aaa accounting` command results in which of the following?

    A. The access server waits for the user's remote profile, stored on their PC, to be uploaded.

    B. The access server waits for the AAA server to acknowledge receipt of the start log entry.

    C. The access server waits for acknowledgment of all AAA communications.

    D. None of the above.

16. Which of the following are examples of client protocols? (Select all that apply.)

    A. CHAP

    B. PPP

    C. TACACS+

    D. RADIUS

17. Which of the following are examples of server (central site) protocols? (Select all that apply.)

    A. TACACS+

    B. PAP

    C. Kerberos V

    D. L2F

18. If the TACACS+ protocol fails to find a server, the user or administrator is always locked out of the access device unless which of the following is true?

    A. They have the enable secret password.

    B. The `enable` keyword was used.

    C. They press Ctrl+Alt+Del on their workstation.

    D. Telnet from a preauthorized host is used.

19. TACACS+ communicates via which of the following?

    A. TCP

    B. UDP

    C. SPX

    D. CDP

20. It is possible to select multiple authentication methods. For example, the administrator could configure TACACS+ to be used, but upon failure the access server's local enable password could be used. Is the previous statement accurate?

    A. Yes, with the `enable` parameter.

    B. Yes, with the `tacacs failure` command.

    C. Yes, with the `backup authentication` command.

    D. No, it is not possible, and administrators should maintain a backup TACACS+ server.

Answers to Written Lab

1. aaa new-model
2. tacacs-server host 192.168.72.5
3. tacacs-server key password
4. aaa accounting exec stop-only radius
5. aaa accounting exec wait-start radius
6. aaa accounting system tacacs+
7. username George password curious
8. tacacs-server host 192.168.2.1 tacacs-server host 192.168.90.1
9. aaa accounting exec wait-start tacacs+
10. aaa authentication enable radius tacacs+

Answers to Review Questions

1. C. Recall that although the function provides an audit trail, the service is called accounting. Cisco is not above slight word alterations on their exams.

2. A. A TACACS+ server can be configured to restrict enable commands on a per-user basis. Note that TACACS+ is not required.

3. B. The administrator will be locked out of the router because there is no username database or security server.

4. A. Authentication obtains the username and validates the user's identity with a password or other authentication process.

5. B. Recall that packet mode is generally used for pass-through packets, such as PPP. Character mode is associated with the login and enable services.

6. D. CiscoSecure is Cisco's AAA server, providing all of the noted services.

7. A. To authorize access, the system must identify the user. Authentication provides this service.

8. B. Recall that usernames and other information can be stored on the router locally—the benefit of the security servers is that the usernames and passwords are stored centrally.

9. D. This question is tricky because of like words. Virtual profiles allow for interface and user-specific configuration options.

10. C. There are two tricks to this question. The first requires knowing the name of the service that provides logging—accounting. The second requires knowing the parameter that governs the service—start-stop. Note that this question is useful for teaching a common trick for guessing the answer on a test. Look at the repetition found in the answers—auditing and begin-end appear only once, which makes those answers unlikely. The last answer adds PPP, which was not part of the question.

11. C. Unlike the previous question, this one is just tough. You might have been tricked into thinking that the **aaa** prefix was necessary simply because it appeared in three choices. The first answer is also a trick because the command is correct except for this prefix.

12. B. By recording the duration of access, a company could implement a charge-back billing system.

13. C. CiscoSecure has no such restriction on clients.

14. B. Administrators need to be cautious when they are deploying aggressive intrusion detection methods because they can lead to denial-of-service attacks.

15. B.   This question could be regarded as tricky, but you remembered the syntax of the commands in the chapter—right?

16. A, B.   TACACS+ and RADIUS are server protocols. Remember that CHAP operates over PPP, so if you remembered CHAP as a client protocol, PPP also must be included.

17. A, C.   PAP and L2F are not server protocols because they operate between the client and server.

18. B.   The `enable` keyword allows the local TACACS+ service to time out and then uses the local enable password. Note that the administrator could also reload the router and break in locally.

19. A.   TACACS+ uses the connection-oriented IP protocol (TCP).

20. A.   The `enable` parameter allows the enable password to be used in the event of a TACACS+, or other security, server failure.

Glossary

AAA Authentication, authorization, and accounting: A Cisco description of the processes that are required to provide a remote access security solution. Each is implemented separately but relies on the others for functionality.

access control Used by Cisco routers to control packets as they pass through a router. Access lists are created and then applied to router interfaces to accomplish this.

access list A set of test conditions kept by routers that determines "interesting traffic" to and from the router for various services on the network.

access method The manner in which network devices approach gaining access to the network itself.

access rate Defines the bandwidth rate of the circuit. For example, the access rate of a T-1 circuit is 1.544Mbps. In Frame Relay and other technologies, there might be a fractional T-1 connection—256Kbps, for example—however, the access rate and clock rate are still 1.544Mbps.

access server Also known as a "network access server," it is a communications process connecting asynchronous devices to a LAN or WAN through network and terminal emulation software, providing synchronous or asynchronous routing of supported protocols.

accounting One of the three components in AAA. Accounting provides auditing and logging functions to the security model.

ACK Acknowledgment: Verification sent from one network device to another, signifying that an event has occurred. *Compare with: NAK.*

address mapping By translating network addresses from one format to another, this methodology permits different protocols to operate interchangeably. *See also: address resolution.*

address mask A bit combination descriptor identifying which portion of an address refers to the network or subnet and which part refers to the host. Sometimes simply called the "mask." *See also: subnet mask.*

address resolution The process used for resolving differences between computer addressing schemes. Address resolution typically defines a method for tracing Network Layer (Layer 3) addresses to Data Link Layer (Layer 2) addresses. *See also: address mapping.*

administrative distance A number between 0 and 255 that expresses the value of trustworthiness of a routing information source. The lower the number, the higher the integrity rating.

algorithm A set of rules or processes used to solve a problem. In networking, algorithms are typically used for finding the best route for traffic from a source to its destination.

AMI Alternate mark inversion: A line-code type on T1 and E1 circuits that shows 0s as "01" during each bit cell and 1s as "11" or "00" alternately, during each bit cell. The sending device must maintain ones density in AMI but not independently of the data stream. *Compare with: B8ZS. See also: ones density.*

analog connection Provides signaling via an infinitely variable waveform. This differs from a digital connection, in which a definite waveform defines values. Traditional phone service is an analog connection.

analog dial-up   Refers to traditional modem-based connections.

analog transmission   Signal messaging whereby information is represented by various combinations of signal amplitude, frequency, and phase.

Application Layer   This layer provides functions for users or their programs and is highly specific to the application being performed. It provides the services that user applications use to communicate over the network, and it is the layer in which user-access network processes reside. *See also: Data Link Layer, Network Layer, Physical Layer, Presentation Layer, Session Layer,* and *Transport Layer.*

ARP   Address Resolution Protocol: Defined in RFC 826, the protocol that traces IP addresses to MAC addresses. *See also: RARP.*

ASCII   American Standard Code for Information Interchange: An 8-bit code for representing characters, consisting of 7 data bits plus 1 parity bit.

asynchronous connection   Defines the start and stop of each octet. As a result, each byte in asynchronous connections requires 2 bytes of overhead. Synchronous connections use a synchronous clock to mark the start and stop of each character.

asynchronous transmission   Digital signals sent without precise timing, usually with different frequencies and phase relationships. Asynchronous transmissions generally enclose individual characters in control bits (called start bits and stop bits) that show the beginning and end of each character. *Compare with: synchronous transmission.*

authentication   The first component in the AAA model. Users are typically authenticated via a username and password, which are used to uniquely identify them.

authorization   The act of permitting access to a resource based on authentication information in the AAA model.

auxiliary port   The asynchronous port on the back of Cisco routers that enables you to dial into the router and make console configuration settings. It also can be used for dial-on-demand routing (DDR).

B8ZS   Binary 8-zero substitution: A line-code type, interpreted at the remote end of the connection, that uses a special code substitution whenever eight consecutive zeros are transmitted over the link on T1 and E1 circuits. This technique assures ones density independent of the data stream. Also known as "bipolar 8-zero substitution." *Compare with: AMI. See also: ones density.*

bandwidth   The gap between the highest and lowest frequencies employed by network signals. More commonly, it refers to the rated throughput capacity of a network protocol or medium.

baud   Synonymous with bits per second (bps), if each signal element represents 1 bit. It is a unit of signaling speed equivalent to the number of separate signal elements transmitted per second.

B channel   Bearer channel: A full-duplex, 64Kbps channel in ISDN that transmits user data. *Compare with: D channel.*

bearer service   Used by service providers to provide DS0 service to ISDN customers. A DS0 is one 64K channel. An ISDN bearer service provides either two DS0s, called two bearer channels for a Basic Rate Interface (BRI), or 23 DS0s, called a Primary Rate Interface (PRI).

BECN   Backward Explicit Congestion Notification: BECN is a bit set by a Frame Relay switch in frames opposite the data that experienced congestion. A DTE that receives frames with the BECN might ask higher-level protocols to take necessary flow-control measures. *Compare with: FECN.*

binary   A two-state numbering method that uses 1s and 0s. The binary numbering system underlies all digital representation of information.

BoD   Bandwidth on Demand: This function enables an additional connection to be used to increase the amount of bandwidth available for a particular connection.

BRI   Basic Rate Interface: The ISDN interface that facilitates circuit-switched communication between video, data, and voice; it is made up of two B channels (64Kbps each) and one D channel (16Kbps). *Compare with: PRI. See also: ISDN.*

broadcast   A data frame or packet that is transmitted to every node on the local network segment (as defined by the broadcast domain). Broadcasts are known by their broadcast address, which is a destination network and host address with all the bits turned on. Also called "local broadcast."

brute force attack   Bombards the resource with attempted connections until successful. The most common brute force attack repeatedly tries different passwords until finding a match that is then used to compromise the network.

buffer   A storage area dedicated to handling data while in transit. Buffers are used to receive/ store sporadic deliveries of data bursts, usually received from faster devices, thereby compensating for the variations in processing speed. Incoming information is stored until everything is received prior to sending data. Also known as an "information buffer."

cable modem   Not actually an analog device, like an asynchronous modem, but rather a customer access device for linking to a broadband cable network. These devices are typically bridges that have a coax connection to link to the cable network and a 10-BaseT Ethernet connection to link to the user's PC.

CD   Carrier Detect: A signal indicating that an interface is active or that a connection generated by a modem has been established.

CDP   Cisco Discovery Protocol: Cisco's proprietary protocol that is used to tell a neighboring Cisco device about the type of hardware, software version, and active interfaces that the Cisco device is using. CDP is used between devices and is not routable.

challenge   Provides authentication in Challenge Handshake Authentication Protocol (CHAP) as part of the handshake process. This numerically unique query is sent to authenticate the user without sending the password unencrypted across the wire.

channelized E-1   Operating at 2.048Mbps, an access link that is sectioned into thirty B channels and one D channel, supporting dial-on-demand routing (DDR), Frame Relay, and X.25. *Compare with: channelized T-1.*

channelized T-1   Operating at 1.544Mbps, an access link that is sectioned into twenty-three B channels and one D channel of 64Kbps each, where individual channels or groups of channels connect to various destinations, supporting dial-on-demand routing (DDR), Frame Relay, and X.25. *Compare with: channelized E-1.*

CHAP   Challenge Handshake Authentication Protocol: Supported on lines using PPP encapsulation, it is a security feature that identifies the remote end, helping keep out unauthorized users. After CHAP is performed, the router or access server determines whether a given user is permitted access. It is a newer, more secure protocol than Password Authentication Protocol (PAP). *Compare with: PAP.*

character mode connections   Typically terminated at the access server, these connections include Telnet and console connections.

checksum   A test for ensuring the integrity of sent data. It is a number calculated from a series of values taken through a sequence of mathematical functions, typically placed at the end of the data from which it is calculated and then recalculated at the receiving end for verification. *Compare with: CRC.*

CIR   Committed Information Rate: Averaged over a minimum span of time and measured in bits per second (bps), a Frame Relay network's agreed-upon minimum rate of transferring information.

circuit switching   Used with dial-up networks such as PPP and ISDN. Passes data, but needs to set up the connection first—just like making a phone call.

Cisco IOS software   Cisco Internetwork Operating System software: The kernel of the Cisco line of routers and switches that supplies shared functionality, scalability, and security for all products under its CiscoFusion architecture.

Class A network   Part of the Internet Protocol hierarchical addressing scheme. Class A networks have only 8 bits for defining networks and 24 bits for defining hosts on each network.

Class B network   Part of the Internet Protocol hierarchical addressing scheme. Class B networks have 16 bits for defining networks and 16 bits for defining hosts on each network.

Class C network   Part of the Internet Protocol hierarchical addressing scheme. Class C networks have 24 bits for defining networks and only 8 bits for defining hosts on each network.

CLI   Command Line Interface: Enables you to configure Cisco routers and switches with maximum flexibility.

clocking   Used in synchronous connections to provide a marker for the start and end of data bytes. This is similar to the beat of a drum, with a person speaking only when the drum is silent.

CO   (1) Central office: the local telephone company office where all loops in a certain area connect and where circuit switching of subscriber lines occurs. (2) Carrier operations: the carrier network that traffic will traverse to get from one site to another. Sometimes called the "CO cloud."

compression   A technique to send more data across a link than would be normally permitted by representing repetitious strings of data with a single marker. *See also: Predictor* and *Stac.*

console port Typically an RJ-45 port on Cisco routers and switches that allows Command-line interface capability.

CRC Cyclic redundancy check: A methodology that detects errors, whereby the frame recipient makes a calculation by dividing frame contents with a prime binary divisor and compares the remainder to a value stored in the frame by the sending node. *Compare with: checksum.*

CSU Channel Service Unit: A digital mechanism that connects end-user equipment to the local digital telephone loop. Frequently referred to along with the data service unit as "DSU/CSU." *See also: DSU.*

custom queuing Used by the Cisco router IOS to provide a queuing method to slower serial links. Custom queuing enables an administrator to configure the type of traffic that will have priority over the link.

data compression *See: compression.*

Data Link Layer Layer 2 of the OSI Reference Model, it ensures the trustworthy transmission of data across a physical link and is primarily concerned with physical addressing, line discipline, network topology, error notification, ordered delivery of frames, and flow control. The IEEE has further segmented this layer into the MAC sublayer and the LLC (Logical Link Control) sublayer. Also known as the "Link Layer." *See also: Application Layer, Network Layer, Physical Layer, Presentation Layer, Session Layer,* and *Transport Layer.*

DCE Data Communications Equipment (as defined by the EIA) or data circuit-terminating equipment (as defined by the ITU-T): The mechanisms and links of a communications network that make up the network portion of the user-to-network interface, such as modems. The DCE supplies the physical connection to the network, forwards traffic, and provides a clocking signal to synchronize data transmission between DTE and DCE devices. *See also: DTE.*

D channel Data channel: A full-duplex, 16Kbps (BRI) or 64Kbps (PRI) ISDN channel. *Compare with: B channel.*

DDR Dial-on-demand routing: A technique that enables a router to automatically initiate and end a circuit-switched session per the requirements of the sending station. By mimicking keepalives, the router fools the end station into treating the session as active. DDR permits routing over ISDN or telephone lines via a modem or external ISDN terminal adapter.

DE Discard Eligibility: Used in Frame Relay networks to tell a switch that a frame can be discarded if the switch is too busy. The DE is a field in the frame that is turned on by transmitting routers if the Committed Information Rate (CIR) is oversubscribed or set to 0.

DE bit Marks a frame as discard-eligible on a Frame Relay network. If a serial link is congested and the Frame Relay network has passed the Committed Information Rate (CIR), the DE bit will always be on.

default route The static routing table entry used to direct frames whose next hop is not spelled out in the dynamic routing table.

delay The time elapsed between a sender's initiation of a transaction and the first response they receive. Also, the time needed to move a packet from its source to its destination over a path. *See also: latency.*

demodulation   A series of steps that return a modulated signal to its original form. When receiving, a modem demodulates an analog signal to its original digital form (and, conversely, modulates the digital data it sends into an analog signal). *See also: modem* and *modulation.*

denial-of-service attack   Also known as a DoS. Blocks access to a network resource by saturating the device with attacking data. Typically, this is targeted against the link (particularly lower-bandwidth links) or the server. DDoS attacks, or distributed denial-of-service attacks, use multiple originating attacking resources to saturate a more capable resource.

destination address   The address for the network devices that will receive a packet.

dial backup   Dial backup connections are typically used to provide redundancy to Frame Relay connections. The backup link is activated over an analog modem.

DLCI   Data link connection identifier: Used to identify virtual circuits in a Frame Relay network.

DNS   Domain Name Server: Used to resolve host names to IP addresses.

DSL   Digital Subscriber Line: Provides broadband services over a single copper pair, typically to residential customers. Most vendors are providing DSL services at up to 6Mbps downstream; however, the technology can support 52Mbps service.

DSR   Data Set Ready: When a DCE is powered up and ready to run, this EIA/TIA-232 interface circuit is also engaged.

DSU   Data Service Unit: This device is used to adapt the physical interface on a Data Terminal Equipment (DTE) mechanism to a transmission facility such as T1 or E1 and is also responsible for signal timing. It is commonly grouped with the channel service unit and referred to as the "DSU/CSU." *See also: CSU.*

DTE   Data Terminal Equipment: Any device located at the user end of a user-network interface serving as a destination, a source, or both. DTE includes devices such as multiplexers, protocol translators, and computers. The connection to a data network is made through Data Communications Equipment (DCE) such as a modem, using the clocking signals generated by that device. *See also: DCE.*

DTR   Data terminal ready: An activated EIA/TIA-232 circuit communicating to the DCE the state of preparedness of the DTE to transmit or receive data.

E-1   Generally used in Europe, a wide-area digital transmission scheme carrying data at 2.048Mbps. E-1 transmission lines are available for lease from common carriers for private use.

encapsulation   The technique used by layered protocols in which a layer adds header information to the Protocol Data Unit (PDU) from the layer above. As an example, in Internet terminology, a packet would contain a header from the Physical Layer, followed by a header from the Network Layer (Internet Protocol), followed by a header from the Transport Layer (Transmission Control Protocol), followed by the application protocol data.

encryption   The conversion of information into a scrambled form that effectively disguises it to prevent unauthorized access. Every encryption scheme uses some well-defined algorithm, which is reversed at the receiving end by an opposite algorithm in a process known as decryption.

error correction   Uses a checksum to detect bit errors in the data stream.

ESF   Extended Super Frame: Made up of 24 frames with 192 bits each, with the 193rd bit providing other functions including timing. This is an enhanced version of SF. *See also: SF.*

extended IP access list   IP access list that filters the network by logical address, protocol field in the Network Layer header, and even the port field in the Transport Layer header.

FECN   Forward Explicit Congestion Notification: A bit set by a Frame Relay network that informs the DTE receptor that congestion was encountered along the path from source to destination. A device receiving frames with the FECN bit set can ask higher-priority protocols to take flow-control action as needed. *Compare with: BECN.*

firewall   A barrier purposefully erected between any connected public networks and a private network, made up of a router or access server, or several routers or access servers, that uses access lists and other methods to ensure the security of the private network.

Flash   Electronically Erasable Programmable Read-Only Memory (EEPROM). Used to hold the Cisco IOS in a router by default.

flow control   A methodology used to ensure that receiving units are not overwhelmed with data from sending devices. Pacing, as flow control is called in IBM networks, means that when buffers at a receiving unit are full, a message is transmitted to the sending unit to temporarily halt transmissions until all the data in the receiving buffer has been processed and the buffer is again ready for action.

frame   A logical unit of information sent by the Data Link Layer over a transmission medium. The term often refers to the header and trailer, employed for synchronization and error control, that surround the data contained in the unit.

Frame Relay   A more efficient replacement of the X.25 protocol (an unrelated packet relay technology that guarantees data delivery). Frame Relay is an industry-standard, shared-access, best-effort, switched Data Link Layer encapsulation that services multiple virtual circuits and protocols between connected mechanisms.

Frame Relay switching   Device at a service provider that provides packet switching for Frame Relay packets.

framing   Encapsulation at the Data Link Layer of the OSI model. It is called framing because the packet is encapsulated with both a header and a trailer.

frequency   The number of cycles of an alternating current signal per time unit, measured in hertz (cycles per second).

Group of Four   Used by Cisco Local Management Interface on Frame Relay networks to manage the Permanent Virtual Circuits (PVCs). It was made up of the following companies: Digital Equipment Corporation (DEC), Cisco, Northern Telecom (Nortel), and StrataCom.

handshake   Any series of transmissions exchanged between two or more devices on a network to ensure synchronized operations.

HDLC High-Level Data Link Control: Using frame characters, including checksums, HDLC designates a method for data encapsulation on synchronous serial links and is the default encapsulation for Cisco routers. HDLC is a bit-oriented synchronous Data Link Layer protocol created by ISO and derived from SDLC. However, most HDLC vendor implementations (including Cisco's) are proprietary.

helper address The unicast address specified that instructs the Cisco router to change the client's local broadcast request for a service into a directed unicast to the server.

host address Logical address configured by an administrator or server on a device. Logically identifies this device on an internetwork.

ICMP Internet Control Message Protocol: Documented in RFC 792, it is a Network Layer Internet protocol for the purpose of reporting errors and providing information pertinent to IP packet procedures.

Internet The global "network of networks," whose popularity continues to explode. Originally a tool for collaborative academic research, it has become a medium for exchanging and distributing information of all kinds. The Internet's need to link disparate computer platforms and technologies has led to the development of uniform protocols and standards that have also found widespread use within corporate LANs. *See also: TCP/IP.*

internet Before the rise of the Internet, this lowercase form was shorthand for "internetwork" in the generic sense. Now rarely used. *See also: internetwork.*

internetwork Any group of private networks interconnected by routers and other mechanisms, typically operating as a single entity.

intruder detection Systems that operate by monitoring the data flow for characteristics consistent with security threats. In this manner, an intruder can be monitored or blocked from access. One trigger for an intruder detection system is multiple ping packets from a single resource in a brief period of time.

Inverse ARP Inverse Address Resolution Protocol: A technique by which dynamic mappings are constructed in a network, enabling a device such as a router to locate the logical network address and associate it with a Permanent Virtual Circuit (PVC). Commonly used in Frame Relay to determine the far-end node's TCP/IP address by sending the Inverse ARP request to the local DLCI.

IP Internet Protocol: Defined in RFC 791, it is a Network Layer protocol that is part of the TCP/IP stack and allows connectionless service. IP furnishes an array of features for addressing, type-of-service specification, fragmentation and reassembly, and security.

IP address Often called an "Internet address," this is an address uniquely identifying any device (host) on the Internet (or any TCP/IP network). Each address consists of four octets (32 bits), represented as decimal numbers separated by periods (a format known as "dotted-decimal"). Every address is made up of a network number, an optional subnetwork number, and a host number. The network and subnetwork numbers together are used for routing, while the host number addresses an individual host within the network or subnetwork. The network and subnetwork information is extracted from the IP address by using the subnet mask. There are five classes of IP addresses (A–E), which allocate different numbers of bits to the network, subnetwork, and host portions of the address. *See also: IP* and *subnet mask.*

IPCP   IP Control Protocol: The protocol used to establish and configure IP over PPP. *See also: IP and PPP.*

IPX   Internetwork Packet Exchange: Network Layer protocol (Layer 3) used in Novell NetWare networks for transferring information from servers to workstations. Similar to IP and XNS.

IPXCP   IPX Control Protocol: The protocol used to establish and configure IPX over PPP. *See also: IPX and PPP.*

ISDN   Integrated Services Digital Network: Offered as a service by telephone companies, a communication protocol that enables telephone networks to carry data, voice, and other digital traffic. *See also: BRI and PRI.*

ITU-T   International Telecommunications Union-Telecommunication Standardization Sector: This is a group of engineers that develops worldwide standards for telecommunications technologies. Formerly known as the CCITT.

LAPB   Link Accessed Procedure, Balanced: A bit-oriented Data Link Layer protocol that is part of the X.25 stack and has its origin in Synchronous Data Link Control (SDLC). *See also: X.25.*

LAPD   Link Access Procedure, Data. The ISDN Data Link Layer protocol used specifically for the D channel and defined by ITU-T recommendations Q.920 and Q.921. LAPD evolved from LAPB and is created to comply with the signaling requirements of ISDN basic access.

latency   Broadly, the time it takes a data packet to get from one location to another. In specific networking contexts, it can mean either (1) the time elapsed (delay) between the execution of a device's request for network access and the time the mechanism actually is permitted transmission, or (2) the time elapsed between a mechanism's receipt of a frame and the time that frame is forwarded out of the destination port. *See also: delay.*

LCP   Link Control Protocol: The protocol designed to establish, configure, and test data link connections for use by PPP. *See also: PPP.*

leased lines   Permanent connections between two points leased from the telephone companies.

link compression   *See: compression.*

LMI   Local Management Interface: An enhancement to the original Frame Relay specification. Among the features it provides are a keepalive mechanism, a multicast mechanism, global addressing, and a status mechanism.

local loop   Connection from a demarcation point to the closest switching office.

LZW algorithm   A data compression process named for its inventors, Lempel, Ziv, and Welch. The algorithm works by finding longer and longer strings of data to compress with shorter representations.

MAC address   Media access control address: A Data Link Layer hardware address that every port or device needs to connect to a LAN segment. These addresses are used by various devices in the network for accurate location of logical addresses. MAC addresses are defined by the IEEE standard, and their length is six characters, typically using the burned-in address (BIA) of the local LAN interface. Variously called "hardware address," "physical address," "burned-in address," or "MAC-layer address."

maximum rate   The maximum permitted data throughput on a particular virtual circuit, equal to the total of insured and uninsured traffic from the traffic source. Should traffic congestion occur, uninsured information might be deleted from the path. Measured in bits or cells per second, the maximum rate represents the highest throughput of data the virtual circuit is ever able to deliver and cannot exceed the media rate.

MMP   Multichassis Multilink Protocol: A protocol that supplies multilink PPP (MPPP) support across multiple routers and access servers. MMP enables several routers and access servers to work as a single, large dial-up pool with one network address and ISDN access number. MMP successfully supports packet fragmenting and reassembly when the user connection is split between two physical access devices.

modem   Modulator-demodulator: A device that converts digital signals to analog and vice versa so that digital information can be transmitted over analog communication facilities, such as voice-grade telephone lines. This is achieved by converting digital signals at the source to analog for transmission and reconverting the analog signals back into digital form at the destination. *See also: modulation* and *demodulation.*

modemcap database   Stores modem initialization strings on the router for use in auto-detection and configuration.

modem eliminator   A mechanism that makes possible a connection between two DTE devices without modems by simulating the commands and physical signaling required.

modulation   The process of modifying some characteristic of an electrical signal, such as amplitude (AM) or frequency (FM), in order to represent digital or analog information. *See also: demodulation* and *modem.*

MP bonding   Multilink Protocol bonding: The process of linking two or more physical connections into a single logical channel. This can use two or more analog lines and two or more modems, for example.

MTU   Maximum transmission unit: The largest packet size, measured in bytes, that an interface can handle.

NAK   Negative acknowledgment: A response sent from a receiver, telling the sender that the information was not received or contained errors. *Compare with: ACK.*

NAT   Network Address Translation: An algorithm instrumental in minimizing the requirement for globally unique IP addresses, permitting an organization whose addresses are not all globally unique to connect to the Internet, regardless, by translating those addresses into globally routable address space.

network address   Used with the logical network addresses to identify the network segment in an internetwork. Logical addresses are hierarchical in nature and have at least two parts: network and host. An example of a hierarchical address is 172.16.10.5, where 172.16 is the network and 10.5 is the host address.

Network Layer   In the OSI Reference Model, it is Layer 3—the layer in which routing is implemented, enabling connections and path selection between two end systems. *See also: Application Layer, Data Link Layer, Physical Layer, Presentation Layer, Session Layer,* and *Transport Layer.*

NIC Network interface card: An electronic circuit board placed in a computer. The NIC provides network communication to a LAN.

NT1 Network Termination type 1: An ISDN designation for devices that understand ISDN standards.

NT2 Network Termination type 2: An ISDN designation for devices that do not understand ISDN standards. To use an NT2, you must use a Terminal Adapter (TA).

NVRAM Nonvolatile RAM: Random-access memory that keeps its contents intact while power is turned off.

OC Optical Carrier: A series of physical protocols, designated as OC-1, OC-2, OC-3, and so on, for SONET optical signal transmissions. OC signal levels place Synchronous Transport Signal STS frames on a multimode fiber-optic line at various speeds, of which 51.84Mbps is the lowest (OC-1). Each subsequent protocol runs at a speed divisible by 51.84. *See also: SONET.*

octet A numbering system used to identify a section of a dotted decimal IP address. Also referred to as a "byte."

ones density A method of signaling that ensures there is always a voltage change on the circuit to ensure accurate clocking. The DSU/CSU retrieves the clocking information from data that passes through it. For this scheme to work, the data needs to be encoded to contain at least one binary 1 for each 8 bits transmitted. *See also: CSU and DSU.*

one-time challenge tokens Provide a single-use password. This prevents replay attacks and snooping; however, it also requires the user to have a device that provides the token. This physical component of the security model prevents hackers from guessing or obtaining the user's password.

OSI Reference Model Open Systems Interconnection Reference Model: A conceptual model defined by the International Organization for Standardization (ISO), describing how any combination of devices can be connected for the purpose of communication. The OSI model divides the task into seven functional layers, forming a hierarchy with the applications at the top and the physical medium at the bottom, and it defines the functions each layer must provide. *See also: Application Layer, Data Link Layer, Network Layer, Physical Layer, Presentation Layer, Session Layer,* and *Transport Layer.*

out-of-band signaling Within a network, any transmission that uses physical channels or frequencies separate from those ordinarily used for data transfer. For example, the initial configuration of a Cisco Catalyst switch requires an out-of-band connection via a console port.

packet In data communications, the basic logical unit of information transferred. A packet consists of a certain number of data bytes, wrapped or encapsulated in headers and/or trailers that contain information about where the packet came from, where it's going, and so on. The various protocols involved in sending a transmission add their own layers of header information, which the corresponding protocols in receiving devices then interpret.

packet mode connections Typically passed through the router or remote access device. This includes PPP sessions.

packet switch   A physical device that makes it possible for a communication channel to share several connections. Its functions include finding the most efficient transmission path for packets.

packet switching   A networking technology based on the transmission of data in packets. Dividing a continuous stream of data into small units—packets—enables data from multiple devices on a network to share the same communication channel simultaneously but also requires the use of precise routing information.

PAD   Packet assembler/disassembler: Used to buffer incoming data that is coming in faster than the receiving device can handle it. Typically, it is used only in X.25 networks.

PAP   Password Authentication Protocol: In Point-to-Point Protocol (PPP) networks, a method of validating connection requests. The requesting (remote) device must send an authentication request, containing a password and ID, to the local router when attempting to connect. Unlike the more secure CHAP (Challenge Handshake Authentication Protocol), PAP sends the password unencrypted and does not attempt to verify whether the user is authorized to access the requested resource; it merely identifies the remote end. *Compare with: CHAP.*

parity checking   A method of error-checking in data transmissions. An extra bit (the parity bit) is added to each character or data word so that the sum of the bits will be either an odd number (in odd parity) or an even number (even parity).

PAT   Port Address Translation: Enables a single IP address to represent multiple resources by altering the source TCP or UDP port number.

payload compression   Reduces the number of bytes required to accurately represent the original data stream. Header compression is also possible. *See also: compression.*

PDN   Public Data Network: Offers the public access to computer communication networks operated by private concerns or government agencies, generally for a fee. Small organizations can take advantage of PDNs, aiding them in creating WANs without investing in long-distance equipment and circuitry.

Physical Layer   The lowest layer—Layer 1—in the OSI Reference Model, it is responsible for converting data packets from the Data Link Layer (Layer 2) into electrical signals. Physical Layer protocols and standards define, for example, the type of cable and connectors to be used, including their pin assignments and the encoding scheme for signaling 0 and 1 values. *See also: Application Layer, Data Link Layer, Network Layer, Presentation Layer, Session Layer,* and *Transport Layer.*

ping   Packet Internet groper: A Unix-based Internet diagnostic tool, consisting of a message sent to test the accessibility of a particular device on the IP network. The acronym (from which the "full name" was formed) reflects the underlying metaphor of submarine sonar. Just as the sonar operator sends out a signal and waits to hear it echo ("ping") back from a submerged object, the network user can ping another node on the network and wait to see whether it responds.

PLP   Packet Layer Protocol: Occasionally called X.25 Level 3 or X.25 Protocol, a Network Layer protocol that is part of the X.25 stack.

POTS   Plain old telephone service: Refers to the traditional analog phone service found in most installations.

PPP   Point-to-Point Protocol: The protocol most commonly used for dial-up Internet access, superseding the earlier Serial Line Internet Protocol (SLIP). Its features include address notification, authentication via CHAP or PAP, support for multiple protocols, and link monitoring. PPP has two layers: the Link Control Protocol (LCP) establishes, configures, and tests a link; then any of the various Network Control Protocol (NCPs) transport traffic for a specific protocol suite, such as IPX. *See also: CHAP, PAP,* and *SLIP and LCP.*

PPP callback   Point-to-Point Protocol callback: Supports callback to a predetermined number to augment security.

Predictor   A compression technique supported by Cisco. *See also: compression.*

Presentation Layer   Layer 6 of the OSI Reference Model, it defines how data is formatted, presented, encoded, and converted for use by software at the Application Layer. *See also: Application Layer, Data Link Layer, Network Layer, Physical Layer, Session Layer,* and *Transport Layer.*

PRI   Primary Rate Interface: A type of ISDN connection between a PBX and a long-distance carrier, which is made up of a single 64Kbps D channel in addition to 23 (T1) or 30 (E1) B channels. *Compare with BRI. See also: ISDN.*

priority queuing   A routing function in which frames temporarily placed in an interface output queue are assigned priorities based on traits such as packet size or type of interface.

process switching   As a packet arrives on a router to be forwarded, it's copied to the router's process buffer, and the router performs a lookup on the Layer 3 address. Using the route table, an exit interface is associated with the destination address. The processor forwards the packet with the added new information to the exit interface, while the router initializes the fast-switching cache. Subsequent packets bound for the same destination address follow the same path as the first packet.

propagation delay   The time it takes data to traverse a network from its source to its destination.

protocol   In networking, the specification of a set of rules for a particular type of communication. The term is also used to refer to the software that implements a protocol.

PSE   Packet Switch Exchange: The X.25 term for a switch.

PSN   Packet-Switching Network: Any network that uses packet-switching technology. Also known as Packet-Switched Data Network (PSDN). *See also: packet switching.*

PSTN   Public Switched Telephone Network: Colloquially referred to as "plain old telephone service" (POTS). A term that describes the assortment of telephone networks and services available globally.

PVC   Permanent Virtual Circuit: In a Frame Relay network, a logical connection, defined in software, that is maintained permanently. *Compare with: SVC. See also: virtual circuit.*

QoS   Quality of service: A set of metrics used to measure the quality of transmission and service availability of any given transmission system.

queue Broadly, any list of elements arranged in an orderly fashion and ready for processing, such as a line of people waiting to enter a movie theater. In routing, it refers to a backlog of information packets waiting in line to be transmitted over a router interface.

queuing A quality-of-service process that enables packets to be forwarded from the router based on administratively defined parameters. This can be used for time-sensitive protocols.

R reference point Used with ISDN networks to identify the connection between an NT1 and an S/T device. The S/T device converts the 4-wire network to the 2-wire ISDN standard network.

RADIUS Remote Access Dial-In User Service: A protocol that is used to communicate between the remote access device and an authentication server. Sometimes an authentication server running RADIUS is called a RADIUS server.

RAM Random access memory: Used by all computers to store information. Cisco routers use RAM to store packet buffers and routing tables, along with the hardware addresses cache.

RARP Reverse Address Resolution Protocol: The protocol within the TCP/IP stack that maps MAC addresses to IP addresses. *See also: ARP.*

rate queue A value, assigned to one or more virtual circuits, that specifies the speed at which an individual virtual circuit will transmit data to the remote end. Every rate queue identifies a segment of the total bandwidth available on an ATM link. The sum of all rate queues should not exceed the total available bandwidth.

reference point Used to define an area in an ISDN network. Providers use reference points to find problems in the ISDN network.

reliability The measure of a connection's quality. It is one of the metrics that can be used to make routing decisions.

reload An event or command that causes Cisco routers to reboot.

remote access A generic term that defines connectivity to distant resources by using one of many technologies, as appropriate.

reverse Telnet Maps a Telnet port to a physical port on the router or access device. This enables the administrator to connect to a modem or other device attached to the port.

RFC Request For Comment: Presents and defines standards in the networking industry.

RJ connector Registered jack connector: Is used with twisted-pair wiring to connect the copper wire to network interface cards, switches, and hubs.

robbed bit signaling Used in Primary Rate Interface (PRI) clocking mechanisms.

ROM Read-only memory: Chip used in computers to help boot the device. Cisco routers use a ROM chip to load the bootstrap, which runs a power-on self-test, and then find and load the IOS in flash memory by default.

router A Network Layer mechanism, either software or hardware, using one or more metrics to choose the best path for transmission of network traffic. Sending packets between networks by routers is based on the information provided by the Network Layers. Historically, this device has sometimes been called a "gateway."

routing The process of forwarding logically addressed packets from their local subnetwork toward their ultimate destination. In large networks, the numerous intermediary destinations a packet might travel before reaching its destination can make routing very complex.

RTS Request To Send: An EIA/TIA-232 control signal requesting permission to transmit data on a communication line.

S reference point ISDN reference point that works with a T reference point to convert a 4-wire ISDN network to the 2-wire ISDN network needed to communicate with the ISDN switches at the network provider.

scripts Predefines commands that should be issued in sequence, typically to complete a connection or accomplish a repetitive task.

security policy Documents that define a business's requirements and processes to protect corporate data. A security policy might be as generic as "no file transfers allowed" or as specific as "FTP puts allowed only to server *X*."

security server A centralized device that authenticates access requests, typically via a protocol such as TACACS+ or RADIUS.

server Hardware and software that provide network services to clients.

Session Layer Layer 5 of the OSI Reference Model, responsible for creating, managing, and terminating sessions between applications and overseeing data exchange between Presentation Layer entities. *See also: Application Layer*, *Data Link Layer*, *Network Layer*, *Physical Layer*, *Presentation Layer*, and *Transport Layer*.

set-based Set-based routers and switches use the `set` command to configure devices. Cisco is moving away from set-based commands and is using the command-line interface (CLI) on all new devices.

SF Super Frame: Also called a "D4 frame"; consists of 12 frames with 192 bits each, and the 193rd bit providing other functions including error checking. SF is frequently used on T1 circuits. A newer version of the technology is Extended Super Frame (ESF), which uses 24 frames. *See also: ESF*.

sliding window The method of flow control used by TCP, as well as several Data Link Layer protocols. This method places a buffer between the receiving application and the network data flow. The "window" available for accepting data is the size of the buffer minus the amount of data already there. This window increases in size as the application reads data from it and decreases as new data is sent. The receiver sends the transmitter announcements of the current window size, and it can stop accepting data until the window increases above a certain threshold.

SLIP Serial Line Internet Protocol: An industry standard serial encapsulation for point-to-point connections that supports only a single routed protocol, TCP/IP. SLIP is the predecessor to PPP. *See also: PPP*.

SMTP   Simple Mail Transfer Protocol: A protocol used on the Internet to provide electronic mail services.

socket   (1) A software structure that operates within a network device as a destination point for communications. (2) In AppleTalk networks, an entity at a specific location within a node; AppleTalk sockets are conceptually similar to TCP/IP ports.

SOHO   Small office/home office: A contemporary term for remote users.

SONET   Synchronous Optical Network: The ANSI standard for synchronous transmission on fiber-optic media, developed at Bell Labs. It specifies a base signal rate of 51.84Mbps and a set of multiples of that rate, known as Optical Carrier levels, up to 2.5Gbps.

SPID   Service Profile Identifier: A number assigned by service providers or local telephone companies and assigned by administrators to a BRI port. SPIDs are used to determine subscription services of a device connected via ISDN. ISDN devices use SPID when accessing the telephone company switch that initializes the link to a service provider.

split horizon   Useful for preventing routing loops. A type of distance-vector routing rule stating that information about routes is prevented from leaving the router interface through which that information was received.

Stac   A compression method developed by Stacker Corporation for use over serial links. *See also: compression.*

standard IP access list   IP access list that uses only the source IP addresses to filter a network.

static route   A route whose information is purposefully entered into the routing table and can take priority over those chosen by dynamic routing protocols.

statistical multiplexing   Multiplexing in general is a technique that enables data from multiple logical channels to be sent across a single physical channel. Statistical multiplexing dynamically assigns bandwidth only to input channels that are active, optimizing available bandwidth so that more devices can be connected than with other multiplexing techniques. Also known as statistical time-division multiplexing or stat mux.

subchannel   A frequency-based subdivision that creates a separate broadband communications channel.

subinterface   One of many virtual interfaces available on a single physical interface.

subnet   *See: subnetwork.*

subnet address   The portion of an IP address that is specifically identified by the subnet mask as the subnetwork. *See also: IP address, subnetwork,* and *subnet mask.*

subnet mask   Also simply known as "mask," a 32-bit address mask used in IP to identify the bits of an IP address that are used for the subnet address. Using a mask, the router does not need to examine all 32 bits, only those selected by the mask. *See also: address mask, IP address,* and *subnetwork.*

subnetwork (1) Any network that is part of a larger IP network and is identified by a subnet address. A network administrator segments a network into subnetworks in order to provide a hierarchical, multilevel routing structure and at the same time protect the subnetwork from the addressing complexity of networks that are attached. Also known as a "subnet." *See also: IP address, subnet mask,* and *subnet address.* (2) In OSI networks, the term specifically refers to a collection of End-Systems and Intermediate Systems controlled by only one administrative domain, using a solitary network connection protocol.

SVC Switched Virtual Circuit: A dynamically established virtual circuit, created on demand and dissolved as soon as transmission is over and the circuit is no longer needed. In ATM terminology, it is referred to as a "switched virtual connection." *Compare with: PVC. See also: virtual circuit.*

switch (1) In networking, a device responsible for multiple functions such as filtering, flooding, and sending frames. It works by using the destination address of individual frames. Switches operate at the Data Link Layer of the OSI model. (2) Broadly, any electronic/mechanical device enabling connections to be established as needed and terminated if no longer necessary.

synchronous transmission Signals transmitted digitally with precision clocking. This transmission requires a common clock signal (a timing reference) between the communicating devices in order to coordinate their transmissions. *Compare with: asynchronous transmission.*

T reference point Used with an S reference point to change a 4-wire ISDN network to a 2-wire ISDN network.

T-1 Digital WAN that uses 24 DS0s at 64K each to create a bandwidth of 1.536Mbps, minus clocking overhead, providing 1.544Mbps of usable bandwidth.

T-3 Digital WAN that can provide bandwidth of 44.763Mbps.

TACACS+ Enhanced Terminal Access Controller Access Control System: An enhanced version of TACACS, this protocol is similar to RADIUS.

TCP Transmission Control Protocol: A connection-oriented protocol that is defined at the Transport Layer of the OSI Reference Model. Provides reliable delivery of data.

TCP header compression A compression process that compresses only the TCP header information, which is typically repetitive. This does not compress the user data. *See also: compression.*

TCP/IP Transmission Control Protocol/Internet Protocol. The suite of protocols underlying the Internet. TCP and IP are the most widely known protocols in that suite. *See also: Internet, IP,* and *TCP.*

TDM Time division multiplexing: A technique for assigning bandwidth on a single wire, based on preassigned time slots, to data from several channels. Bandwidth is allotted to each channel regardless of a station's ability to send data.

TE Terminal Equipment: Any peripheral device that is ISDN compatible and attached to a network, such as a telephone or computer. TE can also stand for Terminal Endpoint.

TE1 Terminal Equipment 1: A device with a 4-wire, twisted-pair digital interface. Most modern ISDN devices are of this type. TE1s are ISDN-ready and understand ISDN signaling techniques.

TE2 Terminal Equipment 2: These devices do not understand ISDN signaling techniques, and a terminal adapter must be used to convert the signaling. TE2s are not ISDN-ready and do not understand ISDN signaling techniques.

telco A common abbreviation for the telephone company.

Telnet The standard terminal emulation protocol within the TCP/IP protocol stack. It is a method of remote terminal connection, enabling users to log in to remote networks and use those resources as if they were locally connected. Telnet is defined in RFC 854.

terminal adapter A hardware interface between a computer without a native ISDN interface and an ISDN line. In effect, a device to connect a standard async interface to a nonnative ISDN device, emulating a modem. A terminal adapter must be used with a TE2. Abbreviated as TA.

terminal emulation The use of software, installed on a PC or LAN server, that enables the PC to function as if it were a "dumb" terminal directly attached to a particular type of mainframe.

TFTP Trivial File Transfer Protocol: Conceptually, a stripped-down version of FTP, it's the protocol of choice if you know exactly what you want and where it's to be found. TFTP doesn't provide the abundance of functions that FTP does. In particular, it has no directory browsing abilities; it can do nothing but send and receive files.

Thinnet Also called 10Base2. Bus network that uses a thin coax cable and runs Ethernet media access up to 185 meters.

toll network WAN network that uses the Public Switched Telephone Network (PSTN) to send packets.

trace IP command used to trace the path a packet takes through an internetwork.

traffic shaping Used on Frame Relay networks to provide priorities for data.

Transport Layer Layer 4 of the OSI Reference Model, used for reliable communication between end-nodes over the network. The Transport Layer provides mechanisms used for establishing, maintaining, and terminating virtual circuits, detecting and recovering transport faults, and controlling the flow of information. *See also: Application Layer*, *Data Link Layer*, *Network Layer*, *Physical Layer*, *Presentation Layer*, and *Session Layer*.

U reference point Reference point between a TE1 and an ISDN network. The U reference point understands ISDN signaling techniques and uses a 2-wire connection.

UART Universal Asynchronous Receiver/Transmitter: A chip that governs asynchronous communications. Its primary function is to buffer incoming data; however, it also buffers outbound bits.

UDP User Datagram Protocol: A connectionless Transport Layer protocol in the TCP/IP protocol stack that simply enables datagrams to be exchanged without acknowledgments or delivery guarantees, requiring other protocols to handle error processing and retransmission. UDP is defined in RFC 768.

unnumbered frames   HDLC frames used for control-management purposes, such as link startup and shutdown or mode specification.

UTP   Unshielded twisted-pair: Copper wiring used in small-to-large networks to connect host devices to hubs and switches. Also used to connect a switch to a switch, or a hub to a hub.

virtual circuit   Abbreviated VC, a logical circuit devised to ensure reliable communication between two devices on a network. Defined by a Virtual Path Connection (VPC)/Virtual Channel Identifier (VCI) pair, a virtual circuit can be permanent (PVC) or switched (SVC). Virtual circuits are used in Frame Relay and X.25. Known as a "virtual channel" in ATM. *See also:* PVC and SVC.

VLSM   Variable-length subnet mask: Helps optimize available address space and specify a different subnet mask for the same network number on various subnets. Also commonly referred to as "subnetting a subnet."

VPN   Virtual private network: A method of encrypting point-to-point logical connections across a public network, such as the Internet. This provides secure communications across a public network.

WAN   Wide area network: A designation used to connect LANs together across a Data Communications Equipment (DCE) network. Typically, a WAN is a leased line or dial-up connection across a PSTN network. Examples of WAN protocols include Frame Relay, PPP, ISDN, and HDLC.

weighted fair queuing   Default queuing method on serial links for all Cisco routers. WFQ has been further augmented with Class-Based Weighted Fair Queuing, which allows for classification.

wildcard   Used with access-list, supernetting, and OSPF configurations. Wildcards are designations used to identify a range of subnets.

windowing   Flow-control method used with TCP at the Transport Layer of the OSI model.

X.25   An ITU-T packet-relay standard that defines communication between DTE and DCE network devices. X.25 uses a reliable Data Link Layer protocol called LAPB. X.25 also uses PLP at the Network Layer. X.25 has mostly been replaced by Frame Relay.

X.25 protocol   The first packet-switching network, which provides more error correction functionality than more modern protocols.

Index

Note to the Reader: Throughout this index **boldfaced** page numbers indicate primary discussions of a topic. *Italicized* page numbers indicate illustrations.

A

AAA (authentication, authorization, and accounting), 360, **363–364**, **367–368**
accounting in, **365**, **374–376**
authentication in, **364**, **368–370**
authorization in, **364–365**, **370–373**
defined, 388
aaa accounting command command, 375
aaa accounting connection command, 375
aaa accounting exec command, 368–369, 375
aaa accounting function command, 375–376
aaa accounting network command, 375
aaa accounting system command, 375
aaa authentication command, 366
aaa authentication enable command, 368–369
aaa authentication login command, 368–369
aaa authentication ppp user command, 367
aaa authorization command, 366
aaa authorization commands command, 373
aaa authorization config-commands command, 373
aaa authorization exec command, 373
aaa authorization function command, 374
aaa authorization network command, 373
aaa authorization network tacacs+ command, 367
aaa authorization reverse-access command, 373
aaa new-model command, 368–369
aarp option, 303

access control
components in, **361–363**
defined, 388
access-list command, 239, 338, 340
access lists
DDR with, **179–180**
defined, 388
access methods, 388
access modes in routers, **365–367**
access rates
defined, 388
in Frame Relay performance, **260**
access servers, 362
configuring, **82**
for dedicated and interactive PPP, **83**
for local devices, **83–89**, *84–85*, *87*, *90*
defined, 388
accounting, 360
configuring, **374–376**
defined, 388
ACK (acknowledgments), 388
Active connection state in LMI, 258
active number in WFQ, 298
Address field
in LAPD, **157–158**, *157*
in PPP, **80**
Address Extension field, 158
address mapping, 388
address masks, 388
address resolution, 388
Address Resolution Protocol (ARP), 389
administrative distance, 388
ADSL (Asymmetric Digital Subscriber Line), 9, **214–215**
Advanced Connection Settings dialog box, 132, *132*
Advanced Encryption Standard (AES), 236

Advanced options
    for allowed network protocols, **133**
    for dial-up connection clients, **130–131**
Advanced Research Projects Agency
        (ARPA), 326
AES (Advanced Encryption Standard), 236
AHs (Authentication Headers), 236
ALERTING messages, 164
algorithms, 388
Allowed Network Protocols section, **133**
alternate mark inversion (AMI), 388
Always On/Dynamic ISDN (AO/DI), 152
American Standard Code for Information
        Interchange (ASCII), 389
AMI (alternate mark inversion), 388
analog connections
    cabling in, **26–27**
    defined, 388
    with modems, 50
analog dial-up, 389
analog ports, 32
analog transmissions, 389
ANI (Automatic Number Identification), 153
ANSI LMI version, 258
AO/DI (Always On/Dynamic ISDN), 152
apollo option, 303
appletalk option, 303
Application Layer, 389
applications in WAN protocol selection,
        20–21
arap command, 365
Architecture for Voice, Video, and
        Integrated Data (AVVID), 29
ARP (Address Resolution Protocol), 389
arp option, 304
ARPA (Advanced Research Projects
        Agency), 326
ASCII (American Standard Code for
        Information Interchange), 389
Asymmetric Digital Subscriber Line
        (ADSL), 9, **214–215**
async dynamic address command, 85

async mode dedicated command, 83
async mode interactive command, 83
async packet-mode connections, 366
asynchronous connections, 50
    cabling in, **26–27**
    configuring, **58–65**
    defined, 389
    dial-up
        characteristics of, **16–22**
        uses for, **4–5**
    exam essentials, **66–67**
    hands-on labs, **68–70**
    key terms, **67**
    modems for, **50–53**, *51*
        configuring, **58–65**
        modulation standards for, **55–57**
        signaling and cabling, **53**
    review questions, **71–76**
    summary, **65–66**
    written lab, **68**, **74**
asynchronous transmissions, 389
AT (attention) commands, 59, **62–63**
ATM (Asynchronous Transfer Mode), 4
    as encapsulation type, **14**
    uses for, **11**
    for VPNs, 240
Authenticate-Request packets,
        172–173, *172*
authentication, 360
    configuring, **368–370**
    defined, 389
    in ISDN, **171**
        CHAP, **173–175**, *173*, *175*
        PAP, **171–173**, *172*
    in PPP, **91–93**, *91–93*
authentication, authorization, and
        accounting (AAA), 360, **363–364**,
        367–368
    accounting in, 365, **374–376**
    authentication in, **364**, **368–370**
    authorization in, **364–365**, **370–373**
    defined, 388

Authentication Headers (AHs), 236
authorization, 360
    configuring, **370–373**
    defined, 389
autodiscovery function, 58
automatic modem configuration, **58**
    commands for, **59–61**
    verifying and troubleshooting, **61–62**
Automatic Number Identification
    (ANI), 153
autoselect command, 82
auxiliary ports, 389
availability in WAN protocol selection, **17**
AVVID (Architecture for Voice, Video,
    and Integrated Data), 29

B

B (bearer) channels
    defined, 389
    in ISDN, 150
B8ZS (binary 8-zero substitution) code, 389
backup delay command, 185
backup interface bri0 command, 182
backup load command, 190–191
Backward Explicit Congestion Notification
    (BECN) bit
    defined, 390
    in Frame Relay, 261–262, 274
bandwidth
    defined, 389
    in DSL, **214–215**
    in WAN protocol selection, **17–18**
Bandwidth on Demand (BoD)
    configuring, **190–191**
    defined, 390
Basic Rate Interface (BRI), 5, **150–152**, *151*
    cabling in, 27
    defined, 390
    hands-on lab for, **200–203**, *200*
    packet-mode connections, 366

BASIC switch types, 152
baud
    in asynchronous modem connections, 61
    defined, 389
bearer (B) channels
    defined, 389
    in ISDN, 150
Bearer Capability output, 165
bearer services
    defined, 390
    in Frame Relay, 252
BECN (Backward Explicit Congestion
    Notification) bit
    defined, 390
    in Frame Relay, 261–262, 274
binary 8-zero substitution (B8ZS) code, 389
binary numbering, 390
bit stuffing, 79
BoD (Bandwidth on Demand)
    configuring, **190–191**
    defined, 390
bonding, 33
BRI (Basic Rate Interface), 5, **150–152**, *151*
    cabling in, **27**
    defined, 390
    hands-on lab for, **200–203**, *200*
    packet-mode connections, 366
BRI0 B1 LED, 37, *37*
BRI0 B2 LED, 37, *37*
Bridge-Group Virtual Interface (BVI), 220
bridge option in queuing, 304
broadcasts, 390
brute force attacks
    CiscoSecure for, 363
    defined, 390
bstun option, 304
buffers, 390
bursting in Frame Relay, **260–261**, *261*, 276
BVI (Bridge-Group Virtual Interface), 220
byte-count command, 305
byte-count queues, **305–307**

C

&C AT command, 63

C/R (Command/Response) field, 158

cable modems, 10–11, 232–233, *233*

characteristics of, 16–22

Cisco Cable Manager, 235

Cisco product line, 234–235

defined, 390

DOCSIS for, 233–234

exam essentials, 240–241

hands-on lab, 242–243, 248–249

key terms, 241

review questions, 244–247, 250

summary, 240–241

written lab, 242, 247

cabling and assembling WANs, 26

company site equipment
identification, 28

internetworking and interface options,
26–28

verifying network installations, 35–39,
36–38

CALL PROCEEDING messages, 164

Call Reference Value (CRV)
information, 159

call setup and teardown in ISDN,
163–166, *164*

callbacks, PPP, 93–97, 400

Called Number Identification, 153

Called Party Number output, 166

Calling Line ID (CLID), 153

Callref output, 165

CAR (Committed Access Rate)
queuing, 310

Carrier Detect (CD) signal
defined, 390

in DTE to DCE signaling, 54

carrier operations (CO), 391

catalyst switch configuration, 369–370

CBWFQ (Class-Based Weighted Fair
Queuing), 309

CCM (Cisco Cable Manager), 235

CD (Carrier Detect) signal
defined, 390

in DTE to DCE signaling, 54

CDMA (code division multiple access), 12

CDP (Cisco Discovery Protocol)
defined, 390

operation of, 105

cdp option in queuing, 304

cellular WAN connections, 11–13

central office (CO), 391

central sites, 29

Cisco 3600 platform, 29–30

Cisco 3700 platform, 30

Cisco 7000/7200/7500 platforms, 30

Cisco AS5x00 platform, 30

verifying, 35–37, *36*

CH1 LED, 38, *38*

CH1 RXD LED, 38, *38*

CH1 TXD LED, 38, *38*

CH2 LED, 38, *38*

CH2 RXD LED, 38, *38*

CH2 TXD LED, 38, *38*

Challenge Handshake Authentication
Protocol (CHAP)
defined, 391

in ISDN, **173–175**, *173*, *175*

in PPP, 81, **92–93**

challenges, 390

channel-group command, 193

Channel ID output, 166

Channel Service Units (CSUs), 392

Channel type parameter, 192

channelized E-1
configuring, **194–195**

defined, 390

channelized T-1, 27

configuring, **192–194**

defined, 391

CHAP (Challenge Authentication
Protocol)
defined, 391

in ISDN, **173–175**, *173*, *175*
in PPP, 81, **92–93**
chap pap keyword, 92
character-mode connections
    commands for, **365–366**
    defined, 391
checksums
    defined, 391
    FCS fields for, 82
CIFS (Common Internet File System), 310
CIR (Committed Information Rate)
    defined, 391
    in Frame Relay, **6–7**, **260**, **276–277**
circuit switching, 391
Cisco Discovery Protocol (CDP)
    defined, 390
    operation of, 105
Cisco IOS software, 391
cisco option in Frame Relay, 259
Cisco products, **23–24**
    700 series, **32**, **346–347**
    766 routers, **38–39**, *38*
    800 series, **34**
    1000 series, **35**
    1600 platform, **31**, **37**, *37*
    1700 platform, **31**
    2500 platform, **31**
    2600xM platform, **31**
    3600 platform, **29–30**
    3640 routers, **36–37**, *36*
    3700 platform, **30**
    7000/7200/7500 platforms, **30**
    AS5x00 platform, **30**
    Cisco Cable Manager, **235**
    CiscoSecure, **362–363**
    fixed interface routers, **24–25**
    modular interface routers, **25**
    selection tools for, **25–26**
Cisco standard for LMI, 258
CiscoSecure product, **362–363**
Class A networks, 391

Class B networks, 391
Class-Based Weighted Fair Queuing
    (CBWFQ), **309**
Class C networks, 391
clear ip nat translation command, 343
clear ip nat translation inside command, 343
clear ip nat translation outside
    command, 343
Clear To Send (CTS) wire, 54
clearing NAT translation entries, **343**
CLI (Command Line Interface), 391
CLID (Calling Line ID), 153
clients
    in dial-up connections, **124**
        Dial-Up Networking for,
            124–125, *125*
        Make New Connection Wizard for,
            125–127, *125–127*
        properties for, **127–134**, *128–130*,
            132, 134–135
    in remote access, 361
clock rate command, 273
clocking
    for asynchronous connections, 50–51
    defined, 391
CO (carrier operations), 391
CO (central office), 391
COAX (coaxial cable), 232, *233*
code division multiple access (CDMA), 12
Code field, 173–175, *173*
Command accounting type, 374
command command for character-mode
    connections, 365
Command Line Interface (CLI), 391
Command/Response (C/R) field, 158
Committed Access Rate (CAR)
    queuing, **310**
Committed Information Rate (CIR)
    defined, 391
    in Frame Relay, **6–7**, **260**, **276–277**
committed rate measurement interval, 260

Common Internet File System
   (CIFS), 310
company site equipment identification, **28**
   central sites, **29–30**
   remote branches, **31**
   telecommuter, **32**
compress command, 98
Compressed Serial Line Internet Protocol
   (CSLIP), 129
compressedtcp option, 304
compression, **310–311**, *311*
   in Cisco 700 platform, 33
   considerations for, **313**
   defined, 391
   exam essentials, **315–316**
   hands-on lab, **317–318**, *317*
   key terms, **316**
   link, **312–313**
   in modulation, **56–57**
   payload, 312
   PPP, **97–99**
   review questions, **319–324**
   status of, **314**
   summary, **314–315**
   TCP header, **311–312**
   written lab, **316**, **322**
config-map-class command, 275
configuring
   AAA
      accounting, **374–376**
      authentication, **368–370**
      authorization, **370–373**
   asynchronous modem connections, 58
      automatic, **58–62**
      manual, **62–65**
   BoD, **190–191**
   channelized T1/E1, **192–195**
   DDR, **176–179**
   dial-up connection clients
      Dial-Up Networking for,
         124–125, *125*

Make New Connection Wizard for,
      125–127, *125–127*
   properties for, **127–134**, *128–130*,
      132, 134–135
DSL, **218–220**
dynamic addressing, **84–87**, *84–85, 87*
Frame Relay, **259**
IPSec, **237–239**
ISDN, **166–167**
   dialer interface, **169–171**, **177**
   legacy interface, **167–169**
multilink, **99–101**, *99–101*
NAT, **336–341**
PAT, **345–347**
queuing
   custom, **302–307**
   priority, **299–300**
   Weighted Fair Queuing, **296**
traffic shaping, **275–276**
conflict logging, 86
congestion control in Frame Relay,
   260–263, *261*
congestive-discard-threshold parameter, 296
CONNECT messages, 164
CONNECT ACKNOWLEDGE
   messages, 164
Connection accounting type, 374
connection command, 365
connection properties for dial-up clients,
   127–128
   General tab, **128**, *128*
   Multilink tab, **134**, *135*
   Scripting tab, **134**, *134*
   Server Types tab, **128–133**, *129–130*
connections, asynchronous. *See*
   asynchronous connections
console ports, 392
contention in DSL, **214–215**
Control field
   in LAPD, *157*, **158–159**
   in PPP, 80

convergence with modems, 52
conversations in WFQ, **295–296**
costs in WAN protocol selection, **18–19**
CPE (Customer Premises Equipment), 256
CPU cycles in compression, 313
CPU utilization, 98
CRC (cyclic redundancy check)
    defined, 392
    in LAPD, 160
CRV (Call Reference Value)
    information, 159
crypto IPSec transform-set command, 238
crypto isakmp key command, 238
crypto isakmp policy command, 237
crypto map command, 238–239
CSLIP (Compressed Serial Line Internet
    Protocol), 129
CSUs (Channel Service Units), 392
CTS (Clear To Send) wire, 54
custom option in WFQ, 297
custom queuing, 292, **301–302**, *302*
    configuring, **302–307**
    defined, 392
Customer Premises Equipment (CPE), 256
cyclic redundancy check (CRC)
    defined, 392
    in LAPD, 160

D

D (data) channels
    defined, 392
    in ISDN, 150
&D AT command, 63
Data Communications Equipment (DCE)
    defined, 392
    with DTE connections, 51, *51*, 54
    in Frame Relay, 253
    modems as, 50
data compression. *See* compression

Data Encryption Standard (DES), 237
data exchange phase in PVCs, 255
Data field in CHAP packets, 173, *173*
data link connection identifiers (DLCIs)
    defined, 393
    in Frame Relay, **255–258**, *256–257*
    mapping, **256–258**, *257*
Data Link Layer, 392
Data Over Cable Service Interface
    Specification (DOCSIS), **233–234**
Data Service Units (DSUs), 393
Data Set Ready (DSR) circuits, 393
Data Terminal Equipment (DTE)
    with DCE connections, 51, *51*, 54
    defined, 393
    in Frame Relay, 253
    locking speed of, **135–136**, *136*
    routers as, 50
data terminal ready (DTR) circuits
    defined, 393
    in DTE to DCE signaling, 54
DCE (Data Communications Equipment)
    defined, 392
    with DTE connections, 51, *51*, 54
    in Frame Relay, 253
    modems as, 50
DDR (dial-on-demand routing), **175–176**
    with access lists, **179–180**
    configuring, **176–179**
    defined, 392
    hands-on lab, **197–200**, *198*
    optional commands in, **179**
    for verifying ISDN operations, **180**
DE (Discard Eligibility), 392
DE (Discard Eligibility) bits
    defined, 392
    in Frame Relay bursting, 260
debug dialer command, 180
debug frame-relay lmi Command,
    269–270
debug frame-relay packet command, 270

debug ip nat command, 342
debug isdn q921 command, **160–162**, 180
debug isdn q931 command, **164–166**, 180
debug ppp authentication command, **101–102**, 175
debug ppp negotiation command, **102–106**
debug ppp packet command, **106–109**
decnet option, 304
decnet_node option, 304
decnet_router-l1 option, 304
decnet_router-l2 option, 304
dedicated PPP, **83**
default option
    in custom queuing, 303
    in PAT, 345
default routes, 392
delays
    defined, 392
    in NAT, 330
Deleted connection state in LMI, 258
demodulation, 393
denial-of-service (DoS) attacks
    dealing with, 363
    defined, 393
DES (Data Encryption Standard), 237
destination addresses, 393
DHCP (Dynamic Host Configuration Protocol), **84–87**, *87*
    in Cisco 700 platform, 33
    lease length in, **88–89**, *90*
    operation of, **87–88**
dial backup, **181**, *181*
    defined, 393
    setting up, **181–183**
    testing, **183–190**
dial-on-demand routing (DDR), **175–176**
    with access lists, **179–180**
    configuring, **176–179**
    defined, 392
    hands-on labs, **197–200**, *198*
    optional commands in, **179**
    for verifying ISDN operations, **180**

Dial-up Connection Properties dialog box, 87, *87*
dial-up networking
    configuring clients, **124**
        Dial-Up Networking for, **124–125**, *125*
        Make New Connection Wizard for, **125–127**, *125–127*
        properties for, **127–134**, *128–130*, *132*, *134–135*
    uses for, **122–123**
    verifying, **137**, *137*
    with Windows 95/98, **123**
Dial-Up Networking dialog box, 124–125, *125*
Dial-Up Networking Wizard, 125
dialer-group command, 177, 179, 190
dialer hold-queue command, 179, 190
dialer idle-timeout command, 179
dialer information, **177**
dialer interface in ISDN configuration, **169–171**
dialer-list command, 176–177, 179, 190
dialer-list 1 protocol ip permit command, 171
dialer load-threshold command, 179
dialer map command, 96–97, 167–169, 177
dialer pool-member command, 170–171
dialer profiles, 185
dialer string command, 169–170, 177
Differentiated Services Code Point (DSCP), 309
digital connections in DTE, 50
Digital Subscriber Line. *See* DSL (Digital Subscriber Line)
Digital Subscriber Line Access Multiplexer (DSLAM), 212
directory numbers (DNs), 151
Discard Eligibility (DE), 392

Discard Eligibility (DE) bits
  defined, 392
  in Frame Relay bursting, 260
Discard Eligibility lists, 262
DISCONNECT messages, 164, 166
distributed compression process, 99
DLCIs (data link connection identifiers)
  defined, 393
  in Frame Relay, **255–258**, *256–257*
  mapping, **256–258**, *257*
dlsw option, 304
DNs (directory numbers), 151
DNS (Domain Name Server), 393
DOCSIS (Data Over Cable Service
    Interface Specification), **233–234**
DoS (denial-of-service) attacks
  dealing with, 363
  defined, 393
downstream traffic with cable modems, 10
DSCP (Differentiated Services Code
    Point), 309
DSL (Digital Subscriber Line), **7–10**, *8*,
    212–213, *213*
  ADSL, **214–215**
  characteristics of, **16–22**
  configuring, **218–220**
  defined, 393
  exam essentials, **222**
  G.lite, **215–216**
  hands-on lab, **223**, **228**
  HDSL, **216**
  ISDN DSL, **216**
  key terms, **223**
  review questions, **224–227**, **229**
  routers for, **217–218**
  SDSL, **216**
  summary, **221–222**
  troubleshooting, **220–221**
  type summary, **217**
  variations of, **213–214**
  VDSL, **216**
  written lab, **223**, **228**

DSLAM (Digital Subscriber Line Access
    Multiplexer), 212
DSR (Data Set Ready) circuits, 393
DSUs (Data Service Units), 393
DTE (Data Terminal Equipment)
  with DCE connections, 51, *51*, 54
  defined, 393
  in Frame Relay, 253
  locking speed of, **135–136**, *136*
  routers as, 50
DTR (data terminal ready) circuits
  defined, 393
  in DTE to DCE signaling, 54
dynamic addressing
  configuring, **84–87**, *84–85*, *87*
  in PPP, **83–84**
Dynamic Host Configuration Protocol
    (DHCP), **84–87**, *87*
  in Cisco 700 platform, 33
  lease length in, **88–89**, *90*
  operation of, **87–88**
Dynamic Multiple Encapsulation, 192
dynamic NAT, 329, **338–339**
dynamic-queues parameter, 296

E

E-1 services, **28**
  capacity of, 153
  configuring, **194–195**
  defined, 393
e-mail, dial-up networking for, 122
E protocols in ISDN, 156
E reference points, 156
Edit Extra Device dialog box, 134, *135*
egress in Frame Relay, 253
802.11 standards, **11–12**
802.1q standard, 239
EIR (Excess Information Rate), 274
enable command, 365
Enable Software Compression option, 131

Encapsulating Security Payload (ESP), 236
encapsulation
    defined, 393
    WAN protocols. *See* WANs (wide area
      networks)
encapsulation command, 170
encapsulation frame-relay command, 259
encapsulation ppp command, 91, 100
encryption
    in compression, 313
    defined, 393
end-to-end addresses in NAT, 330
end-to-end reachability in PAT, 344
Enhanced Terminal Access Controller
    Access Control System (TACACS+)
      protocol
    in authentication, 361
    configuration file, 371–373
    configuring, **379**
    defined, 404
error correction
    defined, 394
    in modulation, **57**
ESF (Extended Super Frame), 394
ESP (Encapsulating Security Payload), 236
ET (Exchange Termination), 155
Ethernet, 32
exam essentials
    asynchronous connections, **66–67**
    cable modems, **240–241**
    DSL, **222**
    Frame Relay, **278**
    ISDN, **195–196**
    Microsoft Windows 95/98/2000/XP,
      138–139
    NAT and PAT, **348–349**
    PPP, **110–111**
    queuing and compression, **315–316**
    remote access, **39–40**
    security, **377–378**
    VPNs, **240–241**
Excess Information Rate (EIR), 274

Exchange Termination (ET), 155
EXEC accounting type, 374
exec command, 365
extended IP access lists, 394
Extended Super Frame (ESF), 394
extended translation entries, 328
EZ-ISDN switch types, 152

F

&F AT command, 63
fair option, 297
fair-queue command, 296–297
fast paths, 342
FCS (Frame Check Sequence) field, **82**
FECN (Forward Explicit Congestion
    Notification) bits
    defined, 394
    in Frame Relay, 261–262
Fiber Optics Transmission Systems
    (FOTS), 151
file synchronization, 122
firewalls, 394
fixed interface routers, **24–25**
Flag field
    in LAPD, 157, *157*
    in PPP, **79**
Flash memory, 394
flow control, 394
flowcontrol command, 64
Forward Explicit Congestion Notification
    (FECN) bits
    defined, 394
    in Frame Relay, 261–262
FOTS (Fiber Optics Transmission
    Systems), 151
fragments keyword, 304
Frame Check Sequence (FCS) field, **82**
frame-relay adaptive-shaping becn
    command, 275
frame-relay class name command, 276

frame-relay custom-queue-list number command, 275
frame-relay de-group command, 262–263
frame-relay de-list command, 262
frame-relay intf-type command, 272–273
frame-relay lmi type command, 272
frame-relay map command, 257–258
frame-relay priority-group number command, 275
Frame Relay protocol, **6**, **16**, **252–253**
  cabling in, **28**
  characteristics of, **16–22**
  configuring, **259**
  congestion control in, **260–263**, *261*
  defined, 394
  DLCIs in, **255–258**, *256–257*
  exam essentials, **278**
  hands-on labs, **280**, *280*
    subinterfaces, **280–281**
    traffic shaping, **282**
  history of, **253**
  key terms, **279**
  LMI for, **258–259**, *259*
  performance of, **260–262**, *261*
  point-to-point and multipoint interfaces in, **263–266**
  review questions, **283–286**, **289–290**
  summary, **277–278**
  switching in, **270–273**, *271*, 394
  traffic shaping in, **274–277**
  verifying, **266–270**
  virtual circuits in, **253–255**, *254*
  for VPNs, **240**
  written lab, **279–280**, **287–288**
frame-relay switching command, 273
frame-relay traffic-rate average command, 275
frame-relay traffic-shaping command, 276
Frame type parameter, 192
frames, 394
framing, 394
Framing parameter, 194

frequency, 394
front panel LEDs
  Cisco 766 routers, **38–39**, *38*
  Cisco 1600 routers, **37**, *37*
  Cisco 3640 routers, **36–37**, *36*
ftp option, 345
function groups in ISDN, **154–155**, *154*

G

G.lite, **215–216**
General tab for dial-up clients, **128**, *128*
Generic Router Encapsulation (GRE), 239
global IP addresses in NAT, 328
Global System for Mobile Communications (GSM), 12
GND wire, 54
GRE (Generic Router Encapsulation), 239
group-async packet-mode connections, 366
group command, 237
Group of Four, 394
GSM (Global System for Mobile Communications), 12
gt keyword, 304

H

hands-on labs
  asynchronous connections, **68–70**
  cable modems, **242–243**, **248–249**
  DSL, **223**, **228**
  Frame Relay, **280**, *280*
    subinterfaces, **280–281**
    traffic shaping, **282**
  ISDN, **197**
    DDR, **197–200**, *198*
    PRI and BRI, **200–203**, *200*
  NAT and PAT, **350–351**

PPP, 112–113
queuing and compression, **317–318**, *317*
security, **379**
VPNs, **242–243**, **248–249**
handshakes, 394
hash md command, 237
HCL (hardware compatibility list), 126
HDLC (High-Level Data Link Control)
characteristics of, **14**
defined, 395
HDSL (high bit-rate DSL), 9, **216**
helper addresses
defined, 395
IP, 86
HFC (Hybrid Fiber/COAX) devices,
232, *233*
high bit-rate DSL (HDSL), 9, **216**
High-Level Data Link Control (HDLC)
characteristics of, **14**
defined, 395
host addresses, 395
hotelling installations, 89
http option, 345
Hybrid Fiber/COAX (HFC) devices,
232, *233*

I

I protocols in ISDN, 156
IARP (Inverse ARP)
defined, 395
for DLCI mapping, 258
ICMP (Internet Control Message
Protocol), 395
IDASSN output, 162
IDCKRP output, 162
IDCKRQ output, 161, 163
Identifier field, 173–175, *173*
idle phase in PVCs, 255
IDREM output, 162
IDREQ output, 162–163

IDSL (ISDN-based DSL), 9
ietf option, 259
IKE (Internet Key Exchange), 236
Inactive connection state in LMI, 258
INFOc output, 162
Information field
in LAPD, *157*, **159–160**
in PPP, 82
Information Transfer format, 158
ingress in Frame Relay, 253
inside global IP addresses in NAT, 328
configuring, **338–339**
overloading, **333–334**, *333*
inside local IP addresses in NAT
translating, **332–333**, *332*
working with, 327
inside networks in NAT, 327
Integrated Routing and Bridging
(IRB), 220
Integrated Services Digital Network. *See*
ISDN (Integrated Services Digital
Network)
interactive PPP, **83**
interesting traffic in DDR, **176–177**
interface addressing options for local
devices, **83**
DHCP lease length, **88–89**, *90*
DHCP operation, **87–88**
dynamic addressing, **84–87**, *84–85*, *87*
interface command, 265
interface async16 ppp authentication
command, 367
interface cable-modem0 command, 239
interface dialer command, 185
interface Ethernet0 command, 238
interface option in custom queuing, 303
International Telecommunications
Union-Telecommunication (ITU-T)
group
defined, 396
for LMI, 258
Internet, 395

Internet Control Message Protocol
  (ICMP), 395
Internet Key Exchange (IKE), 236
Internet Protocol (IP), 395
internets, 395
Internetwork Packet Exchange (IPX)
    protocol
  in Cisco 700 platform, 33
  defined, 396
internetworking and interface options, **26**
  asynchronous and analog connections,
    26–27
  Frame Relay, **28**
  ISDN, **27–28**
internetworks, 395
intruder detection
  for brute force attacks, 363
  defined, 395
Inverse Address Resolution Protocol
    (Inverse ARP)
  defined, 395
  for DLCI mapping, 258
IP (Internet Protocol), 395
ip address command
  in IPSec, 238
  in ISDN, 170
IP addresses, **85–87**
  defined, 395
  DHCP for, **84–87**, *87*
    lease length in, **88–89**, *90*
    operation of, **87–88**
  limitations of, 326
  NAT for. *See* NAT (Network Address
    Translation)
IP Control Protocol (IPCP), 396
ip dhcp database command, 86
ip dhcp excluded-address low-address
    command, 86
ip dhcp-server command, 86
ip nat inside command, 337, 341
ip nat inside source list command, 340

ip nat inside source static
    command, 337
ip nat outside command, 337, 341
ip nat outside source list command, 341
ip nat pool command, **338–339**
ip nat pool insidepool command, 340
ip nat pool outsidepool command, 340
ip option in queuing, 304
IP routing in Cisco 700 platform, 33
ip tcp header-compression command,
    98, 312
IP unnumbered options, **83**
IPCP (IP Control Protocol), 396
IPSec, **235–236**
  configuring, **237–239**
  for VPNs, 240
IPX (Internetwork Packet Exchange)
    protocol
  in Cisco 700 platform, 33
  defined, 396
IPXCP (IPX Control Protocol), 396
IRB (Integrated Routing and
    Bridging), 220
ISDN (Integrated Services Digital
    Network), **5**
  authentication in, **171**
    CHAP, **173–175**, *173*, *175*
    PAP, **171–173**, *172*
  Bandwidth on Demand, **190–191**
  BRI, **5**, **150–152**, *151*
    cabling in, **27**
    defined, 390
    hands-on lab for, **200–203**, *200*
    packet-mode connections, 366
  call setup and teardown in,
    163–166, *164*
  channelized T-1/E-1, **192–195**
  characteristics of, **16–22**
  configuring, **166–167**
    dialer interface, **169–171**, 177
    legacy interface, **167–169**

DDR in. *See* DDR (dial-on-demand routing)
defined, **396**
dial backup, **181**, *181*
   setting up, **181–183**
   testing, **183–190**
exam essentials, **195–196**
function groups, **154–155**, *154*
hands-on labs, **197**
   DDR, **197–200**, *198*
   PRI and BRI, **200–203**, *200*
key terms, **196**
LAPD frames in, **157–160**, *157*, *159*
Layer 2 negotiation in, **160–163**
line options for, **150–151**
   Basic BRI, *151*
   BRI, **151–152**
   PRI, **153**
ordering, **166–167**
PRI, **5**, **150**, **153**
   cabling in, **27–28**
   configuring, **192–194**
   defined, **400**
   hands-on labs, **200–203**, *200*
   packet-mode connections, **366**
protocols for, **156–157**
reference points, **155–156**, *155*
review questions, **204–207**, **209–210**
summary, **195**
written lab, **197**, **207–208**
ISDN-based DSL (IDSL), **9**, **216**
isdn disconnect interface command, 180
ISDN interface in Cisco 700 platform, 32
ITU-T (International Telecommunications Union-Telecommunication) group
   defined, **396**
   for LMI, 258

K

key terms
   asynchronous connections, **67**

cable modems, **241**
DSL, **223**
Frame Relay, **279**
ISDN, **196**
Microsoft Windows *95/98/2000/XP*, **139**
NAT and PAT, **349**
PPP, **111**
queuing and compression, **316**
remote access, **41**
security, **378**
VPNs, **241**
Keypad facility output, 166
known values in modem connections, 62

L

L1 AT command, 63
L2TP (Layer 2 Tunneling Protocol), 240
LAN LED, 38, *38*
LAN activity LED, 37, *37*
LAN collision LED, 37, *37*
LAN RXD LED, 38, *38*
LAN TXD LED, 38, *38*
LAPB (Link Accessed Procedure, Balanced) protocol, 396
LAPD (Link Access Procedure, Data) protocol
   defined, **396**
   frames in, **157–160**, *157*, *159*
last mile, 13
latency
   defined, **396**
   in NAT, 330
launching terminal windows, **136–137**, *136*
Layer 2 negotiation, **160–163**
Layer 2 Tunneling Protocol (L2TP), 240
LCP (Link Control Protocol)
   defined, **396**
   in PPP, 79
leased lines, **7**
   cable modems, **10–11**
   characteristics of, **16–22**

defined, 396
Digital Subscriber Line, **7–10**, *8*
leases in DHCP, **88–89**, *90*
LEDs
Cisco 766 routers, **38–39**, *38*
Cisco 1600 routers, 37, *37*
Cisco 3640 routers, **36–37**, *36*
Legacy DDR Hub configuration, 175
Legacy DDR Spoke configuration, 175
legacy interface in ISDN configuration,
167–169
Length information
in CHAP packets, 173, *173*, 175
in LAPD, 159
lifetime command, 238
limit option, 305
line command, 64–65
LINE LED, 38, *38*
Linecode parameter
in E-1, 194
in PRI, 192
Link Access Procedure, Data (LAPD)
protocol
defined, 396
frames in, **157–160**, *157*, *159*
Link Accessed Procedure, Balanced (LAPB)
protocol, 396
link compression
defined, 396
working with, **312–313**
Link Control Protocol (LCP)
defined, 396
in PPP, 79
list keyword, 304
llc2 option, 304
LLQ (low latency queuing), **309**
LMI (Local Management Interface)
defined, 396
for Frame Relay, **258–259**, *259*
load-threshold command, 178
local devices, interface addressing options
for, **83–89**, *84–85*, *87*, *90*

local IP addresses in NAT, 327–328
local loops, 396
Local Management Interface (LMI)
defined, 396
for Frame Relay, **258–259**, *259*
local significance in virtual circuits, 254
Local Termination (LT), 155
locking DTE speed, **135–136**, *136*
log files for dial-up clients, **131–133**
Log On to Network option, 131
login command
for asynchronous routers, 64
for character-mode connections, 365
low latency queuing (LLQ), **309**
lowest-custom option, 303
LT (Local Termination), 155
lt keyword, 304
LZW algorithm
for compression, 57
defined, 396

M

MAC addresses, 396
Make New Connection Wizard, **125–127**,
125–127
manageability in WAN protocol selection,
19–20
management in Cisco 700 platform, 33
Mandatory and Optional Information
Elements field, 160
manual modem configuration, **62–65**
map-class frame-relay command, 275
mapping
address, 388
DLCIs, **256–258**, *257*
in NAT, 329
match address command, 238
match-host parameter, 339
max active number, 298
max total number, 298

maximum rate, 397
maximum transmission units (MTUs), 397
media converters, 54
memory for compression, 313
Message field, 175
Message Type information, 160
Microsoft Point-to-Point Compression
    (MPPC), 98, 311
Microsoft Windows 95/98/2000/XP, 121
    dial-up networking. *See* dial-up
        networking
    exam essentials, **138–139**
    key terms, **139**
    launching terminal windows,
        136–137, *136*
    locking DTE speed, **135–136**, *136*
    review questions, **140–145**
    summary, **137–138**
    verifying dial-Up connections, **137**, *137*
    written lab, **139**, **143**
MMP (Multichassis Multilink Protocol)
    defined, 397
    purpose of, 100, *101*
MO AT command, 63
modem command, 64
modem autoconfigure discovery
    command, **61**
modem autoconfigure type command, **59–60**
modem compression, 313
modem eliminators, 397
modem input command, 62
Modem Properties dialog box, 136, *136*
modemcap database, 59, 397
modemcap edit command, **60–61**
modems
    for asynchronous communication,
        50–53, *51*
        configuring, **58–65**
        modulation standards for, **55–57**
        signaling and cabling, 53
    cable. *See* cable modems
    defined, 397

modular interface routers, **25**
modulation
    defined, 397
    standards for, **55–56**
        data compression, **56–57**
        error correction, **57**
monitoring PAT, **347–348**
MP (Multilink Protocol), 100
MP (Multilink Protocol) bonding
    in Cisco 700 platform, 33
    defined, 397
MPLS (Multi Protocol Label Switching)
    for VPNs, 240
    for WAN services, 22
MPP (Multilink Multipoint Protocol), 134
MPPC (Microsoft Point-to-Point
    Compression), 98, 311
MTUs (maximum transmission
    units), 397
Multi Protocol Label Switching (MPLS)
    for VPNs, 240
    for WAN services, 22
Multichassis Multilink Protocol (MMP)
    defined, 397
    purpose of, 100, *101*
multilink in PPP, **99–101**, *99–101*
Multilink Multipoint Protocol
    (MPP), 134
Multilink Protocol (MP), 100
Multilink Protocol (MP) bonding
    in Cisco 700 platform, 33
    defined, 397
Multilink tab, **134**, *135*
multinational support, 33
multipoint interfaces, **263–266**, *264*

N

NAK (negative acknowledgments), 397
Name field in CHAP packets, 174
nasi command, 365

NAT (Network Address Translation),
326–327
advantages of, **329**
clearing translation entries in, **343**
configuring, **336–341**
defined, 397
disadvantages of, **330**
exam essentials, **348–349**
hands-on lab, **350–351**
IPSec with, 236
key terms, **349**
operation of, **328–329**, *328*
overlapping networks in, **335–336**
overloading inside global addresses in,
333–334, *333*
review questions, **352–355, 357–358**
summary, **348**
TCP load distribution in, **334–335**, *335*
terminology, **327–328**
traffic types in, **330–331**
translating inside local addresses in,
332–333, *332*
troubleshooting, **342–343**
verifying, **341–342**
written lab, **349–350, 356**
NBAR (Network-Based Application
Recognition), 308
NCPs (Network Control Protocols), 79
negative acknowledgments (NAK), 397
Network accounting type, 374
Network Activity LED, 36, *36*
Network Address Translation. *See* NAT
(Network Address Translation)
network addresses, 397
Network-Based Application Recognition
(NBAR), 308
Network Control Protocols (NCPs), 79
network installations, **35**
central site, **35–37**, *36*
remote branch, **37**, *37*
telecommuter, **38–39**, *38*
network interface cards (NICs), 398

Network Layer, 397
Network Termination type 1 (NT1)
in BRI, 154
defined, 398
Network Termination type 2 (NT2)
in BRI, 155
defined, 398
Next Level Communications systems, 8
NICs (network interface cards), 398
no async mode command, 83
no ip dhcp conflict logging command, 86
no ip forward-protocol command, 86
no modemcap edit command, 61
nonvolatile RAM (NVRAM), 398
NRN server type, 129
NT1 (Network Termination type 1)
in BRI, 154
defined, 398
NT1 LED, 38, *38*
NT2 (Network Termination type 2)
in BRI, 155
defined, 398
NTT switch types, 152
NVRAM (nonvolatile RAM), 398

O

OAM (Operation, Administration, and
Management) cells, 219
OC (Optical Carrier) protocols, 398
octets, 398
off option in PAT, 345
one-time challenge tokens
defined, 398
for passwords, 362
ones density signaling, 398
Operation, Administration, and
Management (OAM) cells, 219
Optical Carrier (OC) protocols, 398
Options tab for terminal windows,
136–137, *136*

OSI Reference Model, 398
out-of-band signaling, 398
outside global IP addresses in NAT, 328
outside local IP addresses in NAT, 328
outside networks in NAT, 327
outsourcing, **24, 34**
overlapping address translation,
      340–341
overlapping networks in NAT operations,
      335–336
overloading inside global addresses,
      333–334, *333*
oversubscription
      in DSL, **214–215**
      in Frame Relay, 262

P

packet assembler/disassembler (PAD), 399
Packet Internet groper (ping) tool
      defined, 399
      for ISDN, 180
Packet Layer Protocol (PLP), 399
packet-mode connections
      commands for, **366–367**
      defined, 398
Packet Switch Exchange (PSE), 400
packet switches, 399
packet switching, 399
Packet-Switching Networks (PSNs), 400
packet switching protocols, 252
packets
      Authenticate-Request, **172–173**, *172*
      CHAP, 173–175, *173*
      defined, 398
      PAP, **171–172**
PAD (packet assembler/disassembler), 399
PAP (Password Authentication Protocol)
      defined, 399
      in ISDN, **171–173**, *172*
      in PPP, 81, **91–92**, *91*

pap chap keyword, 92
parity checking, 399
passive parameter, 312
Passwd-Length field, 172
Password Authentication Protocol (PAP)
      defined, 399
      in ISDN, **171–173**, *172*
      in PPP, 81, **91–92**, *91*
password command, 64
Password field, 172
PAT (Port Address Translation), **344**
      in Cisco 700 platform, 33
      configuring, **345–347**
      defined, 399
      disadvantages of, **344–345**
      exam essentials, **348–349**
      hands-on lab, **350–351**
      key terms, **349**
      monitoring, **347–348**
      review questions, **352–355, 357–358**
      summary, **348**
      written lab, **349–350, 356**
patches, 124
payload compression, 312, 399
PC Card LEDs, 36, *36*
PCM (Pulse Code Modulation), 149
PCMCIA LEDs, 36, *36*
pd output, 165
PDNs (Public Data Networks), 399
peer default ip address command, 86
Peer-ID field, 172
Peer-ID Length field, 172
per-interface compression, 312
per-virtual-circuit compression, 312
performance of Frame Relay,
      260–262, *261*
Permanent Virtual Circuits (PVCs)
      defined, 400
      in Frame relay, 6–7, **255**
PH1 LED, 38, *38*
PH2 LED, 38, *38*
Physical Layer, 399

physical-layer async command, *65*

ping (Packet Internet groper) tool
   defined, 399
   for ISDN, 180

plain old telephone service (POTS)
   defined, 400
   operation of, 149

PLP (Packet Layer Protocol), 399

point-to-point interfaces, **263–266**, *264*

Point-to-Point Protocol. *See* PPP
   (Point-to-Point Protocol)

policies
   queuing, **293**, *293*
   security, 362

Port Address Translation. *See* PAT (Port
   Address Translation)

port density, 29

port option, 345

port types, 29

ports in Cisco 700 platform, 32

POTS (plain old telephone service)
   defined, 400
   operation of, 149

PPP (Point-to-Point Protocol), **15**, 78
   architecture, **78–79**, *79*
      Address field, **80**
      Control field, **80**
      Flag field, **79**
      Frame Check Sequence field, **82**
      Information field, **82**
      Protocol field, **80–81**
   callbacks, **93–97**, 400
   CHAP authentication in, **92–93**,
      92–93
   compression, **97–99**
   configuring access servers, **82**
      for dedicated and interactive PPP, **83**
      for local devices, **83–89**, *84–85*,
         87, *90*
   defined, 400
   exam essentials, **110–111**
   hands-on labs, **112–113**

key terms, **111**

multilink in, **99–101**, *99–101*

review questions, **114–119**

summary, **109–110**

verifying and troubleshooting, **101**
      debug ppp authentication command,
         101–102
      debug ppp negotiation command,
         102–106
      debug ppp packet command,
         106–109

written lab, **111–112**, **117**

ppp authentication command, 91–92

ppp callback accept command, 94

ppp callback request command, 94

ppp multilink command, 100, 179

PPP server type, 129

predictor option, 98

Predictor technique
   for compress, 98
   defined, 400
   for link compression, 312

prefix-length command, 339

Presentation Layer, 400

PRI (Primary Rate Interface), **5**,
   150, **153**
   cabling in, **27–28**
   configuring, **192–194**
   defined, 400
   hands-on lab, **200–203**, *200*
   packet-mode connections, 366

pri-group timeslots command, 192–194

PRIMARY switch types, 153

priorities
   in priority queuing, **298**, *298*
   in Weighted Fair Queuing, **295**,
      295, 297

priority-group command, 299–300

priority-list list-number default
   command, 299

priority-list list-number interface
   interface-type command, 299

priority-list list-number protocol
  command, 299
priority-list list-number queue-limit
  command, 299
priority option, 297
priority queuing, 292
  configuring, **299–300**
  defined, 400
  priorities in, **298**, *298*
  verifying, **301**
process switching, 400
profiles, virtual, **376–377**
propagation delay, 400
Protocol field, **80–81**
Protocol Discriminator field, 159
protocols
  in custom queuing, 303
  defined, 400
  for ISDN, **156–157**
PSE (Packet Switch Exchange), 400
PSNs (Packet-Switching Networks), 400
PSTNs (Public Switched Telephone
  Networks), 400
Public Data Networks (PDNs), 399
Pulse Code Modulation (PCM), 149
PVCs (Permanent Virtual Circuits)
  defined, 400
  in Frame relay, 6–7, **255**

Q

Q protocols in ISDN, 156
&Q6 AT command, 63
QoS (quality of service)
  defined, 400
  in WAN protocol selection, **21**
queue-list commands, 303, 306–307
queue option, 303, 305
queues, 401
queuing, **292–293**
  Class-Based Weighted Fair Queuing, **309**

Committed Access Rate, 310
custom queuing, **301–307**, *302*
defined, 401
exam essentials, **315–316**
in Frame Relay, 274
hands-on lab, **317–318**, *317*
key terms, **316**
low latency queuing, 309
options, **294**, *294*
policies for, **293**, *293*
priority queuing, **298–301**, *298*
review questions, 319–324
summary, **314–315**
traffic prioritization in, 293
Weighted Fair Queuing, **295–298**, *295*
written lab, **316, 322**

R

R reference points, 401
RADIUS (Remote Access Dial-In User
  Service) protocol
  in authentication, 361
  defined, 401
RAM (random access memory), 401
RARP (Reverse Address Resolution
  Protocol), 401
rate queues, 401
RD LED, 38, *38*
read-only memory (ROM), 401
recompressed option, 98
Record a Log File for This Connection
  option, 131
reference points
  defined, 401
  ISDN, **155–156**, *155*
RELEASE messages, 164
RELEASE COMPLETE messages, 164
reliability
  defined, 401
  in WAN protocol selection, **21–22**

reloading, 401
remote access, 2–3
    cabling and assembling WANs, 26
        company site equipment
            identification, 28
        internetworking and interface
            options, 26–28
        verifying network installations,
            35–39, 36–38
    Cisco products, 23
        fixed interface routers, 24–25
        modular interface routers, 25
        selection tools for, 25–26
    defined, 401
    exam essentials, 39–40
    key terms, 41
    review questions, 43–48
    summary, 39
    WANs in. *See* WANs (wide area
        networks)
    written lab, 42, 46
Remote Access Dial-In User Service
    (RADIUS) protocol
    in authentication, 361
    defined, 401
remote branch equipment
    platforms for, 31
    verifying, 37, 37
remote control, dial-up networking
    for, 122
Request To Send (RTS) signal
    defined, 402
    in DTE to DCE signaling, 54
Requests for Comments (RFCs)
    defined, 401
    for PPP, 78–79
Require Data Encryption option, 131
Require Encrypted Password option, 131
reservable-queues parameter, 296
Resource accounting type, 374
Reverse Address Resolution Protocol
    (RARP), 401

reverse Telnet, 401
review questions
    asynchronous connections, 71–76
    cable modems, 244–247, 250
    DSL, 224–227, 229
    Frame Relay, 283–286, 289–290
    ISDN, 204–207, 209–210
    Microsoft Windows 95/98/2000/XP,
        140–145
    NAT and PAT, 352–355, 357–358
    PPP, 114–119
    queuing and compression, 319–324
    remote access, 43–48
    security, 380–383, 385–386
    VPNs, 244–247, 250
RFCs (Requests for Comments)
    defined, 401
    for PPP, 78–79
RI (Ring Indication) wire, 54
RIP (Routing Information Protocol), 34
RJ connectors, 401
robbed bit signaling, 401
ROM (read-only memory), 401
router access modes, 365
    character-mode connections,
        365–366
    packet-mode connections, 366–367
routers
    authentication configuration for, 369
    defined, 401–402
    for DSL, 217–218
    in Frame Relay congestion control,
        262–263
routing, 402
Routing Information Protocol (RIP), 34
RPS LED, 36, 36
RRx output, 162
RTS (Request To Send) signal, 402
    defined, 402
    in DTE to DCE signaling, 54
RX output, 161, 165
RXD wire, 54

S

S reference points
   defined, 402
   in ISDN, 156
S/T interfaces, 156
SABME output, 161
SAPI (Service Access Point Identifier) field,
   157–158
sapi output, 161
Scripting tab for dial-up clients, **134**, *134*
scripts, 402
SDH (Synchronous Digital Hierarchy), 151
SDSL (symmetric DSL), 9, **216**
secondary command, 169
Secure Sockets Layer (SSL), 240
security, 360
   AAA, 360, **363–364**, **367–368**
      accounting in, 365, **374–376**
      authentication in, **364**, **368–370**
      authorization in, **364–365**, **370–373**
      defined, 388
   access control solutions, **361–363**
   exam essentials, **377–378**
   hands-on lab, **379**
   IPSec, **235–236**
      configuring, **237–239**
      for VPNs, 240
   key terms, **378**
   review questions, **380–383**, **385–386**
   router access modes, **365–367**
   summary, **377**
   terminology for, **360–361**
   virtual profiles for, **376–377**
   in WAN protocol selection, **22–23**
   written lab, **378–379**, **384**
security policies, 362, 402
security servers, **361–362**, 402
selection tools for Cisco products, **25–26**
Serial command, 169

Serial Line Internet Protocol (SLIP)
   defined, 402
   purpose of, **15**
serial packet-mode connections, 366
Server Types tab for dial-up clients,
   128–133, *129–130*
servers
   defined, 402
   DHCP, 88
Service Access Point Identifier (SAPI) field,
   157–158
service dhcp command, 87
service packs, 124
Service Profile Identifiers (SPIDs)
   defined, 403
   in ISDN, 151
Session Layer, 402
set authentication enable command, 370
set authentication login command, 370
set-based routers and switches, 402
set ip pat on command, 345
set ip pat porthandler command, 345
set peer command, 238
set tacacs attempts command, 369
set tacacs directedrequest command, 370
set tacacs key command, 370
set tacacs server command, 369
set tacacs timeout command, 370
set transform-set command, 238
SETUP messages, 164
SETUP output, 165
SF (Super Frame), 402
show compress command, 314
show config command, 370
show dialer command, 180, 186
show frame-relay lmi command, **269**
show frame-relay map command,
   268–269
show frame-relay pvc command,
   267–268, 276

show frame-relay route command, 272
show interface command, **266–267**
show ip nat statistics command, 342
show ip nat translation command, 341
show ip nat translation verbose
  command, 342
show ip pat command, 347–348
show ip route command, 180
show isdn active command, 180
show isdn status command, 180,
  182–183, 185
show line command, 137
show modemcap command, 59–60
show process cpu command, 98
show queue command, 297
show queueing command, 297
show queueing priority command, 301
show running-config command, 276
signaling, **53–55**
Simple Mail Transfer Protocol
  (SMTP), 403
simple translation entries in NAT, 328
site equipment identification, **28**
  central site, **29–30**
  remote branch, **31**
  telecommuter, **32**
sliding window method, 402
SLIP (Serial Line Internet Protocol)
  defined, 402
  purpose of, **15**
SLIP server type, 130
slow paths, 342
small offices/home offices (SOHOs),
  148–149, 403
SMTP (Simple Mail Transfer Protocol),
  403
smtp option in PAT, 345
snapshot routing, 34
sniffers, 343
SO=1 AT command, 63
sockets, 403

SOHOs (small offices/home offices),
  148–149, 403
SONET (Synchronous Optical Network)
  standard
  defined, 403
  for fiber optics, 151
source list list-number interface
  command, 339
speed command, 64
SPIDs (Service Profile Identifiers)
  defined, 403
  in ISDN, 151
split horizon
  defined, 403
  in Frame Relay, 264, *264*
splitterless DSL, 215
splitters in DSL, 214–215
SSL (Secure Sockets Layer), 240
Stac option, 98
Stac technique
  for compress, 98
  defined, 403
  for link compression, 312
standard IP access lists, 403
Stat-TDM (statistical time-division
  multiplexing), 255
static addressing options, **83**
static NAT, **337**
static routes, 403
static translation in NAT, 329
statistical multiplexing, 403
statistical time-division multiplexing
  (Stat-TDM), 255
stopbits command, 64
stun option, 303
subchannels, 403
subinterfaces
  defined, 403
  in Frame Relay, 264, *264*
  hands-on lab, **280–281**
subnet addresses, 403

subnet masks, 403
subnetworks, 404
Super Frame (SF), 402
Supervisory format, 158–159
supported NAT traffic types, **330–331**
SVCs (Switched Virtual Circuits)
    defined, 404
    in Frame relay, 7, **254–255**
switch options
    BRI, **152**
    PRI, **153**
switches
    defined, 404
    in Frame Relay, **261–262**,
        270–273, *271*
symmetric DSL (SDSL), 9, **216**
Synchronous Digital Hierarchy
    (SDH), 151
Synchronous Optical Network (SONET)
    standard
    defined, 403
    for fiber optics, 151
synchronous transmissions, 404
System accounting type, 374
System LED, 36, *36*
System OK LED, 37, *37*
System PWR LED, 37, *37*

T

T-1 circuits, 27, 153
    configuring, **192–194**
    defined, 404
T-3 WANs, 404
T reference points
    defined, 404
    in ISDN, 156
TACACS+ (Enhanced Terminal Access
    Controller Access Control System)
    protocol
    in authentication, 361

configuration file, **371–373**
configuring, **379**
defined, 404
tacacs-server host command, 368–369
tacacs-server key command, 368–369
TAs (Terminal Adapters)
    in BRI, 155
    defined, 405
TCP (Transmission Control Protocol)
    defined, 404
    in NAT, 329
TCP header compression
    defined, 404
    operation of, **311–312**
TCP/IP (Transmission Control Protocol/
    Internet Protocol), 404
TCP/IP Properties dialog box, 85–86, *85*
TCP/IP Settings dialog box, 84, *84*
tcp keyword, 304
TCP load distribution
    configuring, **338–339**
    in NAT, **334–335**, *335*
TDM (time division multiplexing)
    defined, 404
    in Frame Relay, 255
    with modems, 52
    in POTS, 149
TE (Terminal Equipment) devices, 404
TE1 (Terminal Equipment 1) devices
    in BRI, 154
    defined, 405
TE2 (Terminal Equipment 2) devices
    in BRI, 154
    defined, 405
TEI (Terminal Endpoint Identifier)
    field, 158
telcos, 405
telecommuter equipment, **32**
    Cisco 700 series, **32**
    Cisco 800 series, **34**
    Cisco 1000 series, **35**
    verifying, **38–39**, *38*

telephone service support, 34

telnet command, 180

telnet option, 345

Telnet protocol, 405

Terminal Access Controller Access Control
System (TACACS+), protocol
in authentication, 361
configuration file, **371–373**
configuring, **379**
defined, 404

Terminal Adapters (TAs)
in BRI, 155
defined, 405

terminal emulation, 405

Terminal Endpoint Identifier (TEI)
field, 158

Terminal Endpoints (TEs), 160

Terminal Equipment (TE) devices, 404

Terminal Equipment 1 (TE1) devices
in BRI, 154
defined, 405

Terminal Equipment 2 (TE2) devices
in BRI, 154
defined, 405

terminal windows, launching,
136–137, *136*

TEs (Terminal Endpoints), 160

testing dial backups, **183–190**

TFTP (Trivial File Transfer
Protocol), 405

Thinnet networks
and cable modems, 148
defined, 405

time division multiplexing (TDM)
defined, 404
in Frame Relay, 255
with modems, 52
in POTS, 149

toll networks, 405

TOS (Type of Service), 309

trace command, 405

traffic prioritization, **293**

traffic shaping in Frame Relay, **274–277**
defined, 405
hands-on labs, **282**

traffic types in NAT, **330–331**

translating inside local addresses,
332–333, *332*

Transmission Control Protocol (TCP)
defined, 404
in NAT, 329

Transmission Control Protocol/Internet
Protocol (TCP/IP), 404

transport input command, 64

transport input all command, 62

Transport Layer, 405

Transport mode in IPSec, 236

Triple Data Encryption Standard
(3DES), 236

Trivial File Transfer Protocol
(TFTP), 405

troubleshooting, 342
asynchronous modem connections,
61–62
DSL, **220–221**
NAT, **342–343**
PPP, **101**
debug ppp authentication command,
101–102
debug ppp negotiation command,
102–106
debug ppp packet command,
106–109

Tunnel mode in IPSec, 236

TX output, 161, 165

TXD wire, 54

Type of Service (TOS), 309

U

U reference points
defined, 405
in ISDN, 156

UAf output, 162
UART (Universal Asynchronous Receiver/
    Transmitter) chips
  characteristics of, 53
  defined, 405
UBR (unspecified bit rate), 219
UDP (User Datagram Protocol),
    405–406
udp keyword in queuing, 304
Universal Asynchronous Receiver
    Transmitter (UART) chips
  characteristics of, 53
  defined, 405
Unnumbered format in LAPD, 159
unnumbered frames, 406
unshielded twisted-pair (UTP)
    wiring, 406
unspecified bit rate (UBR), 219
unsupported NAT traffic types, 331
upstream traffic with cable modems, 10
User Datagram Protocol (UDP),
    405–406
username command, 366
username name password command,
    92–93, 174
UTP (unshielded twisted-pair)
    wiring, 406

V

V reference points, 156
Value field, 174
Value-Size field, 174
variable-length subnet masks
    (VLSMs), 406
VCs (virtual circuits)
  defined, 406
  in Frame Relay, 253–255, *254*
  for VPNs, 239
VDSL (Very-High Data Rate DSL),
    9, **216**

verifying
  asynchronous modem connections,
    61–62
  dial-up connections, **137**, *137*
  Frame Relay, **266–270**
  ISDN operations, **180**
  NAT, **341–342**
  network installations, 35
    central site, **35–37**, *36*
    remote branch, **37**, *37*
    telecommuter, **38–39**, *38*
  PPP, **101**
    debug ppp authentication command,
      101–102
    debug ppp negotiation command,
      102–106
    debug ppp packet command,
      106–109
  priority queuing, **301**
  Weighted Fair Queuing, **297–298**
Very-High Data Rate DSL (VDSL),
    9, **216**
virtual circuits (VCs)
  defined, 406
  in Frame Relay, **253–255**, *254*
  for VPNs, 239
virtual dialer interfaces, 185
Virtual Path Identifiers (VPIs), 219
virtual private networks. *See* VPNs (virtual
    private networks)
virtual profiles, **376–377**
VLSMs (variable-length subnet
    masks), 406
VN3 switch types
  in BRI, 152
  in PRI, 153
VPIs (Virtual Path Identifiers), 219
VPNs (virtual private networks), **235**
  defined, 406
  for DSL, 219
  encryption with, 53

exam essentials, 240–241
hands-on lab, 242–243, 248–249
IPSec for, 235–239
key terms, 241
review questions, 244–247, 250
summary, 240–241
technologies for, 239–240
for WANs, 23
written lab, 242, 247

W

WANs (wide area networks)
connection types in, 3
asynchronous dial-Up, 4
ATM, 11
Frame Relay, 6
ISDN, 5
leased lines, 7–11, *8*
summary, 13
wireless and cellular, 11–13
X.25, 5
defined, 406
encapsulation protocols for, 14
ATM, 14
Frame Relay, 16
HDLC, 14
PPP, 15
SLIP, 15
X.25, 15–16
protocol selection factors in, 16–17
applications in use, 20–21
availability, 17
bandwidth, 17–18
cost, 18–19
manageability, 19–20
quality of service, 21
reliability, 21–22
security, 22–23
in remote access, 2

WFQ (Weighted Fair Queuing),
292, 295
configuring, 296
conversations in, 295–296
defined, 406
priorities in, 295, *295*
verifying, 297–298
WIC ACT LED, 37, *37*
WIC CD LED, 37, *37*
wide area networks. *See* WANs (wide area networks)
wildcards, 406
windowing, 406
Windows for Workgroups server type, 130
Windows NT server type, 130
Windows operating systems. *See* Microsoft Windows 95/98/2000/XP
wins option, 345
wireless WAN connections, 11–13
written labs
asynchronous connections, 68, 74
cable modems, 242, 247
DSL, 223, 228
Frame Relay, 279–280, 287–288
ISDN, 197, 207–208
Microsoft Windows 95/98/2000/XP, 139, 143
NAT and PAT, 349–350, 356
PPP, 111–112, 117
queuing and compression, 316, 322
remote access, 42, 46
security, 378–379, 384
VPNs, 242, 247

X

X.25 protocol, 5, 15–16
characteristics of, 16–22
defined, 406
X.25 standard, 406

The Official
Juniper™ Networks Certification Study Guides
From Sybex

The Juniper Networks Technical Certification Program offers a four-tiered certification program that validates knowledge and skills related to Juniper Networks technologies:

- JNCIA (Juniper Networks Certified Internet Associate)
- JNCIS (Juniper Networks Certified Internet Specialist)
- JNCIP (Juniper Networks Certified Internet Professional)
- JNCIE (Juniper Networks Certified Internet Expert)

The JNCIA and JNCIS certifications require candidates to pass written exams, while the JNCIP and JNCIE certifications require candidates to pass one-day hands-on laboratory exams.

The Only OFFICIAL Juniper Networks Study Guides Are From Sybex

Written and reviewed by Juniper employees, the Juniper Networks Study Guides are the only official Study Guides for the Juniper Networks Technical Certification Program. Each book provides in-depth coverage of all exam objectives and detailed perspectives and insights into working with Juniper Networks technologies in the real world.

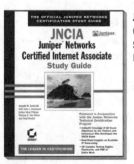

JNCIA: Juniper Networks Certified Internet Associate Study Guide
ISBN: 0-7821-4071-8

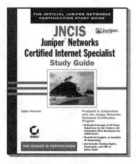

JNCIS: Juniper Networks Certified Internet Specialist Study Guide
ISBN: 0-7821-4072-6

JNCIP: Juniper Networks Certified Internet Professional Study Guide
ISBN: 0-7821-4073-4

JNCIE: Juniper Networks Certified Internet Expert Study Guide
ISBN: 0-7821-4069-6

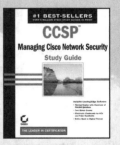

Project Management Skills for all Levels

TELL US WHAT YOU THINK!

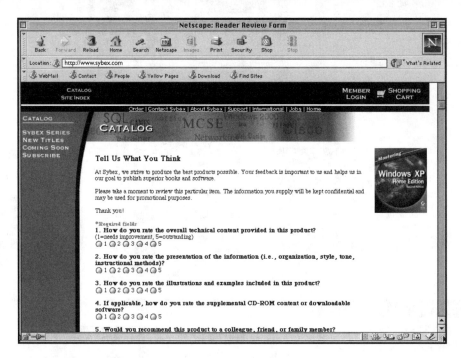

Your feedback is critical to our efforts to provide you with the best books and software on the market. Tell us what you think about the products you've purchased. It's simple:

1. Go to the Sybex website.
2. Find your book by typing the ISBN or title into the Search field.
3. Click on the book title when it appears.
4. Click **Submit a Review.**
5. Fill out the questionnaire and comments.
6. Click **Submit.**

With your feedback, we can continue to publish the highest quality computer books and software products that today's busy IT professionals deserve.

www.sybex.com

SYBEX Inc. • 1151 Marina Village Parkway, Alameda, CA 94501 • 510-523-8233

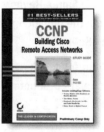